THE NEW WORLD ORDER BOOK

ABOUT THE AUTHOR

 **Nick Redfern** is the author of 30 books on UFOs and crypto-zoology, including *Monster Files; The Real Men in Black; The NASA Conspiracies;* and *Strange Secrets.* He has appeared on more than 70 TV shows, including: the BBC's *Out of This World;* the SyFy Channel's *Proof Positive;* and the History Channel's *Monster Quest.*

THE NEW

WORLD

ORDER

BOOK

NICK REDFERN

VISIBLE
INK
PRESS

Detroit

ALSO FROM VISIBLE INK PRESS

Conspiracies and Secret Societies: The Complete Dossier, 2nd edition
by Brad Steiger and Sherry Hansen Steiger
ISBN: 978-1-57859-368-2

Demons, the Devil, and Fallen Angels
by Marie D. Jones and Larry Flaxman
ISBN: 978-1-57859-613-3

The Dream Encyclopedia, 2nd edition
by James R Lewis, Ph.D., and Evelyn Dorothy Oliver, Ph.D.
ISBN: 978-1-57859-216-6

The Dream Interpretation Dictionary: Symbols, Signs, and Meanings
by J. M. DeBord
ISBN: 978-1-57859-637-9

The Encyclopedia of Religious Phenomena
by J. Gordon Melton
ISBN: 978-1-57859-209-8

The Fortune-Telling Book: The Encyclopedia of Divination and Soothsaying
by Raymond Buckland
ISBN: 978-1-57859-147-3

The Government UFO Files: The Conspiracy of Cover-Up
by Kevin D. Randle
ISBN: 978-1-57859-477-1

Hidden Realms, Lost Civilizations, and Beings from Other Worlds
by Jerome Clark
ISBN: 978-1-57859-175-6

The Horror Show Guide: The Ultimate Frightfest of Movies
by Mike May
ISBN: 978-1-57859-420-7

The Illuminati: The Secret Society That Hijacked the World
by Jim Marrs
ISBN: 978-1-57859-619-5

The Monster Book: Creatures, Beasts, and Fiends of Nature
by Nick Redfern
ISBN: 978-1-57859-575-4

The New World Order Book
by Nick Redfern
ISBN: 978-1-57859-615-7

Real Aliens, Space Beings, and Creatures from Other Worlds,
by Brad Steiger and Sherry Hansen Steiger
ISBN: 978-1-57859-333-0

Real Encounters, Different Dimensions, and Otherworldly Beings
by Brad Steiger with Sherry Hansen Steiger
ISBN: 978-1-57859-455-9

Real Ghosts, Restless Spirits, and Haunted Places, 2nd edition
by Brad Steiger
ISBN: 978-1-57859-401-6

Real Miracles, Divine Intervention, and Feats of Incredible Survival
by Brad Steiger and Sherry Hansen Steiger
ISBN: 978-1-57859-214-2

Real Monsters, Gruesome Critters, and Beasts from the Darkside
by Brad Steiger and Sherry Hansen Steiger
ISBN: 978-1-57859-220-3

Real Vampires, Night Stalkers, and Creatures from the Darkside
by Brad Steiger
ISBN: 978-1-57859-255-5

Real Visitors, Voices from Beyond, and Parallel Dimensions
by Brad Steiger and Sherry Hansen Steiger
ISBN: 978-1-57859-541-9

Real Zombies, the Living Dead, and Creatures of the Apocalypse
by Brad Steiger
ISBN: 978-1-57859-296-8

The Religion Book: Places, Prophets, Saints, and Seers
by Jim Willis
ISBN: 978-1-57859-151-0

The Sci-Fi Movie Guide: The Universe of Film from Alien to Zardoz
by Chris Barsanti
ISBN: 978-1-57859-503-7

Secret History: Conspiracies from Ancient Aliens to the New World Order
by Nick Redfern
ISBN: 978-1-57859-479-5

Secret Societies: The Complete Guide to Histories, Rites, and Rituals
by Nick Redfern
ISBN: 978-1-57859-483-2

The Spirit Book: The Encyclopedia of Clairvoyance, Channeling, and Spirit Communication
by Raymond Buckland
ISBN: 978-1-57859-172-5

Supernatural Gods: Spiritual Mysteries, Psychic Experiences, and Scientific Truths
by Jim Willis
ISBN: 978-1-57859-660-7

UFO Dossier: 100 Years of Government Secrets, Conspiracies, and Cover-Ups
by Kevin D. Randle
ISBN: 978-1-57859-564-8

Unexplained! Strange Sightings, Incredible Occurrences, and Puzzling Physical Phenomena, 3rd edition
by Jerome Clark
ISBN: 978-1-57859-344-6

The Vampire Book: The Encyclopedia of the Undead, 3rd edition
by J. Gordon Melton
ISBN: 978-1-57859-281-4

The Werewolf Book: The Encyclopedia of Shape-Shifting Beings, 2nd edition
by Brad Steiger
ISBN: 978-1-57859-367-5

The Witch Book: The Encyclopedia of Witchcraft, Wicca, and Neo-paganism
by Raymond Buckland
ISBN: 978-1-57859-114-5

The Zombie Book: The Encyclopedia of the Living Dead
by Nick Redfern and Brad Steiger
ISBN: 978-1-57859-504-4

"REAL NIGHTMARES" E-BOOKS BY BRAD STEIGER

Book 1: *True and Truly Scary Unexplained Phenomenon*

Book 2: *The Unexplained Phenomena and Tales of the Unknown*

Book 3: *Things That Go Bump in the Night*

Book 4: *Things That Prowl and Growl in the Night*

Book 5: *Fiends That Want Your Blood*

Book 6: *Unexpected Visitors and Unwanted Guests*

Book 7: *Dark and Deadly Demons*

Book 8: *Phantoms, Apparitions, and Ghosts*

Book 9: *Alien Strangers and Foreign Worlds*

Book 10: *Ghastly and Grisly Spooks*

Book 11: *Secret Schemes and Conspiring Cabals*

Book 12: *Freaks, Fiends, and Evil Spirits*

PLEASE VISIT US AT VISIBLEINKPRESS.COM

The New World Order Book

Visible Ink Press®
43311 Joy Rd., #414
Canton, MI 48187-2075

Visible Ink Press is a registered trademark of Visible Ink Press LLC.

Most Visible Ink Press books are available at special quantity discounts when purchased in bulk by corporations, organizations, or groups. Customized printings, special imprints, messages, and excerpts can be produced to meet your needs. For more information, contact Special Markets Director, Visible Ink Press, www.visibleink.com, or 734-667-3211.

Managing Editor: Kevin S. Hile
Art Director: Mary Claire Krzewinski
Typesetting: Marco Divita
Proofreaders: Aarti Stephens and Shoshana Hurwitz
Indexer: Larry Baker

Front cover images: Photo of Edward Snowden (Gage Skidmore); Anonymous member at Occupy Wall Street protest (David Shankbone); security camera (Shutterstock); Great Seal of the United States and Skull and Bones logo (public domain).

Back cover images: Shutterstock.

ISBN: 978-1-57859-615-7
ePub ISBN: 978-1-57859-669-0
PDF ISBN: 978-1-57859-668-3

Cataloging-in-Publication Data is on file at the Library of Congress.

Printed in the United States of America.

10 9 8 7 6 5 4 3 2 1

CONTENTS

Photo Sources   [xiii]

Acknowledgments   [xv]

Introduction   [xvii]

A

Alchemy   1
Alzheimer's   2
American Vision   4
Anthrax Attack   5
Anti-Globalization Movement   7
Area 51   9
Assange, Julian   12
Avian Flu   13

B

Banking Deaths   17
Barcoding the Population   18
Benjamin Franklin True Patriot Act   20
Bilderberg Group   21
Bilderberg's Role in the New
   World Order   23
bin Laden, Osama   24
Biochips   27
Black Helicopters   28
Blair, Tony   32
Bohemian Club   34

Bohemian Grove Secrecy   36
Border Closings   38
Brave New World   40
Bretton Woods System   42
Brexit   44
Bush, George H. W., 1990 Speech . .   46
Bush, George H. W., 1991 Speech . .   48
Bush, Jeb   50

C

Cashless Society   51
Chemtrails   53
China   56
Civil Unrest   58
Climate Change   59
Clinton, Hillary   61
Club of Rome   63
Cold War Statements   64
Coleman, Dr. John   66
Collins Elite   67
Committee of 300   69
Council for National Policy   72
Council on Foreign Relations   73
Count of St. Germain   74

Coup d'Etat 76
Curfews 77

D

Defense Advanced Research Projects
  Agency (DARPA) 79
Denver Airport 83
Department of Homeland Security . . 85
Diana, Princess of Wales's Death . . 86
Dick, Philip K., and the Nazi Plot . . 87
Dirty Bomb 89
Disarming the United States 90
Doctors' Deaths 92
Dugway Proving Ground 94
Dumbing Down the Population . . . 96

E

Ebola 99
Economic and Monetary Union
  of the European Union 101
Electromagnetic Pulse Disaster . . 103
Eschatology 105
European Union 107
Experiments on the Brain 109
Extraterrestrial New World Order . . 110

F

Federal Emergency Management
  Agency (FEMA) 113
Federalism 115
Five Eyes 116
Fluoride 117
Fort Detrick 120
Fourth Reich 122
Freedom of Information Act
  Erosion 124
Freemasons 126

G–H

Goff, Kenneth 129
Gorbachev, Mikhail 131
Government Communications
  Headquarters 133
"Harrison Bergeron" 134
Hicks, Fredereick C. 136

Homeschooling 137
Human Replacements 138
The Hunger Games 139

I

Illuminati 143
Illuminati and the New World
  Order 145
Immortality for the Elite 147
Insect Drones 149
Internet Censoring 150
Internet Sabotage 152
iPhone Spying 154

J–K

John Birch Society 157
Journalism at Risk 158
Kelly, David 160
Kennedy, John F., Assassination . 163
Kennedy, Robert F. 166
King, Martin Luther, Jr. 169
Kissinger, Henry 171

L–M

Lederberg, Joshua 175
Lennon, John, Murder 177
Library Spying 180
Marconi Electric Systems 182
Martial Law 185
Men in Black 187
Microbiologist Deaths 189
Microchips 192
Militarization of the Police 194
Mind Control 197
Mind Manipulation 198
MKDelta 200
MKNaomi 202
Monatomic Gold Powder 203
Monroe, Marilyn 205
Mood-altering Drugs 207
Mr. Robot 209

N

NATO 211
New World Order in the 1990s . . . 214

9/11 215
1984 217
None Dare Call It Conspiracy 220
Nuclear Winter 222

O

Obesity 227
Octopus 229
Off the Grid 231
One World Currency 233
Origins of the New World Order . . 235
Orwellian 237
Overpopulation 238

P

Patriot Act 243
Pearl Harbor and the New World
  Order Parallels 245
Perpetual War 248
Pine Gap 251
Population Culling 252
PRISM Program 255
Project Blue Beam 256
Project for the New American
  Century 258
Putin, Trump, and the New World
  Order 260

R

Rabies 263
RAND Corporation 264
Reagan's View of a World United
  by UFOs 267
Religion 269
Report from Iron Mountain 271
Reptilians 274
Reptilians and Sex 276
Restore the Fourth 278
Revelations 280
Rex 84 281
Rh Negatives 284
Robertson, Pat 286
Roswell 288

S

Sanders, Bernie 293
7/7 294
The Singularity and Artificial
  Evolution 297
Skull and Bones 299
Smart TV Spies 301
Snowden, Edward 303
Social Security Administration
  Arms Purchases 305
Spanish Flu Pandemic 306
Spraying Cities 308
Superviruses 309
Survivalists 310

T

Talbott, Strobe 313
Television 315
Tor Project 317
Tracking Your Online Purchases . . 318
Trilateral Commission 319
Trump, Donald 321
Trump, Donald, Speech 322
Trump's New World Order 324
Trump's Wall 327
2016 Presidential Election Stolen . 328
2030 Agenda 330

U

Ufologists and Spying 333
UFOs in Ottawa 334
UFOs of the New World Order . . . 336
UK Independence Party 342
United Nations Army 344
United Nations Population Plot . . 346
U.S. Constitution Erosion 348
U.S. Militia 349

V

V for Vendetta 351
Veterans Today 353
Viruses 354
Voting Restrictions 355

W–Z

Wackenhut Corporation 359
Walking Corpse Syndrome 360
Walmart Conspiracy 362
Watch Lists 364
Water Control 365
Weapons of Mass Destruction . . . 367
Weathermen 370

Webcam Spying 372
Webster, Nesta Helen 374
Wells, H.G. 375
WikiLeaks 377
World Bank 379
World Order 383
World War III 386
Zero Hour 391

Further Reading   [393]

Index   [419]

Photo Sources

Branch of the National Union of Journalists: p. 218.

Central Intelligence Agency: p. 201.

Coolcaesar (Wikicommons): pp. 266, 339.

Dallas Dispatch-Journal: p. 130.

James D. Forrester: p. 296.

HMman (Wikicommons): p. 64.

David Jolley: p. 95.

Jrtayloriv (Wikicommons): p. 74.

Lyndon B. Johnson Library/Yoichi R. Okamoto: p. 167.

Michiel1972 (Wikicommons): p. 22.

Jack Mitchell: p. 178.

National Institutes of Health: p. 176.

National Portrait Gallery: p. 376.

New York Sunday News: p. 206.

Paparazzo Presents: p. 288.

Paul Mellon Collection, Yale Center for British Art, Yale University: p. 70.

Shutterstock: pp. 14, 19, 25, 29, 33, 39, 43, 45, 50, 52, 54, 57, 60, 62, 77, 78, 83, 91, 97, 100, 106, 108, 111, 114, 119, 127, 132, 137, 140, 148, 150, 153, 155, 159, 165, 172, 181, 186, 188, 191, 193, 196, 199, 202, 208, 213, 216, 223, 228, 232, 234, 238, 239, 246, 249, 260, 268, 275, 285, 290, 298, 302, 304, 305, 310, 316, 318, 321, 323, 329, 335, 343, 345, 352, 356, 363, 366, 368, 373, 387, 390.

David G. Silvers: p. 12.

16Mcannettes (Wikicommons): p. 81.

Gage Skidmore: p. 326.

Skyring (Wikicommons): p. 252.

Trilateral Commission: p. 320.

Alexis Tsipras, Prime Minister of Greece: p. 314.

U.K. Government: p. 117.

U.S. Air Force: p. 104.

U.S. Army: pp. 6, 307.

U.S. Department of Defense: pp. 47, 65, 162.

U.S. Department of Homeland Security: p. 85.

U.S. Federal Government: pp. 86, 123, 125, 170.

U.S. Senate Historical Office: p. 31.

Wikicommons: p. 10.

WikiLeaks: p. 378.

Wikophile1 (Wikicommons): p. 35.

WNET-TV/ PBS: p. 136.

Zntrip (Wikicommons): p. 3.

Public domain: pp. 41, 144, 300.

Acknowledgments

I would like to offer my sincere thanks to the following: my agent, Lisa Hagan, and Roger Janecke, Kevin Hile, and everyone else at Visible Ink Press.

INTRODUCTION

On January 16, 1991, President George H. W. Bush said, regarding *Operation Desert Storm* (the first war in Iraq), "We have before us the opportunity to forge for ourselves and for future generations a new world order—a world where the rule of law, not the law of the jungle, governs the conduct of nations. When we are successful—and we will be—we have a real chance at this new world order, an order in which a credible United Nations can use its peacekeeping role to fulfill the promise and vision of the U.N.'s founders."

Nineteen ninety-one was not the first time the emotive term "New World Order" was used by a politician. It was, however, the first time that it caught the attention of millions. Unsurprisingly, it provoked a great deal of debate in relation to what it meant for us and for the future. While we are assured by our leaders that any potential NWO will be wholly benign and beneficial in nature, *all* of the facts strongly suggest otherwise.

The New World Order is not just about modelling the future, however. It's also about dumbing-down the population to ensure they become ignorant of the past. Consider these quotes on that very issue. Julian Barnes, the author of the best-selling *The Sense of an Ending*, said: "History is that certainty produced at the point where the imperfections of memory meet the inadequacies of documentation."

In his classic novel *Ulysses*, James Joyce wrote: "History … is a nightmare from which I am trying to awake."

Aldous Huxley remarked: "That men do not learn very much from the lessons of history is the most important of all the lessons that history has to teach."

George Orwell warned us: "The most effective way to destroy people is to deny and obliterate their own understanding of their history."

"If you don't know history, then you don't know anything. You are a leaf that doesn't know it is part of a tree," wrote Michael Crichton in *Jurassic Park*.

"History will be kind to me for I intend to write it," bragged Britain's Prime Minister Sir Winston Churchill.

As for the New World Order and its cohorts in the domain of powerful, secret societies, take careful note of the following. President Woodrow Wilson noted: "Some of the biggest men in the United States, in the field of commerce and manufacture, are afraid of somebody, afraid of something. They know there is a power somewhere so organized, so subtle, so watchful, so interlocked, so complete, so pervasive, that they better not speak above their breath when they speak of condemnation of it."

The Duke of Brunswick, the Grand Master of World Freemasonry warned: "I have been convinced that we, as an order, have come under the power of some very evil occult order, profoundly versed in Science, both occult and otherwise, though not infallible, their methods being black magic, that is to say, electromagnetic power, hypnotism, and powerful suggestion. We are convinced that the order is being controlled by some Sun Order, after the nature of the Illuminati, if not by that order itself."

Senator Daniel K. Inouye said: "There exists a shadowy government with its own Air Force, its own Navy, its own fund raising mechanism, and the ability to pursue its own ideas of national interest, free from all checks and balances; free from law itself."

Sir Thomas Moore offered this: "Everywhere do I perceive a certain conspiracy of rich men seeking their own advantage under that name and pretext of commonwealth."

In *The New World Order Book*, you will find two hundred examples of why we should be suspicious of the looming NWO. They will show readers the true goals of the NWO are the enslavement of the human race, the abolishment of individual nations, and the creation of a one-world government overseen by a ruthless, global elite.

ALCHEMY

Within the field of New World Order (NWO) research, there is a theory that the NWO elite have mastered the ancient art of alchemy. Brad Steiger, an authority on alchemy, says: "A 'respectable burgher of North Holland' appeared 'modest and simple' to the alchemist Helvetius one day in 1666. It was the stranger's incredible knowledge that startled and inspired the alchemists of Helvetius's day, and though these learned and determined men never did acquire the philosopher's stone that would transmute lead into gold, they did fashion the seeds of the science of chemistry that has accomplished so many transmutations of the human environment and the human condition in the last three hundred years.

"Out of the smoky laboratories of the alchemists, Albert le Grand produced potassium lye; Raymond Lully prepared bicarbonate of potassium; Paracelsus described zinc and introduced chemical compounds in medicine; Blaise Vigenere discovered benzoic acid; Basil Valentine perfected sulfuric acid; and Johann Friedrich Boetticher became the first European to produce porcelain.

"While each of the above is an important discovery, there are rumors that lying amidst the musty pages of certain ancient alchemical laboratories there are recorded experiments with photography, radio transmission, phonography, and aerial flight.

"Throughout the Middle Ages and the Renaissance, there were many scholars who claimed that they had received late-night visits from mysterious members of a secret society that had accomplished the transmutation of metals, the means of prolonging life, the knowledge to see and to hear what was occurring in distant places, and the ability to travel across the heavens in heavier-than-air vehicles.

"Numerous occult groups have been created around the belief that centuries ago a secret society achieved a high level of scientific knowledge that they carefully guarded from the rest of humanity. According to these occultists, certain men of genius in ancient Egypt and Persia were given access to the records of the advanced technologies of the antediluvian world of Atlantis. Many hundreds of years ago, these ancient masters learned to duplicate many of the feats of the Titans of the lost continent."

Those same "ancient masters," it is believed, may have shared their secrets with powerful figures who eventually became members of the New World Order.

ALZHEIMER'S

Is the New World Order seeking to try to massively increase the number of people suffering from Alzheimer's disease across the United States? The reason: to lower population levels and create a situation where millions upon millions die prematurely or are rendered helpless due to the crippling, deadly effects of this horrific disease. If it sounds too terrible to contemplate, consider the following:

In the mid-1980s, the first signs of a terrifying condition began to surface in the heart of the British countryside. It was a condition that targeted cattle and made them behave in a distinctly zombie-like fashion, before finally killing the animals in deeply distressing fashion. Its official name is Bovine Spongiform Encephalopathy (BSE). Unofficially, but far more infamously, it is known as Mad Cow Disease. BSE is caused by a prion—a protein-based agent that attacks and affects the normal function of cells. Worse still, just like the fictional zombie virus of so many movies, prion-inducing BSE is utterly unstoppable and incurable. By 1987, the British government recognized that it had not just a problem on its hands but a *major* problem, too. Not only that, the government acted in a wholly unforgivable fashion by secretly putting the beef industry, the economy, and profits way ahead of public safety.

In the same way that, in typically fictional format, infected people feed upon the uninfected survivors of the zombie apocalypse, the same can be said about the origins of BSE: it was spread by cows eating cows. To the horror of the British public—who had previously, and utterly outrageously, been kept in the dark—it was finally revealed by the government that, for years, the dis-

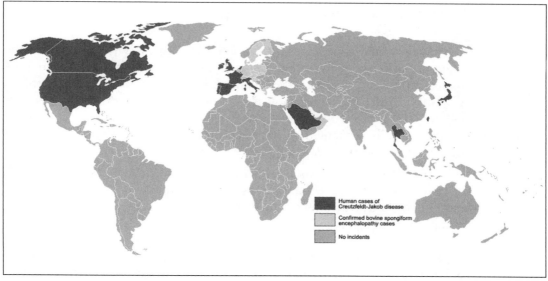

The above map indicates countries with reported Mad Cow Disease and those that also have confirmed cases of human Creutzfeldt-Jacob Disease.

carded remains of millions of cattle that were put to death in British slaughterhouses had been ground to a pulp and used to create cattle feed. It was, for the animal kingdom at least, *Soylent Green* come to hideous reality. And that's when the problems started.

It quickly became very easy to spot a zombie cow: they shuffled rather than walked; their personalities began to change; they exhibited behavior that varied from confusion to outright *rage*; and they quickly became unmanageable under normal circumstances. As the crisis grew, an even more terrifying development surfaced: the infection jumped to the human population in the form of what is termed Creutzfeldt-Jacob Disease, or CJD, which can *also* provoke sudden outbursts of rage. The utterly panicked British government took the only option it felt was available.

With close to an estimated 200,000 cattle infected, officialdom decided to play things safe by systematically wiping out no fewer than 4.4 million cows all across the nation. While such actions were seen as horrific, they were also perceived as necessary to ensure that chaos and death did not spread even further. For some, however, it was all too little and too late.

Although the cannibalization process was brought to a halt by the government in the late 1980s, around 200 British people have since died from what is termed variant CJD (or vCJD), the result of eating BSE-contaminated meat. On top of that, the significant increase in Alzheimer's disease in the UK in recent years has given rise to the highly disturbing theory that many of those presumed to have Alzheimer's were misdiagnosed. They may be suffering from vCJD.

Well, wouldn't an autopsy show evidence of vCJD? Yes, it would, *if* the brain of the deceased individual was examined carefully. Indeed, studying the brains of the dead, or testing the blood, are the only sure ways to fully confirm vCJD. But here's the thing: most people suspected of having Alzheimer's are not tested for vCJD. If a person was diagnosed with Alzheimer's, then their death is usually attributed to complications arising from the disease, rather than anything stranger or suspicious.

In other words, in most patients where an Alzheimer's diagnosis has already been put forward, an autopsy is not done. I know this, as my own mother died of Alzheimer's. Since she was diagnosed with the disease, an autopsy was not perceived as being necessary after her death to check for something else that might have led to similar symptoms. Thus, with a lack of large-scale autopsying of presumed Alzheimer's victims, we have no real way of knowing, exactly, how many were possibly misdiagnosed or who are the victims of a ruthless program of the New World Order to lower population levels.

One only has to take a look at statistics in the United States to see that something strange is afoot. Colm Kelleher, an investigative writer who has pursued this issue carefully, believes that the massive increase in Alzeheimer's is sinister in the extreme. The *Las Vegas Mercury* said of Kelleher's work: "Kelleher points to a 9,000 percent increase in the domestic diagnosis of Alzheimer's disease since 1979. That year, according to statistics from the Centers for Disease Control, 653 people died of Alzheimer's disease in the United States. Twenty-three years later, in 2002, 58,785 people died of Alzheimer's. To him, it's an increase that cannot be explained simply by an aging population and advanced diagnosis techniques."

AMERICAN VISION

The brainchild of a man named Steve Schiffman, American Vision was established in 1978 and operates out of Powder Springs, Georgia. Essentially, its mandate, in its own words, is focused upon "equipping and empowering Christians to restore America's foundation." It's a relatively small group: today, it's overseen by its current president, Gary DeMar, and a staff of just one dozen. Its primary approach is to fly the flag of Christian reconstructionism and postmillennialism. It believes in "developing family oriented biblical worldviews" and holds a yearly conference, the "Worldview Conference."

The teachings of American Vision are steeped in controversy: Gary DeMar has gone on record as stating that with a "reconstructed government," the periodic execution of what he terms "sodomites" would actually benefit U.S. society. His warped justification reads like this: "The law that requires the death penalty for homosexual acts effectively drives the perversion of homosexuality underground, back into the closet."

Given this very disturbing stance—namely, suggesting that it's perfectly fine to execute American citizens because of their sexual preferences—it's worrying to note that American Vision provides its reading material for "Christian schools and home schoolers," something which exposes more and more impressionable minds to DeMar's ideas. Equally controversial, American Vision believes that one goal which should be strived for, in particular, is "the execution of abortionists and parents who hire them."

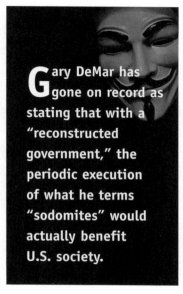

Gary DeMar has gone on record as stating that with a "reconstructed government," the periodic execution of what he terms "sodomites" would actually benefit U.S. society.

To say that the United States living under the type of control that DeMar envisions would be a grim world is not an exaggeration. American Vision calls for the end of its current political structure. In its place will exist, as Brad Steiger notes, "a theocratic government completely dominated by Christians who will strictly enforce Old Testament prohibitions."

ANTHRAX ATTACK

Exactly one week after the terrible, nation-changing events that have since become known as 9/11, the United States was plunged into another, equally fraught and fear-filled, situation. It became known as Amerithrax. This was the official title of the subsequent FBI investigation into the affair, during which anonymously mailed envelopes containing deadly anthrax spores were sent to significant individuals and bodies in the world of politics and the media.

It was an affair of deeply conspiratorial proportions and one that, in a most curious fashion, predates 9/11 itself. It is a seldom discussed fact that on the night of September 11, the then vice president, Dick Cheney—along with members of his staff—was given an antibiotic called Ciprofloxacin. It has the ability to treat, and offer protection from, a wide and varied body of bacterial infections and conditions, including anthrax. We are assured that it is purely coincidental that the vice president was given protection from anthrax exposure just seven days before Amerithrax began.

On September 18, no fewer than five letters—sent by sources then unknown—arrived at the offices of *NBC News*, *ABC News*, the *National Enquirer*, *CBS News*, and the *New York Post*. Or, rather, it's *presumed* that is the case. While the letters sent to *NBC News* and the *New York Post* certainly were found and recovered for forensic analysis by the FBI, the remaining three were not found—ever. That staff at *ABC News*, *CBS News*, and the *National Enquirer* was quickly infected by anthrax has led to the assumption that letters were the delivery method involved, too. That may well be the case. Certainly, it's a logical, solid assumption, but it is still an unproved assumption. Matters, however, had barely begun.

On October 9, things were taken to an entirely new level when two Democratic senators—Tom Daschle and Patrick Leahy (of South Dakota and Vermont, respectively)—were also the recipients of envelopes containing potentially deadly anthrax spores. There was such concern that the U.S. government briefly shut down its own mail service. Ultimately, around two dozen people were infected, and five died, all as a result of the series of letters mailed between September 18 and October 9, 2001. As for where, exactly, the letters were mailed from, the most likely location was a box situated just a short distance from Princeton University. The hunt was immediately on for the culprit or culprits.

The FBI concluded that the guilty party was Dr. Bruce Edwards Ivins. He was a microbiologist, also employed at the Fort Detrick-based U.S. Army Medical Research Institute of Infectious Diseases (USAMRIID), and someone who had held his position for almost two decades. Rather ironically, Ivins played a significant role in analyzing the very anthrax samples that had caused so much chaos and death in late 2001. And they were analyses that Ivins conducted for the FBI, no less. Such was the respect that Ivins had achieved among his colleagues that in 2003, he received the Decoration for Exceptional Civilian Service award from the Department of Defense. It is presently the highest award that the DoD can give to a civilian employee.

A 2003 photo shows Dr. Bruce Edwards Ivins at an awards ceremony two years after being a suspect in the anthrax attacks. He later died of an apparent suicide.

In the summer of 2008, the FBI finally advised Ivins that he was very likely going to be charged with committing one of the worst terrorist attacks in American history. It did not happen, however. On July 27, 2008, Ivins committed suicide (an overdose of codeine and Tylenol™). His weapon of choice was a significant and deadly amount of Tylenol, which took its fatal toll on his kidneys and liver. For the FBI, the case was closed. The FBI may not have got its man, so to speak, but the verdict was that Ivins was almost certainly the guilty party. Not everyone agreed with the FBI, however. In fact, a substantial, and highly credible, body of people didn't.

One of those who stood up in support of Ivins was Dr. Henry S. Heine, who worked with Ivins at USAMRIID. Heine very vocally rejected the idea that Ivins could have perfected such a strain of anthrax and avoided any and all detection in the process. He also maintained that within USAMRIID, and "among the senior scientists," absolutely "no-one believes" that Ivins was responsible.

There is one other notable factor in this strange saga: Some conspiracy theorists suggest that the Bush Administration played at least some role in the anthrax affair, either officially or off the record. It revolves around the aforementioned Democratic senators Tom Daschle and Patrick Leahy. It's important to note the time frame when the anthrax attacks occurred: late 2001. This was the very time when President Bush was pushing to have the Patriot Act passed—an act perceived as being vital to the long-term goals of the New World Order and specifically so in relation to spying on the populace in *1984* style.

Neither Daschle nor Leahy had much love for the controversial act. Daschle, the Senate majority leader, did not believe they should rush the bill through without giving it—and all its many and varied implications—deep thought and study. And, as the Senate majority leader, Daschle held significant sway over the amount of time the act would likely take to pass.

Moving on to Senator Leahy, only five days before Amerithrax erupted, he openly accused the Bush presidency of reneging on a certain agreement contained in the bill. Just like Daschle, Leahy had the ability to majorly slow down the passing of the Patriot Act. However, this did not happen. On October 24—after significant media outlets and two senators were targeted by the anthrax attacker—the Patriot Act was passed, and all without the Senate actually reading it.

Unfortunately for the American people, the NWO had achieved one of its major goals: the passing of a truly creepy piece of legislation that effectively ensured just about anything and everything could be done and justified in the name of national security. The privacy of the population was no more.

ANTIGLOBALIZATION MOVEMENT

*W*ake Up World says: "Under the New World Order, the ritual of inviting 'civil society' leaders into the inner circles of power—while simultaneously repressing the rank and file—serves several important functions. First, it says to the World that the critics of globalization 'must make concessions' to earn the right to mingle. Second, it conveys the illusion that while the global elites should—under what is euphemistically called democracy—be subject to criticism, they nonetheless rule legitimately. And third, it says 'there is no alternative' to globalization: fundamental change is not possible, and the most we can hope is to engage with these rulers in an ineffective 'give and take.'

"While the 'Globalizers' may adopt a few progressive phrases to demonstrate they have good intentions, their fundamental goals are not challenged. And what this 'civil society mingling' does is to reinforce the clutch of the corporate establishment while weakening and dividing the protest movement."

All of which brings us to the matter of the *anti*-globalizers.

Democracy Uprising notes of this particular issue: "Anti-globalization Movement is a disputed term referring to the international social movement network that gained widespread media attention after protests against the World Trade Organization (WTO) in Seattle, WA, in late November and early December 1999. Activists and scholars debate whether it constitutes a single social movement or represents a collection of allied groups, a 'movement of movements.' Including diverse constituencies with a range of ideological orientations, the global movement is broadly critical of the policies of economic neoliberalism, or 'corporate globalization,' that has guided international trade and development since the closing decades of the 20th century. Varied communities organizing against the local and national consequences of neoliberal policies, especially in the global South, connect their actions with this wider effort. Movement constituents include trade unionists, environmentalists, anarchists, land rights and indigenous rights activists, organizations promoting human rights and sustainable development, opponents of privatization, and anti-sweatshop campaigners. These groups charge that the policies of corporate globalization have exacerbated global poverty and increased inequality."

In 2002, political activist Noam Chomsky stated: "The term 'globalization' has been appropriated by the powerful to refer to a specific form of international economic integration, one based on investor rights, with the interests of people incidental. That is why the business press, in its more honest moments, refers to the 'free trade agreements' as 'free investment agreements' (*Wall St. Journal*). Accordingly, advocates of other forms of globalization are described as 'anti-globalization;' and some, unfortunately, even accept this term, though it is a term of propaganda that should be dismissed with ridicule. No sane person is opposed to globalization, that is, international integration. Surely not the left and the workers' movements, which were founded on the principle of international solidarity—that is, globalization in a form that attends to the rights of people, not private power systems."

AREA 51

There can be very few people who have not heard of its infamous name. Many will be familiar with the extraordinary claims of what, allegedly, goes on there. Located in the Nevada desert, it's a place that is saturated in secrecy, cloaked in conspiracy theories, and, according to many, is home to Uncle Sam's very own, highly classified collection of dead aliens, crashed UFOs, and extra-terrestrial technology. Highly fortified and guarded by personnel who have the right to use "deadly force" to protect its secrets, it is Area 51. A far more intriguing theory, however, suggests that the UFO technology at Area 51 is home-grown. That's to say, plans are in place to unleash into the skies of our planet squadrons of what *look* like alien spacecraft, but which, in reality, are part of an incredible ruse to fake an alien invasion—an invasion that will allow the New World Order to justify the implementation of worldwide martial law.

It may not be exactly jaw-dropping to learn that the origins of Area 51 began with none other than the Central Intelligence Agency (CIA). Although the CIA was established in 1947, it was not until the 1950s that serious consideration was given to constructing a secret, out-of-the-way, well-protected installation from which highly classified research could be undertaken. Given the time frame, the Cold War era of the 1950s, the U.S. government knew that it had to take steps to ensure that, at the very least, a balance of power existed between the United States and the former Soviet Union.

Richard M. Bissell, Jr., was a CIA officer who, from 1961 to 1962, held down the job of first co-director of the super-secret National Reconnaissance Office (NRO), which operates much of the United States' satellite-based surveillance technology. Back in the early 1950s, before his NRO career began, Bissell realized that there was a pressing need to keep careful watch on what the Soviets were doing, specifically in terms of constructing new military bases, atomic facilities, and aircraft that might pose distinct and serious threats to the security of the United States. So, a plan was initiated to develop a fleet of aircraft—reconnaissance planes designed to fly very fast and very high—that could secretly spy on the Soviets by penetrating their airspace and securing high-resolution photographs of what they were up to. The aircraft was the Lockheed U-2, and the operation was codenamed Project Aquatone.

Obviously, secrecy was paramount and the definite name of the game. Since intelligence data had shown the Soviets had spies in place all across the United States, even within seemingly secure military facilities and aircraft research centers, a decision was taken to have the project developed not at an existing plant or installation but at an entirely new one, specifically built for

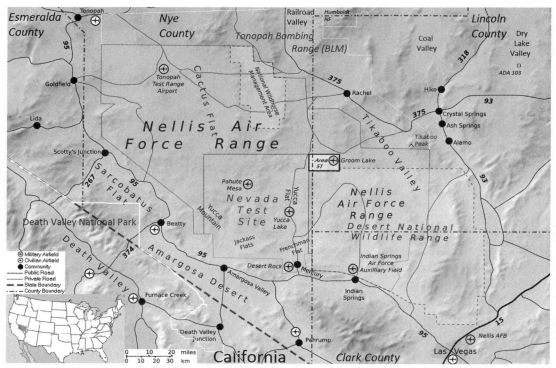

Shown here roughly in the center of a map of federal lands, Area 51 is a remote part of Edwards AFB.

the task. Richard M. Bissell, Jr., was the man who made it all happen. The first thing that Bissell did was to make a careful study of a detailed map of the entire United States. He was looking for somewhere out of the way, largely inaccessible, easily protected, and that would offer a panoramic view of the surrounding landscape—in the event that communist spies attempted to engage in a bit of localized espionage.

One of the people Bissell approached was a man named Clarence "Kelly" Johnson, a brilliant aircraft engineer and designer and the brains behind both the U-2 and the SR-71 *Blackbird*. Johnson scouted out various places in the United States, eventually settling on one that he felt most fit the bill that Bissell and the CIA were looking for. In Johnson's own words regarding a scouting operation of the site in question: "We flew over it and within thirty seconds, you knew that was the place. It was right by a dry lake. Man alive, we looked at that lake, and we all looked at each other. It was another Edwards, so we wheeled around, landed on that lake, taxied up to one end of it. It was a perfect natural landing field … as smooth as a billiard table without anything being done to it."

Johnson was, of course, talking about Groom Lake. Area 51 was about to be born.

Given that the location was blisteringly hot, inhospitable in the extreme, and filled with nothing but desert, dry beds, and mountains, something had to be done to entice people to come out and work there. Johnson had a brainstorm: he decided to christen the site Paradise Ranch. It paid off. Things got moving in the first week of 1955 when a group of surveyors arrived onsite, primarily to figure out the logistics involved in constructing a huge, 5,000-foot-long runway. It wasn't just the construction of the primary runway that began in earnest; the building of workplaces, a couple of rudimentary hangars, and even more rudimentary places to house the workers commenced. In other words, back then, Area 51 was little more than a desert equivalent of a North Pole outpost. As the months progressed, however, the workers were blessed with a couple of sports halls and a small cinema.

To ensure that the Russians didn't get word of what was afoot at the base, careful steps were taken to ensure that at any and every given moment, the numbers of people onsite were kept to the bare minimum. It meant that hardly anyone would stay for lengthy periods of time (all of the workers would be flown in from, and back to, the Lockheed plant), and discussion of what was going on less than 100 miles from Las Vegas was strictly off-limits. The secrecy level was amped up even further when, in July 1955, two things happened: (a) a small, permanent CIA presence was established; and (b) the very first U-2 made its arrival at the base, having been secretly flown in aboard a large, cargo aircraft that was leased out to the CIA. Only days afterward, the first of a near-unending series of flights began between Lockheed's Burbank facility and Area 51.

In the years that followed, such groundbreaking aircraft as the *Blackbird*, and the A-12 were tested, refined, and flown at Area 51—all in an attempt to find ways to keep the Soviet threat to a minimum.

In the years that followed, such groundbreaking aircraft as the U-2, the *Blackbird*, and the A-12 were tested, refined, and flown at Area 51—all in an attempt to find ways to keep the Soviet threat to a minimum. To cope with concerns that the Soviets might try to figure out what was going on by making high-level flights over Area 51, just two weeks into 1962, highly classified legislation was prepared by the Federal Aviation Administration to block airspace in the vicinity to everyone without official clearance. There was a good reason for this: February 1962 marked the date on which the first A-12 was flown into Area 51 for testing.

By the 1970s, Area 51's finest were focusing a great deal on what has since become known as stealth technology—in essence, the ability to render an aircraft invisible to radar. Much of the highly classified research that led to the construction and deployment of the Lockheed F-117 *Nighthawk* (more popularly known as the stealth fighter) and the Northrop B-2 *Spirit* (better known as the stealth bomber) was undertaken out at Area 51. By this time, a countless number of aircraft hangars, underground labs, facilities built into the sides of the surrounding mountains, and new runways were part and parcel of Area 51.

For the most part, no one—aside from those elite figures in the military, the intelligence community, and the government—knew anything of Area 51 from its creation in the 1950s right up until the latter part of the 1980s. The late 1980s, however, was when everything changed, and Area 51 became not just a big name but somewhere that was forever thereafter inextricably tied to the UFO phenomenon. But are those UFOs extraterrestrial in origin? Or are they the creation of the New World Order, preparing to begin a faked alien invasion when the time is deemed right?

ASSANGE, JULIAN

Born in Australia in 1971, Julian Assange is someone most widely known for being the editor-in-chief of WikiLeaks—a group which has released into the public domain an untold number of official, secret documents from a wide and varied body of sources, the vast majority of which were obtained illegally and as a result of computer-hacking. There are interesting links between Assange and the New World Order, as we shall soon see.

While Assange is most assuredly associated with WikiLeaks, his involvement in hacking dates back to the 1980s. In the latter part of that decade, Assange used the hacker handle Mendax. It was during this period that Assange hooked up with two other hackers—Prime Suspect and Trax—and created a body of hackers called the International Subversives. It is known, for sure, that the International Subversives hacked into—among many others—the systems of NASA, various organizations within the U.S. Navy, the Pentagon, and Stanford University.

Controversy continued to follow Assange: in the latter part of 1991, he was arrested by police authorities in Australia,

Computer programmer Julian Assange founded the controversial WikiLeaks site in 2006.

chiefly as a result of his online penetrations of a Canadian telecommunications company called Nortel. Assange was lucky that he was not jailed as a result, given that, initially, he faced no fewer than thirty-one charges. Fortunately for Assange, a plea bargain allowed him to walk away with a relatively small fine.

As the 1990s came to a close, Assange began to focus more and more on the secret work of the U.S. National Security Agency (NSA) and established an unused online domain, leaks.org. In this time frame, Assange made cryptic comments about the work of the NSA and how it was undertaking widespread surveillance and spying on the public. He said, without naming the NSA—but it's clear that's who he was talking about—that "Everyone's overseas phone calls are or may soon be tapped, transcribed and archived in the bowels of an unaccountable foreign spy agency."

In the mid-2000s Assange became a household name. It was all as a result of WikiLeaks, which Assange established in 2006. From the very beginning, WikiLeaks placed into the public domain massive numbers of pages of classified material, the subjects of which ranged from the Iraq War, the hostilities in Afghanistan, and—during the 2016 U.S. presidential election—the emails of presidential candidate Hillary Clinton's campaign manager, John Podesta.

In 2010, the U.S. government took sizable steps to try to bring Wiki-Leaks revelations to a halt. Arguments were made that WikiLeaks had compromised U.S. national security, that Assange had placed the United States and its allies into states of jeopardy. This was soon followed by plans to have Assange extradited to Sweden, amid claims of rape. Worried that any attempt to have him arrested might result in his being handed over to American authorities, Assange chose to hand himself over to UK police in December 2010. The next development came in August 2012, when Assange was provided asylum by the government of Ecuador. To this day, Assange remains within the London, England-based embassy of Ecuador. All of which brings us to the matter of the New World Order. (*See also the entry on* "WikiLeaks.")

AVIAN FLU

In 2005, President George W. Bush made the following statement regarding fears of bird flu erupting in the United States: "If we had an outbreak somewhere in the United States, do we not then quarantine that part of the country? And how do you, then, enforce a quarantine? It's one thing to shut down airplanes. It's another thing to prevent people from coming in to get exposed to the avian flu. And who best to be able to affect a quarantine? One option is the use of a military that's able to plan and move."

Bush's words raised eyebrows in both the mainstream media and the domain of conspiracy theorizing. The media suggested Bush was overreacting by making semi-veiled allusions to martial law and military occupations of infected zones. Conspiracy theorists suspected that the Bush Administration was planning on using fears of avian flu breaking out all across America as a means to invoke martial law and possibly even keep it in place for an extensive time, maybe even near permanently.

Although the current number of people who, on a worldwide basis, have died from avian flu is only in the hundreds, that situation could change both significantly and drastically—something which brings us to the world of bird flu-based conspiracies and the New World Order.

President George W. Bush made statements that sounded as if he might impose martial law on areas of the United States where bird flu infections had spread.

In February 2008, an extraordinary story surfaced out of Indonesia. The nation's health minister, Dr. Siti Fadilah Supari, hit the headlines with her book *It's Time for the World to Change: The Divine Hand Behind Avian Influenza*. One particular part of the book made the world's media sit up and take notice. It was the allegation that the U.S. government was secretly working to transform bird flu into a deadly, biological weapon. This charge was fully endorsed by Indonesian President Susilo Bambang Yudhoyono.

Supari became deeply worried by the fact that the World Health Organization shared samples with the U.S. national laboratory in Los Alamos, New Mexico, where nuclear weapons are developed. Supari additionally commented: "Whether they use it to make vaccine or develop chemical weapons, would depend on the need and interest of the U.S. government. It is indeed a very dangerous situation for the destiny of humanity. It is a matter of choice whether to use the material for vaccines or biological weapon development."

One year later, an Austrian journalist named Jane Bürgermeister filed criminal charges against a number of official bodies and agencies, including the FBI, the United Nations, the World Health Organization, and even President Obama.

It was Bürgermeister's contention that a vast conspiracy was in the making, one that involved the development of a form of bird flu that (a) was designed to spread all across the planet; and (b) would kill billions in no time at all. In other words, Bürgermeister believed she had uncovered a plot to, in stark essence, cull the herd—to keep populations low and under manageable control by a martial law-obsessed New World Order.

In Bürgermeister's words: "There is evidence that an international corporate criminal syndicate, which has annexed high government office at Federal and State level, is intent on carrying out a mass genocide against the people of the United States by using an artificial (genetic) flu pandemic virus and forced vaccine program to cause mass death and injury and depopulate America in order to transfer control of the United States to the United Nations and affiliated security forces (UN troops from countries such as China, Canada, the UK and Mexico)."

She added: "There is proof that many organizations—World Health Organization, UN as well as vaccine companies such as Baxter and Novartis—are part of a single system under the control of a core criminal group, who give the strategic leadership, and who have also funded the development, manufacturing and release of artificial viruses in order to justify mass vaccinations with a bioweapon substance in order to eliminate the people of the USA, and so gain control of the assets, resources etc., of North America.

"The motivation for the crime is classical robbery followed by murder although the scale and method are new in history. The core group sets its strategic goals and operative priorities in secret using committees such as the Trilateral Commission, and in person to person contact in the annual Bilderberg meeting."

Although Bürgermeister's suit proved unsuccessful in terms of bringing to justice what she perceived to be the guilty parties, she continues her work to expose what she believes is a malignant, worldwide plot—operated by a New World Order—to drastically change the face, and size, of human civilization.

BANKING DEATHS

The New World Order is clearly determined to create a world bank of a kind never before seen, which will control and hold the savings of everyone on the planet. What might happen to those in the banking community who dare to go against this dangerous plot? They might pay with their lives. It looks like that may already be happening.

In 2016 the *Free Thought Project* informed its readers: "In 2015 there was a popular 'conspiracy theory' floating around the Internet after a rash of mysterious 'suicides' by high profile banking professions. What once looked like wild speculation is now beginning to resemble a vast criminal conspiracy connected to the Libor, interest-rigging scandal. Over forty international bankers allegedly killed themselves over a two-year period in the wake of a major international scandal that implicated financial firms across the globe. However, three of these seemingly unrelated suicides seem to share common threads related to their connections to Deutsche Bank. These three banker suicides, in New York, London, and Siena, Italy, took place within seventeen months of each other in 2013/14 in what investigators labeled as a series of unrelated suicides."

They continued: "Financial regulators in both Europe and the U.S. in 2013 began a probe that would ultimately become known as the Libor scandal, in which London bankers conspired to rig the London Interbank Offered Rate, which determines the interest banks charged on mortgages, personal and auto loans. The scandal rocked the financial world and cost a consortium of international banks, including Deutsche Bank, about $20 billion in fines."

One of those who died under unusual circumstances, in March 2013, was David Rossi, a fifty-one-year-old communications director at the world's oldest bank, Italian Monte dei Paschi di Siena. The bank was verging on disaster as a result of massive losses in the financial crisis of 2008. Rossi fell to his death on March 6, 2013. *The New York Times* said of Rossi's death: "A devastating security video shows Rossi landing on the pavement on his back, facing the building—an odd position more likely to occur when a body is pushed from a window. The footage shows the three-story fall didn't kill Rossi instantly. For almost 20 minutes, the banker lay on the dimly lit cobblestones, occasionally moving an arm and leg. As he lay dying, two murky figures appear. Two men appear and one walks over to gaze at the banker. He offers no aid or comfort and doesn't call for help before turning around and calmly walking out of the alley. About an hour later, a co-worker discovered Rossi's body. The arms were bruised and he sustained a head wound that, according to the local medical examiner's report, suggested there might have been a struggle prior to his fall."

And there is this from *Wall Street on Parade*, from April 2014: "It doesn't get any more Orwellian than this: Wall Street mega banks crash the U.S. financial system in 2008. Hundreds of thousands of financial industry workers lose their jobs. Then, beginning late last year, a rash of suspicious deaths start to occur among current and former bank employees. Next we learn that four of the Wall Street mega banks likely hold over $680 billion face amount of life insurance on their workers, payable to the banks, not the families. We ask their Federal regulator for the details of this life insurance under a Freedom of Information Act request and we're told the information constitutes 'trade secrets.'"

Clearly, powerful figures do not want the media too close to uncovering the truth of this dark and deadly aspect of the banking business. Powerful figures within the New World Order? Who else?

BARCODING THE POPULATION

David Mikkelson, writing at Snopes, says: "THE EAN-13 barcode system is used in 85 countries, making it the most popular product scanning system of its kind in the world. It works by representing numbers as a series of seven vertical lines. Each of the seven lines is either black or white, and the sequence of lines forms a pattern which is recognized as a particular digit when scanned by a computer. Every product is assigned a unique thirteen-digit number (ten digits for the product itself, a check digit, and a couple of flag characters to indicate which organization assigned the number)."

Is it just "product scanning" that barcoding is noted for, though? Right now, at least, it is. But, under the control of a New World Order, there might be another kind of "product" that gets barcoded. It's called the human race. Science fiction author Elizabeth Moon told the BBC in 2012: "I would insist on every individual having a unique ID permanently attached—a barcode if you will—an implanted chip to provide an easy, fast inexpensive way to identify individuals."

As well as insisting that such a program should go ahead, Moon suggests that the coding should begin at birth. She added: "Having such a unique barcode would have many advantages. In war soldiers could easily differentiate legitimate targets in a population from non-combatants. This could prevent mistakes in identity, mistakes that result in the deaths of innocent bystanders. Weapons systems would record the code of the use, identifying how fired which shot and leading to more accountability in the field. Anonymity would be impossible as would mistaken identity making it easier to place responsibility accurately, not only in war but also in non-combat situations far from the war."

The *New York Daily News* says on this emotive and sinister issue: "The proposal isn't too far-fetched—it is already technically possible to 'barcode' a human—but does it violate our rights to privacy?" The answer is: yes, of course it does!

The American Civil Liberties Union says of this inflammatory affair: "To have a record of everywhere you go and everything you do would be a frightening thing. Once we let the government and businesses go down the road of nosing around in our lives, we're going to quickly lose all our privacy."

The Inquirer echoes these concerns: "The idea of implanting a microchip into a person, whose personal identity data and sensitive private information are on the chip (which could also pinpoint the exact real-time location of the wearer) is creating a lot of controversy. There is concern among various sectors of society that this 'human bar coding' would curtail individual civil liberties and violate the person's constitutional freedom and right to privacy, confidentiality,

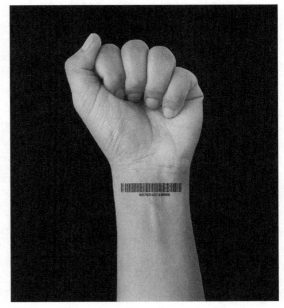

Will we all have to get barcodes tattooed on our flesh one day just like products in a grocery store?

security and safety. There is also the fear that this technology could be used by unscrupulous people or criminals, by competing corporations, or even by some agencies in the government, for illegal information gathering or surveillance, or for some immoral objectives."

BENJAMIN FRANKLIN TRUE PATRIOT ACT

The Benjamin Franklin True Patriot Act "is a bill introduced in the United States House of Representatives intended to review the previously passed USA PATRIOT Act. The bill was referred to subcommittees where it languished without action taken before the end of the 108th United States Congress. The bill will have to be reintroduced in order to be considered again.

"The bill was sponsored by Representatives Dennis Kucinich (D-Ohio) and Ron Paul (R-Texas), with 27 co-sponsors, all Democrats except for Ron Paul. The intent was to review the USA PATRIOT Act to make sure it does not 'inappropriately undermine civil liberties.' Its name, as described in Sec. 2, No. 1, refers to Benjamin Franklin's famous quote, 'Those who would give up Essential Liberty, to purchase a little temporary Safety, deserve neither Liberty nor Safety.'

"The act had the goal of creating a 90-day review period in which parts of Sections 4-10 of the USA PATRIOT Act could be removed. These aspects would include: the use of roving wiretaps, secret record searches, detention and deportation of noncitizens, monitoring of religious institutions and the requirement that airport baggage screeners be U.S. citizens. This bill was presented to the House on September 24, 2003, and was referred to subcommittees for consideration. No action was taken before the end of the 108th Congress. The bill will need to be re-introduced in order to be considered again. The proposed bill drew an angry response from the Justice Department who called their efforts 'misguided' and 'silly' and accused the sponsors of trying to promote fear through misinformation."

The Benjamin Franklin True Patriot Act was among the bills that sought to cap the ability of the Patriot Act to intrude into, and limit, the rights of U.S. citizens and residents. It's a sign of the power that those who wanted the act passed yielded, since neither bill had any bearing on the power of the Patriot Act—it failed. The government responded by, in 2003, creating what was known as the Domestic Security Enhancement Act, which, in essence, was an outgrowth of, and an amendment to, the original Patriot Act. When copies were leaked to the media, it caused a sensation, despite assertions from officialdom that it was nothing more than a concept for change, rather than a literal, soon-to-be-in-place plan.

It was specifically thanks to the Center for Public Integrity that the document (draft or otherwise) surfaced. The CPI notes: "The Center for Public Integrity was founded in 1989 by Charles Lewis. We are one of the country's oldest and largest nonpartisan, nonprofit investigative news organizations. Our mission: To serve democracy by revealing abuses of power, corruption and betrayal of public trust by powerful public and private institutions, using the tools of investigative journalism."

In the first week of February 2003, the CPI acquired the document, which contained two key amendments: the government planned to (a) increase its ability to intrude into the lives of American citizens; and (b) make it more and more difficult for courts to deny the instigation of the amendments. It is, almost certainly, due to the actions of the CPI—who quickly posted the document to their website—that the "draft" was pulled.

The Benjamin Franklin True Patriot Act was among the bills that sought to cap the ability of the Patriot Act to intrude into, and limit, the rights of U.S. citizens and residents.

Had it gone through, in its original form, it would have allowed for (a) the collection of DNA from people suspected of having terrorist links—even if wholly unproven; (b) the legal ability to undertake so-called search-and-surveillance overseas without the need of any kind of court-order; and (c) extensions and modifications to the death penalty; the New World Order's definitive wet dream.

BILDERBERG GROUP

Whenever a discussion or debate occurs on the matter of secret societies, seldom is the Bilderberg Group left out of the equation. In fact, the exact opposite is the case: it's likely to be near the top of the list of talking points. And there are very good reasons for that, too.

SourceWatch says of the Bilderberg Group: "The name came from the group's first meeting place at the Hotel de Bilderberg, in the small Dutch town of Oosterbeek. Bilderberg was founded by Joseph Retinger, Prince Bernhard of the Netherlands, and Belgian Prime Minister Paul Van Zeeland and is comprised of representatives from North America and Western Europe. Since 1954, the group's secret meetings have included most of the top ruling class players from Western Europe and America. Until he was implicated in the Lockheed bribery scandal in 1976, Prince Bernhard served as chairman. Now, Bilderberg is a symbol of world management by Atlanticist elites. Some observers feel that it borders on the conspiratorial, while others are primarily interested in its implications for power structure research. Bilderberg participants from the U.S. are almost always members of the Council on Foreign Relations (CFR). Since 1973, Japanese elites have been brought into the fold through a third overlapping group, the Trilateral Commission."

According to Richard J. Aldrich, a political lecturer at Nottingham University, the Bilderberg Group is an "informal secretive transatlantic council of key decision makers, developed between 1952 and 1954.... It brought leading European and American personalities together once a year for informal discussions of their differences.... The formation of the American branch was entrusted to General Dwight D. Eisenhower's psychological warfare coordinator, C.D. Jackson and the first meeting was funded by the Central Intelligence Agency (CIA)."

When, in 2004, the Bilderberg Group celebrated its fiftieth anniversary, the BBC profiled the organization. In doing so, they significantly noted the aura of mystery surrounding both it and its members. The BBC didn't shy away from discussing the issue of alleged Bilderberg-orchestrated conspiracies, either: "What sets Bilderberg apart from other high-powered get-togethers, such as the annual World Economic Forum (WEF), is its mystique. Not a word of what is

The Bilderberg Hotel in Oosterbeek, Netherlands, is where the powerful elite of Europe and North America meet annually.

said at Bilderberg meetings can be breathed outside. No reporters are invited in and while confidential minutes of meetings are taken, names are not noted. In the void created by such aloofness, an extraordinary conspiracy theory has grown up around the group that alleges the fate of the world is largely decided by Bilderberg. In [the former] Yugoslavia, leading Serbs have blamed Bilderberg for triggering the war which led to the downfall of Slobodan Milosevic. The Oklahoma City bomber Timothy McVeigh, the London nail-bomber David Copeland and Osama Bin Laden are all said to have bought into the theory that Bilderberg pulls the strings with which national governments dance."

Daniel Estulin, who has deeply and carefully studied the work and history of Bilderberg, says: "Slowly, one by one, I have penetrated the layers of secrecy surrounding the Bilderberg Group, but I could not have done this without help of 'conscientious objectors' from inside, as well as outside, the Group's membership. Imagine a private club where presidents, prime ministers, international bankers and generals rub shoulders, where gracious royal chaperones ensure everyone gets along, and where the people running the wars, markets, and Europe (and America) say what they never dare say in public."

Perhaps most chilling of all are the following words of Henry Kissinger, which were made at the Bilderberg Group meeting in 1992: "Today, Americans would be outraged if UN troops entered Los Angeles to restore order; tomorrow, they will be grateful. This is especially true if they were told there was an outside threat from beyond, whether real or promulgated, that threatened our very existence. It is then that all people of the world will plead with world leaders to deliver them from this evil ... individual rights will be willingly relinquished for the guarantee of their well-being granted to them by their world government."

For the sake of everyone, let's hope that Henry Kissinger is way off the mark.

BILDERBERG'S ROLE IN THE NEW WORLD ORDER

On June 10, 2016, the UK's *Express* newspaper ran an article with the eye-catching title of "Inside Bilderberg: Leaders and Elite Meet in 'Illuminati' Style to Decide New World Order." Its author, Jon Austin, said: "The world's most secretive gathering of global leaders and elites begins yesterday—with prime ministers and presidents, bankers and former heads of the CIA and MI6 topping the guest list. The 64th annual Bilderberg Conference is being held in Dresden, Germany, from today until Saturday sending ardent Illuminati New World Order conspiracy theorists crazy. If ever the powers that be wanted to fuel a theory there is a secret sect above the elected rulers of the world's top nations, then Bilderberg is how to do it. Inside, no journalists are allowed in and there is no opening or closing press conferences or statements. On top of this no minutes are taken and attendees are urged not to discuss what goes on inside with anyone else. The organizers of the Bilderberg meetings, claim it is just the world's biggest lobby group and talking shop."

Austin added: "Conspiracy theorists claim the Illuminati (think Freemasons on acid) is a worldwide secret organization which really runs the world above the global leaders we see in office. Various versions of the conspiracy claim the Illuminati is involved in the Occult, and it seeks to impose a New World Order on us mere mortals that will enslave the general population. They are the secret organization often accused of being behind the so-called inside job terror plots such as 9/11 or the Paris attacks this year, in order to gain public support for various wars in the Middle East. Last October, Express.co.uk exclusively revealed that former Whitby town councillor Simon Parkes had claimed to have stopped 'black magic wizards from the Illuminati' working at the CERN Large Hadron Collider from opening up a portal to another dimension that would have allowed Satan into our world."

BIN LADEN, OSAMA

Did the New World Order brilliantly orchestrate a ruse to have us all believe that Osama bin Laden was taken out—as in permanently? Possibly because he was an NWO lackey, one who acted as a patsy to justify the invasion of Afghanistan and Iraq? And, with his work done, was bin Laden removed from the picture when the New World plans were firmly in place? Or, does he still live, in secret, with a significant NWO slush-fund at his side? It was, and to this day remains, one of the most controversial and mystery-filled killings of all time. It is a saga filled with conspiracy theories, with intense doubts about the official version of events, and with shadowy and powerful players with even more shadowy and powerful agendas. We are talking about the May 2011 killing of Osama bin Laden. Or, as many conspiracy theorists prefer it: the *alleged* killing of Osama bin Laden. Before we get to matters shrouded in cover-up and chicanery, let's take a look at the official story of bin Laden's final hours. It goes like this.

Osama bin Laden—the brains behind al-Qaeda and the events of September 11, 2001—was shot and killed on May 2, 2011, by U.S. Navy Seals attached to the U.S. Naval Special Warfare Development Group. Or, as they are far better known: Team Six. Shrouded in overwhelming secrecy, the goal of the project—which was controlled by the CIA and designated the title of "Operation Neptune Spear"—was to launch a team from Afghanistan and have them make their stealthy way into neighboring Pakistan.

Upon crossing the border, the project called for the Seals to take out bin Laden in his fortified base of operations—at Abbottabad, Pakistan. The operation was apparently a complete success: bin Laden was quickly located and salvo upon salvo of bullets ensured he would no longer pose a threat to the free world. The body of bin Laden was then carefully examined to confirm it really was him, after which the corpse was hastily, and secretly, buried at sea.

It's abundantly obvious why so many conspiracy theorists expressed deep doubts and cynicism about bin Laden's alleged

Pakistani supporters of Osama bin Laden hold up a portrait of the terrorist leader.

killing. Absolutely no solid evidence—in terms of photographs of bin Laden's corpse, film footage taken at the scene, DNA, audiorecordings, documents, images shot at the funeral at sea, or statements from the team involved—was ever presented to the world to see and scrutinize, not even in the slightest. Was this because of fears of bin Laden being turned into a martyr? Or, incredibly, was it because the official story was nothing less than a bald-faced lie?

It's important to be aware it wasn't just conspiracy theorists that noted certain inconsistencies in the version of events we are told was the truth. Even the United States' media expressed puzzlement as it sought to uncover something, *anything*, to try to confirm the story. The likes of Fox News, CBS News, Reuters, Citizens United, to Associated Press all did their very best to use the Freedom of Information Act to force open the doors of secrecy. Each and every one of them failed spectacularly. Then, when it was revealed that close to half an hour of the live feed that recorded the raid on bin Laden's compound was mysteriously missing, people *really* began to wonder what the truth was.

The government knew that it had to make a statement, and it did. The official line was that the decision not to reveal any photographs showing the body of bin Laden was simply because they were overly graphic, displayed him riddled with bullets, and were perceived as too shocking for mainstream audiences. This was a scenario that received a degree of backing and support from Jim Inhofe; he was both a senator (with the Republican Party) and a member of the Senate Armed Services Committee. Inhofe went on record as saying he had seen certain images of bin Laden—after death. He came straight to the point and said the photos were "gruesome." Inhofe was in no doubt about the authenticity of the pictures, which he had viewed at some point before May 11.

Since the government admitted that imagery did exist and Inhofe confirmed he had seen it, further steps were taken by the media to try to secure the priceless data. One of the most interesting developments came in April 2012. That was when Judicial Watch—a group that was determined to get the bottom of the puzzle—had its case against the Department of Defense thrown out of court. The U.S. Federal Court tossed out Judicial Watch's argument that the terms of the Freedom of Information Act should allow for the release of evidence of bin Laden's death. The court disagreed. Judicial Watch was far from happy: "The court got it terribly wrong. There is no provision under the Freedom of Information Act that allows documents to be kept secret because their release might offend our terrorist enemies. We will appeal."

Most people, by now, will not be surprised to know that appealing made absolutely no difference whatsoever.

So much for the overwhelmingly unsuccessful attempts to get hard evidence of Osama bin Laden's death, but what about that burial at sea? Simply an attempt to ensure that one of the world's most hated men never had a grave that his followers were able to turn into a shrine? Or, was the story merely that—a story? And, if so, was it a tale created as a convenient way to explain why there *was* no corpse? Maybe there never had been a corpse. Certainly, that was the view of many within conspiracy-themed domains.

As with the matter of the photographs, let's first begin with the government's position—and statements—on the sunken body of bin Laden. The Obama Administration has explained its position on why the body of the notorious terrorist was buried at sea. It relates to Muslim traditions. Within Muslim culture, the dead must be buried inside one day, that's to say, twenty-four hours. The problem with bin Laden, the White House said, was that given the unique circumstances, it became clear there would not be sufficient time to (a) raid bin Laden's compound, (b) kill him, (c) have his DNA confirmed, (d) prepare the body, and (e) then bury it according to Muslim traditions, all within one day. So, the only option was to quickly have bin Laden's corpse taken out to sea and dumped as soon as possible.

A famous and controversial radio host made his thoughts very clear. It was Alex Jones, host of Austin, Texas-based *The Alex Jones Show*, and someone whose YouTube page has been viewed on an astonishing *400 million-plus* occasions.

When he was interviewed on *Russia Today*, Jones revealed that a contact in the White House—unnamed, unfortunately, although some might say predictably—had told him that bin Laden died more than a decade earlier. The story continued that the body of the terrorist was carefully preserved—in liquid nitrogen, no less—until such a time when he would be "rolled out" and his death announced.

Even respected politicians were determined to have their say. The Canadian deputy Leader of the Opposition and MP, Thomas Mulcair, was careful and tactful in his words, but they left very little room for doubt with regard to his views on the matter: "I don't think from what I've heard that those pictures exist."

BIOCHIPS

In the 1950s and 1960s, a large number of experiments in behavior modification were conducted in the United States, and it is well known that electrical implants were inserted into the brains of animals and people. Later, when new techniques in influencing brain functions became a priority to military and intelligence services, secret experiments were conducted with such unwilling guinea pigs as inmates of prisons, mental patients, handicapped children, the elderly, and just about any and all groups considered expendable. It is an area of research that would have the control-obsessed New World Order practically hyperventilating.

Rauni-Leena Luukanen-Kilde, M.D., a former chief medical officer in Finland, has stated that mysterious brain implants, the size of one centimeter, began showing up in X-rays in the 1980s. In a few years, implants were found the size of a grain of rice. Dr. Luukanen-Kilde stated that the implants were made of silicon, later of gallium arsenide. Today, such implants are small enough that it is nearly impossible to detect or remove them. They can easily be inserted into the neck or back during surgical operations, with or without the consent of the subject.

It has been stated that within a few years, all Americans will be forced to receive a programmable biochip implant somewhere in their body—a key aspect of the New World Order agenda. The biochip is most likely to be implanted on the back of the right or left hand so it will be easy to scan at stores. The biochip will also be used as a universal type of identification card. A number will be assigned at birth and will follow that person throughout their life. Eventually, every newborn will be injected with a microchip, which will identify the person for the rest of his or her life.

Initially, people will be informed that the biochip will be used largely for purposes of identification. The reality is that the implant will be linked to a massive supercomputer system that will make it possible for government agencies to maintain surveillance of all citizens by ground sensors and satellites.

Today's microchips operate by means of low-frequency radio waves that target them. With the help of satellites, the implanted person can be followed anywhere. Their brain functions may be remotely monitored by supercomputers and even altered through the changing of frequencies. Even worse, say the alarmists, once the surveillance system is in place, the biochips will be implemented to transform every man, woman, and child into a controlled slave, for these devices will make it possible for outside intelligences to influence a person's brain cell conversations and to talk directly with the individual's brain neurons. Through cybernetic biochip brain implants, people may be forced to think and to act exactly as government intelligence agencies have preprogrammed them to think and behave.

The technology exists right now to create a New World Order served by zombie-like masses. Secret government agencies could easily utilize covert neurological communication systems in order to subvert independent thinking and to control social and political activity.

The National Security Agency's (NSA) electronic surveillance system can simultaneously follow the unique bioelectrical resonance brain frequency of millions of people. The NSA's signals intelligence (SIGINT) group can remotely monitor information from human brains by decoding the evoked potentials (3.50 hertz, 5 milliwatts) emitted by the brain. Electromagnetic frequency (EMF) brain-stimulation signals can be sent to the brains of specific individuals, causing the desired effects to be experienced by the target.

A U.S. Navy research laboratory, funded by intelligence services, has achieved the incredible breakthrough of uniting living brain cells with microchips. When such a chip is injected into a man's or a woman's brain, he or she instantly becomes a living vegetable and a subservient slave.

Experts have said that a micromillimeter microchip may be placed into the optical nerve of the eye and raw neuroimpulses from the brain which embody the experiences, smells, sights, and voice of the implanted subject. These neuroimpulses may be stored in a computer and may be projected back to the person's brain via the microchip to be re-experienced. A computer operator can send electromagnetic messages to the target's nervous system, thereby inducing hallucinations. Beyond all science fiction scenarios, we could become a nation of New World Order-controlled zombies.

BLACK HELICOPTERS

In 1995, the late Jim Keith, a conspiracy theorist who died in questionable circumstances in 1999, wrote a book titled *Black Helicopters: Strike Force for* *the New World Order*. It was Keith's belief that a secret arm of the U.S. military—with ties to those in politics, big businesses, and secret societies and those who wished to see the world placed under the control of the NWO—was secretly building and stockpiling a massive number of black, unmarked helicopters. In Keith's view, they will, in the very near future, amount to becoming the eyes and the ears of a radically altered police force when the New World Order comes into being.

There can be very few people—if, indeed, any—with an interest in UFOs, conspiracies, cover-ups, and strange and sinister goings-on of a distinctly weird nature who have not heard of these mysterious helicopters that seem to play an integral—albeit admittedly unclear—role in perceived UFO-connected events. And one of the biggest misconceptions about this deeply weird phenomenon is that those same mysterious helicopters are lacking in official documentation. Actually, not so at all. In fact, exactly the opposite. If you know where to go looking.

The FBI's now-declassified files on cattle mutilations in 1970s U.S.A. make for fascinating reading and demonstrate that the Bureau had a deep awareness of the presence of the enigmatic helicopters in affairs of the mute kind. On August 29, 1975, Floyd K. Haskell, a senator from Colorado, wrote an impassioned letter to Theodore P. Rosack, a special agent in charge of the FBI in Denver, Colorado, imploring the FBI to make a full investigation into the cattle mutilations in an attempt to resolve the matter once and for all.

Haskell said: "For several months my office has been receiving reports of cattle mutilations throughout Colorado and other western states. At least 130 cases in Colorado alone have been reported to local officials and the Colorado Bureau of Investigation (CBI); the CBI has verified that the incidents have occurred for the last two years in nine states. The ranchers and rural residents of Colorado are concerned and frightened by these incidents. The bizarre mutilations are frightening in themselves: in virtually all the cases, the left ear, rectum and sex organ of each animal has been cut away and the blood drained from the carcass, but with no traces of blood left on the ground and no footprints."

And there was an unmarked helicopter out in force in Colorado, too, as Senator

One conspiracy theorist speculated that the U.S. government is stockpiling black helicopters for the purpose of using them in an oppressive police force.

Haskell was only too well aware: "In Colorado's Morgan County area there has [sic] also been reports that a helicopter was used by those who mutilated the carcasses of the cattle, and several persons have reported being chased by a similar helicopter. Because I am gravely concerned by this situation, I am asking that the Federal Bureau of Investigation enter the case. Although the CBI has been investigating the incidents, and local officials also have been involved, the lack of a central unified direction has frustrated the investigation."

He continued: "It seems to have progressed little, except for the recognition at long last that the incidents must be taken seriously. Now it appears that ranchers are arming themselves to protect their livestock, as well as their families and themselves, because they are frustrated by the unsuccessful investigation. Clearly something must be done before someone gets hurt."

The loss of livestock in at least twenty-one states under similar circumstances suggested that an interstate operation was being coordinated. Senator Haskell closed his letter by urging the FBI to begin its investigation as soon as possible. Haskell forced the issue by issuing a press release, informing the media that he had asked the FBI to investigate the mutilations. This caused the *Denver Post* newspaper to take up the senator's plea on September 3: "If the Bureau will not enter the investigation of the mysterious livestock deaths in Colorado and some adjacent states then Senator Floyd Haskell should take the matter to Congress for resolution." Aware of previous FBI statements that the killings were not within the Bureau's jurisdiction, the *Denver Post* stated firmly: "The incidents are too widespread—and potentially too dangerous to public order—to ignore. Narrow interpretations of what the FBI's role is vis-a-vis state authority are not adequate to the need."

The issue of possible disregard for the law should the Bureau not wish to become involved was also high on the *Post's* agenda: "There is already federal involvement. Consider this: Because of the gun-happy frame of mind developing in eastern Colorado (where most of the incidents have been occurring), the US Bureau of Land Management (BLM) has had to cancel a helicopter inventory of its lands in six counties. BLM officials are simply afraid their helicopters might be shot down by ranchers and others frightened by cattle deaths."

On the day after publication, special agents Rosack and Sebesta of the Colorado FBI made a visit to the offices of the *Denver Post*, where, in a meeting with three *Post* representatives, Charles R. Buxton, Lee Olson, and Robert Partridge, they spelled out the FBI's position with respect to mutilations: "Unless the FBI has investigative jurisdiction under Federal statute, we cannot enter any investigation."

One week later, on September 11, Senator Haskell telephoned Clarence M. Kelley at the FBI to discuss the issue of cattle and animal mutilation and the possibility of the FBI becoming involved in determining who, exactly, was responsible. Again, the FBI asserted that this was a matter outside of its jurisdiction. The Bureau noted: "Senator Haskell [said that] he understood our statutory limitations but he wished there was something we could do," reported an FBI official, R. J. Gallagher. Haskell had additional reasons for wanting the mutilation issue resolved swiftly, as Gallagher recorded in an internal memorandum of September 12, 1975: "Senator Haskell recontacted me this afternoon and said that he had received a call from Dane Edwards, editor of the paper in Brush, Colorado, who furnished information that U.S. Army helicopters had been seen in the vicinity of where some of the cattle were mutilated and that he, Edwards, had been threatened but Senator Haskell did not know what sort of threats Edwards had received or by whom. He was advised that this information would be furnished to our Denver Office and that Denver would closely follow the situation."

The FBI ultimately determined that the unidentified helicopter issue was also outside of its jurisdiction. Curiously, however, during this same time frame, numerous reports of both UFOs and unidentified hel-

Colorado senator Floyd Haskell grew increasingly suspicious of the cattle mutilations and black helicopter sightings in his state.

icopters surfaced in the immediate vicinity of strategic military installations around the United States, and there is evidence that someone within the FBI was fully aware of this and was taking more than a cursory interest in these sightings.

Proof comes via a number of Air Force reports forwarded to the FBI only weeks after its contact with Senator Haskell. One report from December 1975 states: "On 7 Nov 75 an off duty missile launch officer reported that unidentified aircraft resembling a helicopter had approached and hovered near a USAF missile launch control facility, near Lewistown. Source explained that at about 0020, 7 Nov 75, source and his deputy officer had just retired from crew rest in the Soft Support Building (SSB) at the LCF, when both heard the sound of a helicopter rotor above the SSB. The Deputy observed two red-and-white lights on the front of the aircraft, a white light on the bottom, and a white light on the rear.

"On 7 Nov 75, Roscoe E. III, Captain, 341 Strategic Missile Wing, advised that during the hours of 6-7 Nov 75, two adjacent LCFs, approximately 50 miles south of aforementioned LCF, reported moving lights as unidentified flying objects (UFO). During this period there were no reports of helicopter noises from personnel at these LCFs.

"This office was recently notified of a message received by security police MAFB, MT., detailing a similar nocturnal approach by a helicopter at a USAF weapons storage area located at another USAF base in the Northern Tier states. Local authorities denied the use of their helicopters during the period 6-7 Nov 75."

It's curious that these reports were of interest to the FBI, given the statements made to Senator Haskell that the unidentified helicopter sightings reported in Colorado were outside of the FBI's jurisdiction.

It is also notable that an unauthenticated document made available to researcher William Moore (coauthor with Charles Berlitz of a 1980 book, *The Roswell Incident*) refers to the Northern Tier helicopter and UFO sightings of 1975 and expresses concern that, in view of the fact that the media had picked up on the stories, there was a need on the part of some authority to develop an effective disinformation plan to counter the developing interest that was surrounding the sightings.

More than four decades after the events of 1975, the black helicopters are still being seen—and in ever-growing numbers, too, strongly suggesting that the time frame for their leading role in the looming New World Order is getting closer and closer.

BLAIR, TONY

On January 6, 2003, then British Prime Minister Tony Blair gave a speech before British ambassadors in London that significantly focused on the matter of a New World Order. Blair stated: "A country always has to know its place in the world. For Britain this is of special importance. At the end of the 19th century we were an imperial power. A century later the empire was gone. Naturally, and despite the pride of our victory in World War Two, our definition seemed less certain. Our change in circumstances affected our confidence and self-belief. Yet today I have no doubt what our place is and how we should use it.

"What are our strengths? Part of the EU; and G8; permanent members of the UN security council; the closest ally of the US; our brilliant armed forces; membership of NATO; the reach given by our past; the Commonwealth; the links with Japan, China, Russia and ties of history with virtually every nation in

Asia and Latin America; our diplomacy—I do believe our foreign service is the best there is; our language.

"What is the nature of the world in which these strengths can be deployed? The world has never been more interdependent. Economic and security shocks spread like contagion. I learnt this graphically in the 1998 financial crisis; everyone knows it after September 11. Nations recognize more than ever before that the challenges have to be met in part, at least, collectively. Also culture and communication driven by technological revolution are deepening the sense of a global community. Look at the FCO [Foreign Office] strategic goals you set out in your paper. Each of them has a direct domestic impact. Yet each of them— whether free trade through the WTO [World Trade Organization], combating climate change or the threats to our security— *can only be overcome by collaboration across national frontiers.*"

Prime Minister Blair added that "the world today has one overriding common interest: to make progress with order; to ensure that change is accompanied by stability. The common threat is chaos. That

Former British Prime Minister Tony Blair recognized the growing trend toward a New World Order being established in the international community.

threat can come from terrorism, producing a train of events that pits nations against each other. It can come through irresponsible and repressive states gaining access to WMD [weapons of mass destruction]. It can come through the world splitting into rival poles of power; the US in one corner; anti-US forces in another. It can come from pent-up feelings of injustice and alienation, from the divisions between the world's richer and its poorer nations. The threat is not change. *The world and many countries in it need to change.* It is change through disorder, because then the consequences of change cannot be managed."

Blair proceeded to set out what specific role the UK would have in a future, changed world. He told the audience before him: "This has been understood, at least inchoately, ever since the fall of the Berlin Wall. Then the call was for a new world order. But a new order presumes a new consensus. It presumes a shared agenda and a global partnership to do it.

"Here's where Britain's place lies. We can only play a part in helping this—to suggest more would be grandiose and absurd—but it is an important part. Our very strengths, our history equip us to play a role as a unifier around a consensus for achieving both our goals and those of the wider world.

"Stating our aims is relatively easy and they would be shared by many other countries: security from terrorism and WMD; elimination of regional conflicts that can afflict us; a stable world economy; free trade; action against climate change; aid and development. Jack set them out clearly yesterday. The question is: how as a matter of diplomacy do we achieve them? What are the principles of foreign policy that should guide us?

"First, we should remain the closest ally of the US, and as allies influence them to continue broadening their agenda. We are the ally of the US not because they are powerful, but because we share their values."

Blair had more to say, too: "The values we stand for: freedom, human rights, the rule of law, democracy, are all universal values. Given a chance, the world over, people want them. But they have to be pursued alongside another value: justice, the belief in opportunity for all. Without justice, the values I describe can be portrayed as 'Western values;' globalization becomes a battering ram for Western commerce and culture; the order we want is seen by much of the world as 'their' order not 'ours.'"

Prime Minister Blair concluded as follows: "Now is the moment to make our future as exciting in impact, *if different in character*, as our history."

BOHEMIAN CLUB

Created in the nineteenth century—in April 1872, to be precise—the Bohemian Club is an integral part of the New World Order. Launched in San Francisco, California, it began as an organization in which like-minded figures in the world of the arts could get together. Indeed, San Francisco remains its home to this very day. Its bases of operations are San Francisco's Union Square and Bohemian Grove, in Sonoma County. Although the Bohemian Club initially invited the likes of poets, writers, playwrights, and painters into the fold, it wasn't long at all before powerful figures in the fields of politics, business, and the military became members. Eventually, as circumstances and history have shown, they would come to dominate it.

In 1862, the *Westminster Review* described Bohemianism as follows: "The term *Bohemian* has come to be very commonly accepted in our day as the description of a certain kind of literary gypsy, no matter in what language he speaks, or what city he inhabits. A Bohemian is simply an artist or 'littérateur' who, consciously or unconsciously, secedes from conventionality in life and in art."

As for the specific origins of the Bohemian Club, a concise explanation of its beginnings came from Michael Henry de Young, the owner of the *San Francisco Chronicle* newspaper. In 1915, de Young said: "The Bohemian Club was organized in the *Chronicle* office by Tommy Newcombe, Sutherland, Dan O'Connell, Harry Dam and others who were members of the staff. The boys wanted a place where they could get together after work, and they took a room on Sacramento Street below Kearny. That was the start of the Bohemian Club, and it was not an unmixed blessing for the *Chronicle* because the boys would go there sometimes when they should have reported at the office. Very often when Dan O'Connell sat down to a good dinner there he would forget that he had a pocketful of notes for an important story."

It's interesting to note that the de Young family had its very own ties to powerful and famous figures: Michael Henry de Young's grandfather, Benjamin

The headquarters of the Bohemian Club at the corner of Post and Taylor streets in San Francisco. There is also a second headquarters at Bohemian Grove in Sonoma County.

Morange, was the minister from France to Spain under none other than Napoleon Bonaparte.

It is deeply ironic that the group became known as the Bohemian Club. Over time, the number of members who could rightly call themselves Bohemians fell to the point where they were eventually in the minority. The majority soon became those aforementioned politicians, businessmen, and military figures. U.S. presidents—and more than a few of them—would enter the fold, too. We're talking about the likes of President George H.W. Bush, publisher William Randolph Hearst, former National Security Agency director Bobby Ray Inman, Henry Kissinger, and President Ronald Reagan.

The Bohemian Club is most well known—arguably, infamously well known—for its annual, two-week-long get-together at Bohemian Grove, located in Monte Rio, California. While the club's public image is that of a group of like-minded figures getting together and hanging out at Bohemian Grove, that's far from the case. Indeed, behind the closed doors of Bohemian Grove, the club quickly transforms into a definitive secret society, replete with bizarre rituals and initiation rites—as we shall now see.

BOHEMIAN GROVE SECRECY

A search on the Internet reveals that there is often confusion surrounding the Bohemian Club and Bohemian Grove. It's actually quite simple: the former is the name of the group, whereas Bohemian Grove is the location at which the members meet. Bohemian Grove is a huge compound, running close to 3,000 acres in size, and is located on the Russian River in Sonoma County, California. And just about everything that goes on there is shrouded in secrecy. It's also shrouded in Douglas firs and redwoods, all of which help keep prying eyes at bay. And, Bohemian Grove is also a place dominated by controversy, as Brad Steiger notes: "Conspiracy theorists state that the principal theme of the annual meeting is celebration of patriarchy, racism, and class privilege."

The *Washington Post* reveals some notable facts about Bohemian Grove: "The club is so hush-hush that little can be definitively said about it, but much of what we know today is from those who have infiltrated the camp, including Texas-based filmmaker Alex Jones. In 2000, Jones and his cameraman entered the camp with a hidden camera and were able to film a Bohemian Grove ceremony, Cremation of the Care. During the ceremony, members wear costumes and cremate a coffin effigy called 'Care' before a 40-foot-owl, in deference to the surrounding Redwood trees."

Then, we have this from *Bohemian Grove Exposed*: "They secretly meet for seventeen days each July in a remote 'sacred grove' of ancient redwood trees in the deep forests surrounding San Francisco. Some 1,500 in number, their membership roll is kept secret, but includes the super-rich, blood dynasty member families of the Illuminati; heavy-hitting corporate chieftains and high government officials. Mingling among them are a number of Hollywood movie stars, Broadway producers, famous entertainers, musicians, authors, painters and poets. Great statesmen and—so we're told—gentlemen.

"Stories have come out of the Grove about wild homosexual orgies, male and female prostitutes being engaged in what can only be described as extreme sexual games, young children being exploited in unspeakable ways, up to and including cold-blooded ritual murder. There are stories involving actual human sacrifice on the 'altar' of the owl God statue. Understandably, it's all very hard to believe."

Mike Clelland is someone who made a careful study of Bohemian Grove and its history and activities. He says: "The club emblem is an owl with the motto *Weaving Spiders Come Not Here*. This seems to trace back to Greek mythology. Arachne was a mortal woman who boasted that her weaving skill was greater than that of Athena. A contest took place, and Arachne's weaving was filled with imagery depicting ways that the gods had misled and abused mortals. Athena, goddess of wisdom and crafts, saw that Arachne's creation was not only mocking the gods, but it was far more beautiful than her own. Enraged, Athena turned Arachne into a spider. The scientific term for spiders, arachnids, goes back to the myth of Arachne.

"Starting in 1887, there has been an annual play performed by Bohemian members, often at the foot of the sinister looking giant stone owl. Roles for women are played by men, since women are not allowed as club members. The 1906 performance of *The Owl and Care, A Spectacle*, seems to be the only play with the word owl in its title. Curiously, it was performed the same year as the great San Francisco Earthquake.

"This giant stone owl (although some reports describe it made of cement) is commonly known as Moloch, named after a god of the Canaanites, an evil deity that required the sacrifice of human children. But the ancient literature presents Moloch as a bull, and not an owl. No easy answers, but since the Bohemian Club is shrouded under so many layers of secrecy, it is easy to assume the worst. Given the state of the world today, many of these assumptions might be true."

The final words go to President Richard M. Nixon: "Anybody can be President of the United States, but very few can ever have any hope of becoming President of the Bohemian Club."

BORDER CLOSINGS

While the ultimate goal of the New World Order is to create a world that falls under the auspices of one unified government, there is very little doubt that the same NWO is seeking to isolate and control the United States via several disturbing ways. They include encouraging obesity and lethargy, dumbing down the population, and isolating the United States from the rest of the world. Two ways in which Americans may find themselves separate from everyone else are by (a) the process of bit by bit making it more and more difficult for people to travel to the United States; and (b) closing down borders and selling horror stories to the U.S. population as to what might happen to them if they are thinking of spending time overseas. Such a situation could very well—in just a few decades—see the United States turned into a country that is utterly controlled by the New World Order and which has no interest in the rest of the planet, a situation that would easily allow for complete control over the masses.

In April 2002, *World Press Review* stated: "Since Sept. 11, Americans have been forcefully awakened to an awareness of their immense vulnerability. And today they are questioning the effectiveness of their national security. The effects of this unrest could be felt only weeks after the terrorist attacks: Their borders were immediately militarized to control their now-fragile national security, and they are now carrying out investigations to block the entry of new terrorists.

"Since five of the 19 hijackers entered the United States through the long and little-guarded border with Canada, attitudes have changed. While the southern U.S. border is super-militarized, patrolled by 9,000 guards to cover 41 ports of entry, the northern border (3,987 miles long, with 115 ports of entry) is patrolled by only 340 officers. Now the government has decided to reinforce surveillance there and has authorized the transfer of 100 agents from the southern to the northern border. There has even been a proposal to establish a North American perimeter to harmonize migratory policies, border security, and customs norms between the United States and Canada."

The controversy continues to rage. Thirteen years later, Jeff Berwick, writing for *The Dollar Vigilante*, offered the following: "We've reported over the years how the U.S. government has instituted nefarious capital controls via the Foreign Account Tax Compliance Act (FATCA) which makes it very difficult for Americans to open bank accounts outside of the US. And currently thrown into the Developing a Reliable and Innovative Vision for the Economy (DRIVE) Act is an inclusion that the U.S. government can revoke your passport if they think you owe more than $50,000 in taxes. As well, we've reported how numerous US international airports have cash-sniffing dogs checking those trying to leave the country with some money. Meanwhile, in the Presidential debates, the argument appears to be who can build a bigger wall on the Mexican border. And candidate, Ben Carson, said just this week that he wants US troops to patrol the Canadian border. Now, the U.S. government has begun to place iris scanners at the Mexican border to check the identity of those leaving the US and going to Mexico."

Berwick also said: "Examine the situation more closely and the security measures being passed and implemented are aimed at law-abiding citizens not so-called terrorists. The endless ratcheting up of security measures is indicative of a failed state, one where representatives and a larger group of shadowy power brokers intend to loot what is left of civil society on the way to recreating new states that are as yet un-looted."

Former CIA and NSA director, General Michael Hayden notes the dangers and consequences that might come if borders are closed to everyone: "It's not possible, it's not wise, and it wouldn't help. The issue in Brussels, beyond the hideous crime that's been committed, is a sense of alienation of a significant fraction of the Belgian population that does not feel contact, integration with, assimilation into Belgian society. I don't think we strengthen our hand

Parts of the U.S.–Mexico border already have daunting barriers, such as this wall between Tijuana, Mexico, and San Diego, California. U.S. President Donald Trump wants to completely seal the full length of this border as well as ban Muslims from immigrating from selected countries.

to take what has been a winning hand that we are assimilating and suddenly closing our borders to one of the world's great monotheisms. Why would we actually try to undercut an aspect of our character that up to this point has actually made us safer?"

The *Close the Border Petition* states: "Americans are tired of the Violence, Drugs, Trash, Disease, and Deaths caused by illegal aliens and illegal immigrants which cross the border between the United States and Mexico. We stand United in our Desire to Close the Border with Mexico against more injustices to our National Constitution, our National Lands and most especially the injustices being committed on the Citizens of the United States of America. This is not a petition against race or culture, this petition is an attempt to ease if not end the fear and destruction spreading throughout our wonderful Nation. We feel our Nation has been invaded and our U.S. government has become complacent and ineffective. We The People have a solution, close the border until tighter security can be put in place."

While there is no doubt that the world is a dangerous place, the process of isolating the United States from the rest of the world—via the building of huge walls—actually plays right into the heart of the New World agenda: a nation that is isolated, and unaware of what is afoot in the rest of the world, is a nation that can be very easily controlled, manipulated, and, ultimately, enslaved.

See also the entry "Trump's Wall."

BRAVE NEW WORLD

In 1931, Aldous Huxley wrote one of the most important novels ever on the scenario of a nightmarish, futuristic world in which the human race, society, and civilization are very different from what we see today—but which could become all too real. Its title: *Brave New World*. Huxley is also well remembered for his 1954 publication, *The Doors of Perception*, which tells of Huxley's experiences with mescaline in 1953, a book that directly led Jim Morrison to name his legendary band the Doors.

As for *Brave New World*, it is a book that Huxley wrote in quick time, a deeply focused four-month period. It was quickly picked up and published the very next year. This is hardly surprising as Huxley was already a respected and noted writer, with four books already under his belt. Whereas the renowned sci-fi/fantasy author H. G. Wells—who penned such books as *The War of the Worlds* and *The Island of Dr. Moreau*—saw the future as both bright and positive, Huxley did not. He feared that human society would be transformed into what, today, we might term the worst New World Order conceivable. For Wells, a Utopia was on the horizon. For Huxley, however, there was nothing but a dystopia looming large.

To be sure, human civilization in *Brave New World* is grim in the extreme—at least, from our perspective, today. Set in the year 2540, Huxley's novel makes it very clear from the outset that our society is long gone. In its place is what is termed the World State—it is, as its title suggests, an all-powerful, all-dominating body of people who hold firm and solid sway over the world's population.

Rather disturbingly, we see some of the issues and trends that Huxley described already creeping into society. For example, there is the deliberate dumbing down of society, something which is clearly afoot in the real world. One only has to take a look at certain politicians, who cannot even find the likes of Iran or Iraq on a map, or who cannot name even a single overseas world

British author and philosopher Aldous Huxley was most famous for his dystopian novel *Brave New World*.

leader. Indeed, in *Brave New World,* people are encouraged not to ask questions, not to go against authority, to avoid reading books—particularly ones deemed inflammatory—and to even limit personal initiative.

On top of that, there is another, equally nightmarish, situation: people no longer give birth. Instead, fetuses are grown in vast factory-like environments. Families, of the kind we have, no longer exist. Family bonds, therefore, are extinct. And death comes for everyone at the age of sixty—something which is welcomed by the mindless masses. Or, at least, some of them are near mindless: others are quite the opposite.

There are five groups of people—Alpha, Beta, Gamma, Delta, and Epsilon—of wildly varying degrees of intelligence. They range from the elite to those who are treated as subnormal slaves. There is a specific reason for this: while the Alpha and Beta people grow and mature in normal states, the other three are subjected to chemical conditioning, which limits their IQ and intelligence.

It should be noted, however, that the brave new world which Huxley plunges the reader into is not overseen by fascist, jackbooted thugs of the kind that will likely perform a major role in the creation of a New World Order. In his story, no one cares about culture, history, personal growth, freedom, education, literature: the very things that define our society. In the twenty-sixth century, all of that is gone. Instead, there is a world population controlled by a mind-altering drug called Soma—which, in name, at least, exists today—and an addiction to sex. Which, for many, may not be perceived as a bad thing! However, what we see in *Brave New World* is a human race which is, effectively, enslaved by its own ignorance and which wallows in a lack of initiative or creativity. It is also a race which doesn't ask questions—not because it fears state-sponsored backlash but simply because it does not even care about such things. For the people of *Brave New World*, ignorance really is bliss.

The final word goes to the late Neil Postman, an acclaimed writer who penned such books as *Amusing Ourselves to Death* and *The End of Education*. He had thought-provoking words regarding Huxley's *Brave New World* and George Orwell's equally chilling novel, *1984*: "What Orwell feared were those who would ban books. What Huxley feared was that there would be no reason to ban a book, for there would be no one who wanted to read one. Orwell feared those who would deprive us of information. Huxley feared those who would give us so much that we would be reduced to passivity and egotism. Orwell feared that the truth would be concealed from us. Huxley feared the truth would be drowned in a sea of irrelevance. Orwell feared we would become a captive culture. Huxley feared we would become a trivial culture...."

BRETTON WOODS SYSTEM

Created in the mid-1940s and having taken its title from the town of Bretton Woods, New Hampshire, the Bretton Woods system was designed to ensure that financial transactions ran smoothly on a global basis, particularly so for the United States, Japan, the U.K., Australia, Canada, and much of Europe. The system resulted in the establishment of today's International Monetary Fund (IMF), which was also created in the 1940s—specifically in 1944. Today's World Bank would not exist had it not been for the implementation of the Bretton Woods system.

In a *Time* article, M.J. Stephey said of the IMF and the World Bank: "The former was designed to monitor exchange rates and lend reserve currencies to nations with trade deficits, the latter to provide underdeveloped nations with needed capital although each institution's role has changed over time."

Much of the work was driven by a pressing need to rebuild the nations whose cities and landscapes were ravaged by Nazi Germany. The Bretton

Woods system allowed for the stabilization of rates of exchange at an international level and encouraged worldwide trade—all of which resulted in prompt reconstruction of much of Europe, as well as Japan.

By encouraging the aforementioned nations to purchase American dollars, and by tying the dollar to gold, Stephey stated, "[T]he golden age of the U.S. dollar began."

Of the 1944 meeting, the BBC revealed the following: "The meeting was part of the process led by the US to create a new international world order based on the rule of law, which also led to the creation of the United Nations and the strengthening of other international organizations. The delegates focused on two key issues: how to establish a stable system of exchange rates, and how to pay for rebuilding the war-damaged economies of Europe. And they established two international organizations to deal with these problems. The International Monetary Fund was set up to enforce a set of fixed exchange rates that were linked to the dollar....

"Attempts to forge a new Bretton Woods agreement on currencies in the 1970s failed, although the IMF still retained its role of helping countries cope with major currency crises—including Britain in 1976. The breakdown of Bretton Woods had two consequences. On the one hand, it led European countries to begin seriously considering closer monetary co-operation, which ultimately

The World Bank headquarters in Washington, D.C., is located on Pennsylvania Avenue and 18th Street. The bank lends money to foreign nations, but increasingly it has been viewed as a mechanism for creating a world order to dominate less wealthy political states.

led to the creation of the euro in 1999. And it led to the creation of the G7, the informal group of the world's leading economies, which helped to coordinate currency adjustment in the Plaza and Louvre Accords in the 1980s."

PBS *News Hour* offers the following: "Bretton Woods was truly a fascinating saga, but it was most surely not the triumph of economic thinking and international comity it is often painted to be. An ascendant anti-colonial superpower, the United States, used its economic leverage over an insolvent allied imperial power, Great Britain, to set the terms by which the latter would cede its dwindling dominion over the rules and norms of foreign trade and finance. Britain cooperated because the overriding aim of survival seemed to dictate the course.

"The monetary architecture that Harry White designed, and powered through an international gathering of dollar-starved allies, ultimately fell of its own contradictions: The United States could not simultaneously keep the world adequately supplied with dollars and sustain the large gold reserves required by its gold-convertibility commitment. The IMF, the institution through which it was launched, though, endures—however much its objectives have metamorphosed—and many hope that it can be a catalyst for a new and more enduring 'Bretton Woods.'

"Yet history suggests that a new cooperative monetary architecture will not emerge until the United States, the world's largest creditor nation in the 1940s, but now the world's largest debtor, and China, today's dominant creditor nation, each comes to the conclusion that the consequences of muddling on, without the prospect of correcting the endemic imbalances between them, are too great. Even more daunting are the requirements for building an enduring system; monetary nationalism was the downfall of the last great effort in 1944." (*See also the entry "World Bank"*)

BREXIT

When, in the summer of 2016, the people of the UK voted to leave the European Union, it was a clear blow to the ever-growing New World Order, the reason being that a unified Europe is something that is at the heart of the NWO's agenda: namely, trying to ensure that individual nations become a thing of the past and are replaced by giant bodies along the lines of the EU—with the final intent being a world where no nations exist at all, just one world government overseeing everyone. There is no doubt that the NWO was shocked to its core by the actions of the UK population—even more so when the government of the UK accepted the vote without any disagreement and which led to the immediate resignation of Prime Minister David Cameron.

So what, exactly, are the implications for the New World Order, in the wake of the Brexit affair? Before we get to that question, let us first take a look at what Brexit is and how the UK came to leave the European Union. The BBC says: "It is a word that has become used as a shorthand way of saying the UK leaving the EU—merging the words Britain and exit to get Brexit, in a same way as a possible Greek exit from the euro was dubbed Grexit in the past. A referendum—a vote in which everyone (or nearly everyone) of voting age can take part—was held on Thursday 23 June, to decide whether the UK should leave or remain in the European Union. Leave won by 52% to 48%. The referendum turnout was 71.8%, with more than 30 million people voting.

"The former home secretary [Theresa May] took over from David Cameron, who resigned on the day after losing the referendum. Like Mr. Cameron, Mrs. May was against Britain leaving the EU but she says she will respect the will of the people. She has said 'Brexit means Brexit' but there is still a lot of debate about what that will mean in practice especially on the two key issues of how British firms do business in the European Union and what curbs are brought in on the rights of European Union nationals to live and work in the UK."

In an article titled "Brexit Signals the End of the New World Order," Joseph Murray wrote: "We Americans have July 4th, and the Brits now have June 23rd. In the words of Nigel Farage, leader of the UKIP and top proponent for the United Kingdom to leave the European Union, the Brexit vote was Britain's 'Independence Day.' June 23rd will be the day that the British people filed their papers to divorce a global bureaucracy that buried national sovereignty in bureaucratic red tape. After constant failures that left many Brits without jobs and living in a nation being colonized by migrants with no attachment to British culture, enough was enough. After almost three decades of rule, globalism was witnessing a Judgment Day and Brexit represents a nationalistic movement that has laid in wait for two decades."

Murray had more to say: "Whether the protectors of the NWO admit it or not, the world is changing. Brexit won, the Scots—though defeated—will be rejuvenated in their quest for independence, Venice wants to break away from Italy, and Catalonia is giddy to secede from Spain. The old tribes of the West are getting together for a reunion."

Prime Minister David Cameron resigned from office when Great Britain voted to exit the European Union.

The Daily Wire ran an article that was in agreement with Joseph Murray. On June 24, 2016, its main headline read: "Brexit is the End of the New World Order as We Know It, and I Feel Fine." In part, the article noted: "The common takeaway from the left seems to be that Britain's reversion to nationalism represents the rise of ethnic xenophobia and foreign policy isolationism. That's largely because the left sees nationalism itself as an incurable evil. They believe, as Hannah Arendt once wrote, that 'tribal nationalism … denies theoretically the very possibility of a common mankind long before it is used to destroy the humanity of man.' But they don't see that not all nationalism is tribal—nationalism can also be civilizational. *That* is why Britain once embraced the EU, but now rejects it."

Veterans Today had their say, too: "The New World Order plan to impose bankster-driven global tyranny took a huge hit Friday morning as news of the Brexit victory stunned markets, political leaders and pundits. They obviously hadn't planned on this. Polls before the vote showed "leave" down 52%–48%. Given the likelihood of pro-"remain" election fraud—the skids for which had been greased by the elimination of exit polls—a pro-Brexit result seemed mathematically impossible. So … what happened? That is undoubtedly what the Rothschilds and their minions are asking themselves as they take a much-needed break from cackling and rubbing their hands together in glee at the cascading successes of their planetary hostile takeover operation, and instead get to experience a tiny fraction of the anxiety that their victims everywhere have been living with for centuries."

What all of this shows, and as the media sources cited above demonstrate, is that when people band together—in their millions—and create a collective force in the process, things can be achieved that are in our favor and not in favor of the New World Order.

BUSH, GEORGE H. W., 1990 SPEECH

On September 11, 1990, President George H.W. Bush made a now-historic speech that significantly highlighted the concept of a New World Order, as well as an understanding of the term, to the American public. His speech was, of course, prompted by the invasion of Kuwait by the Iraqi forces of Saddam Hussein.

The president said: "We gather tonight, witness to events in the Persian Gulf as significant as they are tragic. In the early morning hours of August 2d, following negotiations and promises by Iraq's dictator Saddam Hussein not to use force, a powerful Iraqi army invaded its trusting and much weaker neighbor, Kuwait. Within 3 days, 120,000 Iraqi troops with 850 tanks had poured into Kuwait and moved south to threaten Saudi Arabia. It was then that I decided to act to check that aggression.

"At this moment, our brave servicemen and women stand watch in that distant desert and on distant seas, side by side with the forces of more than 20 other nations. They are some of the finest men and women of the United States of America. And they're doing one terrific job. These valiant Americans were ready at a moment's notice to leave their spouses and their children, to serve on the front line halfway around the world. They remind us who keeps America strong: they do. In the trying circumstances of the Gulf, the morale of our service men and women is excellent. In the face of danger, they're brave, they're well-trained, and dedicated."

President Bush soon introduced to the United States—and, as a result of international news coverage, to the entire planet, too—the idea of a New World Order. He stated: "We stand today at a unique and extraordinary moment. The crisis in the Persian Gulf, as grave as it is, also offers a rare opportunity to move toward an historic period of cooperation. *Out of these troubled times, our fifth objective—a new world order*—can emerge: a new era—freer from the threat of terror, stronger in the pursuit of justice, and more secure in the quest for peace. An era in which the nations of the world, East and West, North and South, can prosper and live in harmony. A hundred generations have searched for this elusive path to peace, while a thousand wars raged across the span of human endeavor. Today that new world is struggling to be born, a world quite different from the one we've known. A world where the rule of law supplants the rule of the jungle. A world in which nations recognize the shared responsibility for freedom and justice. A world where the strong respect the rights of the weak. This is the vision that I shared with President Gorbachev in Helsinki. He and other leaders from Europe, the Gulf, and around the world understand that how we manage this crisis today could shape the future for generations to come.

"The test we face is great, and so are the stakes. *This is the first assault on the new world that we seek*, the first test of our mettle. Had we not responded to this first provocation with clarity of purpose, if we do not continue to demonstrate our determination, it would be a signal to actual and potential despots around the world. America and the world

President George H. W. Bush (seen here with First Lady Barbara Bush and U.S. Supreme Court Justice Clarence Thomas) announced a New World Order as he ordered war against Iraq's Saddam Hussein.

must defend common vital interests—and we will. America and the world must support the rule of law—and we will. America and the world must stand up to aggression—and we will. And one thing more: In the pursuit of these goals America will not be intimidated."

We also have this, from the very same speech: "Once again, Americans have stepped forward to share a tearful goodbye with their families before leaving for a strange and distant shore. *At this very moment, they serve together with Arabs, Europeans, Asians, and Africans in defense of principle and the dream of a new world order.* That's why they sweat and toil in the sand and the heat and the sun. If they can come together under such adversity, if old adversaries like the Soviet Union and the United States can work in common cause, then surely we who are so fortunate to be in this great Chamber—Democrats, Republicans, liberals, conservatives—can come together to fulfill our responsibilities here."

It truly was a significant moment in the plan to create a New World Order for the people of Earth.

BUSH, GEORGE H. W., 1991 SPEECH

On January 29, 1991—and expanding on his speech of September 11, 1990—President George H.W. Bush made another historic speech about events in the Middle East that led to the first Gulf War of 1990. It is a speech that, for many—and particularly so the public—led to the ultimate defining of the New World Order. In his speech, Bush said, in part: "I come to this House of the people to speak to you and all Americans, certain that we stand at a defining hour. Halfway around the world, we are engaged in a great struggle in the skies and on the seas and sands. We know why we're there: We are Americans, part of something larger than ourselves. For two centuries, we've done the hard work of freedom. And tonight, we lead the world in facing down a threat to decency and humanity.

"What is at stake is more than one small country; *it is a big idea: a new world order, where diverse nations are drawn together in common cause to achieve the universal aspirations of mankind*—peace and security, freedom, and the rule of law. Such is a world worthy of our struggle and worthy of our children's future.

"The community of nations has resolutely gathered to condemn and repel lawless aggression. Saddam Hussein's unprovoked invasion—his ruthless, systematic rape of a peaceful neighbor—violated everything the community of nations holds dear. The world has said this aggression would not stand, and it will not stand. Together, we have resisted the trap of appeasement, cynicism, and isolation that gives temptation to tyrants. The world has answered Saddam's invasion with 12 United Nations resolutions, starting with a demand for Iraq's immediate and unconditional withdrawal, and backed up by forces from 28 countries of 6 continents. With few exceptions, *the world now stands as one*."

President Bush continued: "The conviction and courage we see in the Persian Gulf today is simply the American character in action. The indomitable spirit that is contributing to this victory for world peace and justice is the same spirit that gives us the power and the potential to meet our toughest challenges at home. We are resolute and resourceful. If we can selflessly confront the evil for the sake of good in a land so far away, then surely we can make this land all that it should be. If anyone tells you that America's best days are behind her, they're looking the wrong way. Tonight I come before this House and the American people with an appeal for renewal. This is not merely a call for new government initiatives; it is a call for new initiatives in government, in our communities, and from every American to prepare for the next American century."

The president also stated: "The courage and success of the RAF pilots, of the Kuwaiti, Saudi, French, the Canadians, the Italians, the pilots of Qatar and Bahrain—all are proof that for the first time since World War II, the international community is united. *The leadership of the United Nations, once only a hoped-for ideal, is now confirming its founders' vision.*

"I am heartened that we are not being asked to bear alone the financial burdens of this struggle. Last year, our friends and allies provided the bulk of the economic costs of Desert Shield. And now, having received commitments of over $40 billion for the first 3 months of 1991, I am confident they will do no less as we move through Desert Storm.

"But the world has to wonder what the dictator of Iraq is thinking. If he thinks that by targeting innocent civilians in Israel and Saudi Arabia, that he will gain advantage, he is dead wrong. If he thinks that he will advance his cause through tragic and despicable environmental terrorism, he is dead wrong. And if he thinks that by abusing the coalition prisoners of war he will benefit, he is dead wrong.

"We will succeed in the Gulf. And when we do, the world community will have sent an enduring warning to any dictator or despot, present or future, who contemplates outlaw aggression.

"*The world can, therefore, seize this opportunity to fulfill the long-held promise of a new world order*, where brutality will go unrewarded and aggression will meet collective resistance.

"Yes, the United States bears a major share of leadership in this effort. Among the nations of the world, only the United States of America has both the moral standing and the means to back it up. We're the only nation on this Earth that could assemble the forces of peace. This is the burden of leadership and the strength that has made America the beacon of freedom in a searching world."

President Bush concluded: "Let future generations understand the burden and the blessings of freedom. Let them say we stood where duty required us to stand. Let them know that, together, we affirmed America and the world as a community of conscience. The winds of change are with us now. The forces of freedom are together, united. We move toward the next century more confident than ever that we have the will at home and abroad to do what must be done—the hard work of freedom.

"May God bless the United States of America. Thank you very, very much."

The concept of a New World Order was now firmly cemented in the minds of millions—if not billions—of people, all around the world.

BUSH, JEB

In 2016, *New World Disorder* reported the following: "Jeb Bush found himself in the awkward position of having to answer for his father's legendary statements on the need to create a 'new world order.' The topic was raised by a questioner at a town-hall meeting in Laconia, New Hampshire, Wednesday where Bush was campaigning for next week's GOP primary. A man stood up and asked the former Florida governor: 'Your father spoke of a new world order. If elected, specifically, how will you continue to move the country toward this goal?' Bush seemed taken aback, stumbling over his words and, at first, refusing to answer the question. 'I don't know. I don't have any intention to, uh, lead … I don't know what that means to you so I'm not going to answer it. It makes me nervous to.… It might mean something different to you than it means to me.' But he quickly found his footing and provided a long, rambling explanation of national security and the importance of the United States staying 'engaged' in the world."

Jeb Bush, a former governor of Florida, brother of President George W. and son of President George H. W. Bush, was also at one point associated with the New World Order.

C

CASHLESS SOCIETY

According to the website *True Conspiracies,* "A one world dictatorship and new monetary system will soon prevail. Therefore existing savings may be declared worthless. Deceiving people into investing money in multinationals and banks will give the powerful greater power, and they will soon take our money and not give it back. An individual would be better to withdraw it and use for a good purpose, such as by helping those in need and informing people of the truth.

"We are heading for a cashless society, where soon everyone will be forced to have a mark on their right hand or forehead to buy or sell." The article goes on to relate how this was predicted in the Bible as the mark of the Beast, only in the modern age, this mark would be a computer chip embedded inside people. "There is strong evidence that the Illuminati have well planned this system of a satanic one-world government," the article concludes, adding that average citizens will be brainwashed into thinking the chips are great ideas for preventing fraud and other crimes.

While the religious aspects of the scenario described above are open to debate, there is very little doubt that we are, indeed, heading toward a future in which cash does not play a role. Some might say that doing everything electronically will be to the benefit of everyone. It will not. The only ones who will benefit are the New World Order overlords and their minions.

"The darker aspect of a cashless society, is one which few are debating or discussing, but is actually the most pivotal in terms of social engineering and transforming communities and societies," remarked Patrick Henningsen on the website *21st Century Wire*. In London, the electronic touch payment Oyster Card was introduced in 2003. Initially for public transport, since that time the card has been co-opted to be used for other functions as the UK beta tests the idea of an all-in-one cashless lifestyle solution.

"Ironically, and alongside biometric chipping now in India, it's the United States, supposedly the birthplace of modern capitalism, who is beta testing its own socialist technocracy. As the ranks of the poor and unemployed grow and dollar inflation rises in America, more and more people are dependent on traditional 'Food Stamp' entitlements in order to feed their families. The US has now introduced its own socialist 'Oyster' to replace the old Food Stamp program. It's called the *'EBT,'* which stands for 'Electronic Benefit Transfer,' as a means of transferring money from the central government to people living below the poverty line."

Keep Henningsen's following words firmly in your minds: "It has long been the dream of collectivists and technocratic elites to eliminate the semi-unregulated cash economy and black markets in order to maximize taxation and to fully control markets. If the cashless society is ushered in, they will have near complete control over the lives of individual people. The financial collapse which began in 2007–2008 was merely the opening gambit of the elite criminal class, a mere warm-up for things to come. With the next collapse we may see a centrally controlled global digital currency gaining its final foothold."

London's Oyster Card was originally meant to be used for the city's public transportation system, but it now can be used for a wide variety of transactions.

Finally, take careful note of the words of Matthew Lynn, of the U.K.'s *Telegraph* newspaper. On August 31, 2015, he wrote: "From today, France is banning the use of cash for transactions worth more than €1,000, or slightly more than £700. On one level, that is about combating crime and terrorism. But on another, it is also part of a growing movement among academics and now governments to gradually ban the use of cash completely."

Lynn added: "More importantly, cash is about freedom. There are surely limits to the control over society we wish to hand over to governments and central banks? You don't need to be a fully paid-up libertarian to question whether, in a world where we already worry about the amount of data that Facebook and Google can gather about us, we really want the banks and the state to know every single detail of what we are spending our money on and where. It is easy to surrender that freedom—but it will be a lot harder to get back.

"People have used notes and coins for several thousand years. The earliest go all the way back to the Iron Age. If they wither away because people prefer using their phones or their cards, then that is fine. No one wants to stand in the way of technological innovation. But outlawing cash? That is surely a step too far—and we might miss it when it's gone far more than we realize."

CHEMTRAILS

The controversy of chemtrails has attracted the attention of conspiracy theorists, the mainstream media, the U.S. Air Force, and the governments of both the United Kingdom and Canada. On the one hand, there are those who suggest it's all a matter of conspiratorial nonsense and fear mongering. On the other hand, it's perceived by many as something dark and deadly, something that may even threaten our very existence as a species.

The official line is that chemtrails—in essence, trails in the sky, left by large aircraft—are simply regular contrails of the kind that can be seen in the skies at pretty much anytime and pretty much everywhere. They are created when a high-flying aircraft reaches an altitude cold enough to cause exhaust vapor to transform into crystals of ice, something that causes them to look like long trails of cloudlike vapor.

The unofficial view, however, is very different. It suggests that chemtrails are nothing less than prime evidence that someone is pumping massive amounts of potentially deadly chemicals into the atmosphere. The theories as to why such actions might be taking place include spreading widespread illness and death as a means to lower the planet's ever-growing population levels—an issue that the New World Order sees as being imperative to its long-term goals.

In 1999, the New Mexico attorney general's office contacted New Mexicans for Science and Reason (NMSR) member Kim Johnson to help answer questions from constituents regarding the alleged dangers of "chemtrails." After his investigation, Johnson told the attorney general: "I have viewed a number of photos purporting to be of aircraft spraying the chemical or biological material into the atmosphere. I have also discussed these letters with another scien-

There seems to be no escape from chemtrails these days. Whether you are in the city or the countryside, the white streaks seem to criss-cross our skies everywhere.

tist familiar with upper atmospheric phenomena from Sandia National Laboratory and a retired general and fighter pilot who is an Air Force Hall of Fame Member. In summary, there is no evidence that these 'chemtrails' are other than expected, normal contrails from jet aircraft that vary in their shapes, duration, and general presentation based on prevailing weather conditions."

At the height of the controversy, chemtrails researcher Ken Adachi said: "Chemtrail spraying seems to be heaviest and most constant over North America and most countries of eastern Europe. Some countries in Asia are being sprayed (Japan and Korea), but the greatest exception to any chemtrail activity whatsoever is China. The Chinese are being spared completely because China is being groomed by the NWO to replace the United States as the leading nation of the world, both economically and militarily."

Adachi also noted something that suggested it wasn't the entire human race that was under assault, but possibly just specific portions of it: "It is being reported that people with average or below average immunity are experiencing pneumonia-like respiratory symptoms, while people with stronger immunity are only experiencing slight discomfort for a day or two or no symptoms at all. Some people have gotten very ill and the symptoms seem to keep returning after a short period of improvement. It's possible that some of these sprayings might contain special bioengineered pathogens designed to affect only certain racial groups."

Even the world of mainstream media couldn't ignore the chemtrails. *USA Today* writer Traci Watson said in 2001: "Federal bureaucracies have gotten thousands of phone calls, e-mails and letters in recent years from people demanding to know what is being sprayed and why. Some of the missives are threatening.

"It's impossible to tell how many supporters these ideas have attracted, but the people who believe them say they're tired of getting the brush-off from officials. And they're tired of health problems they blame on 'spraying.'

"'This is blatant. This is in your face,' says Philip Marie Sr., a retired nuclear quality engineer from Bartlett, N.H., who says the sky above his quiet town is often crisscrossed with 'spray' trails.

"'No one will address it,' he says. 'Everyone stonewalls this thing.'"

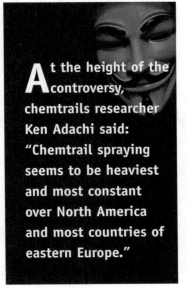

At the height of the controversy, chemtrails researcher Ken Adachi said: "Chemtrail spraying seems to be heaviest and most constant over North America and most countries of eastern Europe."

Moving on to 2008, one of the most well-known and respected investigators of conspiracy theories, Jim Marrs, said: "Chemtrails often occur at altitudes and in conditions where it would be impossible for a contrail to form." He noted that a 2007 investigation undertaken by a television station in Louisiana—KSLA—revealed something startling. According to Marrs, investigative reporter Jeff Ferrell tested water captured under a crosshatch of alleged chemtrails. According to Ferrell, and referenced by Marrs, "KSLA News 12 had the sample tested at a lab. The results: high level of barium, 6.8 parts per million, (ppm). That's more than three times the toxic level set by the Environmental Protection Agency."

The results were disputed by physicist David E. Thomas, who concluded the errors were simply the result of bad math on the part of Ferrell. That Thomas was a contributing editor to the *Skeptical Inquirer* left many of the chemtrail proponents … well … skeptical.

Today, the debate over chemtrails continues to rage on. As prime evidence of this, visitors to *The Sheep Killers* website are told: "Our health is under attack as evidenced by the skyrocketing rates of chemtrail induced lung cancer, asthma and pulmonary/respiratory problems. Our natural environment and planetary weather systems are under attack resulting in freak lightning strikes, bizarre weather, 20% less sunlight reaching the Earth's surface, the alarming, nearly complete collapse in certain areas of the west coast marine ecosystem and the creation of some of the largest tornadoes and hurricanes on record. Our skies are increasingly hazed over with fake barium/aluminum particulate, ethylene dibromide chemtrail clouds. Whether in the atmosphere or in the ocean this added particulate matter is a hazard to the health of every living thing on this planet."

CHINA

As one of the major players on the world stage—both economically and militarily—there is no doubt that the People's Republic of China will play a major role in a New World Order. But what, exactly, might that role be? In 2002, Martin Sieff, a *UPI* senior news analyst, stated: "There was a cloud no larger than the size of a man's hand in the sky of U.S. global leadership at the annual NATO Security Conference, or Wehrkunde, in Munich, Germany, this weekend. But it will get bigger. It was the quiet emergence of China as the leader of a potentially global block dedicated to oppose the United States.

"When Vice Foreign Minister Wang Yi of China addressed the prestigious annual forum of NATO defense ministers in this historic Bavarian city, he heralded the Shanghai Cooperation Organization, founded only last June, as the crucial 'new security concept' necessary to guarantee peace and stability in Central Asia, and to lead the fight there against terrorism.

"So important was this idea of a 'new security concept' to Chinese policy that Wang used the phrase four times in his formal speech."

Yi himself said: "Fighting terrorism needs to address both its symptoms and root caused. An important prerequisite in this connection is to resolve the question of development and narrow the gap between the North and the South," adding that it was time to create a "fair and equitable new world order."

He added: "China is ready to strengthen its coordination and cooperation with all other countries in the conduct of international affairs, security included, and work vigorously toward a world that enjoys lasting peace and universal prosperity with a fair and equitable new international order."

In 2016, fourteen years later, eyes were still on China, specifically with regard to how it will likely play a significant position in the NWO. *The New American* has had a great deal to offer on this issue, including the following: "As Communist China prepares to host and lead the 'Group of 20' G20 summit for the first time next month, the regime is boasting about its 'leading role' in 'global economic governance' and building up 'the international order.' Bringing together the world's 20 most powerful governments and dictatorships to plot humanity's future, the Chinese Communist Party's leaders and propaganda organs have been celebrating that emerging new world order—and their major role within it. At the upcoming summit, the regime also vowed to work with other G20 members to develop policies that will 'steer the world economy into the future' toward a 'green global economy' under the United Nations Agenda 2030 plan for humanity."

The New American also notes: "The official comments about Beijing's growing global influence follow years of promoting what the barbaric Chinese autocracy and its allies around the world often describe as a 'New World Order.' If the plot is not stopped, liberty, Western civilization, national independence, and Judeo-Christian values are all in danger. So far, though, top Western globalists and establishment players in the United States and Europe have been enabling the Communist Chinese dictatorship every step of the way. Beijing's role in steering and hosting the 2016 G20 summit is simply the latest symptom of an ongoing process. Indeed, billionaire Rothschild protégé George Soros said some years ago that the regime even needs to 'own' the 'New World Order' in the same way that the United States owned the old order."

Wang Yi, the vice foreign minister of China, has stated he is in favor of cooperation with other nations to form a new style of world security to protect against terrorism.

Also in 2016, *National Interest* said: "China's rapid ascent to great-power status has, more than any other international development, raised concerns about the future of the liberal international order. Forged in the ashes of the Second World War, that order has enabled a seven-decade period of great-power peace, the expansion of democratic rule and a massive increase in global prosperity. Now, it seems, world order is under threat—not least from China's rising power. While Beijing has thus far avoided active military aggression and refrained from exclusionary economic arrangements, American policymakers worry quite openly about China's challenge to the underlying rules of the road. They hope that Beijing will embrace the existing pillars of global order and even work to support them; they fear that China will prove revisionist, seeking to undermine the rules-based order and fashion an illiberal alternative that excludes the United States."

In 2016, *China Topix* told its readers: "Chinese president Xi Jinping has called on Russia to join China in forming a 'New World Order' dominated by both countries that he expects to realize in the next 10 years. In a vitriolic speech delivered at the 95th anniversary of the founding of the Chinese Communist Party this July, Xi urged Russia and its president Vladimir Putin to join China in a military alliance that will render NATO (the North Atlantic Treaty Organization) 'powerless' and 'put an end to the imperialist desires of the West.' This China–Russia alliance is intended to put more pressure on the United States, China's main antagonist in the South China Sea, by stretching

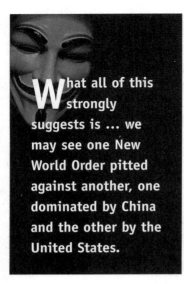

What all of this strongly suggests is ... we may see one New World Order pitted against another, one dominated by China and the other by the United States.

its military forces even thinner with more naval deployments to Europe. But more important for China, a military alliance with Russia along the lines of NATO will mean Russia will be obligated to fight alongside China should a war break out in Asia against the U.S.

"'The world is on the verge of radical change,' said Xi to his communist comrades. 'We see how the European Union is gradually collapsing, as is the U.S. economy—it is all over for the new world order.'"

What all of this strongly suggests is that we may not see the rise and takeover of the New World Order that we have been warned about. Rather, we may see one New World Order pitted against another, one dominated by China and the other by the United States.

CIVIL UNREST

It might sound like just about the wildest science-fiction-like scenario of all, but it most assuredly was not. It was nothing less than astounding reality. On Halloween 2012, at Mission Bay, San Diego, elements of the U.S. Marines, along with an elite unit of U.S. Navy personnel, took part in a training mission that revolved around a tumultuous, but fictional, zombie onslaught. And it was all taken very seriously, too, as was evidenced by the words of one Brad Barker, the president of the Halo Corporation—a security-based organization that was formed in 2006 and that is comprised of personnel with backgrounds in special operations, intelligence, and national security. Barker told the media: "This is a very real exercise. This is not some type of big costume party."

Echoing the deadly seriousness of the exercise was none other than retired U.S. Air Force four-star general, former CIA director, and former National Security Agency director Michael Hayden. On top of that, more than one thousand military personnel, dozens of police officers, and a sizeable number of government officials all took part in the event, which occurred on more than forty acres of land that was specifically transformed into, among other things, an Iraqi-style town.

Barker admitted, rather intriguingly: "No doubt when a zombie apocalypse occurs, it's going to be a federal incident, so we're making it happen." He also noted that, from his own personal perspective at least, there was one major downside to the publicity that had bene given to the exercise of the undead: "Every whack job in the world" was emailing and phoning, demanding to know what, exactly, was afoot and why.

Officially, the scenario of a zombie outbreak, that the military had to quash at all costs, was utilized because of the enormous popularity in which the risen dead are presently bathing and basking. Adding the flesh-eating abominations to the mix, in the collective mind of the Halo Corporation anyway, was a sure way of alerting people's attention to the importance of being prepared for a real disaster, such as one caused by war, by terrorists, or by the harshness of Mother Nature herself. Some New World Order researchers suggested the program was really launched to get the American people more and more acclimatized to seeing an ever-growing military presence in the United States—a presence that will one day, following the agenda of the New World Order, seize control of the nation.

It is especially noteworthy that Michael Hayden is a former director of the National Security Agency: in September 2013, it was revealed in the media that the Big Brother-style NSA secretly refers to the millions of Americans who own iPhones as "zombies." In that sense, the probability is high that in the Halloween 2012 exercise, the zombies were metaphors for the American people—a disturbing thought, to say the least.

CLIMATE CHANGE

One might wonder what the issue of climate change has to do with the New World Order. The answer is: a great deal and more than many might think. NASA—the National Aeronautics and Space Administration—says of this controversial topic: "The Earth's climate has changed throughout history. Just in the last 650,000 years there have been seven cycles of glacial advance and retreat, with the abrupt end of the last ice age about 7,000 years ago marking the beginning of the modern climate era—and of human civilization. Most of these climate changes are attributed to very small variations in Earth's orbit that change the amount of solar energy our planet receives."

As for the situation today, NASA tells us: "The current warming trend is of particular significance because most of it is very likely human-induced and proceeding at a rate that is unprecedented in the past 1,300 years. Earth-orbiting satellites and other technological advances have enabled scientists to see the big picture, collecting many different types of information about our planet and its climate on a global scale. This body of data, collected over many years, reveals the signals of a changing climate. The heat-trapping nature of carbon dioxide and other gases was demonstrated in the mid-19th century. Their

Climate change has become a hot political topic, and protests are becoming more common as average people see their lives and those of future generations threatened.

ability to affect the transfer of infrared energy through the atmosphere is the scientific basis of many instruments flown by NASA. There is no question that increased levels of greenhouse gases must cause the Earth to warm in response. Ice cores drawn from Greenland, Antarctica, and tropical mountain glaciers show that the Earth's climate responds to changes in greenhouse gas levels. They also show that in the past, large changes in climate have happened very quickly, geologically speaking: in tens of years, not in millions or even thousands."

All of which brings us to the New World Order.

RT said on May 8, 2015: "The Australian prime minister's chief business adviser says that climate change is a ruse led by the United Nations to create a new world order under the agency's control. The statement coincided with a visit from the U.N.'s top climate negotiator. Maurice Newman, chairman of Prime Minister Tony Abbott's business advisory council, said the UN is using false models which show sustained temperature increases because it wants to end democracy and impose authoritarian rule.

"'It's a well-kept secret, but 95 percent of the climate models we are told prove the link between human CO2 emissions and catastrophic global warming have been found, after nearly two decades of temperature stasis, to be in error,' he wrote in an opinion piece published in *The Australian* newspaper on Friday, without providing evidence. 'The real agenda is concentrated political authority. Global warming is the hook,' he said, adding that the UN is against capitalism and freedom and wants to create a 'new world order.'"

Your News Wire offered something similar in May 2016: "Evidence and facts have emerged regarding what the 'extreme austerity measures to combat climate change' that the US Environmental Protection Agency, the Obama administration and other environmental groups want enforced will actually do to the US and world economy. The New World Order and their sock puppets have devised a plan to make the elite richer, while placing a heavy burden on middle and low income earners as part of their sick and twisted master plan to control the human race.

"The EPA Chief concedes there will be no climate impact from the climate rule; it's about 'reinventing a global economy.' The impact of these extreme austerity measures on temperatures will be at best 1/100th of a degree. In other words, what these 'extreme measures' will accomplish 'at best' is a reduced temperature of 0.01C. Meanwhile the price of electricity will dramatically increase which will affect the lowest income Americans the most, and the global economy will be reinvented making the rich richer, and the poor poorer."

Then there is this from *Conscious Life News*, in 2013: "According to Public Policy Polling, which was not paid for or authorized by any campaign or political organization and where surveys were conducted between March 27th and March 30th this year, 37% of the people believe it's a hoax, while 12% are not sure. 58% of Republicans agree that it is a conspiracy, while 77% of Democrats disagree. That's quite a high level of skepticism, which only means that more people are starting to see beyond the shadows and lies of the establishment. It also shows that there is indeed a global awakening going on."

Conscious Life News continues: "During the first U.N. Earth Climate Summit that took place in Rio de Janeiro, Brazil in 1992, one of the speakers was former U.S. Senator Timothy Wirth, who was then representing the Clinton-Gore administration as U.S. undersecretary of state for global issues, and who, addressing the audience said: 'We have got to ride the global warming issue. Even if the theory of global warming is wrong, we will be doing the right thing in terms of economic policy and environmental policy.'

"It's worth noting that Wirth now heads the U.N. Foundation which lobbies for hundreds of billions of U.S. taxpayer dollars to help underdeveloped countries fight climate change.

Also speaking at the same conference, was Deputy Assistant of State Richard Benedick who then headed the policy divisions of the U.S. State Department. He said: 'A global warming treaty (Kyoto) must be implemented even if there is no scientific evidence to back the 'enhanced' greenhouse effect.'"

CLINTON, HILLARY

When it comes to the issue of Hillary Clinton, conspiracy theorists are very much divided on her role in a New World Order. Dave Hodges, of *The Common Sense Show*, is clear on where he stands:

"Forge a false-flag event(s) so volatile and horrific, that the implementation of a complete and authoritarian police state would follow. The police state will be so all-encompassing that George Orwell would be jealous. This is certainly well underway with the abuses of the BLM and EPA being perpetrated against farmers. The constant spying through the NSA is certainly a bold move in that direction. Intellistreets and the intrusiveness of Obamacare represent large steps forward toward a 'Police State America.' In this second phase, the will of the people must be destroyed. All resistance must be crushed. When these goals are complete a President Hillary Clinton will help to usher in World War III. Out of order comes chaos. World War III will usher the prime directive of the criminal elite, namely, depopulation. World War III will kill billions."

Tony Elliott, at *Freedom Outpost*, has this to say: "If Donald Trump's 2016 run for President has done anything, it has awakened many people in America to the fact that the free country they thought they lived in is really a socialist dictatorship. Today, our government in Washington is made up of only one political socialist establishment that masquerades as being both Republican and Democrat with a common goal of world and domestic domination.

"In the US today, we are no longer represented by our elected officials, but dictated to by appointed administrators. This country has not had a fair election since the hanging chad controversy in the Bush/Gore Presidential

It has been said that Hillary Clinton was designated by the ruling elite to be President Obama's heir apparent as far back as the time when Obama won his first election.

election in 2000, mainly due to the switch to electronic balloting making it very easy to manipulate votes to favor the dictatorship's choices for successors. Along with cheating via electronic balloting, we still have blatant finagling by establishment candidates to gain more votes and delegates than candidates not approved by the dictatorship, as we have seen with both the Hillary Clinton campaign and the Ted Cruz campaign."

Salon offers this: "The idea that Hillary Clinton has been empowered by the New World Order to manipulate events to her liking has gone completely mainstream this election cycle. Most conspiracy theorists know well enough to avoid the term 'New World Order' these days. But that's certainly what people like Trump are implying when they argue that the election is somehow being 'rigged' by a conspiracy that incorporates the media, the government, the Democratic Party and probably a bunch of house elves as well."

CLUB OF ROME

The official website of the Club of Rome provides the following information about this organization, a powerful body that has been targeted by New World Order researchers as a direct threat to the future of the human race: "The Club of Rome was founded in 1968 as an informal association of independent leading personalities from politics, business and science, men and women who are long-term thinkers interested in contributing in a systemic interdisciplinary and holistic manner to a better world. The Club of Rome members share a common concern for the future of humanity and the planet.

"The aims of the Club of Rome are: to identify the most crucial problems which will determine the future of humanity through integrated and forward-looking analysis; to evaluate alternative scenarios for the future and to assess risks, choices and opportunities; to develop and propose practical solutions to the challenges identified; to communicate the new insights and knowledge derived from this analysis to decision-makers in the public and private sectors and also to the general public and to stimulate public debate and effective action to improve the prospects for the future."

Not everyone, however, is quite so sure that the Club of Rome is as benevolent as it appears to be. Indeed, some students of conspiracy theories and secret societies believe the group to be downright dangerous and a key player in the creation of a looming New World Order. The Jeremiah Project provides thought-provoking words: "To facilitate the management of the New World Order agenda calls for the elimination of most of the world's population through war, disease, abortion and famine. According to the Club of Rome's

Founded in Rome and now located in Switzerland, the Club of Rome includes politicians and scientists concerned about worldwide issues like climate change and overpopulation.

publications, the common enemy of humanity is man. One of the major goals of the Club of Rome is to reduce the world's population by 2 billion people through war, famine, disease and any other means necessary."

As controversial as this may sound, the Club of Rome makes no bones about the fact that it views man as man's own enemy. Consider the following, stated by the Club of Rome in 1991: "In searching for a new enemy to unite us, we came up with the idea that pollution, the threat of global warming, water shortages, famine and the like would fit the bill.... But in designating them as the enemy, we fall into the trap of mistaking symptoms for causes. All these dangers are caused by human intervention and it is only through changed attitudes and behavior that they can be overcome. The real enemy, then, is humanity itself.'"

COLD WAR STATEMENTS

Long before people like President George H.W. Bush and Henry Kissinger made the term "New World Order" infamous, it was already in use—and particularly at the height of the Cold War. In February 1962, Nelson Rockefeller, former governor of New York, was quoted in a *New York Times* feature with the title of "Rockefeller Bids Free Lands Unite: Calls at Harvard for Drive to Build New World Order." The *NYT* said: "The United Nations, he told an audience at Harvard University, 'has not been able—nor can it be able—to shape a new world order which events so compellingly demand.' The new world order that will answer economic, military, and political problems, he said, 'urgently requires, I believe, that the United States take the leadership among all free peoples to make the underlying concepts and aspirations of national sovereignty truly meaningful through the federal approach.'"

In October 1967, before he was elected president, Richard M. Nixon said: "The developing coherence of Asian regional thinking is reflected in a disposition to consider problems and loyalties in regional terms, and to evolve regional approaches to development needs and to the evolution of a new world order."

In 1974, Richard N. Gardner told *Foreign Affairs*: "If instant world government, Charter review, and a greatly strengthened International Court do not provide the answers, what hope for progress is there? The answer will not satisfy those who seek simple solutions to complex problems, but it comes down essentially to this: The hope for the foreseeable lies, not in building up a few ambitious central institutions of universal membership and general jurisdiction as was envisaged at the end of the last war, but rather in the much more decentralized, disorderly and pragmatic process of inventing or adapting institutions of limited jurisdiction and selected membership to deal with specific problems on a case-by-case basis. In short, the 'house of world order' will have to be built from the bottom up rather than from the top down. It will look like a great 'booming, buzzing confusion,' to use William James' famous description of reality, but an end run around national sovereignty, eroding it piece by piece, will accomplish much more than the old-fashioned frontal assault."

Ambassador Richard Gardner (seated to the right of President Clinton) is shown here at a NATO summit listening to a speech by Secretary of Defense William Cohen. Gardner was a supporter of world government.

On the Creation of a Just World Order is a 1975 book that includes a paper by Richard A. Falk titled "Toward a New World Order: Modest Methods and Drastic Visions." Falk wrote: "The existing order is breaking down at a very rapid rate, and the main uncertainty is whether mankind can exert a positive role in shaping a new world order or is doomed to await collapse in a passive posture. We believe a new order will be born no later than early in the next century and that the death throes of the old and the birth pangs of the new will be a testing time for the human species."

Henry Kissinger, speaking before the United Nations in October 1975, revealed his thoughts on the matter of the New World Order: "My country's history, Mr. President, tells us that it is possible to fashion unity while cherishing diversity, that common action is possible despite the variety of races, interests, and beliefs we see here in this chamber. Progress and peace and justice are attainable. So we say to all peoples and governments: Let us fashion together a new world order."

One month later—November 1975—the New York Times shared this with its readers: "At the old Inter-American Office in the Commerce Building here in Roosevelt's time, as Assistant Secretary of State for Latin American Affairs under President Truman, as chief whip with Adlai Stevenson and Tom Finletter at the founding of the United Nations in San Francisco, Nelson Rockefeller was in the forefront of the struggle to establish not only an American system of political and economic security but a new world order."

Moving into the 1980s, there is this from Mikhail Gorbachev, in 1988: "Further global progress is now possible only through a quest for universal consensus in the movement towards a new world order."

"We believe we are creating the beginning of a new world order coming out of the collapse of the U.S.–Soviet antagonisms," said Brent Scowcroft slightly less than two years after Gorbachev uttered his words.

COLEMAN, DR. JOHN

In 1992, says Three World Wars, "Dr. John Coleman published Conspirators Hierarchy: The Story of the Committee of 300. With laudable scholarship and meticulous research, Dr. Coleman identifies the players and carefully details the New World Order agenda of worldwide domination and control. On page 161 of the Conspirators Hierarchy, Dr. Coleman accurately summarizes the intent and purpose of the Committee of 300."

In Coleman's own words: "A One World Government and one-unit monetary system, under permanent non-elected hereditary oligarchists who self-select from among their numbers in the form of a feudal system as it was in the Middle Ages. In this One World entity, population will be limited by restrictions on the number of children per family, diseases, wars, famines, until 1 billion people who are useful to the ruling class, in areas which will be strictly and clearly defined, remain as the total world population.

"There will be no middle class, only rulers and the servants. All laws will be uniform under a legal system of world courts practicing the same unified code of laws, backed up by a One World Government police force and a One World unified military to enforce laws in all former countries where no national boundaries shall exist. The system will be on the basis of a welfare state; those who are obedient and subservient to the One World Government will be rewarded with the means to live; those who are rebellious will simply be starved to death or be declared outlaws, thus a target for anyone who wishes to kill them. Privately owned firearms or weapons of any kind will be prohibited."

COLLINS ELITE

The idea that the New World Order secretly works with a highly classified, secret group which believes that the UFO phenomenon is one of demonic—rather than extraterrestrial—origins may sound outlandish and unlikely. It is, however, absolute fact. It goes by the name of the Collins Elite, although don't expect the world of officialdom to confirm its existence. At least, not anytime soon. We know, however, that the group exists—and largely thanks to a man named Ray Boeche. He is both a UFO investigator (and a former state director for the Mutual UFO Network, MUFON) and a priest.

It was Boeche's unique connection to two issues that appear wholly unconnected that led to the exposure of the clandestine world of the Collins Elite. It all began in late 1991, when Boeche was contacted by two scientists who were undertaking work for the Pentagon: they were secretly contracted to come on board with the Collins Elite. The purpose of their work was to research the UFO phenomenon, possibly even try to make contact with the entities behind the same phenomenon, via psychic, mind-to-mind means. As their work progressed, however, it became more and more clear to the pair—and to the rest of their colleagues—that the large-headed, black-eyed aliens the Collins Elite assumed they were in contact with were nothing of the sort. They were, the group concluded, nothing less than deceptive demons. They sought Ray Boeche's help due to his knowledge of both the UFO phenomenon and demonology. A meeting was set for November 25, 1991, in Lincoln, Nebraska, at the Cornhusker Hotel—Nebraska being Boeche's home state.

Boeche was definitely the ideal person for the two physicists to speak with as he had long ago discarded the idea that UFOs were extraterrestrial in origin and was firmly in the demonic camp. As Boeche was told by his sources, the Collins Elite did not refer to the creatures as aliens or demons but as "Non-Human Entities," or NHEs. And, in no time at all, it became very clear to them that by trying to psychically contact the NHEs, they had "opened" a "doorway" to menacing creatures from a hellish realm that masqueraded as extraterrestrials to get their grips into the heart of the U.S. government—a kind of supernatural "Trojan Horse," one might be justified in saying.

As Boeche listened, he was told that there had been a number of deaths in the program, bizarre runs of bad luck and unexplained illnesses blighted those on the program—all of which collectively led the Collins Elite to believe they were under demonic attack and had been, essentially, "cursed."

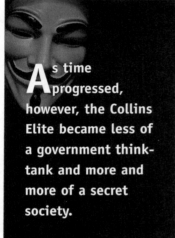

As time progressed, however, the Collins Elite became less of a government think-tank and more and more of a secret society.

With their scientific background, they wanted guidance from someone well versed in matters relative to the concept of hell, the devil, and demonic hierarchies. Boeche was shocked but willing to help. Indeed, he was consulted by the group on a couple of occasions, something which made it very clear to him that the Collins Elite—as well as cleared people in the Pentagon—were deeply concerned about the "door" they had opened and which was showing no signs of closing anytime soon.

Additional revelations demonstrated that, by 1991, the Collins Elite had already been in existence for several decades. However, it was only concern on the group's part about something dark and deadly on the horizon that led them to open their secret doors to Boeche—to a degree, at least. Further research into the strange and unsettling world of the Collins Elite has shown that the late President Ronald Reagan was briefed on the work of the Collins Elite, as were senior personnel in the National Security Agency (NSA), the CIA, and naval intelligence. Ancient manuscripts—such as Reginald C. Thompson's *Devils and Evil Spirits of Babylonia*; Edward Langton's *Essentials of Demonology*; and John Deacon and John Walker's 1601 publication, *Dialogical Discourses of Spirits and Devils*—were carefully studied and scrutinized in an effort to allow the Collins Elite to have a better understanding of what it was they were dealing with.

As time progressed, however, the Collins Elite became less of a government think tank and more and more of a secret society. For example, the members of the group cultivated links with senior and influential figures in the clergy, specifically those who had links to the very heart of the Vatican itself.

Archaeologists—particularly so those who were deeply conversant with ancient Middle Eastern history, legend, folklore, and mythology—were secretly contracted and consulted to further knowledge on the nature and intent of the demonic threat.

The Collins Elite made approaches—apparently successful—to a number of U.S. presidents, including Ronald Reagan, a man who had a deep interest in both UFOs and "End Times" scenarios, both of which were (and still are) integral portions of the belief systems of the Collins Elite. Shadowy meetings with some of the world's most powerful people in the business world were arranged—chiefly to ensure massive, "under-the-table" funding for the group and in a fashion that would ensure budgetary data would not reach the likes of Congress, something which could have potentially blown the whole thing wide open.

Today, the Collins Elite still exists—despite the widespread denials of the U.S. government that it has ever existed. And, in the twenty-first century, the group is a definitive secret society. Entrance to the group is strictly limited to those who move effortlessly between the domains of the Pentagon and the Trilateral Commission, the Department of Defense and fringe archaeologists, the Pope, and those well versed in the black arts.

As the Collins Elite sees it, the group is at the forefront of a worldwide, secret war to prevent a full-scale demonic invasion, Armageddon, the rise of the Antichrist, and a planet and its people plunged into a literal, hellish nightmare. A religion-dominated New World Order, in other words, one which will adhere to iron-fisted Old Testament wrath and thunder.

Time may tell if the theories of this secret network are valid or not. For Ray Boeche, his views on the demonic theory for the UFO phenomenon are held as strongly today as they were when he had that near-unique meeting with two Department of Defense scientists back in November 1991.

COMMITTEE OF 300

A powerful, worldwide network with an alleged sinister goal for humanity, the Committee of 300 was inspired—in terms of its make-up, ideology, and approach to manipulating key events—by the British East India Company's Council of 300, which was created in the early part of the eighteenth century and which was largely funded by opium trading in the Far East. As for the British East India Company, its origins date back to the 1600s, thanks to the influence of the British royal family, which got things moving. Essentially, the

Committee of 300 is at the forefront of a secret program designed to ultimately control the worlds of banking, politics, the economy, and even the size of the Earth's human population. The number "300" comes from a statement made by General Electric's Walter Rathenau. In 1909, he said: "Three hundred men, all of whom know one another, direct the economic destiny of Europe and choose their successors from among themselves."

It's not just Europe, however, that the Committee of 300 has its sights set on controlling—and controlling completely. No, we're talking about the entire planet. The No Cancer Foundation notes of the Committee of 300 that: "The Committee of 300 uses a network of roundtable groups, think tanks and secret societies which control the world's largest financial institutions and governments. The most prominent of these groups include Chatham House, Bilderberg Group, Trilateral Commission, Council on Foreign Relations, Ditchley Foundation, Club of Rome, RAND Corporation, PNAC and of course Freemasonry. The power behind the Committee of 300 is the Anglo-Jewish cousinhood that dominate the financial and political systems of the world. This cous-

East India House in London was the headquarters of the British East India Company, which was really the entity that governed India more than the actual British government.

inhood includes the Rothschild, Rockefeller, Oppenheimer, Goldsmid, Mocatta, Montefiore, Sassoon, Warburg, Samuel, Kadoorie, Franklin, Worms, Stern and Cohen families."

Dr. John Coleman, an expert on the Committee of 300, says that "the Committee of 300 long ago decreed that there shall be a smaller—much smaller—and better world, that is, their idea of what constitutes a better world. The myriads of useless eaters consuming scarce natural resources were to be culled. Industrial progress supports population growth. Therefore the command to multiply and subdue the earth found in Genesis had to be subverted. This called for an attack upon Christianity; the slow but sure disintegration of industrial nation states; the destruction of hundreds of millions of people, referred to by the Committee of 300 as 'surplus population'; and the removal of any leader who dared to stand in the way of the Committee's global planning to reach the foregoing objectives. Not that the U.S. government didn't know, but as it was part of the conspiracy, it helped to keep the lid on information rather than let the truth be known. Queen Elizabeth II is the head of the Committee of 300."

As to how Coleman was exposed to the dark world of the Committee of 300, he reveals: "In my career as a professional intelligence officer, I had many occasions to access highly classified documents, but during service as a political science officer in the field in Angola, West Africa, I had the opportunity to view a series of top secret classified documents which were unusually explicit. What I saw filled me with anger and resentment and launched me on a course from which I have not deviated, namely to uncover what power it is that controls and manages the British and United States governments."

Of the membership of the Committee of 300, "The Atlantean Conspiracy" offers the following. As you'll see, those who have allied themselves to the group are powerful, indeed: "Some notable members of the Committee of 300 include: The British royal family, Dutch royal family, House of Hapsburg, House of Orange, Duke of Alba, Prince Philip Duke of Edinburgh, Lord Carrington, Lord Halifax, Lord Alfred Milner, John Jacob and Waldorf of the Astor Illuminati bloodline, Winston Churchill, Cecil Rhodes, Queen Elizabeth II, Queen Juliana, Queen Beatrix, Queen Magreta, King Haakon of Norway, Colonel Mandel House, Aldous Huxley, John Forbes, Averill Harriman, William and McGeorge Bundy, George Bush, Prescott Bush, Henry Kissinger, J.P. Morgan, Maurice Strong, David Rockefeller, David and Evelyn Rothschild, Paul, Max and Felix Warburg, Ormsby and Al Gore, Bertrand Russell, Sir Earnest and Harry of the Oppenheimer Illuminati bloodline, Warren Buffet, Giuseppe Mazzini, Sir William Hesse, George Schultz, H.G. Wells, and Ted Turner."

COUNCIL FOR NATIONAL POLICY

❝ The Council for National Policy (CNP) brings together the country's most influential conservative leaders in business, government, politics, religion, and academia to hear and learn from policy experts on a wide range of issues. In addition, we provide a forum that allows an open exchange between participants, presenting numerous opportunities to cultivate ideas to help solve America's growing problems."

Those are the words of the Council for National Policy, which U.S. President Ronald Reagan described as a "handful of men and women, individuals of character [who] had a vision. A vision to see the return of righteousness, justice, and truth to our great nation."

Alternet reveals some intriguing and illuminating material about the council: "CNP was founded in 1981 by Tim LaHaye, the right-wing, evangelical political motivator and author of the *Left Behind* serial, which chronicles a fictional Armageddon and second coming (in which the non-believers are left behind while believers are carried off in a rapturous moment without their clothes. It gives an eerie ring to the No Child Left Behind Act). LaHaye's empire includes his fingerprints on a number of evangelically oriented, right-wing political action groups, his wife Beverly's Concerned Women for America, along with the twelve *Left Behind* novels, which, according to the author's own website, have sold 55 million copies worldwide since their introduction in 1995."

Then, we have these words from *SourceWatch* which offers even more thought-provoking information: "The Council for National Policy (CNP) is a shadowy, secretive group dubbed 'Sith Lords of the Ultra-Right' by the liberal blog *DailyKos*. Mark Crispin Miller called CNP a 'highly secretive ... theocratic organization—what they want is basically religious rule.'"

The website *Public Eye*, which is the official page of the Council for National Policy, goes a step further and adds more than a bit of controversial data to the story: "Clothed in secrecy since its founding in 1981, the Council for National Policy is a virtual who's who of the Hard Right. Its membership comprises the Right's Washington operatives and politicians, its financiers, and its hard-core religious arm. The Hard Right utilizes the CNP's three-times-a-year secret meetings to plan its strategy for implementing the radical right agenda. It is here that the organizers and activists meet with the financial backers who put up the money to carry out their agenda.

"Because CNP rules state that 'meetings are closed to the media and the general public' and 'our membership list is strictly confidential and should not be shared outside the Council,' the mainstream press knows very little about the CNP. Through this site, and the *Freedom Writer*, the Institute for First Amendment Studies is, for the first time, revealing the activities and current membership of the Council for National Policy."

COUNCIL ON FOREIGN RELATIONS

In concise terms, the Council on Foreign Relations describes itself as follows: "The Council on Foreign Relations (CFR) is an independent, nonpartisan membership organization, think tank and publisher. Each of these functions makes CFR an indispensable resource in a complex world."

The CFR, however, is composed of far more than that. Founded in 1921, the group has close to five thousand members, many of whom are prominent politicians, federal judges, members of the intelligence community (and particularly so the CIA), and high-ranking officials from NATO. Then, there's the matter of U.S. presidents. The list of presidents attached to the CFR has included George H. W. Bush, Bill Clinton, Jimmy Carter, Gerald Ford, Richard Nixon, John F. Kennedy, Dwight Eisenhower, and Herbert Hoover. And, as the *Conspiracy Archive* website notes: "If one group is effectively in control of national governments and multinational corporations; promotes world government through control of media, foundation grants, and education; and controls and guides the issues of the day; then they control most options available. The Council on Foreign Relations (CFR), and the financial powers behind it, have done all these things, and promote the 'New World Order,' as they have for over seventy years.

"The CFR is the promotional arm of the Ruling Elite in the United States of America. Most influential politicians, academics and media personalities are members, and it uses its influence to infiltrate the New World Order into American life. Its 'experts' write scholarly pieces to be used in decision making, the academics expound on the wisdom of a united world, and the media members disseminate the message."

The *Jeremiah Project* website provided the following: "Many of its own members admit the CFR goal is to subvert the democratic process. CFR member and Judge Advocate General of the U.S. Navy Admiral Chester Ward wrote 'The main purpose of the (CFR) is promoting the disarmament of US sovereignty and national dependence and submergence into an all powerful, one world government.' This high ranking military officer went on to explain their procedures for influencing policy, claiming: 'Once the ruling members of the CFR shadow government have decided that the U.S. government should adopt a particular policy, the very substantial research facilities of the CFR are put to work to develop

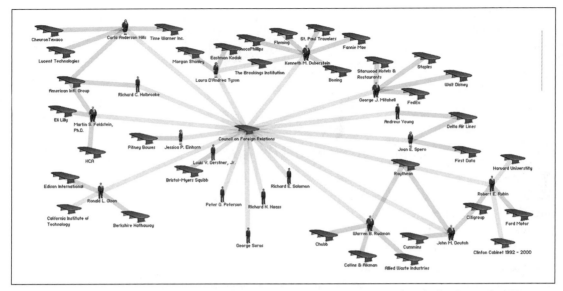

A diagram showing how large U.S. businesses and executives are intertwined with the Council on Foreign Relations.

arguments, intellectual and emotional, to support the new policy and to confound and discredit, intellectually and politically, any opposition.'"

Gary Allen of *None Dare Call It Conspiracy* said of the CFR that it is a subsidiary of the Round Table Group. He continues: "This is the group which designed the United Nations—the first major successful step on the road to a World Superstate. At least forty-seven C.F.R. members were among the American delegates to the founding of the United Nations in San Francisco in 1945.... Today, the C.F.R. remains active in working toward its final goal of a government over all the world—a government which the Insiders and their allies will control. The goal of the C.F.R. is simply to abolish the United States with its Constitutional guarantees of liberty. And they don't even try to hide it. Study No. 7, published by the C.F.R. on November 25, 1959, openly advocates building a new international order [which] must be responsive to world aspirations for peace, for social and economic change."

COUNT OF ST. GERMAIN

One thread throughout the pages of this book suggests the New World Order is seeking to achieve—or may have already have achieved—physical immortality. For them, but not for the rest of us, of course. It has been suggested that a person who may have perfected the secrets of immortality, and who may be a member of the New World Order, is the Count of St. Germain.

So far as can be determined, it was in the very early years of the eighteenth century—around 1705 to 1715—that the Count of St. Germain first surfaced publicly, quickly inserting himself into the world of the rich and powerful of Europe. He did so with amazing ease, too. Those who met the count at the time suggested that he appeared to be in his late thirties or, at the very most, in his early forties. The count preferred to keep his real age—and his true origins—to himself, something which ensured that an air of mystery and intrigue quickly surrounded him. And, as history has shown, it never left him.

Rumors soon began to circulate that the Count of St. Germain was possibly of an elite, royal bloodline. Maybe, even, the ostracized son of a powerful and ancient European family. The count carefully chose to remain enigmatically tight-lipped on such claims. High-society figures flocked to him, women were immediately entranced by him, men envied him, and he soon became the subject of deep interest. That he appeared to have endless amounts of money, which permitted him to travel the globe, seems undeniable. He was clearly very well read, had an expensive and lavish wardrobe, and told of his adventures in Persia (today, Iran), where he learned the secrets of alchemy—the ancient ability to transmute base metals, such as tin, into nothing less than priceless gold. Further rumors swirled around, all pointing in one direction: namely, that the count's exposure to the mysterious domain of alchemy had allowed him to tap into the world of immortality.

While such a scenario is certainly controversial, from the early 1700s to the latter part of that century, the Count of St. Germain did appear to maintain his youthful state, while all of those around him aged, withered, and, finally, died. Indeed, throughout the 1740s, the count traveled widely: throughout Scotland, England, and France. Reportedly, those who had met the count three decades earlier maintained that his appearance had not changed by the mid-1700s. Age-defying or ageless, the count, by now, had taken on legendary status, and his ability to stay young, vigorous, well connected, and rich continued.

An extensive trip to India in 1755 took up much of the count's time, as did a growing friendship with the French king of the day, Louis XV. Officially, the count died on February 27, 1784—still appearing no different from the way he looked in 1705. Students of his life, however, have suggested that his death was simply a convenient and ingenious way for him to adopt a new identity—something which, perhaps, he routinely and regularly did to ensure that no one ever learned of his secrets and his immortal life. Unless, of course, he specifically chose to share his story with others—which, as we'll soon see, may very well have happened. Maybe on more than a few occasions, too.

On this particular matter of the count constantly changing his identity, Maxamillien de Lafayette says of the count: "He was supposed to have been, in previous lives, St. Alban, an English saint of the third or fourth century A.D.; Proclus, a Neoplatonic philosopher who lived during the 5th century A.D.; Roger Bacon, a thirteenth century English philosopher; and Sir Francis Bacon, a philosopher, author, and statesman who lived in the sixteenth century." De Lafayette continues: "Some go as far as associating him with ancient civilizations, such as Atlantis, and Biblical personalities, such as the Prophet Samuel. The Theosophists accepted him as one of their Ascended Masters."

On the matter of Sir Francis Bacon and the count, there's this from the *Crystal Links* website: "According to Elizabeth Clare Prophet, St. Germain ascended on May 1st 1684. Although Sir Francis Bacon is said to have died in 1626, Prophet claims that the body in the coffin at Sir Francis Bacon's funeral was not his own and that he attended his own funeral."

COUP D'ÉTAT

One of the terms that regularly gets tossed around when any mention of the New World Order is made is *coup d'état*. But what, precisely, does it mean? Dictionary.com describes it as follows: "A quick and decisive seizure of governmental power by a strong military or political group. In contrast to a revolution, a *coup d'état*, or coup, does not involve a mass uprising. Rather, in the typical coup, a small group of politicians or generals arrests the incumbent leaders, seizes the national radio and television services, and proclaims itself in power. *Coup d'état* is French for 'stroke of the state' or 'blow to the government.'"

This brings us to the matter of a potential *coup d'état* that brought down the New World Order's favorite figure, Hillary Clinton, in the final days of the 2016 U.S. presidential election. Chuck Ross, at *The Daily Caller* on November 11, 2016, said: "Longtime Clinton insider Sidney Blumenthal claims that a group of 'right-wing agents' in the FBI staged a *coup d'etat* to prevent Hillary Clinton from being elected president. Blumenthal, a former journalist who has been nicknamed 'Grassy Knoll' by some in Clintonworld because of his tendency to latch on to conspiracy theories, made the charge in an interview on Dutch television after Clinton's loss to Donald Trump. 'It was the result of a cabal of right-wing agents of the FBI in the New York office attached to Rudy Giuliani, who was a member of Trump's campaign,' said Blumenthal, who emailed frequently with Clinton while she was secretary of state."

Indeed, on November 11, 2016, the BBC reported the following: "Hillary Clinton has blamed her defeat in the US presidential election on interventions by the FBI director. James Comey's announcement of a new inquiry into her use of email while secretary of state shortly before election day had stopped her campaign's momentum, Mrs. Clinton said. The Democratic candidate was speaking to top party donors in a phone call, which was leaked to the media.

"Mrs. Clinton, who served as Mr. Obama's secretary of state from 2009 to 2013, has been keeping a low profile since conceding victory. On 28 October, Mr Comey informed Congress that the FBI was examining newly discovered emails sent or received by Mrs Clinton, thus reviving an investigation which had been completed in July. Then, on 6 November, two days before the election, Mr. Comey announced in a second letter that he was standing by his original assessment—that Mrs. Clinton should not face criminal charges."

U.S. Secretary of State Hillary Clinton was a darling among those in the New World Order, according to some, and when Donald Trump won, it was considered a *coup d'état.*

Clinton herself said of the following about the situation regarding the election: "There are lots of reasons why an election like this is not successful. But our analysis is that Comey's letter raising doubts that were groundless, baseless, proven to be, stopped our momentum. We dropped, and we had to keep really pushing ahead to regain our advantage."

CURFEWS

In August 2008, the blog entry "Connecting the Dots in the New World Order" said: "War zone security has arrived in the US as cities are shut down at night by police struggling to control a deadly wave of gun crime. David Usborne reports from Hartford, Connecticut: 'The police state has not arrived quite yet but it may feel like it to the residents of some American cities, where a handful of embattled mayors and police chiefs are imposing strict and sometimes sweeping curfews as a last resort to quell new waves of gun violence this summer.

"'We must do this because we cannot and will not tolerate innocent people, especially children, to be victims,' insists Eddie Perez, the Mayor of Hart-

Curfews are becoming increasingly common in the United States and would continue to do so, of course, if a New World Order were to be established.

ford, the capital of Connecticut, where a night-time curfew was introduced last week and will remain in effect for a month for those under 18 years old. Nor are there any apologies from the authorities in Helena-West Helena on the banks of the Mississippi in Arkansas, small pockets of which are under a 24-hour curfew that all ages must respect. Police are enforcing it, moreover, with night-vision goggles and M16 military rifles."

One month later, the same blog reported: "Campaigners have called for a night curfew for children to be extended across Britain after a trial scheme saw crime plunge by 15 percent.

"They said that since Operation Goodnight was introduced around a month ago, there has been a dramatic fall in anti-social behaviour in Redruth, Cornwall. Police asked 600 parents to ensure all children under 16 were indoors by 9 P.M. and those aged ten and under at home by 8 P.M. In the following month 106 crimes were recorded, a fall of 15 on the same period last year."

Curfews continue to be a growing issue, particularly in the United States, as *The Guardian* makes graphically clear: "Conceived as a crime-reduction tactic, curfews were promoted during the 'tough on crime' era of the 1990s. In 1996, President Bill Clinton flew out to Monrovia, California—among the first cities to claim curfew success—to publicly endorse the idea at the local high school. From there, they spread like wildfire and remain in place decades later.

"From Baltimore, which has one of the strictest curfews in the country, to Denver, where curfew enforcement ramps up every summer, the laws are on the books in hundreds of cities across the US. According to available FBI data, there were 2.6m curfew arrests from 1994 and 2012; that's an average of roughly 139,000 annually. Philadelphia alone reported 16,079 violations in 2014—among the highest in the country."

If a New World Order takes over the United States there is very little doubt that curfews will become mandatory in every U.S. city and town.

DEFENSE ADVANCED RESEARCH PROJECTS AGENCY (DARPA)

One of the lesser-known U.S. agencies that is already playing a significant role in the development of the New World Order is the Defense Advanced Research Projects Agency. It is far better known as DARPA. For more than half a century, DARPA's staff have dedicated themselves to one specific goal: creating new and novel technologies that will have a notable bearing on the security of the nation.

The origins of DARPA can be firmly traced back to one of the most significant events in what was known as "The Space Race," namely the October 4, 1957, launch of Sputnik 1 by the Soviets. It was the very first satellite to orbit the Earth. The event sent shockwaves throughout the U.S. government, military, intelligence community, and the worlds of science and technology.

As a result, the U.S. government vowed never again to be second best when it came to the development of advanced technologies. DARPA, unsurprisingly, quickly came into existence. The DARPA website states: "Working with innovators inside and outside of government, DARPA has repeatedly delivered on that mission, transforming revolutionary concepts and even seeming impossibilities into practical capabilities. The ultimate results have included not only game-changing military capabilities such as precision weapons and stealth technology, but also such icons of modern civilian society such as the Internet, automated voice recognition and language translation, and Global Positioning System receivers small enough to embed in myriad consumer devices."

Currently, DARPA employs more than two hundred people, all highly skilled in the fields of burgeoning, new technologies—many of which are destined for use by the U.S. military: the Army, Navy, and Air Force. The agency is known for taking careful steps when it comes to the recruitment of new personnel—particularly those who find themselves working on technology-based programs that may have a significant bearing on American national security.

There is also this from the DARPA website: "Program managers address challenges broadly spanning the spectrum from deep science to systems to capabilities, but ultimately they are driven by the desire to make a difference. They define their programs, set milestones, meet with their performers and assiduously track progress."

Indeed, program managers are integral figures within DARPA. It is their specific goal to closely liaise with office directors and their assistants, particularly so when it comes to ensuring that programs are correctly and successfully executed and implemented. This approach has allowed DARPA to achieve its goals and missions in extraordinarily short periods of time.

There is, however, a dark and disturbing side to DARPA and its work—not to mention its links to the New World Order, as we shall now see.

In 2010, Andrew Wozny of the *Canadian Internet Examiner* said: "No big surprise that DARPA, the military's blue-sky research arm, is the agency behind the lofty five-year program, called Insight. The agency's goal is to replace 'largely manual exploitation and ... chat-based operator interactions' with a system that mines different inputs, including drone footage and on-the-ground intelligence, and quickly stitches together the data to identify potential threats."

Wozny added: "The Pentagon's been investing in super-powered surveillance for years now, and DARPA wants Insight to capitalize on the rapid growth in the recon field.... And ongoing DARPA projects might be rolled into the Insight system too. The agency's solicitation cites a handful, including the recently launched PerSEAS, a program to design complex algorithms that can somehow spot threats based on little more than 'weak evidence.'

"It's the Information Awareness Office by another name. The Information Awareness Office was established by the Defense Advanced Research Projects Agency in January 2002 to bring together several DARPA projects focused on applying surveillance and information technology to track and monitor terrorists and other asymmetric threats to national security, by achieving Total Information Awareness....

"This would be achieved by creating *enormous computer databases* to gather and store the personal information of everyone in the United States, including, personal e-mails, social network analysis, credit card records, phone calls, medical records, and numerous other sources, without any requirement for a search warrant…. Their logo says it all: the New World Order's pyramid and all-seeing Eye. It is the total tracking, total control, and total tyranny program."

In 2013, the situation became even graver. That was when news surfaced that a former director of the Defense Advanced Research Projects Agency (DARPA), Regina Dugan, was championing something that raised both eyebrows and anxiety levels. It was what was described as nothing less than "an edible authentication microchip," one designed to "contain a minute chip that transmits an individual's personal data."

Each chip is able to read a unique signal, one that, if fully embraced, will spell the death-knell for online passwords, passports, driver's licenses, and just about any and all private data. Rather than being implanted into a person's body on a one-time basis, it is inserted into a pill—a pill that a person will be required to swallow every day and that will be "designed to move through the body at the normal process of digestion, and according to engineers working on the device, it can be taken every day for up to a month."

Rather incredibly, the device—which, at the time I write these words, has already been officially approved by the Food and Drug Administration—

is fueled by a battery that uses nothing less than the acid created in the stomach of the individual. When the chip and the acid interact, the former emits a minute signal that can be read by mobile devices, thereby determining and verifying the identity of the person.

As for Regina Dugan, the head of advanced technology at Motorola, she revealed that the company was "working on a microchip inside a pill that users would swallow daily in order obtain the 'superpower' of having their entire body act as a biological authentication system for cellphones, cars, doors and other devices."

In stark terms, the whole human body becomes, as Dugan worded it, "your authentication token."

The *InfoWars* website, which followed the story closely, noted that: "Privacy advocates will wince at the thought, especially given Dugan's former role as head of

Former DARPA head Regina Dugan went on to head Motorola, which is making a microchip to implant in people. Motorola was bought by Google, where Dugan continues to work on the Advanced Technology Projects team.

DARPA, the Pentagon agency that many see as being at the top of the pyramid when it comes to the Big Brother technocracy."

InfoWars also considered that Dugan's claim that just such a pill could be taken an astonishing thirty times a day, every day, for the rest of one's natural life, was "seemingly dubious." They also asked the question: "Would you swallow a Google microchip every day simply to access your cellphone?"

Some might actually do that and much more. Dugan, in a fashion that must surely send chills up and down the spines of sane people everywhere, revealed that Motorola was working to develop a "wearable tattoo," one that could essentially read the human mind by "detecting the unvocalized words in their throat."

John Hewitt, of *Extreme Tech*, explained the science behind this: "It has been known for decades that when you speak to yourself in your inner voice, your brain still sends neural spike volleys to your vocal apparatus, in a similar fashion to when you actually speak aloud."

Dugan apparently already had a method in place that would ensure a sizeable number of young people would eagerly sign up for the "e-tattoo." If it was designed in a fashion that was cool and rebellious, teenagers would quickly be on board, "if only to piss off their parents."

As *InfoWars*' Paul Joseph Watson noted: "The edible microchip and the wearable e-tattoo are prime examples of how transhumanism is being made 'trendy' in an effort to convince the next generation to completely sacrifice whatever privacy they have left in the name of faux rebellion (which is actually cultural conformism) and convenience."

Thankfully, there are others that have warned of the growing threat: "The technology exists to create a totalitarian New World Order," notes Rauni-Leena Luukanen-Kilde, MD, a former chief medical officer in Finland. She adds: "Covert neurological communication systems are in place to counteract independent thinking and to control social and political activity on behalf of self-serving private and military interests. When our brain functions are already connected to supercomputers by means of radio implants and microchips, it will be too late for protest. This threat can be defeated only by educating the public, using available literature on biotelemetry and information exchanged at international congresses."

Greg Szymanski, who has followed the microchipping scandal, asks: "Are you ready for a total elimination of privacy and a robotizing of mankind, as well as an invasion of every thought going through your head? Are you prepared to live in a world in which every newborn baby is micro-chipped? And finally are you ready to have your every move tracked, recorded and placed in Big Brother's data bank?"

THE NEW WORLD ORDER BOOK

DENVER AIRPORT

The official website of the Denver International Airport (DIA) provides the following: "Denver International Airport is the 15th-busiest airport in the world and the fifth-busiest airport in the United States. With more than 53 million passengers traveling through the airport each year, Denver International Airport is one of the busiest airline hubs in the world's largest aviation market. The airport is the primary economic engine for the state of Colorado, generating more than $26 billion for the region annually."

There is, however, another aspect to the Denver Airport, an aspect that takes us right to the heart of the New World Order agenda. *BuzzFeed* provides the following: "When Denver International Airport opened on Feb. 28, 1995, construction had fallen 16 months behind schedule, and $2 billion over budg-

The Denver International Airport is a beautiful work of architecture, but not one without controversy. Construction went $2 billion over budget, and much of that has never been accounted for. There is a network of bunkers underneath it, a mural that has New World Order symbolism, landing strips laid out in the pattern of a swastika, and a dedication stone with the symbol of the Freemasons on it.

et. The final cost of the Denver airport was $4.8 billion, which is a *lot* of money. People wondered what it had gone toward. The airport itself is 35,000 acres, which is almost twice as large as the next biggest U.S. airport."

But, that is not all that *BuzzFeed* has to say: "The airport was dedicated on March 19, 1994, and a capstone was placed inside the airport to memorialize it. This dedication stone displays the Masonic symbol of a compass with a capital G inside. Underneath the symbol, the 'New World Airport Commission' is credited with helping fund and build the airport.

"What is the 'New World Airport Commission'? Airport officials have said that it was a commission for the new 'world airport,' but the wording calls to mind the New World Order conspiracy. New World Order conspiracists believe that there has been a small group of powerful people working together in secret throughout history toward establishing a single all-powerful global government."

Adding to the controversy are a series of unusual murals that can be seen at the Denver Airport. *War on the People* website makes that very clear: "A gas-masked Nazi-alien stabs the dove of peace, a Christian symbol, with a Muslim sabre. The Nazi connection sources from IG Farben, the initial petrochemical cartel based in Germany, connected to the drug industry and the holocaust. The blade is swished through the air leaving a rainbow chemtrail polluting the air of the people below, suffering from the toxicity and genocide. The children are closest to the sword and [an] image much like the 911-twin towers destruction is also depicted."

WonT says: "Against a backdrop of horrific destruction, and the extinction of various species, including whales and sea turtles, only children are seen in the center sobbing over three open caskets. The funeral service is for the Black African people on the left, the Native Red people in the center, and the White Judeo-Christians on the right."

Vigilant Citizen also notes the curious—and, frankly, disturbing—aspects of the Denver International Airport, revealing that "there are so many irregularities surrounding the DIA, that a voluminous book could be written on the subject. The facilities and the art displayed lead many observers to believe that the DIA is much more than an airport: it is literally a New-Age cathedral, full of occult symbolism and references to secret societies. The art at the DIA is NOT an aggregation of odd choices made by people with poor taste, like many people think. It is a cohesive collection of symbolic pieces that reflect the philosophy, the beliefs and the goals of the global elite. The DIA is the largest airport in America and it has cost over 4.8 billion dollars. Everything regarding this airport has been meticulously planned and everything is there for a reason."

So, what is really afoot at the airport? *Vigilant Citizen* suggests something deeply disturbing: "Analysis of the data available makes me reach at least one conclusion: this gigantic structure will eventually become much more than a regular commercial airport. It has the capacity to handle a huge amount of people and vehicles, leading observers to think that the structure might be used as military base and others even add that it will be used as a civilian concentration camp in the near future."

DEPARTMENT OF HOMELAND SECURITY

❚❚ The United States Department of Homeland Security (DHS) is a cabinet department of the United States federal government with responsibilities in public security, roughly comparable to the interior or home ministries of other countries. Its stated missions involve antiterrorism, border security, immigration and customs, cybersecurity, and disaster prevention and management. It was created in response to the September 11 attacks. In fiscal year 2011 it was allocated a budget of $98.8 billion and spent, net, $66.4 billion. With more than 240,000 employees, DHS is the third largest Cabinet department, after the Departments of Defense and Veterans Affairs. Homeland security policy is coordinated at the White House by the Homeland Security Council. Other agencies with significant homeland security responsibilities include the Departments of Health and Human Services, Justice, and Energy."

The quote above is an accurate summary of the history and work of the U.S. Department of Homeland Security. However, some people firmly believe that the DHS will play an integral role in helping to usher in a New World Order.

New World Order Today has addressed this issue and says: "[President] Obama's Executive Order 13603 aka the National Defense Resource Preparedness Act was signed March 16th 2012 and among other things it amended Executive Order 12919 that had been in place since June 1994 by removing a total of 10 references to FEMA.

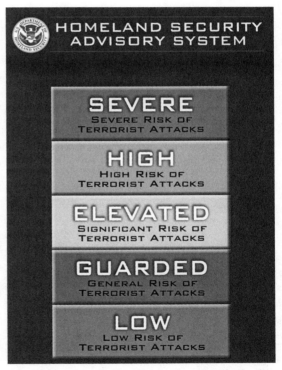

The system used by the Department of Homeland Security to gauge the threat level of a terrorist attack.

These are now referenced to the Department of Homeland Security. The Federal Emergency Management Agency was originally designed to interface with the Department of Defense for civil defense planning and an 'emergency czar' was appointed.

"FEMA/Homeland Security has been given responsibility for disasters, refugee situations, urban riots, and emergency planning for nuclear and toxic incidents. It has the power to suspend laws, move entire populations, arrest and detain citizens without a warrant and hold them without trial. It can seize property, food supplies, transportation systems, and can suspend the Constitution, with a scratch of a pen."

DIANA, PRINCESS OF WALES'S DEATH

When Diana, Princess of Wales, was killed in a car crash in Paris, France, on August 31, 1997, the world was shocked, but, was Diana's death nothing stranger than a tragic accident? Not everyone is quite so sure. Indeed, there is a wealth of material linking Diana's death to the secret activities of certain powerful, clandestine groups. One theory suggests that elite figures within the New World Order were determined to stop a marriage between Diana and Dodi Fayed, a Muslim, at all costs. *Vigilant Citizen* provides the following: "Similarly to the Virgin Mary, Diana had (and still has) legions of followers, worshiping her giving nature and her maternal energy. In other words, she seems to fulfill the almost inherent need in human beings to worship a female goddess, giver of life and filled with compassion. The media has been a key actor in the creation of this icon by documenting every detail of her fairytale wedding, her troubled marriage, her humanitarian activities and, finally, her untimely death. Was Diana picked and groomed to become a sort of a 'modern day Goddess' to ultimately be sacrificed, in accordance with ancient pagan practices? This might sound preposterous to the average National Inquirer reader, but not to the connoisseur of the occult practices of the world elite. Furthermore, numerous clues and symbols have been placed by this group to subtly commemorate the occult nature of Lady Di's death."

Vigilant Citizen continues: "The city of Paris was built by the Merovingians, a

Princess Diana (right) is shown here in June 1997 talking with First Lady Hillary Clinton. The photo was taken two months before Diana's untimely death.

medieval dynasty which ruled France for numerous generations. Before converting to Christianity, the Merovingian religion was a mysterious brand of paganism. The Pont D'Alma Tunnel was a sacred site dedicated to the Moon Goddess Diana, where they used to practice ritual sacrifices. During those ceremonies, it was of an utmost importance that the sacrificed victim died inside the underground temple. The assassination of Diana was a reenactment of this ancient pagan tradition."

As for who, exactly, the Merovingians were, April Holloway provides this: "Mythologized and circumscribed for over 1,500 years, the Merovingians were a powerful Frankish dynasty, which exercised control much of modern-day France, Germany, Switzerland, Austria, and the Low Countries. During the Early Middle Ages, the Merovingian kingdoms were arguably the most powerful and most important polities to emerge after the collapse of the Western Roman Empire, blending Gallo-Roman institutions with Germanic Frankish customs."

IlluminatiWatcher expands on this issue: "The Merovingian dynasty worshiped the goddess Diana, and the murder of Princess Diana is a ritual sacrifice to the goddess Diana. To believe this, we must believe that the Merovingian dynasty secretly retained power up to present day, which isn't too far of a stretch. If the British Royal Family can continue to hold a position of power over the citizens simply because they have a 'superior' blood, perhaps France has Merovingian bloodlines in positions of power unknown to the citizens."

Intriguing words, to say the very least.

DICK, PHILIP K., AND THE NAZI PLOT

One of the foremost figures in the field of science fiction writing, Philip K. Dick, was the author of many novels, including *Do Androids Dream of Electric Sheep?* In 1982, it was made into a blockbuster Hollywood movie, *Blade Runner*. Then, in 2011, Dick's short story from 1954, "Adjustment Team," was made into a hit movie starring Matt Damon, *The Adjustment Bureau*. It's to Dick's relationship to the FBI that we have to turn our attention, however. According to what Dick told the Bureau, in 1972, he had uncovered details of a highly secret Nazi cabal in the United States which was trying to infiltrate the world of science fiction to further its aims and goals—leading up to a New World Order. In other words, science fiction authors were being threatened and bullied by this secret group into promoting Nazi ideologies into their stories.

On October 28, 1972, Dick wrote the following to the FBI: "I am a well-known author of science-fiction novels, one of which dealt with Nazi Germany (called *Man in the High Castle*, it described an 'alternate world' in which the Germans and the Japanese won World War Two and jointly occupied the United States). This novel, published in 1962, won the Hugo Award for Best Novel of the Year and hence was widely read both here and abroad; for example, a Japanese edition printed in Tokyo ran into several editions."

Dick continued and got to the point of his letter: "I bring this to your attention because several months ago I was approached by an individual who I have reason to believe belonged to a covert organization involved in politics, illegal weapons, etc., who put great pressure on me to place coded information in future novels 'to be read by the right people here and there,' as he phrased it. I refused to do this."

The FBI was further told by the famous writer: "The reason why I am contacting you about this now is that it now appears that other science fiction writers may have been so approached by other members of this obviously Anti-American organization and may have yielded to the threats and deceitful statements such as were used on me. Therefore I would like to give you any and all information and help I can regarding this, and I ask that your nearest office contact me as soon as possible."

Dick added: "I heard only one code identification by this individual: Solarcon-6."

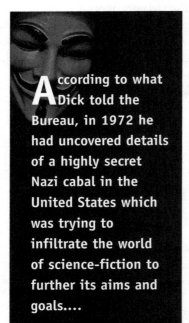

According to what Dick told the Bureau, in 1972 he had uncovered details of a highly secret Nazi cabal in the United States which was trying to infiltrate the world of science-fiction to further its aims and goals....

In further correspondence, Dick revealed that on November 17, 1971, his house—on Hacienda Way, Santa Venetia—was broken into and "extensively robbed." A follow-up break-in occurred in March 1972. Dick said, "My realtor, Mrs. Annie Reagan had stored my things and at least one room of stuff is missing; the bedroom in which the control system of the burglar alarm was located, the one room not covered by the scanner. Obviously it was robbed by someone who intimately knew the layout of the alarm system and how to bypass it."

Dick had a few ideas as to who was responsible: "Only two or three persons that I can recall knew the layout of the burglar alarm system. One was Harold Kinchen, who was under investigation by Air Force Intelligence at Hamilton Field.... It had to do with an attempt on the arsenal of the Air Force Intelligence people at Hamilton on I recall January first of this year."

The story got even more complicated, as Dick revealed: "I have come to know something about the rightwing paramilitary Minutemen illegal people here—they tell me confidentially that from my description of events surrounding that November robbery of my house, the methods used, the activities of Harry Kinchen in particular, it sounds to them like their counterparts up there, and possibly even a neo-Nazi group....

"Kinchen is an ardent Nazi trained in such skills as weapons-use, explosives, wire-tapping, chemistry, psychology, toxins and poisons, electronics, auto repair, sabotage, the manufacture of narcotics."

Over the course of several more months, Dick detailed for the FBI yet further information he believed supported the notion that a highly secret, well funded, cabal of Nazis—a secret society, determined to revive Adolf Hitler's Third Reich—existed in the United States. We may never know to what extent Philip K. Dick was on to something as many of the pages contained within the FBI's files on the man are, to this day, classified under national security legislation, which in itself is highly intriguing for someone who was, chiefly, a writer of sci-fi.

DIRTY BOMB

Within the field of conspiracy-theorizing there is a great deal of talk of the New World Order taking our rights away from us—chiefly as a result of a false flag situation revolving around the detonation of a dirty bomb in a major city. But, what, exactly, is a dirty bomb? Tom Harris, at *How Stuff Works*, explains: "A dirty bomb is an explosive designed to spread dangerous radioactive material over a wide area. When people hear 'bomb' and 'radioactive' in the same sentence, their minds jump to nuclear war pretty quickly. But it turns out that a dirty bomb's primary destructive power would probably be panic, not radiation damage. A dirty bomb is much closer in power to an ordinary explosive than it is to the widespread destructive force of a nuclear bomb. But the fear of contamination could be debilitating, in the same way that 2001's anthrax scare in the United States terrorized much of the American populace, even though only a few people were infected."

But what of this issue of a false flag affair in relation to dirty bombs? In August 2015, *Forbes* noted: "The Western media has decided to carry the story of a dirty bomb purportedly being assembled in Donetsk by rebel forces with the aid of Russian nuclear scientists. The accounts in *The Times* of London, *Newsweek* and Fox News cite Ukrainian intelligence sources, being careful to note that the Ukrainian intelligence cannot be independently verified."

Forbes added: "Kremlin propaganda had already been peddling its own dirty bomb story. Its version accused Ukraine, not the Russian-backed rebels. LiveLeak reported that Ukrainian nationalists were caught trafficking in nuclear materials and radioactive substances with the potential to make a dirty bomb. Fascist Ukrainian organizations, they claim, are behind these nuclear escapades."

Also in 2015, *PressTV* ran an article titled "Israel could use dirty nuke in false flag attack in US: Ex-CIA contractor." In part, the article said: "Israel is testing dirty nuclear bombs in its deserts which could be used in a 'false flag' attack in the United States to implicate Iran, a former CIA and NSA contractor says. 'One has to wonder if they [Israelis] feel that the momentum for realizing 'greater Israel' is going away, and if the world opinion is shifting, which clearly it seems to be ... [then] we have to be concerned with a false flag attack on the United States in order to justify a retaliatory strike against Iran,' said Steven D Kelley.

"'We know that this Israel is actually testing dirty nuclear devices in their desert right now, and we know this has no strategic value other than to be used as a terrorist device in a false flag attack,' he added. 'So this is a very dangerous time.'"

Yes, we are indeed living in a dangerous time. It's a time when the New World Order may be grooming us for a dirty bomb-driven false flag event to control us to even greater levels, to have us living in states of near-neverending fear, and to take away even more of the rights we are entitled to.

DISARMING THE UNITED STATES

If a New World Order-type takeover looks inevitable, it can only take place if the public is unable to fight back against those who are determined to place us in states of almost literal slavery. That means taking away the public's guns. The Second Amendment of the U.S. Constitution makes things explicitly clear: "A well regulated Militia, being necessary to the security of a free State, the right of the people to keep and bear Arms, shall not be infringed."

It hasn't been infringed so far, but that doesn't mean it won't happen.

Truth and Fiction says: "Although Obama hasn't publicly stated he wants a national gun registry and ultimate confiscation, he doesn't have to, we've all known it's 'in the works' and it has now been confirmed. An internal DOJ memo has uncovered Obama's plan to disarm America. This memo surfaced in February but its veracity was in question, until now. NRA spokesman Andrew Arulanandam has confirmed the memo as legitimate. The DOJ memo states the administration 'believes that a gun ban will not work without mandatory gun confiscation' and thinks universal background checks 'won't work without requiring national gun registration.'

A pile of deactivated guns lies waiting for disposal after a government collection program offered to take them from citizens with no questions asked. Some fear the government will one day take all guns from private owners.

USA Today, in 2016, said: "Despite steep declines in violent crimes, an estimated 70 million firearms were added to American arsenals the past two decades, according to a new landmark study on gun ownership. Overall, Americans own an estimated 265 million guns—more than one gun for every American adult, according to the study by researchers at Harvard and Northeastern universities. Half of those guns—133 million—were in the hands of just 3% of American adults, so-called 'super owners' who possessed an average of 17 guns each, it showed."

Clearly, if a NWO force was determined to take on the American public, it would likely find itself in a major battle—and quite literally. The one way that would pave the way for NWO to achieve its goals would be to ensure that Americans are made to hand over their weapons. To what extent the public would simply roll over and capitulate is something that is hard to determine. Nevertheless, rumors are rife that some form of gun confiscation—rather than carefully regulated gun control—is on the horizon.

Mr. Conservative, in 2016, offered his views on this issue: "According to recent reports, Obama's gun control law is based on a 1961 State Department memorandum titled, 'The United States Program For General And Complete Disarmament in a Peaceful World.' That's right, a memorandum on how all second amendment rights will be disavowed and guns will be forcefully removed from citizen possession. It has happened before. During the aftermath of hurricane Katrina, all guns were confiscated in order to ensure residents safety. The truth of the matter was, if you had a gun, it was taken, sometimes leaving honest people with nothing to defend themselves with. An Infantryman told how they would come to the houses late at night, introduce themselves as the National Guard and ask if anyone needed any assistance. After announcing themselves, they kicked in the doors and began to warrentlessly search the premises for firearms. Returning to the document, it states that a UN 'Peace Force' will be constructed in order to 'enforce the peace as the disarmament process proceeds.' Isn't that an oxymoron?—Enforce the peace?"

Freedom Outpost notes: "The United Nations held the 'Sixth Biennial Meeting of States to Consider the Implementation of the Program of Action to Prevent, Combat and Eradicate the Illicit Trade in Small Arms and Light Weapons in All Its Aspects.' This meeting was held June 6–10, 2016 in New York. Located in their 'Draft Outcome' report are many disturbing findings."

Contained in the "Draft Outcome" is the following: "States welcomed the progress made in implementing the Programme of Action and the International Tracing instrument since their adoption, including on the establishment, strengthening and enforcement of national laws, regulations and administrative procedures to prevent the illicit trade and illegal manufacture of small arms and light weapons, the development of national action plans, the establishment of national points of contact, the submission of voluntary national reports and the strengthening of subregional and regional cooperation. They also welcomed progress made in implementing stockpile management and security, the collection and destruction of illicit small arms and light weapons, the marking of small arms and light weapons, technical training and information sharing."

No one wants to see a United States overrun by gun-toting lunatics committing terrible crimes of senseless murder. On the other hand, it is understandable to want a responsible way to protect and defend oneself in the event that a New World Order takes over.

DOCTORS' DEATHS

This book demonstrates that the New World Order is determined to control the pharmaceutical industry and its profits as well as ensuring that as many people as possible are hooked on mind-numbing drugs. Of course, if faced with a threat from the field of alternative health care, it is not at all out of the question that the New World Order might take steps to ensure those who offer alternative health treatments are taken out of circulation—as in permanently.

Disturbingly, that is exactly what we are seeing: holistic doctors are dying at an alarming rate. Let's see what people are saying of this affair.

On July 29, 2015, *Health Impact News* ran an article titled "Is the U.S. Medical Mafia Murdering Alternative Health Doctors Who Have Real Cures Not Approved by the FDA?" It stated: "On June 19, 2015, Dr. [Jeffrey] Bradstreet reportedly shot himself in the chest after his offices were raided by U.S. FDA agents and State of Georgia law enforcement agents. Three days before his death, agents exercised a search warrant to gather information about the use of GcMAF with autistic patients in his clinic. Human GcMAF holds great promise in the treatment of various illnesses including cancer, autism, chronic fatigue and possibly Parkinson's. Since 1990, 59 research papers have been published on GcMAF, 20 of these pertaining to the treatment of cancer."

Freedom Outpost, in October 2015, offered the following from writer Tim Brown: "Back in July, I reported that five holistic doctors had met untimely and suspicious deaths within 30 days and that five more were still missing. Within days of that report, two more doctors were also found dead under suspicious circumstances, which made 7 inside of a month. Now, within the span of 90 days, eleven doctors have been found dead under suspicious circumstances, and just prior to the writing of this article a twelfth holistic doctor, Marie Paas was found dead due to an apparent suicide."

In February 2016, *Natural News* posted a news story with the title of "Wave of holistic doctor deaths continues, as Florida chiropractor suddenly dies despite being 'hearty and healthy.'" The following is an extract from the article, which was the work of staff writer Julie Wilson: "A wave of mysterious deaths continues to plague practitioners in the field of holistic medicine, including chiropractors, herbalists and other alternative healers, with the latest fatality involving a licensed chiropractor who also worked as a full-time teacher. Dr. Rod Floyd, Associate Professor and Faculty-Clinician with the Palmer College of Chiropractic at the Port Orange, Fla. campus, had just celebrated he and his wife's 37th wedding anniversary, when he abruptly passed away in his home late last month."

"50 Holistic Doctors Have Mysteriously Died in the Last Year, but What's Being Done about It?" That was the eye-catching title of an article which appeared at *Truth Theory* in June 2016. The story was intriguing and highlighted thirty-four deaths within the last year. They said: "We'll let you be the judge on whether or not the untimely demise of many of these practitioners is fate or suspect. What matters most is that if these doctors were killed because they're practicing true medicine, the injustice is uncovered and the parties responsible pay for their crimes."

Snopes.com took a different approach and stated: "As of March 2015, there was an estimated range of 897,000 to just over 1,000,000 doctors in the

United States, and per every 100,000 people (of all vocations) each year, approximately 821 die. Going by those numbers alone, between 6,500 and 8,200 medical doctors will statistically die of myriad causes in any given year."

Are we seeing the sinister murder of holistic doctors on a large scale by the New World Order? Or, are people assuming that's the case as a result of looking for threads and links that may not be relevant? In time, we may know for sure.

DUGWAY PROVING GROUND

Is it feasible that the Dugway Proving Ground—working to a New World Order agenda—is planning on unleashing the closest thing one could imagine to a real outbreak of a zombie virus? It sounds outlandish, but it may not be. Located approximately eighty-five miles outside of Salt Lake City, the huge Dugway Proving Ground (DPG) sits squarely within Utah's Great Salt Lake Desert. It is shielded and protected by a huge expanse of mountains that dominate the surrounding landscape. The highly classified work of the DPG falls under the control of the U.S. Army, and its role is to research chemical and biological weaponry from a defensive perspective.

Late on the afternoon of January 27, 2011, the supersecret DPG went into lockdown mode. If you were inside at the time, the doors closed, then you stayed there. And if you were outside, there was no chance of getting in—at all. For the better part of a day, the situation did not change. Despite the tight security, word leaked outside that something of a disastrous nature had occurred, possibly even the mistaken release of a deadly pathogen that could spread across the planet. Was it really that serious? Well, that very much depends on who you ask: the locals, the staff at Dugway, or investigative journalists.

Whistleblowers from Dugway claimed that, yes, it was actually that serious. When an everyday stocktaking of certain dangerous items was undertaken on January 27, 2011, it was found, to the complete and utter consternation of just about everyone on base, that one particular vial wasn't where it should have been. In fact, it wasn't anywhere: it had vanished. Well, what was one little vial in the bigger scheme of things? Actually, one little vial could have amounted to quite a lot.

The vial in question contained nothing less than a deadly chemical warfare agent called VX, which has significant and horrific effects on the human body. Nausea and sweating are just the start. Bizarre twitching follows, as does uncontrollable vomiting. Then there is an accompanying fever, the victim's

The Dugway Proving Ground covers over 2,500 square miles (about 6,500 square kilometers) of the Utah desert. Chemical and biological weapons are maintained and tested here, including deadly anthrax.

nose runs uncontrollably, and breathing becomes labored. Left untreated, the infected are in for quick and horrible deaths.

We are assured, however, that when further checks were made, it was discovered that the deadly vial hadn't vanished, after all. It had simply been mislabeled and placed on the wrong shelf. Problem solved. True or not, we are fortunate that the apocalypse did not begin.

In addition to missing vials of deadly agents, there is the matter of the Dugway Proving Ground's secret connections to the world of the zombie. And, no, that is not a joke. Clairvius Narcisse was a resident of Haiti and a man who claimed that, in 1962, he was zombified and forced to work in a slavelike, mind-controlled fashion on a Haitian plantation owned by his brother. Research undertaken after Narcisse's story came to light, and specifically that done by Wade Davis for his book *The Serpent and the Rainbow*, strongly suggested that Narcisse was rendered into such a bizarre condition after being given a powerful combination of two powerful agents: (a) bufotoxin, which is found in, and extracted from, the paratoid glands of toads; and (b) tetrodotoxin, which can majorly affect the human nervous system. Combined, however, they can render a person into a deathlike state, in which both pulse and blood pressure plummet.

Additional research strongly suggested that Narcisse was then awakened from his "dead" state via Datura Starmonium, which is a form of herbal medicine that can provoke hallucinogenic experiences and amnesia. As a result of this mind-bending cocktail, Narcisse was led to believe by his brother that he,

THE NEW WORLD ORDER BOOK

Narcisse, was a literal zombie who was brought back from the dead. The outcome was that Narcisse began to act like a zombie—and for no less than eighteen years. So, what does all of this have to do with the top-secret world of the Dugway Proving Ground?

When, in late January 2011, there was that aforementioned mishandling of a highly toxic nerve-agent at the DPG, persistent digging by the media revealed that both bufotxin and tetrodotoxin were the subjects of highly classified studies at the secret installation. And what might be the reason for the DPG researching a controversial cocktail that can render a person into a definitively zombie-like state? The likelihood is that staff were seeking to perfect the ultimate tool of control over us by plunging us into states resembling old-school, mind-controlled zombies. The New World Order, to be sure, would find such tools of control most appealing.

DUMBING DOWN THE POPULATION

If there is one thing that the New World Order wants, it's a population that doesn't ask questions—chiefly because it has no idea of what the hell is going on. And, if there is one, sure-fire, way of guaranteeing that the people of Earth will be turned into underintelligent, uninformed, and ignorant masses is by ensuring that a long-term program of "dumbing down" the population goes ahead. The scary thing about this is that it is already happening. Joachim Hagopian, at Global Research, made that abundantly clear in 2014: "The most obvious example of how Americans have been dumbed down is through this nation's failed public education system. At one time not that long ago America reigned supreme as a leading model for the rest of the world providing the best quality free public K-12 education system on the planet. But over the last many decades while much of the rest of the world has been passing us by, it seems an insidious federal agenda has been implemented to condition and brainwash a population of mindless, robotic citizenry that simply does what it's told, and of course the brainwashing commences early in America's schools."

Hagopian also said: "Over numerous decades a grand experiment engaging in social engineering with America's youth has been steadily working to homogenize a lowest common denominator product of sub par mediocrity, creating generations of young Americans who can neither read nor write, nor think for themselves in any critical manner. According to a study last year by the US Department of Education, 19% of US high school graduates cannot read, 21% of adults read below 5th grade level and that these alarming rates have not changed in the last ten years."

Echoing this is *Psychology Today*: "There is a growing and disturbing trend of anti-intellectual elitism in American culture. It's the dismissal of science, the arts, and humanities and their replacement by entertainment, self-righteousness, ignorance, and deliberate gullibility.

"Susan Jacoby, author of *The Age of American Unreason*, says in an article in the *Washington Post*, 'Dumbness, to paraphrase the late senator Daniel Patrick Moynihan, has been steadily defined downward for several decades, by a combination of heretofore irresistible forces. These include the triumph of video culture over print culture; a disjunction between Americans' rising level of formal education and their shaky grasp of basic geography, science and history; and the fusion of anti-rationalism with anti-intellectualism.'"

InfoWars has kept its readers informed of this deliberate eroding of the intelligence levels of the American population. As an example, consider the words of Michael Snyder from 2013: "Have you ever seen the movie *Idiocracy*? It is a movie about an 'average American' that wakes up 500 years in the future only to discover that he is the most intelligent person by far in the 'dumbed down' society that is surrounding him. Unfortunately, that film is a very accu-

The public education system in the United States has been roundly criticized as inadequate, which would be exactly what those in the New World Order would want because smart, educated citizens are considered a threat.

rate metaphor for what has happened to American society today. We have become so 'dumbed down' that we don't even realize what has happened to us. But once in a while something comes along that reminds us of how far we have fallen. In Kentucky, an eighth grade exam from 1912 was recently donated to the Bullitt County History Museum. When I read this exam over, I was shocked at how difficult it was. Could most eighth grade students pass such an exam today? Of course not. In fact, I don't even think that I could pass it. Sadly, this is even more evidence of 'the deliberate dumbing down of America' that former Department of Education official Charlotte Iserbyt is constantly warning us about. The American people are not nearly as mentally sharp as they once were, and with each passing generation it gets even worse."

In May 2016, Clarence B. Jones, writing for the *Huffington Post*, made a number of very good points: "With hundreds of thousands of homeless people sleeping on our sidewalks nationwide, the continuing potential terror threat of ISIS to our homeland, rising health care costs, interest on our national debt being third highest expenditure in our Federal Budget, the highest incarceration rate worldwide, and income and wealth inequality remaining unabated, should we be seriously more concerned about who should be able and qualified to use a public restroom? Have we succumbed to the 'Trumpenization' of America: anything is ok, irrespective of whether or not it is true, immoral, or practically doable in the real existential universe or who it hurts or benefits? Has our national 2016 presidential election become the holographic version of a reality TV show?"

All of this eerily mirrors "Harrison Bergeron" (see the entry in this book titled "Harrison Bergeron"), a story written by Kurt Vonnegut and published in 1961. It tells of a future United States—specifically the year 2081, when the population is dumbed down by the Handicapper General, whose office ensures that everyone is of limited intelligence. It couldn't happen? Unfortunately, and thanks to the machinations of the New World Order, we are already on our way. Unless, of course, the collective population stands up and fights back—which would, of course, be the preferred outcome.

EBOLA

Very few people will forget the atmosphere of fear that gripped the American population in the latter part of 2014, when Ebola hemorrhagic fever surfaced in the United States. and particularly so when people realized that, currently, there is no cure for Ebola. Before we get to the meat of the matter, an important question needs to be answered: what, exactly, is Ebola? The Centers for Disease Control and Prevention (CDC) states: "Ebola, previously known as Ebola hemorrhagic fever, is a rare and deadly disease caused by infection with one of the Ebola virus species. Ebola can cause disease in humans and nonhuman primates (monkeys, gorillas, and chimpanzees). Ebola is caused by infection with a virus of the family *Filoviridae*, genus *Ebolavirus*. There are five identified Ebola virus species, four of which are known to cause disease in humans: Ebola virus (*Zaire ebolavirus*); Sudan virus (*Sudan ebolavirus*); Taï Forest virus (*Taï Forest ebolavirus*, formerly Cùte d'Ivoire ebolavirus*); and Bundibugyo virus (*Bundibugyo ebolavirus*). The fifth, Reston virus (*Reston ebolavirus*), has caused disease in nonhuman primates, but not in humans.

"Ebola viruses are found in several African countries. Ebola was first discovered in 1976 near the Ebola River in what is now the Democratic Republic of the Congo. Since then, outbreaks have appeared sporadically in Africa. The natural reservoir host of Ebola virus remains unknown. However, on the basis of evidence and the nature of similar viruses, researchers believe that the virus is animal-borne and that bats are the most likely reservoir. Four of the five virus strains occur in an animal host native to Africa."

The World Health Organization says of Ebola: "The Ebola virus causes an acute, serious illness which is often fatal if untreated. Ebola virus disease (EVD) first appeared in 1976 in 2 simultaneous outbreaks, one in what is now, Nzara, South Sudan, and the other in Yambuku, Democratic Republic of Congo. The latter occurred in a village near the Ebola River, from which the disease takes its name. The current outbreak in West Africa, (first cases notified in March 2014), is the largest and most complex Ebola outbreak since the Ebola virus was first discovered in 1976. There have been more cases and deaths in this outbreak than all others combined. It has also spread between countries starting in Guinea then spreading across land borders to Sierra Leone and Liberia, by air (1 traveler) to Nigeria and USA (1 traveler), and by land to Senegal (1 traveler) and Mali (2 travelers)."

All of which brings us back to 2014. It all began in September of that year, when a Liberian man, Thomas Eric Duncan, who was visiting family in the Dallas, Texas area, had the dubious honor of being the first person in the United States to show signs of what was suspected as being Ebola. On Sep-

A billboard in Mali warns of the dangers of spreading the Ebola virus.

tember 30, the Centers for Disease Control confirmed what everyone was dreading: Duncan had Ebola, but not for long. He was dead by October 8.

Three days later, one of Duncan's nurses at the Texas Health Presbyterian Hospital Dallas, the facility where he was treated, *also* fell sick with Ebola. Her name was Nina Pham. Seventy-two hours later, *another* nurse, Amber Joy Vinson, was also diagnosed with an Ebola infection. Fortunately, both recovered. A physician named Craig Spencer, who was involved in a project to help West Africans infected with Ebola, was struck by the disease in New York. He, too, recovered. The nation, however, wondered where Ebola would erupt next. The answer was: it didn't erupt anywhere. That was the beginning and the end of the 2014 Ebola outbreak: four cases confirmed in the United States. That's not quite the end of the story, however.

When the initial infection in Texas went from one, to two, then to three, hysterical, nationwide calls went out for the city of Dallas to be quarantined, to be placed in lockdown, for martial law to be imposed to prevent the number of infected from spiraling out of control and spreading the virus across the rest of the Lone Star State, and, ultimately, all across America. It was like something out of the average zombie movie. Massive, unwarranted hysteria was running wildly out of control.

As history has shown, martial law was not declared in Dallas, the city was not placed in unending lockdown mode, and no one was placed in detention camps. For a short time, however, shrill screams on the Internet succeeded in whipping up a frenzy as well as a call for draconian laws to be introduced—as in right now, before it's too late. All of this was caused by the medical plight of just four people—three of whom, it should not be forgotten, went on to make full, lasting recoveries.

It is very easy to see how all of this talk—or, more correctly, screaming and shouting—about martial law, "draconian powers," and "detention camps" could all be secretly exploited by the New World Order, specifically as a means to create fear and hysteria and impose the very draconian powers that the media was screaming about. It is, of course, very important that we take careful notice of such dangerous viruses as Ebola; however, we also need to avoid overusing the fear factor, lest we unwittingly help feed the fear-creating agenda of the New World Order.

ECONOMIC AND MONETARY UNION OF THE EUROPEAN UNION

The Economic and Monetary Union of the European Union is an integral part of the European Union (EU), which is itself working to further the agenda of the New World Order. It states: "Economic and Monetary Union (EMU) represents a major step in the integration of EU economies. It involves the coordination of economic and fiscal policies, a common monetary policy, and a common currency, the euro. Whilst all 28 EU Member States take part in the economic union, some countries have taken integration further and adopted the euro. Together, these countries make up the euro area.

"The decision to form an Economic and Monetary Union was taken by the European Council in the Dutch city of Maastricht in December 1991, and was later enshrined in the Treaty on European Union (the Maastricht Treaty). Economic and Monetary Union takes the EU one step further in its process of economic integration, which started in 1957 when it was founded. Economic integration brings the benefits of greater size, internal efficiency and robustness to the EU economy as a whole and to the economies of the individual Member States. This, in turn, offers opportunities for economic stability, higher growth and more employment—outcomes of direct benefit to EU citizens. In practical terms, EMU means: Coordination of economic policy-making between Member States, coordination of fiscal policies, notably through limits on government debt and deficit, an independent monetary policy run by the European Central Bank (ECB), single rules and supervision of financial Institutions within the euro area, and the single currency and the euro area."

On September 21, 2014, José Manuel Durão Barroso, the president of the European Commission, delivered a speech titled "The European Union in the New World Order." In part, it stated: "Today, when you hear someone discuss 'the new world order,' you may be forgiven for spontaneously thinking: 'World order? That would be a good idea as well.'

"It would certainly seem an improvement on the evolutions we have been seeing recently, in which disorder is the order of the day, and a number of threatening trends can only be described as 'unworldly.' From Eastern Ukraine to Syria and Iraq, some events just don't fit the world view we had been cherishing for years, possibly even decades. And yet, out of all this chaos some kind of order will eventually materialize, and in our defense against such threats we will find the real essence of our governing systems. These evolutions force us, not only to find an effective answer in day-to-day political terms, but also to revisit the very concepts on which our political and societal institutions are based, to reaffirm our commitment to democracy and the rule of law, to redefine our attachment to globalization and international integration, to upgrade our engagement in multilateralism and multiculturalism. Either we will shape the new world order, or we will suffer the consequences."

On the matter of the Monetary Union, Barroso added in his speech: "If the financial and economic crisis highlighted the unprecedented level of global interdependence, the fallout in Europe, in the form of a sovereign debt crisis, revealed not only an unprecedented but even an unexpected level of inter-dependence of the economies—namely but not only—of the euro area.

"Decisions by national governments, but also the economic health of the banking and corporate sectors and of the households in one specific country, irrespective of its economic dimension, proved to have a very strong impact on the situation in other parts of the Monetary Union. So we could no longer avoid being attentive to the spill over effects of the decisions or non-decisions taken by one single country. And to really understand—which is, by the way, in the Lisbon Treaty—that the economic policy of each Member State is indeed a matter of European concern, not only of national concern."

He closed his speech as follows: "Ladies and gentlemen, let me conclude, Interdependence may sometimes lead to free-rider behavior: the benefits of global markets and international stability are taken for granted, while each country's responsibility for such global public goods is all too easily neglected. In the new multipolar world, some even call it a-polar, each power's stake and responsibility will only increase with time. Emerging powers will take an increasing part in decision-making, and will eventually take up a bigger part of the responsibility. They will have no other choice. Order, they too will realise, is something you create, establish, work towards. And I am deeply convinced that the partnership between the US and the EU, which has come to the same conclusion many times in the past, will continue to form the core of that effort in the future as well. Hopefully, we will have a world order based on the principles so important to us: the principle of freedom, justice, rule of law, democracy and human dignity."

ELECTROMAGNETIC PULSE DISASTER

One of the things that could lead us into a New World Order, particularly so if the infrastructure completely collapses—whether as a result of a terrorist attack or a false flag-style situation—is an electromagnetic pulse (EMP) disaster. It is something that surfaces within the media quite regularly, but what, exactly is an EMP disaster, and how could it impact us?

The "2008 Report of the Commission to Assess the Threat to the United States from Electromagnetic Pulse Attack" states in part: "The electromagnetic pulse (EMP) generated by a high altitude nuclear explosion is one of a small number of threats that can hold our society at risk of catastrophic consequences.... A single EMP attack may seriously degrade or shut down a large part of the electric power grid in the geographic area of EMP exposure effective instantaneously. There is also the possibility of functional collapse of grids beyond the exposed

An EMP simulator tests Air Force One to see if it is vulnerable to an electromagnetic pulse attack.

one, as electrical effects propagate from one region to another…. Should significant parts of the electric power infrastructure be lost for any substantial period of time, the Commission believes that the consequences are likely to be catastrophic, and many people may ultimately die for lack of the basic elements necessary to sustain life in dense urban and suburban communities."

The report adds: "In fact, the Commission is deeply concerned that such impacts are likely in the event of an EMP attack unless practical steps are taken to provide protection for critical elements of the electric system and for rapid restoration of electric power, particularly to essential services."

Forbes says of such an apocalyptic situation: "One curious facet of an EMP event is that we wouldn't even feel it pass through our bodies. The EMP would pass unnoticed through us, even as it fried the iPhones and Galaxies in our pockets, knocked out our telecommunications system, rendered our cars and computers without the ability to function, and took out our power grid.

We would have little idea of the dread potentially awaiting us, because there would be no communications. No mobility. Nothing that our highly evolved, sophisticated, and electronic society relies on. That's the bad news."

Secrets of Survival offers a bleak picture: "As a result of just one EMP attack on the U.S., in an instant the nation's power grid will fail as anything with circuits (including most automobiles built since the early 1960s when computerized components became more standard in automobiles) will cease to work. Trains, buses, subway systems and commercial airlines and other modern planes will cease to work also—even the 4,000 or so commercial flights (think Delta, U.S. Airways, Southwest Airlines, and many others) that are in the sky over America at any given time. Our electricity driven society, built on a complex web of intersecting wires and computer circuits, will suddenly come to a standstill. All Hell will probably break loose shortly after."

It's very easy to see how, under such circumstances, we might all be plunged into a New World Order, a system created to take control when all of our technology is forever rendered extinct.

ESCHATOLOGY

There are a significant number of people who believe that the New World Order will come to fruition when the world is faced with a planetwide threat from demonic forces that are at the heart of the UFO phenomenon—as controversial as such a thing sounds. In 2003, a Lincoln, Nebraska, priest named Ray Boeche met with a pair of U.S. Department of Defense physicists who were working on a top-secret program to contact—and even make deals with—demonic things that they termed Non-Human Entities or NHEs. Boeche's informants had their own views on what might be looming large. Boeche says: "They didn't just think that this was a spiritual deception, but that it was possibly something leading to a final deception. In their view—which, theologically, I don't particularly hold—they viewed things much more like that of [Tim] LaHaye and [Jerry B.] Jenkins in the *Left Behind* book-series: the Antichrist will appear, then we are fooled, and Armageddon will then be triggered. That seemed to be their personal feeling about the whole scenario."

Boeche has his own position on Armageddon. "I tend to take the view," he commented, "that many of the prophecies in the Book of Revelation were fulfilled with Rome's destruction of Jerusalem. Orthodox Christianity teaches a physical return of Christ, but that is always considered to be the church's great hope: Christ's returning, a triumphant return. So, from that point of view, the *Left Behind* mentality—that Armageddon is a terrible thing and that

A worldwide crisis of Armageddon-like proportions is just the thing needed for a New World Order to swoop in and take over the planet.

you want to push it off as long as possible—to me doesn't really hold, at least in the historical sense. Christ's eventual return is the culmination of this age and this world, so it's not something to fear. It's something to be welcomed. But, it was viewed by the DoD like that, as a final battle scenario. Their other big fear in the whole thing was: if you have these types of entities who will present themselves as extraterrestrial beings, how is that going to affect the spiritual outlook of the people? Will it sway people from a belief in Christ? Would it have that sort of a spiritual effect?"

And then there is Dan T. Smith, an enigmatic figure on the UFO research scene, whose father was Harvard economist Dan Throop Smith, the Treasury Department's number-one tax advisor during the Eisenhower Administration. Researcher Gary Bekkum said of Dan T. Smith: "His personal meetings have included former and present representatives of the U.S. government intelligence community and their political associates, like Chris Straub, a former member of the Senate Select Committee on Intelligence."

Researcher Vince Johnson, who had the opportunity to speak with Smith on a number of occasions about his ufological views and insider contacts, stated: "According to Smith, UFOs are primarily a psychological/metaphysical phenomenon which are both preparing us and pressuring us to develop our own psi abilities. Not that UFOs are a single type of entity; Smith asserts that there are 'powers and principalities' at work—presumably supernatural entities like angels and demons.

"Furthermore, he said that a radical program of parapsychological research and development is currently underway near Los Alamos, New Mexico. This group's development of psychokinesis, and psychotronics (a term used to denote psychic warfare techniques) represents a danger of eschatological proportions. 'These techniques have been available, but controlled, throughout history. Now, other entities are forcing the issue,' said Smith."

Johnson added: "[Smith] reported that his governmental sources 'hinted at' an eschatological emergency.... When I asked why the CIA was interested in eschatology, he replied that the ramifications of the eschaton event represented a serious threat to national security, and thus, fell into the purview of the intelligence agencies. Smith also revealed that the eschatological issues he raised related directly to the biblical prophecies of the Book of Revelation."

EUROPEAN UNION

According to its own website, the European Union "is a unique economic and political union between 28 European countries that together cover much of the continent. The EU was created in the aftermath of the Second World War. The first steps were to foster economic cooperation: the idea being that countries that trade with one another become economically interdependent and so more likely to avoid conflict. The result was the European Economic Community (EEC), created in 1958, and initially increasing economic cooperation between six countries: Belgium, Germany, France, Italy, Luxembourg and the Netherlands. Since then, a huge single market has been created and continues to develop towards its full potential."

The EU website continues: "What began as a purely economic union has evolved into an organization spanning policy areas, from climate, environment and health to external relations and security, justice and migration. A name change from the European Economic Community (EEC) to the European Union (EU) in 1993 reflected this. The EU is based on the rule of law: everything it does is founded on treaties, voluntarily and democratically agreed by its member countries. The EU is also governed by the principle of representative democracy, with citizens directly represented at Union level in the European Parliament and Member States represented in the European Council and the Council of the EU."

Finally, there is this from the EU: "The EU has delivered more than half a century of peace, stability and prosperity, helped raise living standards and launched a single European currency: the euro. In 2012, the EU was awarded the Nobel Peace Prize for advancing the causes of peace, reconciliation, democracy and human rights in Europe. Thanks to the abolition of border controls between EU countries, people can travel freely throughout most of the continent. And it has become much easier to live, work and travel abroad in Europe. The single or 'internal' market is the EU's main economic engine, enabling most goods, services, money and people to move freely. Another key objective is to develop this huge resource also in other areas like energy, knowledge and capital markets to ensure that Europeans can draw the maximum benefit from it."

There are, however, those who believe that the European Union has a far more sinister agenda. It may very well be an agenda which allies the EU to the New World Order and its short- and long-term goals for worldwide domination.

Bibliotecapleyaes.net makes its position on the European Union–New World Order connection abundantly clear: "[T]he concept of a United Europe is not that different from the concept of a United States. The states in the United States Union were essentially and originally individual sovereign states that joined together in a kind of a union. To say 'United States' is much like saying 'Union of States.' This Awareness indicates that the idea of a union of states was pure and could be very beneficial, but when the union of states get controlled from outside by the United States of America, Incorporated, in Washington D.C., whose jurisdiction in reality should only be its own ten square miles of territory, and when this union of states lets that corporation begin to rule them, because the corporation is capable of giving them large sums of money if they yield to their control, then a problem is developed.

"They are selling their souls to the devil, in a sense. The same can be said for Europe. If these countries, which are sovereign independent countries, join together, and if, in their joining together they allow some external corporation or country or organization or force to begin dictating to them, then they have lost something very important: their own sovereignty, their own right to make their own decisions. This Awareness indicates that first it may be very insignif-

European Union flags wave in front of the Belgium Parliament's building in Brussels. For some, the EU represents peace and stability; for others, it is a sinister threat to independence and freedom.

icant and unimportant. The decisions that are made may not be of great concern, but the time will come when the outside force begins to dictate heavier and heavier policies, imposing restrictions on these independent countries, so that freedoms, which were once commonplace, are no longer allowed."

With the Brexit affair having caused shockwaves throughout the New World Order hierarchy, *Freedom Fighter Times* suggests a new scenario on the part of the NWO as it seeks to recover from what, for us, is a very welcome setback: "France and Germany plan to enact a European Superstate abolishing the EU and formally bringing about the New World Order. According to the signed documents by France and Germany, obtained by TVP; the superpowers of the world better get ready for another contender; the European Superstate. In the West it's America, in the East, it's Russia and China, but now there is a plan to create a monstrous superstate and abolish the EU. In everything that takes place the elite have an agenda. With the Brexit, it would appear as though their agenda is to bring the EU to ruin and implement a superstate. This new superpower would include the combination of France, Germany, and potentially Italy. The countries in the superstate would not be allowed to have their own army or special services. The ES would bring about a unified law and taxation system and abolish the member countries central bank and currency. They would then bring about their own visa administration and enact a common foreign policy with other organizations and counties. Finally, the member countries would have their role within NATO limited."

EXPERIMENTS ON THE BRAIN

As we have seen, there is good evidence to suggest that the widespread use of biochip implants may allow the New World Order to take control of us by, essentially, rendering us helpless. Such technology, and its usage, has a long and controversial history.

According to the MKUltra files, on April 13, 1953, CIA chief Allen Dulles ordered the creation of a program of mind control known as MKUltra to be conducted by Dr. Sydney Gottlieb. Rumors and half truths about new mind-control techniques being used by Soviet, Chinese, and North Korean interrogators on U.S. prisoners of war panicked the CIA into a search for its own sure-fire method of questioning captives. In April 1961, Dr. Gottlieb decided the animal experiments, which he was conducting by implanting electrodes in their brains, were successful and that it was time to experiment with human brains. Information has leaked out concerning experiments with three Viet Cong (VC) prisoners in July 1968.

A team of behaviorists flew into Saigon and traveled to the hospital at Bien Hoa, where the prisoners were being confined. The agents from Sub-project 94 set up their equipment in an enclosed compound, and the team's neurosurgeon and neurologist inserted miniscule electrodes into the brains of the three VC prisoners. After a brief recovery period, the prisoners were armed with knives, and direct electrical stimulation was applied to their brains. The goal of the experiment was to determine if individuals with such electrodes implanted in their brains could be incited to attack and to kill one another. Once again, the agency was seeking a perfect sleeper assassin, a true Manchurian candidate, who could be electronically directed to kill a subject. After a week of enduring electrical shocks to their brains, the prisoners still refused to attack one another. They were summarily executed and their bodies burned.

EXTRATERRESTRIAL NEW WORLD ORDER

Without doubt, the strangest New World Order suggests it won't be the powerful elite of our world who establish a New World Order but aliens. Make mention of the words "alien abduction," and most people will have at least *some* degree of understanding of the term. Since the early 1960s, countless individuals—all across the world—have made astonishing claims to the effect that they have been kidnapped and experimented upon in bizarre fashion by emotionless, dwarfish entities sporting large, bald heads and huge, black, insect-like eyes. Those same, alleged alien entities have become famously known as the Grays. Their helpless and terrified victims are the abductees.

A wealth of theories exists to try to explain what may be afoot when darkness sets in and the creepy Grays surface from their dark, hidden lairs. While the skeptics and the debunkers prefer to relegate everything to the realm of nightmarish dreams, sleep disorders, hoaxing, and fantasy, not everyone is quite so sure that is all which is going on.

Many UFO researchers believe that the spindly Grays are on a significant and serious evolutionary decline and that to try to save their waning species, they secretly harvest DNA, blood, cells, eggs, sperm, and much more from the human race. The sheer nerve of it all! They then use all of this acquired material in sophisticated, gene-splicing-style programs to boost their waning bodies and repair their weakened immune systems.

There is, however, a much darker theory than that. It's a theory that's downright *menacing*.

Many so-called alien abductees—usually when placed in hypnotic states and regressed to the time of the presumed otherworld experience—describe the Grays implanting into their bodies, or under the surface of their skin, small, metallic devices. We are talking here about what have become infamously known as alien implants. If such an astonishing and controversial claim has even a nugget of truth to it, then what might be the purpose of these sinister actions? The answer to that question is not necessarily a positive one.

Some flying saucer sleuths have suggested that the devices allow the aliens to secretly track the movements of the abductees throughout their entire lives— thus permitting their extraterrestrial captors to find them, and extract even more and more cells and DNA, no matter where the people live or to where they might move.

Are aliens known to ufologists as "Grays" abducting people and implanting them with tracking devices? Are they harvesting our body cells and fluids?

There is a mind-blowing variant on this controversial theory. It is one that suggests the implants are put in place to control the minds of the abductees. Imagine, if you will, millions of people, all across the planet, and all implanted with highly sophisticated devices fashioned on another world, one very different from ours. Imagine, too, that the day finally comes when E.T.—a definitively hostile and deceptive creature very far removed from Steven Spielberg's highly annoying and sickly sweet *E.T.*—decides to take over the planet.

However, the aliens don't choose to do so via a massive show of force or by pummeling our cities and landscapes with terrible, futuristic weaponry in *Independence Day*-style. No; instead, they get the abductees to do their dirty work for them. Talk about taking the easy way out. One day, the researchers who adhere to this particular theory believe, all of those millions of currently dormant implants will be "switched on." For all intents and purposes, each and every one of the abductees will then suddenly become a mind-controlled slave to the alien hordes.

In this scenario, we will wake one morning to frightful scenes of utter carnage on the streets as the zombified abductees follow their preprogrammed assignments in violent and crazed fashion, but it won't be occurring just here or there. It will be *everywhere*. It will be on your very doorstep. It will be on the doorsteps of all of us.

The world will be plunged into utter chaos as the *implanted*—rather than the *infected*—do their utmost to wipe out the rest of us for their extraterrestrial masters. And, when the war is finally over and humankind is decimated, the aliens will take over a planet that will be largely free of us but in a fashion that leaves the Earth utterly intact.

In view of the above, should you, one day, encounter groups of alien abductees roaming the cities, it might be wise to follow that one word which so often gets shouted, in fear-filled tones, in just about every zombie movie at some point or another: "Run!"

An alien-controlled New World Order? Could such a sci-fi-like scenario become science fact? Could it be any worse than the NWO that the world's most powerful figures have in store for us?

Federal Emergency Management Agency (FEMA)

The official website of the Federal Emergency Management Agency (FEMA) offers the following history: "For 37 years, FEMA's mission remains: to lead America to prepare for, prevent, respond to and recover from disasters with a vision of 'A Nation Prepared.' On April 1, 1979, President Jimmy Carter signed the executive order that created the Federal Emergency Management Agency (FEMA). From day one, FEMA has remained committed to protecting and serving the American people. That commitment to the people we serve and the belief in our survivor centric mission will never change.

"As of April 2014, FEMA has 14,844 employees across the country—at headquarters, the ten regional offices, the National Emergency Training Center, Center for Domestic Preparedness/Noble Training Center and other locations.

"The Federal Emergency Management Agency coordinates the federal government's role in preparing for, preventing, mitigating the effects of, responding to, and recovering from all domestic disasters, whether natural or man-made, including acts of terror.

"FEMA can trace its beginnings to the Congressional Act of 1803. This act, generally considered the first piece of disaster legislation, provided assistance to a New Hampshire town following an extensive fire. In the century that followed, ad hoc legislation was passed more than 100 times in response to hurricanes, earthquakes, floods and other natural disasters."

There is, allegedly at least, a more sinister side to the work of FEMA. Many conspiracy theorists believe that FEMA is secretly creating a series of nationwide camps into which so-called "undesirables" will be held when the New World Order takeover occurs, "undesirables" meaning anyone who dares to argue with the jackbooted minions of the NWO.

In 2014, *National Report* stated: "The Federal Emergency Management Agency has officially opened their first 'Political Realignment Facility,' more famously known as a 'concentration camp' or 'death camp,' in an area southwest of Willcox, Arizona on Thursday, according to an official FEMA press release. The agency plans on opening another four such facilities in 2015, and plans to have twelve up and running before the 2016 elections.

"The first facility, designated as 'Camp Alpha,' is built on nearly 500 acres of Federal property near the Chiricahua national park in southwest Arizona. FEMA says the camp can hold as many as 10,000 Americans, with barracks-style living accommodations, a large cafeteria, and prison-like security perimeters and features, as well as facilities for FEMA personnel to 'conduct the business of the facility' and both open-air and underground labor facilities to quote 'keep inmates occupied and, when needed, separate.'

"The facilities, which were ordered and authorized through two-dozen executive orders by President Barack Obama the day he took office on January 20th, 2009, will serve as special camps for conservative-leaning Americans who openly dissent against the Obama Administration and the Democratic party, through Facebook status updates, Tweets, blog posts, or in private conversations intercepted by FEMA."

A FEMA truck equipped with satellite communications parks in a hotel lot during the 2012 Hurricane Sandy disaster.

Dave Hodges of *The Common Sense Show* wrote, "Every act of civil disobedience, every act of revolution and every act of tyrannical genocide committed by government, requires a trigger event. For the Nazis, this trigger event included burning down the Reichstag building and blaming the Communists as an excuse to declare martial law. What will be the trigger event for the coming genocidal holocaust committed against American citizens? No one can say for sure. However, the criminal elite are in need of a miracle because they have lost control of much of the population.

"Will it be a series of contrived false flag terror events conducted by ISIS followed by the demise of Clinton in which a lone-nut assassin, with a diary, allegedly acts on behalf of Donald Trump. This could be followed by a declaration of martial law. The people would be in the streets and the roundups would begin in earnest. However, history has proven that government gun confiscations from private citizens are the chest pains prior to the heart attack. In the 20th century, there were 17 major genocides committed against civilian populations resulting in a death toll of around 60 million people. Every one of these genocides was preceded by gun confiscation which rendered the intended victims defenseless against the slaughter that awaited them."

Just about anyone and everyone who owns one or more guns should take very careful heed of the words above. Your one chance to protect yourself and your family may soon be taken away from you.

FEDERALISM

A good, solid explanation of what federalism is comes from *USHistory*, which writes: "Did you ever wonder why you don't need a passport to go from New York to California, but if you were to move from one state to another, you would need a new driver's license? Or why you can use the same currency in all states, but not be subject to the same speed limits? Or why you have to pay both federal and state taxes? The maze of national and state regulations results from federalism—the decision made by the Founders to split power between state and national governments. As James Madison explained in the 'Federalist Papers,' our government is 'neither wholly national nor wholly federal.'

"In creating a federalist system the founders were reacting to both the British government and the Articles of Confederation. The British government was—and remains—a unitary system, or one in which power is concentrated in a central government. In England, government has traditionally been centralized in London, and even though local governments exist, they generally have only those powers granted them by Parliament. The national government is supreme, and grants or retains powers to and from local governments at its whim."

In 2001, the Brookings Institute stated: "The current consensus among savants of American federalism is that, at long last, power is shifting back to the states. The Cold War, which gave Washington politicians a national-security pretext for immersing themselves in local tasks like building bridges and highways, is history. Republican majorities, reputedly solicitous of state sovereignty, have controlled Congress since 1995. They promptly enacted legislation that would supposedly kick the congressional habit of heaping expensive obligations on state and local governments but not appropriating the money to help them comply. A year later, Congress also put the states in charge of handling more of the national welfare program. The Clinton administration not only signed off on this devolution but granted state agencies a degree of discretion in administering Medicaid and in managing some aspects of U.S. environmental policy. Much of the energy stirring public policy these days— from school reform to the reprise of prohibitionism (this time targeting tobacco)—seems to emanate from the statehouses. Perhaps most notably, during the past few years the Supreme Court has handed down several opinions that have sought to shore up prerogatives of the states."

Of course, this is all anathema to the New World Order that is intent on ensuring that every single decision that has a bearing on us, the people, is dictated by them. "Regional government" and "central government" will be outmoded concepts should the New World Order take control.

FIVE EYES

A group of intelligence agencies—all with significant stakes in the New World Order—Five Eyes is described by Privacy International as "a secretive, global surveillance arrangement of States comprised of the United States National Security Agency (NSA), the United Kingdom's Government Communications Headquarters (GCHQ), Canada's Communications Security Establishment Canada (CSEC), the Australian Signals Directorate (ASD), and New Zealand's Government Communications Security Bureau (GCSB). Beginning in 1946, an alliance of five English-speaking countries (the US, the UK, Australia, Canada and New Zealand) developed a series of bilateral agreements over more than a decade that became known as the UKUSA agreement, establishing the Five Eyes alliance for the purpose of sharing intelligence, primarily signals intelligence (SIGINT). For almost 70 years, this secret post-war alliance of five English-speaking countries has been building a global surveillance infrastructure to 'master the Internet' and spy on the world's communications."

Privacy International adds: "Even within the governments of the respective countries, which the intelligence agencies are meant to serve, there has historically been little appreciation for the extent of the arrangement. In fact, it is so secretive that the Australian prime minister reportedly wasn't informed of its existence until 1973 and no government officially acknowledged the arrangement by name until 1999. Few documents have been released detailing the Five Eyes surveillance arrangement … Here's what we do know: under the agreement interception, collection, acquisition, analysis, and decryption is conducted by each of the State parties in their respective parts of the globe, and all intelligence information is shared by default. The agreement is wide in scope and establishes jointly run operations centers where operatives from multiple intelligence agencies of the Five Eyes States work alongside each other."

News.com.au, in February 2016, ran an article titled "Britain's new plan to tackle terrorism both home and abroad with controversial security alliance." It stated: "Britain has warned that terrorism was exploiting mass migration to destabilise and take lives, as it called on its closest allies including Australia to resolve the current 'disparate' international fight against groups like ISIS. British Home Secretary Theresa May said it was that disjointed fight that was allowing extremism to spread and it was time to call on old alliances to be reinvigorated. Ms. May was in Washington to address senior figures of the Five Eyes security alliance, of Britain, the US, Australia, Canada and New Zealand, that was created post World War II and during the Cold War which carried out critical joint signals surveillance and intelligence operations against the Soviets and Eastern Bloc."

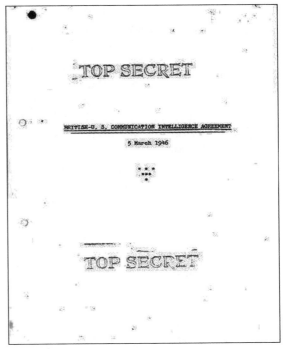

The 1946 agreement between the United States and United Kingdom that established the formation of Five Eyes was only released to the public in 2011.

FLUORIDE

Is the New World Order seeking to poison and control us with fluoride? As controversial as such a thing sounds, it is far from being implausible. It is a theory which has an all too real, verifiable equivalent. In the early 1930s, some of Adolf Hitler's scientists learned of certain experiments with fluoride that were conducted in the UK in which infinitesimal doses of fluoride in drinking water would, in time, reduce an individual's power to resist domination. Since the dosages were small, the victims were unknowingly poisoned, and a specific area of the brain would be narcotized, thereby making the victims submissive to the will of those who wished to govern them—a New World Order dream come true, one might say. The Nazis envisioned worldwide domination via mass medication of drinking water supplies.

The first of the Nazis' secret potions was demonstrated by mixing fluoride in the drinking water in Nazi prison camps in order to subdue the more unruly inmates into calm submission. Repeated experiments indicated that the addition of fluoride appeared to produce notable results in calming the most troublesome of the prisoners. Their early experiments led Nazi scientists to confidently predict that entire cities could be made submissive to the Hitler gospel. Rebellious regions could be made passive and be commanded to enter work programs as if they were near-zombies. On top of that, entire regiments of soldiers could become completely subservient, never questioning their officers, never resisting any order, and never complaining about a lack of comfortable living conditions.

Sodium fluoride is a hazardous waste by-product of the aluminum manufacturing process. The fluoride contamination of the environment comes from the following things: coal combustion, cigarette smoke, pesticides such as cockroach and rat poison, animal feeds, fertilizer, plastics, nonstick cookware, soft drinks, juices, and other drinks (both canned and bottled), and in a massive number of pharmaceutical products, including anesthetics, vitamins, antidepressants, hypnotics, psychiatric drugs, and military nerve gases.

A German chemist who worked in the huge I. G. Farben chemical company testified after the end of World War II that when the Nazis under Hitler decided to go into Poland, the general staff, of the German army planned to accomplish mass control through the process of water medication.

German scientists declared that any person who drank artificially fluoridated water for a period of one year or more would never again be the same person mentally or physically. Large numbers of German soldiers had fluoride introduced into their daily supply of drinking water. It is quite possible that the slavish devotion that so many Nazi troops had to their Fuhrer was due to the submissiveness induced by fluoride.

After fluoride was used on the German people for a number of years, researchers, scientists, doctors, neurosurgeons, and other professionals began to notice, during autopsies, a rise in the presence of the chemical within the human brain. Since fluoride was known to have effects on the right temporal lobe, hippocampus, and the pineal gland, some of the professionals began to ask similar questions: Was the fanatical rise in the worship of the Fuhrer due to the fluoride placed in the water? Had a combination of the chemical and the Fuhrer's fiery speeches that emphasized the German people being the true master race begun to take great effect on large numbers of the public? Had he truly achieved his goal of submissive, compliant zombies with no true will of their own?

Marchers in San Francisco protest fluoridation of drinking water in 2013.

One cannot resist pointing out that in 1945, fluoride was introduced into the public water supply and drinking water of select cities across the United States. Eventually, most cities across North America followed suit, believing that it was the healthy thing to do. The wonder-working benefits of fluoride were taught to dentists and dental hygienists and to children in elementary school health classes. Soon, families across the United States spent extra money and time making dental appointments for their children and themselves in an effort to have strong, healthy, and hopefully cavity-free teeth.

As early as 1954, some doctors suspected and reported fluoride to be harmful. Dr. George L. Waldbott, M.D., observed that his fluoridation patients became forgetful, drowsy, lethargic, and incoherent. Comparable cases of impaired cognition and memory were reported to the government by many other dental professionals. Government reports themselves indicate similar findings of impaired cognition and memory. Contrary to popular belief, fluoride has never been approved by the FDA for ingestion, only for topical use.

Mixing fluoride with drinking water remains controversial. On December 18, 2009, Graham Demeny, who had served fifteen years at the Glenmore Water Treatment Plant in Rockhampton, Queensland, Australia, resigned his position because he questioned the safety of adding fluoride to the city's water supply. Graham told reporter Allan Reinikkaar that until the city began adding fluoride to the water supply, all processes adopted by the city council had made the water clean or safe to consume. Fluoride addition does neither, he said, and questionably compromises the safety aspect.

FORT DETRICK

Ken Adachi, at *NWO Observer*, says: "De Facto US president Barack Hussein Obama, World Health Organization Head Dr. Margaret Chan and Centers for Disease Control and Prevention Director Dr. Thomas R. Frieden are all guilty of conspiring to commit and committing the following high crimes: bio-terrorism, crimes against humanity, genocide and conspiracy to commit mass murder. Bioterrorism is terrorism by intentional release or dissemination of biological agents (bacteria, viruses, or toxins); these may be in a naturally occurring or in a human-modified form.

"According to the US-based Centers for Disease Control and Prevention (CDC): A bioterrorism attack is the deliberate release of viruses, bacteria, or other germs (agents) used to cause illness or death in people, animals, or plants. These agents are typically found in nature, but it is possible that they could be changed to increase their ability to cause disease, make them resistant to current medicines, or to increase their ability to be spread into the environment."

Adachi adds: "Under the Bush administration the U.S. Army replaced its Military Institute of Infectious Diseases at Fort Detrick, Md., 'with a new laboratory that would be a component of a biodefense campus operated by several agencies.' The Army told the Associate Press that the laboratory is intended to continue research that is only meant for defense against biological threats.

"But University of Illinois international law professor Francis Boyle charged the Fort Detrick work would include "acquiring, growing, modifying, storing, packaging and dispersing classical, emerging and genetically engineered pathogens." Those activities, as well as planned study of the properties of pathogens when weaponized, "are unmistakable hallmarks of an offensive weapons program."

This brings up important issues: what, exactly, is Fort Detrick, and what is the nature of its work? *DC Military Archives* states: "The U.S. Biological Laboratories were established at Detrick Field in 1943, achieving pioneering efforts in decontamination, gaseous sterilization, and agent purification.

"Camp Detrick became Fort Detrick in 1956, continuing its mission of biomedical research and its reputation as the world's leading research campus for agents requiring specialty containment. The offensive biological warfare program was disestablished in 1969. The closing of the former biological warfare laboratories gave way to a period of transition in the 1970s. Former laboratories and land were transferred to the Department of Health and Human Services and the National Cancer Research and Development Center was established in 1971, now called the Frederick National Laboratory.

"The installation has since grown in the scope of its operations and now has an interagency campus, which houses all of the military services as well as non-Department of Defense organizations. The installation has matured as a center for advanced biomedical research and development, medical materiel management, and long-haul telecommunications for the White House, Department of Defense, and other governmental agencies. The National Interagency Biodefense Campus is here and co-locates the National Institute of Allergy and Infectious Diseases and the National Biodefense Analysis and Countermeasures Center with the U.S. Army Medical Research Institute of Infectious Diseases, all in an effort to provide opportunities for scientific coordination, education and partnerships."

There is ... a dark side to the work of Fort Detrick, a side which may have a bearing on the agenda of the New World Order to lower population levels.

There is, however, a dark side to the work of Fort Detrick, a side which may have a bearing on the agenda of the New World Order to lower population levels. Sue Arrigo, M.D., says: "As an ex-CIA physician with high level access, I wrote a report for DCI Webster in about 1991 arguing for closure of all the US Bio-Warfare Labs. I did that after reviewing the Ft. Detrick and the CIA's Langley Bio-Warfare Labs's research, looking at their own documents. That review was authorized because Bush, Sr. had sold dangerous Bio-Warfare agents to Hussein, which I ended up having to recover from Iraq. Webster, as a former judge, willing to evaluate the evidence, allowed me to research the field and write a report for him of close to a hundred pages, with one thousand pages of supporting documents.

"Although the focus of my report was why the Bio-Warfare Labs should be closed, the issue of the HIV virus developed by the Ft. Detrick lab formed about 18 pages of my report. At the time I wrote that report, the vaccine for HIV that had been developed in 6 months of work, had already been used by the Cabal since 1983.

"It was a crime against humanity that the virus was unleashed on the world, and it continues to be a crime that the vaccine has been kept secret and for private use only. Meanwhile, the outer research to get to a vaccine is an exercise in how not to arrive at a solution before millions more die. The initial 'hopes' for HIV per its designers was to be able to walk into Africa and take the resources from a ghost continent. They had hyped it as killing everyone there within a year, in their pre-release reports."

FOURTH REICH

Many conspiracy theorists believe that the New World Order will have significant input from a highly secret Fourth Reich, a follow-up to Adolf Hitler's infamous Third Reich of World War II. The Fourth Reich would be a successor to the Nazi era, and it is a term sometimes used by neo-Nazi groups that hope for a return to the days of Aryan supremacy. The phrase is also mentioned by conspiracy theorists, who apply it to any covert groups who hold ideals similar to the Nazis.

At the heart of this secret Third Reich—a potentially large player when the New World Order plays its ace card—is a firm belief that Adolf Hitler did not commit suicide in 1945 but secretly survived the war long enough to establish the roots of a powerful, well-hidden Fourth Reich. Certainly, there is no shortage of such claims.

It's a little-known fact that the FBI, in the postwar era, began to quietly compile what ultimately turned out to be a large dossier of material on claims that Hitler had survived World War II and secretly fled to South America. It's a dossier that has now been declassified and can be accessed at the FBI's website, *The Vault*.

As one might expect to be the case, many of the claims are scant in data, second- and thirdhand in nature, or written by individuals with more time on their hands than sense in their heads. That said, however, one section of the file is particularly intriguing and noteworthy. Incredibly, it suggests that none other than Allan Dulles—who, in World War II, made his mark in the Office of Strategic Services and served as director of the CIA from 1953 to 1961—was complicit in a top-secret program to have Hitler secretly shipped out to South America when the Nazis were defeated.

The files in question refer to stories coming out of Los Angeles, California, which reached the eyes and ears of the L.A. office of the FBI. According to what the FBI was told, two Nazi-controlled submarines made their stealthy way to the Argentinean coastline, where they covertly deposited high-ranking Nazis that had escaped the wrath of the United States, the United Kingdom, and the Soviet Union. One of the most astounding rumors concerning this story was that it was not just high rankers who were making new lives for themselves on the other side of the world. It was *the* most high-ranking Nazi, too: Adolf Hitler, who, allegedly, was by now hunkered down, somewhere, in the heart of the Andes.

The big question is: who was the FBI's informant? Unfortunately, we don't know since his name is excised from the relevant, released documents. Nevertheless, he had a great deal of data to impart, something which definitely made the FBI sit up and take careful notice. It must be noted that the Bureau's source, himself a former Nazi, offered the information—with a promise of more to come—in return for a safe haven in the United States. As to how the person claimed to know that Hitler had survived the war, it was, if true, sensational. The man said he was personally present when the submarines in question reached the coastline of Argentina. Aboard one of them were Adolf Hitler and Eva Braun—neither displaying *any* evidence of bullet wounds or of the effects of cyanide. Quite the opposite: they were vibrant, healthy, and very much alive.

Allen Dulles, the head of the CIA during the early years of the Cold War, is said by some to have been secretly involved in transporting Adolf Hitler safely to South America.

If the story was simply that—a tall tale told to try to secure asylum in the United States—the man had certainly crafted an elaborate story. The FBI's source provided details of the specific villages that Hitler, and the rest of the straggling remnants of the "Master Race," passed through on their way to a safe haven, somewhere in Argentina.

Adding further credence to this, additional files—also declassified under Freedom of Information legislation—revealed that among staff of the U.S. Naval Attaché in Buenos Aires, rumors were circulating that Hitler did not die in Berlin but that he was now hiding out in Argentina.

In 2014, a dramatic, new development happened in the saga of whether or not Adolf Hitler died in Berlin, Germany, in 1945 or secretly made a new life for himself in South America—first in Paraguay and then in Brazil. The new data came from Simoni Renee Guerreiro Dias, the author of a book entitled *Hitler in Brazil—His Life and His Death*. Dias' research suggests that Hitler changed his name to Adolf Leipzig, living out his life in Nossa Senhora do Livramento, a small village approximately fifty kilometers from the Brazilian town of Cuiaba. Supposedly, to the villagers, Hitler was known as the "Old German."

As to how Dias found out this information, the story is a thought-provoking one: during the course of her research, Dias found an old, faded photograph of Adolf Leipzig and then compared it to photos of Hitler. The suggestion is they were one and the same. Additional confirmation came from a nun who had seen Hitler, when he was in his eighties, hospitalized in Cuiaba. Attempts to have Hitler removed from the hospital were denied amid rumors that Vatican officials had the last word on the matter—and the last word, apparently, was that Hitler should remain where he was: out of sight and protected.

At the time of writing, the story is progressing in dramatic fashion: the body of Leipzig has been secured and permission has been given for DNA to be extracted from it. And, to ensure there is comparative material, a relative of Hitler, now living in Israel, has offered to provide a sample of DNA to determine if the two match.

The story is not as unlikely as many might assume. As *Liberty Voice* noted, when the Leipzig–Hitler story surfaced in early 2014: "Thousands of Nazis escaped Germany after the war, including Adolf Eichmann and Josef Mengele. Eichmann and Mengele, two of Hitler's most trusted henchman, both lived in Argentina in the 1940s. The Argentine President, Juan Domingo Peron, did everything that could be done to get the Nazis to South America's second largest country. Argentine agents were sent to Europe to make passage easy by providing falsified travel documents and, in many instances, travel expenses were covered. Even Nazis accused of the most horrific crimes, such as Mengele and Eichmann, were welcomed."

FREEDOM OF INFORMATION ACT EROSION

The Department of Justice says of the Freedom of Information Act: "Since 1967, the Freedom of Information Act (FOIA) has provided the public the right to request access to records from any federal agency. It is often described as the law that keeps citizens in the know about their government. Federal agencies are required to disclose any information requested under the FOIA unless it falls under one of nine exemptions which protect interests such as personal privacy, national security, and law enforcement.

"The FOIA also requires agencies to proactively post online certain categories of information, including frequently requested records. As Congress, the President, and the Supreme Court have all recognized, the FOIA is a vital part of our democracy.

"President Obama and the Department of Justice have directed agencies to apply a presumption of openness in responding to FOIA requests. The

Department of Justice, in its 2009 FOIA Guidelines, emphasized that the President has called on agencies to work in a spirit of cooperation with FOIA requesters. The Office of Information Policy at the Department of Justice oversees agency compliance with these directives and encourages all agencies to fully comply with both the letter and the spirit of the FOIA."

Numerous nations have Freedom of Information Acts, including the U.K., Canada, and Australia. They are all, broadly, similar. There is another similarity, too: the FOIA legislation is now being significantly eroded, specifically by those who prefer we know less and less about government, rather than more and more. Under a New World Order-driven regime, there is no doubt that the FOIA would be radically compromised, if not even completely shut down.

In 2010, the *Daily Gate City* said: "See no evil. Speak no evil. Report no evil. Barely months into what promised to be a new day for freedom of information in Illinois, we seem to be watching that potential in the state's still-anemic Freedom of Information Act eroding, at least from an anecdotal standpoint. The Freedom of Information Act contains the rules for what elected and appointed officials and agencies have to tell the public about what is going on.

"Those principles are a crucial part of what we in the news media rely on to do our jobs and get the information channeled along to the readers, the listeners and the viewers. Through almost-daily use, the press has learned to navigate the sometimes-rocky straits encountered in trying to get this information. But recently, we find ourselves crashing against the rocks of an overused and frequently misinterpreted exemption from disclosure known in legalese as subsection 7(1) but commonly called the 'pending investigation' clause.

"In a beautifully ironic example, Virden police last week asked for the public's help in solving a shooting incident—and then declined to release any information: No gender, no time or location, no suspects or descriptions."

Two years later, Scotland's information commissioner, Rosemary Agnew, offered this: "The current economic situation is leading to an increase in freedom of information requests to authorities, as people naturally want to understand the reasons behind decisions that affect them.

The Freedom of Information Act was signed into law in 1965 by President Lyndon Johnson, taking effect the following year.

"At the same time authorities are finding themselves with fewer resources to respond. My priority as commissioner is to help the public make better-targeted, more effective requests while also developing resources to support public authorities in responding to those requests faster and more efficiently. However, an ever-growing concern is the loss of rights occurring through the delivery of public services by arms-length organizations and third parties. FOI was introduced for a reason: to ensure that the delivery of public services and the spending of public money is transparent, open and accountable. It is simply not acceptable that citizens' rights continue to be eroded through complex changes in the delivery of services. This must be looked at as an immediate priority."

The Californian, in 2015, gave its readers the following, which continues this undeniably disturbing trend: "It's getting harder and more expensive to use public records to hold government officials accountable. Authorities are undermining the laws that are supposed to guarantee citizens' right to information, turning the right to know into just plain 'no.' Associated Press journalists filed hundreds of requests for government files last year, simply trying to use the rights granted under state open records laws and the U.S. Freedom of Information Act. What we discovered reaffirmed what we have seen all too frequently in recent years: The systems created to give citizens information about their government are badly broken and getting worse all the time."

Under a New World Order regime, "broken" and "getting worse" will, in all likelihood, be replaced by "eradicated."

FREEMASONS

The Masonic Service Association of North America says of the world's most famous, secret society: "No one knows with certainty how or when the Masonic Fraternity was formed. A widely accepted theory among Masonic scholars is that it arose from the stonemasons' guilds during the Middle Ages. The language and symbols used in the fraternity's rituals come from this era. The oldest document that makes reference to Masons is the Regius Poem, printed about 1390, which was a copy of an earlier work. In 1717, four lodges in London formed the first Grand Lodge of England, and records from that point on are more complete."

As for that 1390 document, the Masonic Dictionary states: "The manuscript is in the King's Library of the British Museum. It was published in 1840 by James O. Halliwell, and again in 1844, under the title of *The Early History of Freemasonry in England*. The Masonic character of the poem remained unknown until its discovery by Halliwell, who was not a Freemason, because it was catalogued as *A Poem of Moral Duties*. It is now more commonly known as the *Regius Manuscript* because it formed part of the Royal Library commenced by Henry VII and presented to the British Museum by George II."

By 1750, the world of the Masons had come to dominate practically all of Europe and was destined to become a powerful force within the growing America, as the Texas State Historical Association demonstrates: "The Masonic fraternity, brought to the American colonies in the mid-eighteenth century, was well established in all of the United States by 1820. Among the first Americans to migrate to Texas in the 1820s were a number of Masons, including Stephen F. Austin. Austin attempted to organize a Masonic lodge in 1828, when he and six other Masons met at San Felipe and petitioned the Grand York Lodge of Mexico for a charter dispensation. The petition evidently reached Mexico at the height of a quarrel between the 'Yorkinos' and 'Escoceses' (adherents of the Scottish Rite) and disappeared. A more successful effort occurred in the spring of 1835 when Dr. Anson Jones and five others, fearing Mexican reprisals, met secretly under the Masonic Oak near Brazoria and petitioned the Grand Lodge of Louisiana for a charter. The grand master of that state, John Henry Holland, issued the dispensation, and Holland Lodge No. 36 met for the first time on December 27, 1835, with Jones presiding as worshipful master."

The symbol of the Freemasons shows tools of the mason trade and sometimes, as in this case, the letter G, which means God or Geometry or Great Architect, depending upon the source.

Indeed, stateside, the Masons soon gained major footholds. For example, both Benjamin Franklin and George Washington were Masons. That the fraternity had members holding the highest office in the United States, and in quick time, demonstrates the power and influence the Masons wielded. On top of that, Chief Justice John Marshall—the one man, more than any other—who molded the Supreme Court into what it is today was a Mason.

In terms of the modern era, Brad Steiger notes that after the American Revolution, "Freemasonry became extremely powerful in the United States. Lodges sprang up in the smallest of villages, and it became an undeniable sign of prestige in any community to be a member. For businessmen who wished to succeed, it was almost a requirement to join the Masons."

THE NEW WORLD ORDER BOOK

In the wake of the still-unsolved murder in 1826 of a Mason named William Morgan—of Batavia, New York—there was an uprising against the Masons in the United States, chiefly out of fear of the power they wielded, both as a secret society and in terms of being able to stonewall the investigation into the Morgan death. The result, as Brad Steiger says, was that Freemasonry in the United States "never again achieved the social status it had once enjoyed."

And as Steiger also states: "Depending upon the prejudices of the beholder, the Freemasons remain a fraternal group that donates generously to charities—*or an insidious secret society bent on world conquest.*"

G-H

GOFF, KENNETH

Born in Wisconsin in 1914, Kenneth Goff is described in now-declassified FBI files from May 6, 1955, as "a self-styled freelance Evangelist who for the past number of years has been speaking around the U.S. regarding the threat of communism to the U.S."

Lectures that Goff routinely delivered to interested parties included: *Treason in our State Department*; *Should we use the Atom Bomb?*; *Red Secret Plot for Seizure of Denver*; and *Do the Reds Plan to Come by Alaska?*

As the FBI additionally noted: "Also, some of the titles of Goff's books, which he publishes voluminously are: '*Will Russia Invade America?*', '*One World, A Red World,*' and '*Confessions of Stalin's Agent.*'" But, the FBI had other concerns about Goff. He had once been a rabid commie himself, and there were certain figures in the Bureau that believed Goff was not quite the anti-communist that he now professed to be. Rather, there was a suspicion that Goff's had gone deep cover, and his red-hating ravings were merely a collective, ingenious ruse to camouflage his real intent: establishing networks of communist sympathizers across the United States.

The FBI certainly had a fine stash of material on Goff, who, it was recorded, "is a self-admitted former member of the Communist Party" and who "was found guilty by jury trial on February 25, 1948, in United States District Court, District of Columbia, and was fined $100 as a result of the subject's placing anti-communist signs before the Soviet Embassy in Washington, D.C."

The FBI files on Goff also noted: "The *Rocky Mountain News* on October 25, 1951, contained an article stating that three Englewood persons were ordered to appear in Denver Municipal Court as an aftermath of the ripping of the Soviet flag yesterday at Civic Center. Mr. and Mrs. Kenneth Goff were two of these three individuals."

Patriots might say that protesting outside the Soviet embassy and tearing up the Soviet flag were very laudable actions for a U.S. citizen to undertake on their home turf at the height of the fraught and dicey Cold War. The FBI wasn't quite so sure, however: "It has been our concern that Goff always ensures he is seen while displaying anti-Soviet tendencies. [Deleted] has remarked that if Goff is still privately 'of a party mind' this might explain his public displays."

Goff was certainly an interesting character and had made comments in the 1950s about communist-based plans to covertly introduce fluoride into the U.S. water supply to create a "spirit of lethargy" in the nation, and guess what? Goff had a deep interest in flying saucers. Indeed, one of Goff's regular lectures was titled *Traitors in the Pulpit, or What's behind the Flying Saucers—Are They from Russia, Another Planet, or God?* It was not so much from the perspective of UFOs being alien or even Russian, however, that interested Goff. His concern was how the UFO subject could be utilized as a tool of manipulation and control by government.

In his 1959 publication, *Red Shadows*, Goff offered the following to his readers—which, of course, secretly included the FBI: "During the past few years, the flying saucer scare has rapidly become one of the main issues, *used by organizations working for a one-world government* [italics mine], to frighten people into the belief that we will need a super world government to cope with an invasion from another planet. Many means are being used to create a vast amount of imagination in the minds of the general public, concerning the possibilities of an invasion by strange creatures from Mars or Venus."

Orson Welles' 1938 radio broadcast of "War of the Worlds," which was about a Martian invasion, scared many Americans. Kenneth Goff believed that the communists were behind this "test" of radio's power.

He continued: "This drive began early in the 40's, with a radio drama, put on my Orson Welles, which caused panic in many of the larger cities of the East, and resulted in the death of several people. The Orson Welles program of invasion from Mars was used by the Communist Party as a test to find out how the people would react on instructions given out over the radio. It was an important part of the communist rehearsal for the Revolution."

The now infamous Welles broadcast was, of course, based upon H.G. Wells' acclaimed novel *War of the Worlds*. And while, today, it is fashionable and almost de rigueur within ufological circles to suggest that the Welles broadcast and deep conspiracy go together hand in glove, it was far less so in the 1950s. Goff, then, was quite the prophet—and particularly so when one takes into consideration the fact that he had been mouthing off about *War of the Worlds*, a "one-world government," and a secret program to manipulate the public with staged UFO encounters as far back as 1951.

GORBACHEV, MIKHAIL

On December 7, 1988, at the forty-third session of the United Nations General Assembly, Mikhail Gorbachev—the eighth and final leader of the former Soviet Union—made a speech that focused extensively on not just plans for a new world but also for a definitive New World Order. Gorbachev began: "Two great revolutions, the French revolution of 1789 and the Russian revolution of 1917, have exerted a powerful influence on the actual nature of the historical process and radically changed the course of world events. Both of them, each in its own way, have given a gigantic impetus to man's progress. They are also the ones that have formed in many respects the way of thinking which is still prevailing in the public consciousness. That is a very great spiritual wealth, but there emerges before us today a different world, for which it is necessary to seek different roads toward the future, to seek—relying, of course, on accumulated experience—but also seeing the radical differences between that which was yesterday and that which is taking place today."

Gorbachev continued: "The newness of the tasks, and at the same time their difficulty, are not limited to this. Today we have entered an era when progress will be based on the interests of all mankind. Consciousness of this requires that world policy, too, should be determined by the priority of the values of all mankind.

"The history of the past centuries and millennia has been a history of almost ubiquitous wars, and sometimes desperate battles, leading to mutual destruction. They occurred in the clash of social and political interests and national hostility, be it from ideological or religious incompatibility. All that was the case, and even now many still claim that this past—which has not been overcome—is an immutable pattern. However, parallel with the process of wars, hostility, and alienation of peoples and countries, another process, just as objectively conditioned, was in motion and gaining force: The process of the emergence of a mutually connected and integral world."

When he was still leader of the Soviet Union, Mikhail Gorbachev added his voice to the idea of a "New World Order" that would include global government.

And take careful note of this section of Gorbachev's speech: "*Further world progress is now possible only through the search for a consensus of all mankind, in movement toward a new world order* [italics mine]. We have arrived at a frontier at which controlled spontaneity leads to a dead end. The world community must learn to shape and direct the process in such a way as to preserve civilization, to make it safe for all and more pleasant for normal life. It is a question of cooperation that could be more accurately called 'co-creation' and 'co-development.' The formula of development 'at another's expense' is becoming outdated. In light of present realities, genuine progress by infringing upon the rights and liberties of man and peoples, or at the expense of nature, is impossible."

And, finally: "The very tackling of global problems requires a new 'volume' and 'quality' of cooperation by states and sociopolitical currents regardless of ideological and other differences.

"Of course, radical and revolutionary changes are taking place and will continue to take place within individual countries and social structures. This has been and will continue to be the case, but our times are making corrections here, too. Internal transformational processes cannot achieve their national objectives merely by taking "course parallel" with others without using the achievements of the surrounding world and the possibilities of equitable cooperation. In these conditions, interference in those internal processes with the aim of altering them according to someone else's prescription would be all the more destructive for the emergence of a peaceful order. In the past, differences often served as a factor in pulling away from one another. Now they are being given the opportunity to be a factor in mutual enrichment and attraction. Behind differences in social structure, in the way of life, and in the preference for certain values, stand interests. There is no getting away from that, but neither is there any getting away from the need to find a balance of interests within an international framework, which has become a condition for survival and progress. As you ponder all this, you come to the conclusion that if we wish to take account of the lessons of the past and the realities of the present, *if we must reckon with the objective logic of world development, it is necessary to seek—and then seek jointly—an approach toward improving the international situation and building a new world* [italics mine]."

GOVERNMENT COMMUNICATIONS HEADQUARTERS

A massive amount of attention has been given by the world's media on the extent to which the U.S. National Security Agency monitors the social media activity, email activity, and both cell- and landline phones—all of which is to the great satisfaction of New World Order proponents—far less has been said about the UK's equivalent, the Government Communication Headquarters, better known as GCHQ. For those who may be unaware of the nature and work of the agency, a bit of background data is required.

GCHQ's official website states: "Employing over 6,000 people from a range of diverse backgrounds, we strive to keep Britain safe and secure by working with our partners in the Secret Intelligence Service (MI6) and MI5. Our headquarters is based in Cheltenham, with regional hubs in Scarborough, Bude, Harrogate and Manchester.

"Using our expertise and experience GCHQ is part of the team which protects the UK, along with law enforcement and the other intelligence agencies. Working with HMG and industry, we defend government systems from cyber threat, provide support to the Armed Forces and strive to keep the public safe, in real life and online.

"Internet connectivity brings great benefit, but is also exploited by those wishing to cause harm. GCHQ seeks to identify those threats, playing a leading role with government and industry to help protect the UK."

There is far more to the work of GCHQ than all that, however. What GCHQ's website fails to inform visitors of is the sheer extent to which the agency spies on the UK public—in much the same way that the National Security Agency does in the United States.

In February 2015, for example, the UK's *Independent* newspaper informed its readers of the following: "GCHQ unlawfully spied on British citizens, a secretive UK court has ruled. The decision could mean GCHQ will be forced to delete the information it acquired from people that were spied on. The Investigatory Powers Tribunal (IPT), the secretive court that was created to keep Britain's intelligence agencies in check, said that GCHQ's access to information intercepted by the NSA breached human rights laws. The court found that the collection contravened Article 8 of the European Convention on Human Rights, which protects the right to a private and family life. It also breaches Article 6, which protects the right to a fair trial. The breaches open up the possibility of anyone who 'reasonably believes' they were spied on to ask for the information that GCHQ holds on them to be deleted."

Question More had notable things to say on this issue, too: "A Parliamentary report examining the mass collection of private communications by UK security agencies has defended the practice as 'essential.' The Intelligence and Security Committee (ISC) report, published on Thursday, said only a 'tiny' proportion of data collected was ever seen by human eyes. Intelligence agencies 'do not seek to circumvent the law' and must seek the 'specific authorization' of a cabinet minister before spying on individuals in the UK, the ISC said.

"Although the agency collects a vast amount of private information from ordinary citizens, only a 'tiny proportion of this is examined by spies. This 'tiny' proportion still amounts to 'around [deleted] thousand items a day,' the report said in a heavily redacted section."

One year after its earlier report, specifically in October 2016, the *Independent* had more to say on this matter; much more, in fact: "UK spying agencies illegally stored data about the country's citizens for more than a decade, according to a new judgement. The collection of data on everyone's communications was illegal between 1998 and 2015, according to the Investigatory Powers Tribunal, the watchdog for intelligence agencies. But spying agencies will be able to continue collecting data on citizens because of small tweaks to the law that allow them to get around the ruling."

The *Independent* added: "But the spying won't actually have to stop, despite the decision. Last November, the bulk collection program was changed so that the agencies had to disclose more about what they're doing—that made the work legal, despite making no change to how it actually works. Further powers will be given to GCHQ and other spying agencies under the Investigatory Powers Bill, which is currently in its final stages before being passed by Parliament. That law will clear up the regulation of intelligence agencies, but it will also hand over unprecedented powers to those same spying organizations criticized in the new report."

Privacy International said of this outrageous state of affairs: "Today's judgment is a long overdue indictment of UK surveillance agencies riding roughshod over our democracy and secretly spying on a massive scale. There are huge risks associated with the use of bulk communications data. It facilitates the almost instantaneous cataloguing of entire populations' personal data."

George Orwell would be spinning in his grave.

"HARRISON BERGERON"

There is no doubt that the two definitive novels that present New World Order-style scenarios are George Orwell's *1984* and Aldous Huxley's *Brave*

New World. Although the plotlines are very different, both novels are decidedly grim in terms of presenting a futuristic world in which the human population is utterly controlled, watched, and monitored. There is, however, another—less well-known—story that most assuredly is worthy of a place in the pages of this book is "Harrison Bergeron." Just like Orwell's and Huxley's novels, "Harrison Bergeron"—written by acclaimed author Kurt Vonnegut—is focused on a world very much different to that of today but which could easily be looming large on the horizon.

Whereas *1984* and *Brave New World* are full-length novels, "Harrison Bergeron" is a short story. It does not, however, lack anything when it comes to storytelling and getting across to the reader the disturbing nature of the world ahead.

Vonnegut's story is set in the United States during the latter years of the twenty-first century. It is a United States that is now dumbed down to just about the lowest level possible. Intelligence on the part of the general public is not just frowned upon, it is carefully and ruthlessly regulated to the extent that the entire nation is almost dysfunctional—at least, compared to our world of today.

Civil liberty, freedom of speech, and the Constitution of the United States are not what they were. In fact, they are nonexistent. The population is controlled and manipulated by the ominously named Office of the Handicapper General. It is the role of this particular agency to ensure that everyone is equal. In theory, that sounds fine: a body of people who live in a world without poverty, stigma, or problems. In the story, however, equality equates to a nation of stupidity. It is important to note, however, that this is not the fault of the public. In fact, quite the opposite: it is all down to the Handicapper General.

Those who are born with high levels of intelligence are implanted with radio devices that lessen their intelligence and ensure that their otherwise-high IQs are kept in check. People considered overly sexually attractive are made to wear masks. Those who exhibit strength and athleticism are made to haul around heavy weights, effectively preventing them from utilizing their natural abilities. After decades of generation after generation being dumbed down to the lowest levels possible, the people of the United States are little more than cattle. Enter Harrison Bergeron.

He is a young teenager who is tall, athletic, and who possesses a very high IQ: all the things that the United States of 2081 is vehemently against. When Harrison is arrested by the stormtroopers of the U.S. government for being a potential threat to the enforced order of idiocy, his parents, George and Hazel, who are carefully kept in check by the Handicapper General, have no real understanding of what is going on. Instead, they are content to do nothing but watch television in their befuddled states.

The late Kurt Vonnegut was famous for his thought-provoking stories, including the short tale "Harrison Bergeron," which is about a society that is deliberately made stupid and weak.

Harrison realizes that there is something very wrong about late twenty-first-century American society. As a result, he decides to do something about it: he invades a television station, removes all of his own handicaps as well as those of a group of musicians and a ballerina who are performing on what passes for TV-based entertainment. At first, the music is played badly and the dancing is practically nonexistent—thanks to the heavy weights that dancers are forced to haul around.

When, however, Harrison removes their handicaps and proclaims that he can overthrow the oppressive regime, there is a sudden change in mental faculties. That is, until the Handicapper General, Diana Moon Glampers, realizing that the potentially millions of people watching the show may consider removing their very own handicapping technology, arrives at the studio and shoots and kills Harrison. The story ends with Harrison's parents, George and Hazel, barely aware of what has happened to their son as they continue to watch the show.

"Harrison Bergeron" is a chilling story that—taking into consideration the clear dumbing down of society that is afoot right now—could become all too plausible in the decades ahead. Let us hope that millions of real Harrison Bergerons will resist such a terrible change should it ever come to pass in American society.

HICKS, FREDERICK C.

While the term "New World Order" is perceived in many quarters as being terminology only created in the last couple of decades, that is most assuredly not the case. In 1920 Frederick C. Hicks wrote a book titled *The New World Order*. In March of that year, Hicks wrote the following, which is excerpted from the preface to his book: "For the most part, the facts have been allowed to speak for themselves, opinions and prophecies rarely being hazarded; but the study has resulted in the author's personal conviction that the League of Nations should be supported not merely because it provides means for putting war a few steps farther in the background, but because it emphasizes the necessity for cooperation between sovereign states. International cooperation is an end in itself, the benefits of which are felt by the people of all participating states, and incidentally it tends to decrease the number of disputes likely to lead to a rupture."

While Hicks was not a part of any sinister agenda—he genuinely felt that a benign New World Order would be a good thing for the planet and its people—it's very easy to see how the term was hijacked by those who saw "international cooperation" as something that will ultimately result in a one-world government.

HOMESCHOOLING

As we have seen, one of the key and instrumental ways in which the New World Order stands a very good chance of achieving its dangerous and

Might homeschooling be a method to avoid the government-controlled school system?

deadly goals is to dumb down the population. Unfortunately, they are doing a very good job of it, too—as we have seen from current statistics, and particularly with regard to schoolchildren, who today are not so much taught as indoctrinated. An alternative to the Orwellian-like school system does exist, however: it's called homeschooling.

Dr. Samuel L. Blumenfeld says: "Since public school authorities always complain of lack of parental interest in their children's education, it's a great pleasure watching parents at homeschool conventions poring over books, listening attentively to speakers, purchasing curricula. If anything, homeschooling has made these parents intensely interested in the education of their children. This can only benefit the family and the society we live in. America is at a very crucial period in its history. Our national sovereignty is being continually diminished by the New World Order clique that wants us to spearhead the movement into world government. This century of wars has been politically plagued by two insane ideas: communism and world government."

He adds: "American children in American schools are being indoctrinated in world citizenship and away from patriotism, which is called ethnocentrism. But there's a fly in the ointment. It is called homeschooling.... By opting out of the government system, they have rejected the statist claim that children are a state resource, to be exploited and used by the state for the state."

HUMAN REPLACEMENTS

In 1954, a sci-fi story titled "The Body Snatchers" by Jack Finney appeared in serial form in *Colliers Magazine*. In the following year, 1955, it surfaced in full-length book form. One year later, it was made into a classic and excellent piece of big-screen paranoia: *Invasion of the Body Snatchers*, starring Kevin McCarthy. A pretty good remake appeared in 1978, with Donald Sutherland taking the lead role. A not-bad version—*Body Snatchers*—hit the cinemas in 1993. And an awful version was unleashed in 2007 called *The Invasion*.

Most people know the general scenario of the story, even if they haven't seen the film: the Earth is being invaded by hostile extraterrestrial entities. But the takeover of the planet doesn't occur in a laser-guns-blazing, *Independence Day*-style assault. Indeed, not a single UFO is in sight, just a bunch of curious-looking flowers that are springing up all over the place. Things quickly progress, albeit not in a good fashion. People are quietly, systematically, and, one by one, replaced by identical clones of themselves, who are grown in giant-sized pods. The clones, however, are cold, emotionless monsters. And, when they spring to life, the person whose appearance they have adopted dies.

There are those who believe the New World Order may be doing something very similar in the real world. Back in the mid to late 1990s, several British-based UFO investigators (including some from the now defunct newsstand publications of that era, such as *UFO Magazine* and *UFO Reality*) were given the details of a bizarre story that, they were assured by their *Deep Throat*-like sources, was absolutely true.

So, the tale went, late one night, at some point around 1991 or 1992, a number of animal-rights activists broke into Porton Down, Wiltshire, England—one of the most secretive installations in the UK, whose work focuses to a very significant degree on matters of a chemical and biological nature. If a real-life zombie apocalypse ever erupts, none should be surprised if it begins at Porton Down.

When the activists were actively searching for all the many and varied animals they were intent on freeing—mice, rats, monkeys, and so on—they entered a room which was filled with dozens of approximately eight-foot-long containers, all carefully positioned on sturdy tables and all containing seemingly lifeless, or sleeping, duplicates of famous, then-current British politicians. The terrified activists fled Porton Down, never to return. Of course, the outlandish tale has never been verified, and as for the activists, there's not a single one who has gone on the record, but, just maybe, we should keep our eyes on those politicians who have signed up with the New World Order. Maybe they are not what they appear to be.

THE HUNGER GAMES

Wikipedia says of the phenomenally successful "Hunger Games" franchise: "*The Hunger Games* is a trilogy of young adult dystopian novels written by American novelist Suzanne Collins. The series is set in *The Hunger Games* universe, and follows young characters Katniss Everdeen and Peeta Mellark.

"The novels in the trilogy are titled *The Hunger Games* (2008), *Catching Fire* (2009), and *Mockingjay* (2010). The novels have all been developed into films, with the adaptation of *Mockingjay* split into two parts. The first two books in the series were both *New York Times* bestsellers, and *Mockingjay* topped all U.S. bestseller lists upon its release. By the time the film adaptation of the first volume in the trilogy was released in 2012, the publisher had reported over 26 million "Hunger Games" trilogy books in print, including movie tie-in books.

"*The Hunger Games* universe is a dystopia set in Panem, a country consisting of the wealthy Capitol and 12 districts in varying states of poverty.

Author Suzanne Collins poses in front of a poster of her book *The Hunger Games: Catching Fire.*

Every year, children from the districts are selected to participate in a compulsory annual televised death match called The Hunger Games.

"The novels were all well received. In August 2012, the series ranked second, beaten only by the *Harry Potter* series in NPR's poll of the top 100 teen novels, which asked voters to choose their favorite young adult books. On August 17, 2012, Amazon announced *The Hunger Games* trilogy as its top seller, surpassing the record previously held by the *Harry Potter* series. As of 2014, the trilogy has sold more than 65 million copies in the U.S. alone (more than 28 million copies of *The Hunger Games*, more than 19 million copies of *Catching Fire*, and more than 18 million copies of *Mockingjay*). *The Hunger Games* trilogy has been sold into 56 territories in 51 languages to date."

However, *The Hunger Games* and the New World Order-style futuristic world in which the people of the era live has another aspect to it. *The Vigilant Citizen* provides this: "*The Hunger Games* takes place in a context that is strikingly on-par with descriptions of the New World Order as planned by today's global elite. One of the main characteristics of the New World Order is the dissolving of regular nation-states to form a single world government to be ruled by a central power. In *The Hunger Games*, this concept is fully represented as the action takes place in Panem, a totalitarian nation that encompasses the entire North-American territory. The United States and Canada have therefore merged into a single entity, a step that many predict that will happen before the full-on creation of the NWO."

The Vigilant Citizen asks a couple of very interesting questions: "Is *The Hunger Games* giving teenagers a glimpse of a not-too-distant future? It doesn't take a crystal ball to see the elite are trying to take the world in that direction. Is the author Suzanne Collins communicating a strong anti-NWO message to the youth by showing its dangers or is it getting the youth used to the idea?"

In 2014, T.S. Caladan wrote an article with the following title: "Are the Hunger Games Real?" Caladan said: "Could we be once again seeing some form of truthful reflection of what is really going on behind the scenes of Hollywood in the *Hunger Games* series? These films, like many others, often show the unaware public a theatrical play or representation of *what has been actually occurring in secret enclaves*.

"Why *wouldn't* the real elite that run the planet just LOVE the Hunger Games? New World Order obviously financed the series. Examine posters for film #2 'Catching Fire.' We have a pagan ode to the SUN. We have the element of FIRE as in Prometheus stealing from the gods. Later, the main character of Katniss Everdeen transforms into a dark image with wings ('mockingjay'). She represents the Firebird or Phoenix that has risen from its ashes. She is referred to as the 'Girl on Fire' … a rebirth into a new Order. Mason Manly P. Hall wrote that the symbol for America is not the eagle, but (secretly) it is truly the PHOENIX; New World from old. These are all Illuminati themes."

Food for thought, indeed.

ILLUMINATI

Although what is known officially as the Order of the Illuminati did not come into being until the 1700s, the word "Illuminati" has origins that date back to at least the 1400s. In Spain, at that time, those who immersed themselves in the world of the black arts identified occultists, alchemists, and witches as having been given "the light." We're talking about nothing less than a supernatural form of "illumination" which gave them extraordinary powers, hence the term, "Illuminati." As for the Order of the Illuminati, it was created in 1776—specifically on May 1. The man behind the mysterious group was Adam Weishaupt. The location: Ingolstadt, Bavaria. At the time, Weishaupt was approaching his thirties and worked as a professor of religious law. As Brad Steiger notes, Weishaupt "blended mysticism into the workings of the brotherhood in order to make his agenda of republicanism appear to be more mysterious than those of a political reform group."

The group had decidedly small-scale origins: it began with just five members, one being Weishaupt himself. The Illuminati were not destined to stay that way, however. Bit by bit, the group began to grow, to the point where, by 1780, the membership was around five dozen and extended to six cities. Certainly, many were attracted to Weishaupt's group due to the fact that it paralleled the Masons—specifically in relation to levels and orders of hierarchy that could be achieved. Indeed, Weishaupt was careful to point out to his followers that the further they immersed themselves in the domain of the Illuminati, the greater the level of illuminated, supernatural knowledge they would achieve.

History has shown that Weishaupt was not alone in ensuring the Illuminati grew from strength to strength. He was aided to a very significant degree by one Adolph Francis, better known as Baron von Knigge. A renowned and influential figure with an expert knowledge of all things of an occult nature, von Knigge was a powerful individual who had risen through the ranks of the Masons, and he shared Weishaupt's desire for political revolution. In no time, and as a result of von Knigge's contacts and ability to entice others to the cause, the Illuminati grew to a group of several hundred. The Illuminati was not a group open to everyone, however. In fact, quite the opposite: the powerful, the rich, and the well connected were those who Weishaupt and von Knigge worked hard to bring on board. Rituals and rites for those who wished to be a part of Weishaupt's vision were established, as was the wearing of specific clothes—or, as Brad Steiger described them, "bizarre costumes," and, the membership expanded ever further.

By the mid-1780s, the Illuminati was no longer a group with hundreds of followers but thousands. In 1784, however, dissention began in the ranks. It was in April of that year when von Knigge and Weishaupt had a major falling

Adam Weishaupt (left) and Adolph Francis, Baron von Knigge, were leaders of the Bavarian Illuminati in the late eighteenth century.

out, something which led to von Knigge walking away from the group. There was another problem, too: the occult "illumination" that Weishaupt had promised his followers failed to appear. Many of them became disillusioned, suspecting that Weishaupt had very little interest in the domain of the occult, but, in fact, had really sought out the rich and powerful as a means to help his plans for revolution. The outcome was that many walked away from the Illuminati, fearful that it was becoming a manipulative, sinister body with hidden agendas. It wasn't long before the Illuminati was no more. On this issue, let's turn again to Brad Steiger: "In June 1784 Karl Theodor [the Duke of Bavaria] issued an edict outlawing all secret societies in his province. In March 1785 another edict specifically condemned the Illuminati. Weishaupt had already fled to a neighboring province, where he hoped to inspire the loyal members of the Illuminati to continue as a society. In 1787 the duke issued a final edict against the Order of the Illuminati, and Weishaupt apparently faded into obscurity."

Or did it? Does the Illuminati still exist? Is it one of the major bodies in the secret cultivation of a New World Order? These are the questions we will address now.

ILLUMINATI AND THE NEW WORLD ORDER

The Jeremiah Project says: "Many believe the Illuminati are the master-minds behind events that will lead to the establishment of such a New World Order, and see connections between the Illuminati, Freemasonry, the Trilateral Commission, British Emperialism, International Zionism and communism that all lead back to a bid for world domination. In more recent years the Illuminati has allegedly been involved in the assassination of John F. Kennedy and has been at the forefront of indoctrinating the American public into their socialist one-world agenda.

"It is difficult to uncover the facts regarding the modern day role of the Illuminati as most of the information is cloaked in secrecy. What we must do instead is to look at the available evidence and relationships in the context of contemporary world events, and form some common sense conclusions based on that inquiry."

The Jeremiah Project also notes: "The Illuminati was presumed to have been dispersed by the end of the century but some people such as David Icke, Ryan Burke and Morgan Gricar, have argued that the Bavarian Illuminati survived and believe that Illuminati members chose instead to conceal themselves and their plans within the cloak of Freemasonry, under which auspices they continue to thrive. They have maintained a stranglehold on the political, financial and social administration of the United States and other nations acting as a shadowy power behind the throne, controlling world affairs through present day governments and corporations."

Henry Makow reveals an extremely disturbing NWO–Illuminati story: "A woman who was raised in the Illuminati cult describes a powerful secret organization comprising one percent of the U.S. population that has infiltrated all social institutions and is covertly preparing a military takeover. Her revelations cast the 'war on terror' and 'homeland security' in their true light.

"'Svali' is the pseudonym of the woman, age 45, who was a mind 'programmer' for the cult until 1996. She was the sixth head trainer in the San Diego branch and had 30 trainers reporting to her. She has risked her life to warn humanity of the Illuminati's covert power and agenda.

"She describes a sadistic Satanic cult led by the richest and most powerful people in the world. It is largely homosexual and pedophile, practices animal sacrifice and ritual murder. It works 'hand in glove' with the CIA and Freemasonry. It is Aryan supremacist (German is spoken at the top) but welcomes Jewish apostates. It controls the world traffic in drugs, guns, pornography and prostitution. It may be the hand behind political assassination, and 'terrorism,' including Sept. 11, the Maryland sniper and the Bali bomb blast. It has infiltrated government on a local, state and national level; education and financial institutions; religion and the media. Based in Europe, it plans a 'world order' that will make its earlier attempts, Nazism and Communism, look like picnics."

The website *Warning Illuminati* appropriately warns us: "There is a worldwide conspiracy being orchestrated by an extremely powerful and influential group of *genetically related individuals* (at least at the highest echelons) which include many of the world's wealthiest people, top political leaders, and corporate elite, as well as members of the so-called Black Nobility of Europe (dominated by the British Crown) whose goal is to create a One World (fascist) Government, stripped of nationalistic and regional boundaries, that is obedient to their agenda. Their intention is to effect complete and total control over every human being on the planet and to dramatically reduce the world's population by 5.5 Billion people. While the name *New World Order* is a term frequently used today when referring to this group, it's more useful to identify the principal organizations, institutions, and individuals who make up this vast interlocking spiderweb of elite conspirators.

"The Illuminati is the oldest term commonly used to refer to the 13 *bloodline families* (and their offshoots) that make up a major portion of this controlling elite. Most members of the Illuminati are also members in the highest ranks of numerous secretive and occult societies which in many cases extend straight back into the ancient world. The upper levels of the tightly compartmentalized (need-to-know-basis) Illuminati structural pyramid include planning committees and organizations that the public has little or no knowledge of. The upper levels of the Illuminati pyramid include secretive committees with names such as: the Council of 3, the Council of 5, the Council of 7, the Council of 9, the Council of 13, the Council of 33, the Grand Druid Council, the Committee of 300 (also called the "Olympians") and the Committee of 500 among others."

IMMORTALITY FOR THE ELITE

Are the orchestrators behind the New World Order actively seeking to find ways to live forever? As amazing and as science fiction-like as such a scenario might sound, it cannot be entirely ruled out. As someone who writes a lot of books, blog posts, and articles, I get a great deal of feedback from people who check out what I'm doing, and, very often, people want to share information. Sometimes, that information proves easy to investigate and provides new data, insight, and information on cases both old and new. And then there is a different category of story. A *very* different one.

On more than a few occasions, I have been the recipient of fantastic accounts of a mind-blowing nature. The problem, however, is that no matter how deeply I pursued the relevant story, I reached nothing but an endless brick wall. So, I figured I would share with you one of those cases—right here, right now. Of course, I can't say for sure that it isn't the work of a fantasist or a hoaxer, one with an agenda of the very obscure kind. But, by at least putting the data out there, I also figure it may well provoke debate.

It's a story that was told to me in 2012 and which focuses on the not insignificant matter of immortality. We all want to live forever, right? Well, yes, we do. Providing, of course, we can remain at the age of our choosing and not spend our days forever locked into extremely elderly, decrepit mode. As for the story, it was all focused on a hush-hush program that was run out of a particular facility in Utah.

It was a program that allegedly began in 2003 and was prompted by the discovery of certain unspecified, ancient "things" in Baghdad after the invasion of Iraq began. The project had at its heart something both amazing and controversial. It all revolved around nothing less than attempts to bring the human aging process to a halt—and maybe, even … *to reverse it*. This was, however, a very unusual program in the sense that it didn't just rely on modern-day technology and medicine. That may sound odd, but bear with me, and I'll explain what I mean.

The ultimate goal among the rich elite is to be forever young and forever in power.

Yes, the program had a number of brilliant scientists attached to it, but it was also populated by theologians, historians, and archaeologists—who were quietly contracted and hired and subjected to grim nondisclosure agreements. The quest for the truth of immortality was, to a very significant degree, not based around the present or the future but on the *distant past*. Much time was spent digging into accounts of none other than "Manna from Heaven," and the controversies surrounding what has become known as "White Powder Gold," the "Bread of Presence," and "Amrita."

All of these substances have several things in common: (a) they have ancient origins; (b) they have to be ingested; (c) they have the potential to offer perfect health; and (d) they promise neverending life. Of course, it must be stressed that is what legend, mythology, and ancient religious texts tell us. Actually *proving* that these mysterious "things" exist and also proving they can do what we are told they can do is a *very* different matter. So, I did what I always do in these situations, which is to listen very carefully to what the relevant person has to say. True or not, the story was pretty incredible.

Deep underground, scientists who had spent much of their working lives striving to understand why, exactly, the aging process occurs as it does were sat next to biblical experts who were deciphering and interpreting ancient texts on the aforementioned life-extending, digestible substances. Military personnel, who were dutifully ensuring the program ran under the strictest levels of security and safety, rubbed shoulders with modern-day alchemists, who were striving to crack the white powder gold conundrum, and learned souls in the fields of none other than "ancient astronauts" and the Bible's legendary "men of renown" crossed paths with demonologists.

The story continued that at least as late as 2010, absolutely no progress was made, beyond adding to the lore and legend that surrounds tales of immortality and massive life spans in times long gone. Rather ironically, the fact that I was told the project was a 100 percent failure added credibility to the story—for me, at least, it did. You may think otherwise.

To me, it sounds *exactly* like the kind of off-the-wall program that significant dollars might be invested in just in case it might, one day, offer something sensational and literally life changing. That the source of the story specifically *didn't* spin some controversial and conspiratorial tale of a secret, ruling elite living forever was one of the things that makes me think there just might have been something to all this—and perhaps there still is.

INSECT DRONES

On December 23, 2014, on the *Defense One* website, Patrick Tucker told his readers: "The Defense Advanced Projects Research Agency put out a broad agency announcement this week seeking software solutions to help small drones fly better in tight enclosed environments. The Fast Lightweight Autonomy program, the agency said, 'focuses on creating a new class of algorithms to enable small, unmanned aerial vehicles to quickly navigate a labyrinth of rooms, stairways and corridors or other obstacle-filled environments without a remote pilot.'"

He added an important statement: "Urban disaster relief is an 'obvious' application for tiny, self-guided insect robots according to the agency. An equally obvious application, left out of the announcement, *is spy drones that can fly independently into rooms, find a perch, and serve as a fly on the wall in a very real (but robotic) sense of the world.*"

Then, on August 11, 2016, Larisa Brown, the defense correspondent for the U.K's *Daily Mail* newspaper, wrote the following: "A tiny remote-controlled aircraft modelled on an insect will become Britain's latest weapon against terror. The Dragonfly drone—which can fit in the palm of a hand—will spy on enemy positions and gather intelligence for the military and British agents. It is inspired by the biology of a dragonfly, with four flapping wings and four legs to enable it to fly through the air seamlessly and perch on a windowsill to spy on terrorists."

Brown continued: "It is one of the futuristic pieces of kit currently being developed for the Ministry of Defense and the UK's security forces as part of the MoD's new innovation project."

Perhaps more interesting is the response of the *Daily Mail's* readers. Many of them expressed their suspicions that regardless of the words of the newspaper and those of the Ministry of Defense, this new technology would be used to spy on the British public.

One said: "Only the blind would fail to see something that size flying into a room. More likely to be used by the establishment so that Big Brother can keep a closer eye on us."

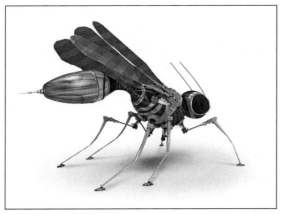

While this is just an artist's concept, governments such as the UK's are developing tiny drones that could easily be used to spy on enemies—or private citizens.

Another stated: "It scares me that they have technology like this but does not surprise me. It is only a matter of time before they will be spying on every one of us just like George Orwell predicted. The thing is, it all happens 'incrementally' so people (especially the sheep on here) don't notice it. Just a little thing here a little thing there. We get used to that, then a new law here another gadget there. And then we can't imagine a world without it. People say 'but we must have this stuff to defeat the criminals and terrorists.' The worst is when the naive sheep say 'if you've got nothing to hide you've got nothing to fear.' They really haven't a clue."

Certainly, the creepiest revelation came from Paul Joseph Watson at *Infowars*. One year before the *Daily Mail* informed its readers of what was afoot, Watson revealed: "Harvard Professor Margo Seltzer warned that miniature mosquito drones will one day forcibly extract your DNA on behalf of the government and insurance companies as she told elitists at the World Economic Forum in Davos that privacy was dead. Seltzer, a professor in computer science at Harvard University, told attendees, 'Privacy as we knew it in the past is no longer feasible.... How we conventionally think of privacy is dead.' Seltzer went on to predict that in the near future, mosquito-sized robots would perpetually monitor individuals as well as collect DNA and biometric information for governments and corporations."

"It's not whether this is going to happen, it's already happening," stated Seltzer, who added: "We live in a surveillance state today." Yes, we do, and the insect drone is just the latest development in the plan to have us all permanently watched by a grave and grim New World Order.

As the New World Order increases its grip on society and its ever-increasing erosion of privacy and freedom, Crane's question is one we will all be asking—and with ever-increasing frequency.

INTERNET CENSORING

In 2012, a BBC writer said: "About 70 countries throughout the world such as China and Iran have been known to use filters to cut their people off from the global web. Foreign news media, websites of political opponents, and pages flagging up human rights abuses are routinely blocked. Social media sites which allow groups to organize themselves online are also targeted and sometimes simply disconnected, as happened during the revolutions in Libya and Egypt."

In a New World Order-driven society, it is all but certain that selected websites, blogs, and social media would suffer adversely—and to the point that, in all probability, they would all but vanish. Indeed, a clampdown on the Internet, and what appears on it, has already begun. Three years after its 2012 statement, the BBC offered the following: "China's President Xi Jinping has called on countries to respect one another's 'cyber sovereignty' and different Internet governance models. Mr Xi said countries had the right to choose how to develop and regulate their Internet. He was speaking at the Beijing-sponsored World Internet Conference held in Zhejiang province. China has been criticized for its strict Internet regulations where it blocks major sites and censors posts. The BBC's John Sudworth, who is at the conference, says the keynote speech by President Xi is a clear sign that *Internet security and control have been elevated to national priorities*."

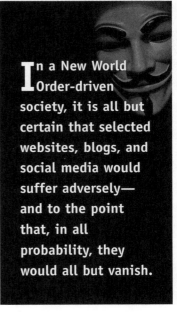

In a New World Order-driven society, it is all but certain that selected websites, blogs, and social media would suffer adversely— and to the point that, in all probability, they would all but vanish.

Then, there is the matter of North Korea, where Kim Jong-un assumed power in 2011 after the death of his father, Kim Jong-il. The *Telegraph* has commented on the situation in Korea, especially on the matter of Internet access. Jeff Stone, writing in *International Business Times*, said in 2012: "The only people to have true Internet access are political leaders and their families, students at elite universities and members of the country's cyber warfare units. This is thought to amount to just a few thousand people. However, just as in the West, it is likely that the government monitors this access and keeps records."

Of course, one might expect to see such ironfisted activity in the likes of North Korea, China, and Russia. But you may be surprised to learn it is already on your doorstep. *Natural News*, in May 2015, stated: "In November 2013, a federal court ruled that the Department of Homeland Security must disclose previously secret plans the massive agency developed for an Internet kill switch— 'Standard Operating Procedure 303,' also known as the 'Internet kill switch' from Homeland Security. These protocols govern shutting down wireless networks to prevent the remote detonation of bombs, the *Washington Times* reported: 'When you throw in the new "Net neutrality" rules, the Department of Justice seizing Internet domains without due process and so forth, you can begin to see how the U.S. is already a long way down the road to Chinese-style censorship.'"

In 2013, *Fox News* reported the following: "The U.S. government asked Google for data on its users more than 31,000 times in 2012, for example. And the government rarely obtained a search warrant first, Google recently revealed; in nearly all cases, the company ended up turning over at least some data."

Moving on to France, we have this from *Heritage.org*: "American Web users' access to Internet content may soon be limited, thanks to a recent decision by French regulators. France's National Commission on Informatics and Liberties (known by its French acronym CNIL) ordered Google to apply the European Union's bizarre 'right-to-be-forgotten' rules on a global basis in a June ruling. The search engine announced at the end of July that it would refuse to comply. If it is nevertheless forced to do so, the result could be unprecedented censorship of Internet content, as well as a dangerous expansion of foreign Web restrictions on Americans.

"The European Union's 'right-to-be-forgotten' rules were first imposed in May of last year in a case decided by the European Court of Justice. The plaintiff, a Spanish citizen named Mario Costeja González, had his house repossessed in 1998 due to a tax debt. A notice of the sale was duly printed in a local paper. A decade later, concerned that the newspaper notice still appeared in search results when his name was Googled, he sued the search engine under the EU privacy law, to force it to filter the story from future search results."

While this particular legislation obviously has its benefits when it comes to personal privacy, it is also a system that is wide open to abuse by the world of officialdom. The U.K. is also clamping down on its citizens, as the *Guardian* reveals: "With minimal argument, a Conservative-led government has given private firms permission to decide what websites we may and may not access. This sets a precedent for state censorship on an enormous scale—all outsourced to the private sector, of course, so that the coalition does not have to hold up its hands to direct responsibility for shutting down freedom of speech."

Is all of this censoring of the Internet, all around the world, merely coincidental? Or, are we seeing the early steps of the New World Order to erode the Internet—and access to it—and effectively destroy its ability to keep us informed of the things we have a right to know about and the things we have a right to discuss? Time may soon tell.

INTERNET SABOTAGE

While the Internet allows—to a massive degree—the New World Order to spy on just about each and every aspect of our online activity, it also allows us to have constant, worldwide contact with just about whoever we wish, and when and where we wish. In that sense, for the NWO, the Internet is very much a double-edged sword: it allows for constant surveillance but also gives us massive freedom, too. That's why there are many theorists who believe that certain factions of the New World Order are seeking to take down the Internet, thereby keeping us largely uninformed of what's going on in the world. Could such a thing actually happen? Does the technology exist to permanently crash the Internet? Let's see.

This was an issue specifically addressed by the BBC in 2015. Journalist Chris Baraniuk said that although "there's never been a case where the whole Internet has gone down, that doesn't mean we shouldn't think about the possibility, though, says Vincent Chan, a professor at the Massachusetts Institute of Technology.

"'I think a massive attack to bring down the whole Internet is actually possible,' he says. He points out that physical attacks on the Internet's infrastructure are unlikely to do much permanent damage. Destroying one node in a 1,000 node network won't take the whole network down, of course. But what if you find a software vulnerability that affects all 1,000 nodes? Then you've got a problem.

"Chan thinks there might be some who would be tempted to attack the Internet in this way. But the consequences of breaking the Internet may not always be properly thought through. 'I think there should be discussions of attack and defense of the Internet as an entity,' he says. 'That's never been discussed before adequately.'"

It's not just the BBC that has recognized this potential for disaster: *TechNewsWorld* offers the following: "Unknown attackers have been testing the defenses of companies that run critical parts of the Internet, possibly to figure out how to take them down, cybersecurity expert Bruce Schneier warned Tuesday. Large nation states—perhaps China or Russia—are the likely culprits, he suggested. 'Nation state actors are going to probe to find weaknesses in all of our technologies,' said Travis Smith, senior security research engineer at Tripwire. They 'want to know what can be done not only in the event of a cyberwar but a kinetic war as well,' he told *TechNewsWorld*."

The highly complicated Internet network is vulnerable to hacking and manipulation by everyone from individual criminals to those working for the New World Order.

TechNewsWorld adds, however, that "a takedown of the entire Internet is not going to happen, contended Martin McKeay, security advocate at Akamai, because 'it's a whole bunch of networks, and you're not going to take it down unless you take down all the circuits. You can take down a company, an organization, or part of a government—but you can't really take down the Internet as a whole."

At least, not yet.

Scientific American, in 2012, spoke with an MIT economist named William Lehr on this very issue: "If, in the future, the U.S. government sought to shut down or limit Internet access, similar workarounds would crop up, and they would grow more sophisticated as the regulatory methods became more extreme—a 'weapons race,' Lehr called it. 'The tools for fighting the war are mostly defensive (fire walls, shutting down interconnects, monitoring, locking up folks who have violated 'laws') but also can be offensive (viruses to attack hostile websites/destroy content, locking folks up preemptively, etc.).

"Lehr added that, while no single government could destroy the Internet everywhere, it could certainly cripple it sufficiently to render its use unattractive for people within its country of governance."

iPhone Spying

The number of people who, today, own iPhones is huge. *CNET* revealed in 2015: "An estimated total of 94 million iPhones were in use in the US at the end of March, including 38 million iPhone 6 and iPhone 6 Plus units, CIRP said Friday. That 38 million figure is made up of 25 million iPhone 6 units and 13 million iPhone 6 models, according to the company's estimates. CIRP also discovered that there are still 8 million iPhone 4S devices in use in the US, despite the handset launching in 2011.

"To put that in some context: Research firm eMarketer estimates 184.2 million people in the US will use a smartphone this year, representing 71.6 percent of mobile phone users and 57.3 percent of the population. By 2018, the firm predicts penetration will reach 82 percent of mobile phone users and 66.9 percent of the US population, with a total of 220 million smartphone users."

This is made all the more alarming by the fact that the U.S. National Security Agency now has the ability to penetrate just about every iPhone on the planet—to the extent that your emails, social-media, activity, and phone calls can all be carefully monitored 24/7. It's a dream come true for the New World Order. For us, it's a nightmare come true.

Andrew Griffin, writing at *The Independent* in 2015, said: "The iPhone has secret spyware that lets governments watch users without their knowledge, according to Edward Snowden. The NSA whistleblower doesn't use a phone because of the secret software, which Snowden's lawyer says can be remotely activated to watch the user. 'Edward never uses an iPhone, he's got a simple phone,' Anatoly Kucherena told Russian news agency RIA Novosti. 'The iPhone has special software that can activate itself without the owner having to press a button and gather information about him, that's why on security grounds he refused to have this phone.'"

If this all sounds like over-the-top paranoia, the bad news is that it's not. Griffin adds: "Apple has been active in making the iPhone harder for security services to spy on, and the company said that iOS 8 made it impossible for law enforcement to extract users' personal data, even if they have a warrant. The company has also been active in campaigning for privacy reform after the Snowden revelations, joining with Facebook and Google to call for changes to the law.

"But recently published files from the NSA showed that British agency GCHQ used the phones UDIDs—the unique identifier that each iPhone has—to track users. While there doesn't seem to be any mention of such spying software in any of the revelations so far, a range of documents are thought to be still unpublished."

But, how could such a thing happen? How are agencies able to achieve this blatant violation of our privacy? *Wired's* Andy Greenberg explains the process—which is chillingly simple when one knows how to do it: "Security researchers posit that if an attacker has a chance to install malware before you shut down your phone, that software could make the phone *look* like it's shutting down—complete with a fake 'slide to power off' screen. Instead of powering down, it enters a low-power mode that leaves its baseband chip—which controls communication with the carrier—on.

"This 'playing dead' state would allow the phone to receive commands, including one to activate its microphone, says Eric

The U.S. National Security Agency has the ability to hack into the millions of iPhone 6s used by Americans today.

McDonald, a hardware engineer in Los Angeles. McDonald is also a member of the Evad3rs, a team of iPhone hackers who created jailbreaks for the two previous iPhone operating systems. If the NSA used an exploit like those McDonald worked on to infect a phone with malware that fakes a shutdown, 'the screen would look black and nothing would happen if you pressed buttons,' he says. 'But it's conceivable that the baseband is still on, or turns on periodically. And it would be very difficult to know whether the phone has been compromised.'"

Thankfully, it's not all bad news. Indeed, steps are being taken to fight back against Big Brother. CNBC says of this specific issue: "Stronger encryption in Apple's iPhones and on websites like Facebook has 'petrified' the U.S. government because it has made it harder to spy on communications, Glenn Greenwald, the writer who first reported on Edward Snowden's stolen files, told CNBC.

"Former National Security Agency (NSA) contractor Edward Snowden caused major shockwaves around the world in 2013 when he unveiled the surveillance body's wide ranging spying practices, which included regularly attempting to snoop into data held by major technology companies. Glenn Greenwald, the man who helped Snowden publish the documents, said that Silicon Valley companies have bolstered the encryption on their products, thereby making it harder for governments to eavesdrop."

J-K

JOHN BIRCH SOCIETY

Rational Wiki says of the New World Order that its "popularization among conspiracy theorists can be traced to over thirty years ago when 'New World Order' appeared in the 1972 book *None Dare Call It Conspiracy* by Gary Allen, a John Birch Society writer. Allen claimed it to be the 'code word' which the International Communist Conspiracy would use when they were ready to unveil their secret plans for a socialist world government. This book was widely read in right-wing conspiracy-minded circles during the 1970s and is probably the source of the hysteria that later erupted over the term."

Before we get to the matter of Gary Allen's book, let's first acquaint ourselves with the John Birch Society (JBS) that he was attached to.

The website of the John Birch Society provides the following on this particular group: "Formed by Robert Welch in December 1958, The John Birch Society takes its name from World War II Army Captain John Birch, an unsung hero. The organization's overall goal is to educate the American people about their country and its enemies, in order to protect our freedom and the nation's independence."

The JBS continues that, since the late 1950s, it has remained "an education and action organization. With organized chapters in all 50 states, the JBS stands firm in its defense of freedom, morality, and the U.S. Constitution. John Birch, our namesake, worked hard to serve God, family, and country. As a solo missionary in China, he brought God's Word to remote villages.

"During WWII, John risked his life to rescue American prisoners and pilots, volunteered for spy missions, and transmitted enemy locations to Allied Forces. As a guiding strength to others, he never lost faith. Tragically, he was murdered by Chinese Communists 10 days after the war ended. John was only 27.

"Robert Welch, a child prodigy, graduated high school at the age of 12 and college at 16. He attended the U.S. Naval Academy and Harvard Law School. Highly educated, Welch became a successful candy manufacturer, retiring in 1956. Robert Welch recognized that the U.S. Constitution and our God-given rights were under attack. As a result, in 1958, he created The John Birch Society, uniting citizens to effectively battle those who threaten our freedoms. Today, The John Birch Society is known as the defender of freedom, as inspired by the selfless John Birch and established by the determined Robert Welch."

Brad Steiger has noted that the influence on U.S. politics by the John Birch Society really came into being in 1964—when there was a major push to have Republican Senator Barry Goldwater elected president of the United States. JBS personnel, says Steiger, "published several widely distributed books that simultaneously promoted conspiracy theories and support for Goldwater. *None Dare Call It Treason*, by John A. Stormer, warned about decay in the public schools and the advance of Communism throughout the world; it sold over 7 million copies."

Steiger also notes: "*A Choice, Not an Echo*, by Phylis Schafly, worried about the Republican Party's being controlled by elitists and Bilderbergers. *The Gravediggers*, coauthored by Schafly and retired rear admiral Chester Ward, revealed that U.S. military strategy had paved the way for Communist conquest of the world."

John Michael Greer, an expert on the domain of secret societies, observes that the John Birch Society "remains a small but vocal presence on the extreme right, while the ideas it launched into popular culture have become central elements of the worldviews of tens of millions of Americans."

The final word goes to the John Birch Society: "By definition, a conspiracy is when two or more people work in secret for evil purposes. The John Birch Society believes this definition fits a number of groups working against the independence of the United States. Extensive study has shown us that history is rarely accidental."

JOURNALISM AT RISK

In the event that a New World Order comes to pass, one of the easiest and—unfortunately—most effective ways to ensure that the public does not get a clear picture of what is afoot is to erode the domain of investigative journalism—something which is already happening and at a shocking speed.

In 2015, the UK's *Telegraph* newspaper offered the following: "Investigative journalism will be 'stopped dead in its tracks' and local newspapers may be 'driven out of business' when new laws restricting Britain's free press come into force next month, a report warns. Media organizations face 'the most substantial threat to press freedom in the modern era' as a result of the 'menacing' laws passed in the wake of the Leveson Inquiry. An independent report into the implications of the Crime and Courts Act, which comes into force on November 3, says that *The Telegraph's* landmark investigation into MPs' expenses would have been all but impossible under the new regime. Campaigners for free speech are demanding the repeal of the 'pernicious' new law."

The Leveson Inquiry—named after Lord Justice Leveson—made the following points: "An independent regulatory body for the press should be established. It should take an active role in promoting high standards, including having the power to investigate serious breaches and sanction newspapers. The new body should be backed by legislation designed to assess whether it is doing its job properly. The legislation would enshrine, for the first time, a legal

A free press that practices investigative journalism will be a thing of the past in a future where the New World Order has taken over.

duty on the government to protect the freedom of the press. An arbitration system should be created through which people who say they have been victims of the press can seek redress without having to go through the courts. Newspapers that refuse to join the new body could face direct regulation by media watchdog Ofcom. The body should be independent of current journalists, the government and commercial concerns, and not include any serving editors, government members or MPs. The body should consider encouraging the press to be as transparent as possible in relation to sources for its stories, if the information is in the public domain. A whistle-blowing hotline should be established for journalists who feel under pressure to do unethical things."

While the UK government welcomed all of this, *Human Rights House* said: "As Leveson indicated himself, the media has a vital role to play in monitoring and reporting the political scene, challenging and criticising and holding to account those in power. If journalists cannot do this robustly and without fear of interference or other political consequences, press freedom is constrained. Beyond this, even 'light' statutory regulation could easily be revisited, toughened and potentially abused once the principle of no government control of the press is breached. The fact that, in Leveson's recommendations, it is left as 'voluntary' for news publishers to decide to join does not mitigate the fact that all those who do join are part of a statutorily established process. 'A media regulatory body anchored by statute cannot be described as voluntary,' said Committee to Protect Journalists Executive Director, Joel Simon."

Journalism.org has made illuminating statements concerning how investigative journalists are likely being watched very closely by the intelligence community: "About two-thirds of IRE journalists (64%) believe that the U.S. government probably has collected data about their own phone calls, emails or online communications. This perception is especially prevalent among those who cover national security, foreign affairs or the federal government. Fully 71% of this group says the government has likely collected this data. Eight-in-ten of all journalists surveyed (80%) express the belief that being a journalist increases the likelihood that their data will be collected by the U.S. government."

If nothing else, this may well sway some journalists from investigating important issues, such as surveillance of social media, invasion of personal privacy, and the ushering in of a New World Order.

KELLY, DAVID

On July 18, 2003, it was widely reported in the media that Dr. David Kelly, a British biological weapons expert, had slashed his own wrists while walking in the woods near his home. Kelly was the British Ministry of Defense's chief scientific officer and the senior adviser to the Proliferation and Arms Control Secretariat and the Foreign Office's Non-Proliferation Department. The senior adviser on biological weapons to the UN biological weapons inspections teams (Unscom) from 1994 to 1999, Kelly was, in the opinion of his peers, preeminent in his field in the world.

Kelly had grave doubts about the claims that Saddam Hussein possessed significant numbers of weapons of mass destruction. Of course, the WMD issue was an integral part of the New World Order's plans to justify an invasion of the Middle East. That Kelly was a prominent figure—and, to the NWO, a troublesome figure—meant that something had to be done to quash his stance and words. Fortunately for the New World Order, Kelly's "suicide" conveniently paved the way for the UK government, led by Tony Blair, to endorse the Bush Administration's plans to launch a full-blown invasion. But was Kelly's death really a suicide? Many suggest not, including some notable figures.

Ten years after Kelly's death, the *Guardian* newspaper ran an article that made it very clear that many were far from happy with the explanation that Kelly took his own life. The *Guardian* said: "Kelly's death led not to an inquest, but a public inquiry by Lord Hutton, which brought a rare glimpse into the secret worlds of Whitehall, British intelligence, the low arts of high politics, and the workings of the BBC....

"The inquiry found that Kelly died after cutting an artery, had taken an overdose of painkillers and had heart disease which left his arteries 'significantly narrowed.' Thus, said experts, less blood loss may have killed the scientist than that needed to kill a healthy man. Among those who have called for an inquest or have doubts it was a suicide are former Tory leader Michael Howard, and Liberal Democrat minister Norman Baker, who wrote a book saying Kelly was most likely murdered. A group of doctors say Hutton's findings should be discarded and a new inquest held. Dr. Stephen Frost said: 'We have lots of evidence.... No coroner in the land would reach a verdict of suicide as Lord Hutton did.'"

Norman Baker, a member of the British parliament, made the following statement: "My investigations have since convinced me that it is nigh-on clinically impossible for Dr. Kelly to have died by his own hand and that both his personality and the other circumstantial evidence strongly militate against suicide.... British diplomat David Broucher told the Hutton inquiry that, some months before Dr. Kelly's death, he had asked him what would happen if Iraq were invaded. Rather chillingly, Dr. Kelly replied that he 'would probably be found dead in the woods.' At the inquiry, this was construed as meaning that he had already had suicidal thoughts. That, of course, is patently absurd. Nobody can seriously suggest that he was suicidal at the time the meeting took

Iraqi leader Saddam Hussein (pictured) was accused of having "weapons of mass destruction." When British biological weapons expert Dr. David Kelly raised doubts about this, it was not long before he "committed suicide."

place—yet Lord Hutton seems to have made his mind up about the way in which Dr. Kelly died before the inquiry even began. The result is a series of gaping, unresolved anomalies. Crucially, in his report, Hutton declared that the principal cause of death was bleeding from a self-inflicted knife wound on Dr. Kelly's left wrist. Yet Dr. Nicholas Hunt, the pathologist who carried out the post-mortem examination on Dr. Kelly, stated that he had cut only one blood vessel—the ulnar artery.

"Since the arteries in the wrist are of matchstick thickness, severing just one of them does not lead to life-threatening blood loss, especially if it is cut crossways, the method apparently adopted by Dr. Kelly, rather than along its length. The artery simply retracts and stops bleeding. As a scientist who would have known more about human anatomy than most, Dr. Kelly was particularly unlikely to have targeted the ulnar artery. Buried deep in the wrist, it can only be accessed through the extremely painful process of cutting through nerves and tendons. It is not common for those who commit suicide to wish to inflict significant pain on themselves as part of the process. In Dr. Kelly's case, the unlikelihood is compounded by the suggestion that his chosen instrument was a blunt pruning knife."

Baker was so convinced that Kelly was murdered, he wrote a book on the subject, *The Strange Death of David Kelly*. Nigel Jones, writing for *The Telegraph*, said: "If Baker's meticulous account is to be believed, what happened on that gentle English hillside was murder most foul, carelessly dressed up to look like suicide."

Jones continues: "Baker fills in the political background to Kelly's death—the duplicities and deceptions advanced to justify the Iraq war; then ticks off the likely suspects for Kelly's death, starting with the nuttiest—no, it wasn't a ritualized pagan killing on a ley line; nor were the Russians guilty. Reluctantly, he even acquits MI6 and the CIA of direct responsibility, while making it clear that both had the capability to carry out the killing and concluding that both probably were aware that it would happen and covered up the fact that it had."

Jones makes it clear, however, that Baker believes very powerful figures—powerful enough to influence and change nations—were most assuredly involved: "followers of the exiled CIA- and MI6-backed 'dissidents' Ahmed Chalabi and Iyad Allawi, cousins both hoping to be installed in power in the wake of a successful Anglo-American invasion."

Jones added: "As Baker rightly comments, proponents of 'conspiracy theories' tend to be dismissed as nutters. His own courageous and well-publicized probing into Kelly's death has been dismissed with the usual 'we don't do that kind of thing, old boy.' But, as this disquieting book makes very clear—unfortunately, we do."

KENNEDY, JOHN F., ASSASSINATION

In 2013, WND asked a highly controversial question: "Was John F. Kennedy assassinated as the first presidential victim of the emerging 'New World Order' championed by former CIA directors Allen Dulles and George H. W. Bush?"

They continued: "Armed with recently declassified documents, New York Times bestselling author Jerome Corsi tackles that question in *Who Really Killed Kennedy* as the 50th anniversary of the assassination approaches. Corsi points out Kennedy had refused to authorize the Navy to launch a military strike from an aircraft carrier to save the faltering U.S.-backed invasion of Cuba known as the Bay of Pigs attack. Kennedy also refused to authorize the use of U.S. military force in Laos and, just before he was assassinated, he had decided to pull out of Vietnam."

In the slightly more than half a century that has now passed since President John F. Kennedy (JFK) was shot and killed in Dealey Plaza, Dallas, Texas, on November 22, 1963, people have put forward a wealth of theories to explain the death of the president who was as hated as he was loved.

On November 29, 1963, an investigation began that still provokes huge debate in conspiracy-themed circles decades after JFK bought the bullet(s). The ten-month-long study was undertaken by the President's Commission on the Assassination of President Kennedy, or, as it is far better, and unofficially, known, the Warren Commission, which took its name from its chairman, Chief Justice Earl Warren. The commission's job was to get to the bottom of the big question that everyone was itching to see answered: who *really* shot JFK? According to the Warren Commission, it was a man named Lee Harvey Oswald. And it was *only* Oswald. Not everyone agreed with that controversial conclusion, however.

In 1978, fourteen years after the Warren Commission laid all the blame firmly on the shoulders of Oswald, the U.S. House Select Committee on Assassinations (HSCA) came to a different conclusion. The lone gunman, said the committee, was not such a lone gunman, after all. President Kennedy's death was the result of nothing less than a full-on conspiracy.

The HSCA agreed with the Warren Commission that Kennedy was killed by Oswald and no one else. The committee went one step further, how-

The commission's job was to get to the bottom of the big question that everyone was itching to see answered: who *really* shot JFK?

ever, by concluding that Oswald was not the only gunman prowling around Dallas on that deadly day.

Forensic analysis suggested to the HSCA's investigators that *four* shots rang out, not the three that the Warren Commission attributed to Oswald. That's to say there was another gunman. In the minds of the HSCA's staff, this mysterious second character completely missed his target. Nevertheless, a pair of shooters meant a conspiracy was at the heart of the JFK assassination. In other words: take that, Warren Commission.

Prior to his death in 1976, Johnny Roselli was a notorious and much-feared figure in the Chicago, Illinois, Mafia. His influence and power extended to the heart of tinseltown and the slots and tables of Vegas. In 1960, Roselli was quietly contacted by a man named Robert Maheu, a former employee of the CIA and the FBI.

A startling proposal was put to Roselli. The CIA, Maheu explained, wanted Roselli's help in taking care of Fidel Castro. In mob-speak, "taking care of" meant "whacking." Thus was born a controversial program that saw the CIA and the mob work together, hand in glove.

As history has shown, Roselli and his goons never did take out Castro. But, say conspiracy theorists, they may have ended the life of JFK, with help from the CIA. The mob was no fan of the Kennedy Administration. Robert Kennedy, as attorney general of the United States, went after the mafia in definitive witch-hunt style. Did the mob decide to return the favor? Maybe it did.

Following Kennedy's killing, Roselli and a number of other mobsters, including Santo Trafficante, Jr., and Carlos Marcello, were suspected of having been implicated. Even the House Select Committee on Assassinations admitted there were "credible associations relating both Lee Harvey Oswald and Jack Ruby to figures having a relationship, albeit tenuous, with Marcello's crime family or organization."

Just perhaps, it's not such a whacked-out theory, after all.

One of the oddest theories concerning the Kennedy assassination tumbled out in the pages of a 1975 book, *Appointment in Dallas*. It was written by

Hugh McDonald, formerly of the LAPD. According to McDonald, Oswald was indeed a patsy, but in a very strange fashion.

Oswald was supposedly told, by shadowy NWO-type sources, that his expertise was needed in Dallas on November 22, 1963. But Oswald wasn't required to kill the president. Quite the contrary, Oswald was told to ensure all his bullets *missed* JFK.

The operation, Oswald was assured, was designed to demonstrate how inadequate the Secret Service was by staging a mock assassination attempt of the president. Unbeknownst to Oswald, however, a team of *real* assassins was in Dealey Plaza. Their bullets, however, did not miss.

The gunmen made quick exits, leaving Oswald as the man guaranteed to take the fall—simply because he really *did* fire bullets across Dealey Plaza. A panicked Oswald, realizing he was set up, fled the scene, thus setting in motion the wheels that led to his arrest and death.

In January 1961, outgoing President Dwight D. Eisenhower made a speech, part of which has become inextricably tied to the murder of JFK. Eisenhower said: "In the councils of government, we must guard against the

The X in the lower-left corner of this photograph marks the spot where President Kennedy was hit by an assassin's bullet in Dallas, Texas.

acquisition of unwarranted influence, whether sought or unsought, by the military-industrial complex."

In the minds of many JFK assassination researchers, it is this military-industrial complex that we should look to for the answers on the fifty-year-old killing of the president. JFK had a vision of creating a state of lasting peace between the United States and the Soviet Union. In short, Kennedy wanted to end the Cold War. We're talking permanently.

Powerful figures in the military, the intelligence community, and companies that raked in millions of dollars in lucrative defense contracts secretly agreed to do the unthinkable. Profits from war were more important than the life and goals of the president.

KENNEDY, ROBERT F.

Ave Hodges says of the 1968 assassination of Robert F. Kennedy (RFK) that in 1968 "Robert Kennedy was still reeling from his older brother's assassination for which the Vietnam War was a major factor which motivated the co-conspirators. RFK was determined to end the war in Vietnam. Robert also posed the threat of being able to reopen his brother's murder and Allan Dulles, Richard Nixon, Gerald Ford, George Bush and David Rockefeller had a lot to worry about if that were ever to happen. RFK had to be stopped with regard to his quest for the Presidency.

"As Robert Kennedy sought the Democratic nomination for the 1968 presidential race, we should take note of the fact that most of his supporters were in their early to mid–20's which comprised the demographics of people most vehemently opposed to the Vietnam War. Therefore, Robert F. Kennedy had a motive to withdraw the forces from Vietnam for political reasons."

Of course, the New World Order, determined to ensure that perpetual war eventually became a reality, could not permit RFK to destabilize their plans. The version of events that is accepted by the U.S. government is that Kennedy was shot and killed in the early hours of June 5, 1968, in Los Angeles, California, by a man named Sirhan Sirhan—and *only* by Sirhan Sirhan. At the time, Kennedy was aggressively campaigning to be the Democratic nominee for president. Sirhan's actions ensured Bobby never, ever held presidential office. Sirhan received a life sentence for murdering Robert Kennedy—which he continues to serve to this day at the San Diego, California-based Richard J. Donovan Correctional Facility.

On the other side of the coin are the claims of deep conspiracy, of mind-controlled assassins, of Manchurian candidates, and of shadowy gunmen—all of whom were determined to ensure that another Kennedy never reached the White House, on the specific orders of those who had grand plans to create a New World Order.

An enthused RFK knew that he had to continue the tidal wave of campaigning, speaking to the voters, and getting the nation behind him if he was to secure the White House for the next four years—at least. This involved Kennedy thanking his campaign team, and followers, in the Embassy Room of the Ambassador Hotel. Had RFK already been elected president, there's a good chance he would have survived the assassination: at the time the Secret Service, specifically in the wake of the assassination of JFK in November 1963, had majorly beefed up the security for the U.S. president. Unfortunately, the Secret Service provided *zero* protection for presidential candidates. As for Kennedy, he had just three people protecting him: a couple of bodyguards and one William Barry, previously with the FBI. Little did he know it, but time was running out for Robert Kennedy—drastically so.

With Kennedy now riding a distinct wave, the original plan—for him to meet with his team and supporters—was put on hold, the reason being that the media demanded a statement from RFK, something that, if done quickly, would still allow the story to make the next day's early morning newspapers. Since this would continue the campaign momentum, Kennedy—following the suggestion of his aide, Fred Dutton—agreed that the best approach was to speak with the media first. To reach that rapidly growing band of media, Dutton directed RFK through the hotel's kitchen—which was the most optimum route.

Kennedy gave the press what they wanted, after which his exit plans suddenly changed. The number of people present, by now, was a definitive throng. Kennedy couldn't even get back to the kitchen via the original route and was forced to take another to finally make it. Kennedy and Karl Uecker, who was the maître d'hôtel, increased their step as they walked along a passageway, one in which Kennedy stopped to shake hands with a busboy named Juan Romero. At that moment, Sirhan Sirhan raced forward, letting loose with a salvo of bullets. Complete and utter chaos broke out

Much like his brother John, Robert F. Kennedy was targeted by the NWO. He was assassinated while on the campaign trail.

as Sirhan's .22 caliber Iver-Johnson Cadet revolver took down Kennedy and injured a number of other people present, including one of RFK's campaign volunteers, Irwin Stroll, and *ABC News'* William Weisel. Sirhan was quickly wrestled to the ground, but it was all to no avail. Kennedy's life was quickly ebbing away—as the media looked on and captured on film the final, grim moments of his life.

But what of RFK's assassin, Sirhan Sirhan: was he really the solitary shooter that he was portrayed as?

Sirhan Sirhan's background is a significant part of the story: he was born in Jerusalem, was a citizen of Jordan, and was vehemently anti-Zionist. That RFK was a noted supporter of the state of Israel deeply grated on Sirhan's mind to the point where loathing of Kennedy eventually turned into outright hatred. This is very clear from Sirhan's very own journal. Under the May 19, 1968, date, he wrote: "My determination to eliminate RFK is becoming more and more of an unshakeable obsession. RFK must die. RFK must be killed. Robert F. Kennedy must be assassinated. Robert F. Kennedy must be assassinated before 5 June 68."

Almost certainly, these words had specific significance to Sirhan. June 5 marked the date on which—one year earlier, in 1965—the so-called Six-Day War, between Israel and its opponents in the Middle East (Syria, Jordan, and Egypt), began.

Since the evidence against Sirhan was seen as being cast-iron, on April 17, 1969, he was found guilty of the murder of Robert Kennedy, something which resulted in him being given a sentence of death—one which was later changed to life imprisonment. But was the evidence really that cast-iron, after all? Not to some, no.

It transpired that doubts about Sirhan's guilt surfaced very soon after he was found guilty of killing RFK. While Sirhan was in San Quentin prison in 1969, he was interviewed by a man named Dr. Eduard Simson-Kallas—an expert in the field of hypnosis, who believed Sirhan was subjected to some form of subliminal programming of the mind-control kind. On top of that, the coroner in the RFK case, Thomas Noguchi, offered his conclusion that the bullet which entered the senator's skull, behind his right ear, was fired at a distance of barely one inch. That suggests that even if Sirhan was a hypnotically controlled assassin, he must have had an accomplice since he was most definitely further away than one inch when he shot Kennedy.

It transpired that doubts about Sirhan's guilt surfaced very soon after he was found guilty of killing RFK.

A mind-controlled assassin—or assassins—of the New World Order is not as far-fetched as it might sound.

KING, MARTIN LUTHER, JR.

Very few people would dispute that Martin Luther King, Jr., was the foremost, leading, and most influential figure in the arena of civil rights in the twentieth century. King, who was born on January 15, 1929, in Atlanta, Georgia, was a man upon whose words millions of African Americans hung—and still do. He changed the face of American society and culture. He was awarded the Nobel Peace Prize in 1964. And he died—before he was even forty—under circumstances that many theorists and researchers believe were dominated by conspiracy and cover-up. Indeed, NWO researchers see the murder of MLK as a significant event in the 1960s-era plans to create a New World Order—an order in which King had no place.

The countdown to King's final moments really began on April 3, 1968. That was when King spoke before an audience at Memphis' Church of God in Christ—which, today, has no fewer than five million, predominantly African American, followers. King told the audience: "I don't know what will happen now. We've got some difficult days ahead. But it doesn't matter with me now, because I've been to the mountain-top. And I don't mind. Like anybody, I would like to live a long life. Longevity has its place. But I'm not concerned about that now. I just want to do God's will. And He's allowed me to go up to the mountain. And I've looked over and I've seen the Promised Land. I may not get there with you. But I want you to know tonight, that we, as a people, will get to the Promised Land. And so I'm happy, tonight. I'm not worried about anything; I'm not fearing any man. My eyes have seen the glory of the coming of the Lord."

It was just one minute after 6:00 P.M. on the evening of April 4 that King's life was violently and viciously taken. At the time in question, King was positioned on a second-floor balcony of the Lorraine Motel. Suddenly, a single, solitary shot rang out. It wrought immediate and irreversible devastation on King: it slammed into his cheek, utterly shattering his right jawbone, breaking into shards a number of vertebrae, and creating a gaping hole in his jugular vein. One of these injuries alone could have proved fatal. With all of them, however, King really didn't stand a chance. He was unconscious even before he hit the balcony floor.

Despite the fact that King was driven, at breakneck speed, to Memphis' St. Joseph Hospital, and despite the very best efforts of the hospital's medical staff, King could not be saved from the reaper. A little more than an hour after he was shot, King was dead.

The official version of events that concerns the shooting of Martin Luther King, Jr., is actually quite straightforward. Not long after that fatal shot rang out, a man named James Earl Ray was seen leaving—with possibly incriminating speed—a lodging house which was situated on the other side of the road from the Lorraine Motel. That Ray, at the time, was renting a room at the house is not a matter of any doubt, nor is the fact that less than a week before the shooting, Ray purchased a rifle, using a bogus name. That very same rifle—along with a pair of binoculars—was found, in a bundle, covered in Ray's fingerprints. It must be noted, too, that Ray had a long and checkered history as a career criminal.

Just like Lee Harvey Oswald, John F. Kennedy's assassin, James Earl Ray, was portrayed as a definitive lone gunman, even by himself. At least, for a short period: only seventy-two hours after admitting to having shot and killed King, Ray, by now in custody, had a sudden and radical change of mind. Not only that, he made some curious statements concerning the assassination of the civil rights legend. According to Ray, while he was not the man who shot and killed King, he was possibly "partially responsible without knowing it." Then there was the matter of a mysterious character known as "Raoul."

According to Ray, he met the enigmatic Raoul in Canada sometime after escaping from the Missouri State Penitentiary. Writer Pan Shannan said of the Ray–Raoul connection that Raoul "quickly began to give James money in exchange for his help with importing some kind of contraband."

The Rev. Dr. Martin Luther King, Jr., is shown here talking with President Lyndon Johnson. King's assassination remains a matter for considerable speculation.

Shannan continued: "In Memphis on April 4th, the afternoon of the murder, Raoul had suggested that James go to a movie, but James declined. After several tries at getting rid of James for awhile, Raoul finally sent him on an errand only minutes before King was shot. James said that he was going to get the worn tires changed on the Mustang but that the man at the tire store was too busy and could not get to it that day. When James returned to the flop-house/Lorraine Motel location, it was surrounded by police cars with flashing lights, and he decided it would be prudent to leave the area, as it certainly was not a place for an escaped con to hanging around."

It was, said Ray, Raoul who told him to purchase the rifle, who instructed Ray to meet with him in Memphis, and who even told Ray in which boarding house he should rent a room. The story continues that, although he did not realize it at the time, Ray was being set up as the fall guy—the patsy—in the assassination. A case for this *can* be made: the bundle containing the rifle and binoculars was dumped in the doorway of a building adjacent to the rooming house.

The website *What Really Happened* notes: "Less than two minutes after the fatal shot was fired, a bundle containing the 30.06 Remington rifle allegedly used in the assassination and some of Ray's belongings was conveniently found in the doorway of the Canipe Amusement Company next door to the boarding house. Ray would have had to fire the shot that killed King from his contorted position in the bathroom, exit the sniper's nest, go to his room to collect his belongings and wrap and tie it all in a bundle, leave his room, run down the stairs and out of the boarding house, stash the bundle next door, and then get away from the scene unnoticed—all within two minutes!"

Brad Steiger suggests that Ray, if he was indeed the culprit, was possibly mind-controlled by sinister, powerful forces: "Dr. William Joseph Bryan, Jr. had programmed individuals when he was with the air force as chief of Medical Survival Training, the air force's covert mind-control section. Bryan, whom some called pompous and arrogant, liked nothing better than to talk about himself and his accomplishments. He was known as an expert on brainwashing, and he served as a consultant on *The Manchurian Candidate*, a motion picture that portrayed a programmed political assassin. In informal discussions, Bryan 'leaked' that he had programmed Sirhan Sirhan and James Earl Ray to commit assassinations and to forget their participation in the act."

KISSINGER, HENRY

In 1991, at Evian, France, Henry Kissinger stated: "Today, America would be outraged if U.N. troops entered Los Angeles to restore order. Tomorrow, they will be grateful. This is especially true if they were told that there was an outside threat from beyond, whether real or promulgated, that threatened our very existence. It is then that all peoples of the world will plead to deliver them from this evil. The one thing every man fears is the unknown. When presented with this scenario, individual rights will be willingly relinquished for the guarantee of their well-being granted to them by the World Government."

Grim and disturbing words, to say the very least. And it doesn't end there, as Alex Newman noted at *The New American* in September 2014: "As awareness grows of the international establishment's globalist plotting against liberty and national sovereignty, problems on the road toward a 'New World Order' are becoming increasingly obvious, and opposition is surging in tandem. It seems that insider bigwigs are getting nervous. Changes in strategy may be forthcoming as a result. Still, as a recent 'analysis' by establishment spokesman Henry Kissinger (shown) makes clear, the powerful forces of globalism and totalitarianism have no intention of backing down from their plot to impose their 'New World Order' on humanity.

"Former Secretary of State and national security adviser Kissinger—a key front man for a powerful movement aiming to impose what he and other globalists refer to as a 'New World Order'—recently outlined some of the establishment's concerns. In a piece published on August 29 in the *Wall Street Journal*, headlined 'Henry Kissinger on the Assembly of a New World Order,' the prominent foreign policy Machiavellian also proposed the acceleration of efforts to impose global governance on humanity."

But who, exactly, is Henry Kissinger? Let's take a look. As Biography.com states: "Born on May 27, 1923, in Fürth, Germany, Henry Kissinger became a Harvard professor before assuming leadership in U.S. foreign policy. He was appointed secretary of state in 1973 by President Richard Nixon and co-won the Nobel Peace Prize for his work in the Vietnam War's Paris accords. He was later critiqued for some of his covert actions at home and abroad. Kissinger is also a prolific author."

Henry Kissinger was U.S. secretary of state under Presidents Richard Nixon and Gerald Ford, but he is still a vocal political pundit, advising President George W. Bush, for example, on terrorist issues.

Over the years and decades, Kissinger has made a number of statements that are just about as disturbing—if not more so—

than his 1991 words concerning how "individual rights will be willingly relinquished." Consider these: "The illegal we do immediately; the unconstitutional takes a little longer.

"The emigration of Jews from the Soviet Union is not an objective of American foreign policy. And if they put Jews into gas chambers in the Soviet Union, it is not an American concern. Maybe a humanitarian concern.

"I don't see why we need to stand by and watch a country go communist due to the irresponsibility of its people. The issues are much too important for the Chilean voters to be left to decide for themselves."

Kissinger clearly realizes that his much-cherished plans for a New World Order are not going as smoothly as he might well prefer. In 2014, he said: "Libya is in civil war, fundamentalist armies are building a self-declared caliphate across Syria and Iraq and Afghanistan's young democracy is on the verge of paralysis. To these troubles are added a resurgence of tensions with Russia and a relationship with China divided between pledges of cooperation and public recrimination. The concept of order that has underpinned the modern era is in crisis."

As for the United Kingdom's exit from the European Union—more famously known as "Brexit"—Kissinger stated: "The cascade of commentary on Britain's decision to leave institutional Europe has described the epochal event primarily in the vocabulary of calamity. However, the coin of the realm for statesmen is not anguish or recrimination; it should be to transform setback into opportunity."

Kissinger's word, "setback," clearly reveals his desire for a unified Europe—no doubt followed by a unified planet. Fortunately, as the Brexit affair showed, the British people chose to rise up and demonstrate to the likes of Kissinger that unification can easily be undone. When people stand together, NWO plans can be systematically sidelined and even derailed. It just requires one and all to stand together in the face of a looming, worldwide dictatorship.

L-M

LEDERBERG, JOSHUA

Should the New World Order initiate a program to unleash a deadly virus—as a means to massively lower the Earth's human population levels—what we need is someone who can counter the attack. A perfect example was the late Joshua Lederberg, a man who deeply understood the seriousness of deadly viruses. Born in New Jersey in 1925, Lederberg obtained his B.A. with honors in zoology at Colombia University and in 1947 was appointed to the position of assistant professor of genetics at the University of Wisconsin. He became a full professor in 1954. Stanford University Medical School entrusted to him the organization of its Department of Genetics and appointed him professor and executive head in 1959.

Lederberg's lifelong research, for which he received the Nobel Prize in 1958 at the age of thirty-three, was in genetic structure and function in microorganisms, and he was actively involved in artificial intelligence research, in computer science, and in NASA's experimental programs seeking life on the planet Mars. Lederberg died in 2008 at the age of eighty-two. In 2012, a crater on Mars was named after Lederberg in his honor.

An eight-page paper written by Lederberg, for *Science*, on August 12, 1960, titled "Exobiology: Approaches to Life beyond the Earth," focused in part on the potential outcome of a virus from another world reaching the Earth and provoking a phenomenally rapid worldwide disaster. "The most dramatic haz-

Nobel Prize winner Joshua Lederberg is a microbiologist who also specializes in artificial intelligence.

ard," said Lederberg, "would be the introduction of a new disease, imperiling human health. What we know of the biology of infection makes this an extremely unlikely possibility. However, a converse argument can also be made that we have evolved our specific defenses against terrestrial bacteria and that we might be less capable of coping with organisms that lack the proteins and carbohydrates by which they could be recognized as foreign. At present the prospects for treating a returning vehicle to neutralize any possible hazard are at best marginal by comparison with the immensity of the risk."

By the mid-1960s, Lederberg was writing a regular column for the *Washington Post* newspaper. Several of those columns are of both note and relevance to Lederberg's words above. On September 24, 1966, Lederberg wrote a feature for the newspaper titled "A Treaty on Germ Warfare." It dealt with his worries about biological warfare and its potential for catastrophic misuse. In part, he stated: "The large scale deployment of infectious agents is a potential threat against the whole species: mutant forms of viruses could well develop that would spread over the Earth's population for a new Black Death."

Cowritten by Lederberg with Carl Sagan and Elliott C. Levinthal, "Contamination of Mars" is an eighteen-page paper that was published by the Smithsonian Institution in June 1967, which primarily focused on ascertaining the potential hazards that the human species might pose to the planet Mars, specifically by way of introducing hostile organisms to the red planet. The paper states: "One serious contingency for release of contained micro-organisms is a crash-landing, and, particularly, a spacecraft impacting Mars with a velocity about 6km/sec will be totally pulverized."

Two years later, on July 13, 1969, Lederberg wrote a letter to the *New York Times* in which he said that the issue of having to "protect the Earth against possible infection from Mars" was a very real one. Let's hope that the nightmarish situation which Lederberg feared—extraterrestrial infection and death on a massive, worldwide scale—never comes to pass.

LENNON, JOHN, MURDER

Paul A. Philips, in an article titled "10 Celebrities Killed by the Ruling Elite for Exposing the Global Conspiracy?" and published on the *New Paradigm* website, says: "It has been alleged that a number of celebrities have been killed for speaking out against the world's ruling elite. Known as the illuminati the world's ruling elite meet in secret societies where they orchestrate their world control over the banks, major corporations, the politicians, the war machine, etc. for global domination and the New World Order one world government. They control the entertainment industry and the price for fame not only demands certain ritual blood sacrifices to prove worthiness, but also remain silent on the organization's existence. Some celebrities over the years however, had not remained silent and it has been said that they were killed by the ruling elite's agents for exposing the global conspiracy."

Philips suggests one of those who fell victim to the New World Order was John Lennon. The countdown to the murder of rock music legend and former Beatle John Lennon arguably began hours before it actually occurred, which was at 10:50 P.M. on December 8, 1980. During the afternoon of Lennon's last day alive, he and Yoko Ono were photographed at their apartment—in New York's Dakota hotel—by Annie Leibowitz, who was there to secure pictures for a *Rolling Stone* magazine story. When the shoot was over, Lennon did a radio interview with San Francisco host Dave Sholin.

With the interview complete, John and Yoko left the hotel and headed to a waiting limousine, which was to take them to the New York-based *Record Plant Studio*. As they strolled toward the vehicle, Lennon was approached by a young, bespectacled man who said absolutely nothing whatsoever. It was Mark Chapman, whose only action was to push a copy of Lennon's *Double Fantasy* album into the hands of the former Beatle. Lennon, always willing to meet with fans, signed the album, which seemingly satisfied Chapman, who went on his way—as did John and Yoko.

It was shortly before 11:00 P.M. that the pair returned to the Dakota hotel. Chapman was still there, hanging around since Lennon gave him an autograph just a few hours earlier. Yoko exited the limousine first, and John followed. Tragedy was only mere moments away. As Lennon passed Chapman—and apparently recognized him from earlier—the words "Mr. Lennon!" rang out. Lennon turned in time to see Chapman assuming a combat-style position and gripping a pistol with both hands. It was all too late, however.

Chapman—who later said that, at that very moment, he heard a voice in his head say "Do it, do it, do it!"—fired on Lennon. Two bullets slammed into his back and two more into his left shoulder. Chapman had chosen his method of killing Lennon carefully. Chapman's pistol was loaded with hollow-tipped bullets, which are designed to cause maximum, pulverizing damage. They did exactly that. Lennon, covered in blood and fatally injured, managed to stagger up the steps of the hotel, collapsing as he uttered the words, "I'm shot." For his part, Chapman simply removed his hat and coat and sat down on the sidewalk.

It became clear to all those present—which included the Dakota's concierge, Jay Hastings, and the doorman, Jose Sanjenis Perdomo, formerly an agent of both Cuba's secret police and the CIA—that Lennon needed emergency attention immediately. Despite the very best efforts of the responding doctors and nurses, Lennon could not be saved. The sheer level of destruction to his internal organs, arteries, and blood vessels sealed his fate back at the Dakota. As for Mark Chapman, although a battery of psychologists deemed him psychotic (five of whom stated he was suffering from full-blown schizophrenia), he was perceived as able to stand trial. He pleaded guilty to the murder of John Lennon and received a sentence of twenty-five years to life. Chapman remains incarcerated, to this day, despite having had seven parole hearings—all of which ended in denials. And now we come to the most controversial aspect of the shooting of John Lennon.

The *Atomic Poet* website notes: "After Mark David Chapman shot and killed John Lennon, he calmly opened up *Catcher in the Rye* and proceeded to read it—before being apprehended. John Hinckley, the man who attempted to kill Ronald Reagan, also was in possession of the book. It is also alleged Lee Harvey Oswald was quite fond of the book, though this is disputed.

Catcher in the Rye has sold 65 million copies. Of the millions who have enjoyed the book, perhaps three have become well-known assassins. Still, we should ask: is there any merit to the book being an assassination trigger?"

But why, exactly, should the book have any bearing—whatsoever—on Mark Chapman's crazed killing of John Lennon? So, conspiracy theorists maintain, trained, mind-controlled assassins—born out of the CIA's controversial MKUltra program—are "switched on" by certain key "trigger words" that appear in the text of *The Catcher in the Rye*.

Lawrence Wilson, MD, notes that a "hypnotist can implant the suggestion that

Former Beatle John Lennon with his wife, Yoko Ono, in 1980, the year he was murdered by Mark David Chapman.

when the phone rings twice, or when the doorbell rings, a post-hypnotic suggestion such as to kill whomever is in the room, even if it is your wife, will go into effect. This is used by some foreign police agencies to train hypnotized assassins."

In other words, and so the theory goes, Mark Chapman was possibly a victim of deep hypnosis on the part of MKUltra/New World Order operatives, but rather than relying on a phone or doorbell ringing, they used *The Catcher in the Rye*—or segments of the text—as the trigger that turned Chapman into a ruthless killer, one who had no control over his deadly actions on December 8, 1980.

The blog *CIA Killed Lennon* records: "While a teenager in Decatur, Georgia, Chapman did a lot of LSD, then found Jesus, and devoted his life to working with the YMCA, which, according to Philip Agee (*CIA Diary*, 1975), was prime recruiting grounds for CIA stations in Latin America. Chapman's YMCA employment records are missing. In June 1975, Chapman volunteered to work in the YMCA office in Beirut, Lebanon, as the civil war erupted. Returning to the US, Chapman was sent to work with newly resettled Vietnamese refugees (and CIA assets) in Fort Chaffee, Arkansas, run by World Vision, an evangelical organization accused of CIA collaboration in Honduras and El Salvador."

To understand why someone may have wished to see John Lennon terminated, we have to turn to the writings of British conspiracy theorist, Jon King: "In his book *Who Killed John Lennon?* author Fenton Bresler presents evidence that the former Beatle's death was not the work of a 'lone nut', but that Mark David Chapman was a CIA asset and that the CIA itself—or a faction within it—was behind the assassination. Bresler cites Lennon's political activism as a primary motive.

"In support of his claim, Bresler quotes late radio host, Mae Brussell, who broke the Watergate scandal, along with *Washington Post* reporters Bob Woodward and Carl Bernstein.

"'It was a conspiracy,' Brussell affirmed. 'Reagan had just won the election. They knew what kind of president he was going to be. There was only one man who could bring out a million people on demonstration in protest at his policies—and that was Lennon.'

"Indeed, a year after Lennon's death, CIA-backed forces famously massacred more than a thousand civilians in El Salvador, where America was busy fighting a particularly dirty war.

"Lennon was opposed to that war, and word is the White House feared he may have spoilt the party had he remained alive and resumed his role as a political activist—which, according to those closest to him, he was planning to do."

LIBRARY SPYING

For those seeking to plunge the world into a dark and disturbing New World Order, one of their first actions will be to keep very careful and close tabs on the newspapers, magazines, and books that we read. Even more disturbing, that process has already begun.

Without doubt the creepiest part of the Patriot Act was that which oversaw the government's legal and wide-reaching ability to monitor the reading habits of every single American citizen. This relates to what are termed National Security Letters, or NSLs. They are, essentially, subpoenas that are used "to protect against international terrorism or clandestine intelligence activities."

Such NSLs can permit agencies to demand access to—and with potential imprisonment for those who do not comply—bank account data, email history and address books, telephone numbers (both called and received), and books bought online and at stores and those borrowed from libraries. All of this falls under Section 215 of the Patriot Act. In a decidedly hazy fashion—that conveniently allows for widespread interpretation on the part of those who employ it—the act notes that certain "tangible things" may be accessed, such as "books, records, papers, documents, and other items."

Four years after the Patriot Act was passed, Library Connection—a Connecticut-based organization—joined forces with the ACLU to highlight and curtail the government's ability to monitor the reading matter of the average American: "Librarians need to understand their country's legal balance between the protection of freedom of expression and the protection of national security. Many librarians believe that the interests of national security, important as they are, have become an excuse for chilling the freedom to read."

The American Civil Liberties Union (ACLU) elaborated on this: "One of the most significant provisions of the Patriot Act makes it far easier for the authorities to gain access to records of citizens' activities being held by a third party. At a time when computerization is leading to the creation of more and more such records, Section 215 of the Patriot Act allows the FBI to force anyone at all—including doctors, libraries, bookstores, universities, and Internet service providers—to turn over records on their clients or customers."

The ACLU also reveals that the judicial oversight of the new powers that the Patriot Act allows for is "essentially non-existent." They continue: "The government must only certify to a judge—with no need for evidence or proof—that such a search meets the statute's broad criteria, and the judge does not even have the authority to reject the application."

The Patriot Act made it easier for the government to spy on people's browsing and check-out history at public libraries.

Surveillance orders, notes the ACLU, "can be based in part on a person's First Amendment activities, such as the books they read, the Websites they visit, or a letter to the editor they have written."

Slate.com has aired its concerns on the matter of the Patriot Act, too: "Post-Patriot Act, third-party holders of your financial, library, travel, video rental, phone, medical, church, synagogue, and mosque records can be searched without your knowledge or consent, providing the government says it's trying to protect against terrorism."

As for the situation in more recent years, in May 2011 at *Wired*, Spencer Ackerman said: "You think you understand how the Patriot Act allows the government to spy on its citizens. Sen. Ron Wyden says it's worse than you know. Congress is set to reauthorize three controversial provisions of the surveillance law as early as Thursday. Wyden (D-Oregon) says that powers they grant the government on their face, the government applies a far broader legal interpretation—an interpretation that the government has conveniently classified, so it cannot be publicly assessed or challenged. But one prominent Patriot-watcher asserts that the secret interpretation empowers the government to deploy 'dragnets' for massive amounts of information on private citizens; the government portrays its data-collection efforts much differently."

In Senator Wyden's own words: "We're getting to a gap between what the public thinks the law says and what the American government secretly thinks the law says. When you've got that kind of a gap, you're going to have a problem on your hands."

Slate.com has also demonstrated that the change in presidency—from George W. Bush to Barack Obama—made very little difference to the power of the Patriot Act: "Sen. Obama voted to reauthorize the Patriot Act in 2005, a decision he defended on the campaign trail in 2008 with the caveat that some provisions contained in Section 215, like allowing the government to go through citizens' library records, 'went way overboard.' But in 2011 President Obama signed a bill to extend the Patriot Act's sunset clause to June 1, 2015—with Section 215 intact in its 2005 form."

Today, the Patriot Act continues to stand, just as it has since 2001. Coming soon to a library near you.

MARCONI ELECTRIC SYSTEMS

Who could have the ability, manpower, and secrecy levels to wipe out some of the world's leading scientists and technicians? The New World Order? Of course. To many, it might sound like the ultimate plotline of the equally ultimate conspiracy thriller: dozens of scientists and technicians—all working on highly classified programs and all linked to one, particular company—dead under highly controversial and unusual circumstances.

It's a controversy that ran from the early 1980s to 1991 and remains unresolved to this very day. And it all revolves around the top-secret work of a company called Marconi Electronic Systems but which, today, exists as a part of BAE Systems Electronics Limited. Its work includes the development of futuristic weaponry and spy-satellite technology.

It was in March 1982 that professor Keith Bowden, whose computer expertise made him a valuable employee of Marconi, lost his life in a car accident. His vehicle left a three-lane highway at high speed and slammed into a railway line. Death was instantaneous. In March 1985, Roger Hill, a draughtsman with Marconi, died of a shotgun blast. His death was deemed a suicide.

Just months later, the body of Jonathan Wash, an employee of a department within British Telecom that had extensive links to Marconi, was found on the sidewalk of an Ivory Coast, West Africa, hotel. Wash fatally fell, or was pushed, from the balcony of his room. That Wash had told friends and family he believed someone was watching and following him, and that he suspected his life was in danger, adds to the suspicions that his death was not due to accident or suicide.

As 1985 became 1986, the death toll increased dramatically. On August 4, 1986, a highly regarded young man named Vimal Bhagvangi Dajibhai jumped from England's Clifton Suspension Bridge into the deep waters below. He did not survive the fall. Dajibhai held a secret clearance with Marconi Underwater Systems, a subsidiary of the main company.

Only around eight weeks later, one of the most grisly of all the Marconi scientist deaths occurred. The victim was a computer programmer, Arshad Sharif. Such was the terrible and bizarre nature of Sharif's death, it even made the news thousands of miles away, in the United States. The *Los Angeles Times* reported that Sharif "died in macabre circumstances ... when he apparently tied one end of a rope around a tree and the other around his neck, then got into his car and stepped on the accelerator. An inquest ruled suicide."

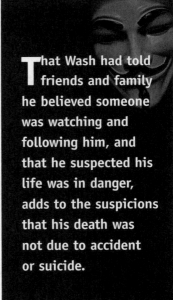

That Wash had told friends and family he believed someone was watching and following him, and that he suspected his life was in danger, adds to the suspicions that his death was not due to accident or suicide.

The coroner in the Sharif case, Donald Hawkins, commented wryly on the fact that Marconi was experiencing an extraordinary number of odd deaths: "As James Bond would say—this is beyond coincidence."

As the months progressed, so did the deaths. The case of Dr. John Brittan was particularly disturbing since he had two run-ins with death, the second of which he did not survive. During Christmas 1986, Brittan ended up in a ditch after his car violently, and inexplicably, lurched across the road. He was lucky to survive.

The Grim Reaper was not happy that Brittan had escaped his icy clutches, however. Less than two weeks into January 1987 (and immediately after Brittan returned to the U.K. from the States, where he was on official, secret business), Brittan's body was found in his garage. He was an unfortunate victim of the effects of deadly carbon monoxide.

Also dead in January 1987 was Richard Pugh, a computer expert who had done work for Marconi and whose death the Ministry of Defense dismissed with the following words: "We have heard about him but he had nothing to do with us."

Then there is the extremely weird saga of Avtar Singh-Gida. An employee of the British Ministry of Defense, who worked on a number of Marconi programs, he vanished from his home in Loughborough, England, right around the same time that Dr. John Brittan died. His family feared the worst. Fortunately, Singh-Gida did not turn up dead. Quite the opposite, in fact: he was found, in Paris, fifteen weeks later. He had no memory of where he was or what he had done in that period.

The deaths of Brittan, Dajibhai, and Sharif—coupled with the odd case of Singh-Gida—prompted a member of Parliament, John Cartwright, to state authoritatively that the deaths "stretch the possibility of mere coincidence too far." Cartwright's words proved to be eerily prophetic.

On February 22, 1987, Peter Peapell, a lecturer at the Royal College of Military Science, who was consulted by Marconi on various projects, was yet another figure whose death was due to carbon monoxide poisoning in his own garage—in the English county of Oxfordshire.

In the same month, David Skeels, a Marconi engineer, was found dead under identical circumstances. Victor Moore was attached to Marconi Space and Defense Systems at the time of his February 1987 death, reportedly of a drug overdose. At the time, he was said to be under investigation by MI5, the British equivalent of the FBI.

Just seven days after Greenhalgh and Gooding died, and only a short distance away, a woman named Shani Warren took her last breath.

One month later, in March 1987, one David Sands killed himself under truly horrific circumstances. He was in the employ of what was called Elliott Automation Space and Advanced Military Systems Ltd.—which just happened to have a working relationship with Marconi at the time. Sands, whose family and colleagues said he was exhibiting no signs of stress or strain, loaded his car with containers of gasoline and drove—at "high voltage," as the police worded it—into an empty restaurant. A fiery death was inevitable.

In April 1987, there was yet another death of an employee of the Royal College of Military Science: Stuart Gooding, whose car slammed head-on into a truck on the island of Cyprus. Colleagues of Gooding expressed doubt at the accidental death verdict. On the very same day that Gooding died, David Greenhalgh died after falling (or being pushed) off a railway bridge at Maidenhead, Berkshire. Greenhalgh just happened to be working on the same program as David Sands.

Just seven days after Greenhalgh and Gooding died, and only a short distance away, a woman named Shani Warren took her last breath. Warren worked for Micro Scope, a company taken over by Marconi just weeks later. Despite being found in just a foot and a half of water and with a gag in her mouth, her feet bound, and her hands tied behind her back, the official verdict was—wholly outrageously—suicide.

May 3, 1987, was the date on which Michael Baker was killed—in a car accident in Dorset, England. He worked on classified programs for Plessey. Twelve years later, Plessy became a part of British Aerospace when the latter combined with Marconi. Ten months after, Trevor Knight, who worked for Marconi Space and Defense Systems in Stanmore, Middlesex, England, died—as had so many others—from carbon monoxide poisoning in his garage.

There were other unexplained deaths in 1988: midway through the year, Brigadier Peter Ferry (a business development manager with Marconi) and Plessey's Alistair Beckham both killed themselves via electrocution. And, finally, there was the mysterious 1991 death of Malcolm Puddy. He had told his bosses at Marconi he had stumbled on something amazing. What that was, no one knows. Within twenty-four hours Puddy was dead. His body was hauled out of a canal near his home.

The grim list of deaths was finally at an end. Theorists suggest the New World Order chose to wipe out the "Star Wars" scientists to ensure that China—at the time, not a huge player in the NWO—did not acquire the technology and unbalance the status quo.

MARTIAL LAW

If the minions of the New World Order seek to take total control of the United States, one way in which this could very easily be achieved is by placing the nation under an unending state of martial law. And what, exactly, might martial law be? Martial law occurs when a military leader takes charge as governor or head of state and removes power from civilian government institutions. It is usually imposed as a temporary measure during times of crisis but can sometimes lead to a military takeover of a country.

"Martial law can be used by governments to enforce their rule over the public. Such incidents may occur after a *coup d'état* (such as Thailand in 2006 and 2014); when threatened by popular protest (China, Tiananmen Square protests of 1989); to suppress political opposition (Poland in 1981); or to stabilize insurrections or perceived insurrections (Canada, The October Crisis of 1970). Martial law may be declared in cases of major natural disasters; however, most countries use a different legal construct, such as a state of emergency.

"Martial law has also been imposed during conflicts, and in cases of occupations, where the absence of any other civil government provides for an unstable population. Examples of this form of military rule include post World War II reconstruction in Germany and Japan as well as the Southern Reconstruction following the U.S. Civil War.

"Typically, the imposition of martial law accompanies curfews, the suspension of civil law, civil rights, habeas corpus, and the application or extension of military law or military justice to civilians. Civilians defying martial law may be subjected to military tribunal (court-martial)."

Could such a thing happen in the United States as a New World Order reaches its end-game strategy? Many say "Yes!"

In July 2016, Scott Adams offered the following thought-provoking scenario: "Let's say Donald Trump wins the election. And let's say Democrats believe everything they say about him—that he's the next Hitler. Wouldn't President Obama be obligated to declare martial law and remain in power?

"I realize this question sounds silly when you first hear it. But keep in mind that Democrats have successfully sold the 'racist strongman' narrative about Trump to their own ranks. If they're right about Trump, we need to start getting serious about planning for martial law, for the good of the country and the world. No one wants another Hitler. And if they're wrong, we still need to plan for martial law because Democrats *think* they are right. That's all it takes."

SOTT (*Signs of the Times*) has its own version of how we might find ourselves in a grim, NWO-driven world: "For decades U.S. law enforcement from the federal to local level has been trained and primed for combat readiness to

Many Americans have taken note that police forces in the United States resemble the military more and more in their dress and equipment. It makes sense if the government is preparing to impose martial law.

THE NEW WORLD ORDER BOOK

wage war against its own citizens, under the pretext to quell the forever imminent civil uprising and volatility about to boil over. Additionally arming 70 federal 'civilian' agencies in the footsteps of militarized police within the EPA, the FDA, the IRS, the Fish and Wildlife Department, the National Oceanic and Atmospheric Administration, Department of Veterans Affairs, even the US Postal Service and Social Security Administration after buying up 6 billion rounds of lethal hollow point bullets speaks volumes of how Obama's leading Americans to the proverbial democide slaughterhouse."

UFP News tells us: "On October 17, 2006, President Bush signed into law, the John Warner Defense Authorization Act. The law allows the President to declare a 'public emergency' at his own discretion, and place federal troops anywhere throughout the United States. Under this law, the President also now has the authority to federalize National Guard troops without the consent of Governors, in order to restore 'public order.' The President can now deploy federal troops to U.S. cities, at will, which eliminates the 1878 Posse Comitatus Act."

We also have this eye-opening extract from what is known as the John Warner Defense Authorization Act: "'Use of the Armed Forces in Major Public Emergencies.' Section 333, 'Major public emergencies; interference with State and Federal law' states that 'the President may employ the armed forces, including the National Guard in Federal service, to restore public order and enforce the laws of the United States when, as a result of a natural disaster, epidemic, or other serious public health emergency, terrorist attack or incident, or other condition in any State or possession of the United States, the President determines that domestic violence has occurred to such an extent that the constituted authorities of the State or possession are incapable of ('refuse' or 'fail' in) maintaining public order, 'in order to suppress, in any State, any insurrection, domestic violence, unlawful combination, or conspiracy.'"

We will end this section of the book with the words of Sergeant Major Dan Page, a former Army Ranger. He says: "The new Constitution is ready to go and they only need the right incident to bring it down. We're not very far away from an event which you would call martial law. That term will never be used, by the way; 'emergency police powers' will be."

MEN IN BLACK

It is intriguing to note that the notorious Men in Black (MIB) of UFO lore have something in common with the New World Order: a connection to the ancient art of alchemy. This has given rise to the theory that the MIB are agents of the New World Order—their mission being to shut down anyone who gets in the way of the NWO agenda and who seeks to uncover the connections between the New World Order and the UFO controversy.

The dark night of Saturday, September 11, 1976, was the decidedly ill-fated evening when the Orchard Beach, Maine, home of a certain Dr. Herbert Hopkins was darkened by a nightmarish MIB. Vampire-like scarcely begins to describe the terrible thing that descended on Hopkins' home. When Hopkins opened the front door, he was confronted by a pale-faced, skinny ghoul, one that was dressed in black, had dark and hostility-filled eyes, and sported the de rigueur fedora hat.

The MIB made it very clear, and extremely quickly, that if Hopkins knew what was good for him, he would immediately cease all of his then-current research into the life and experiences of a reported alien abductee: David Stephens, who lived in nearby Oxford. Hopkins, chilled to the bone, didn't need telling twice. Just for good measure, the undeniably malevolent MIB—in monotone fashion—told Hopkins to take out of the right pocket of his trousers one of the two coins that was in there and hold it in the open palm of his hand. Hopkins didn't even think to wonder how the MIB knew the coins were there; he just did as he was told.

The mysterious Men in Black usually bring up thoughts of UFOs, but they also have a role in the New World Order.

With a detectable threat in his robotic voice, the MIB ordered Hopkins to keep his eyes locked on the coin, which he did. To Hopkins' amazement and horror, something terrifying happened: the coin transmuted. It turned blue in color; it shimmered slightly—as if in a mini heat-haze—and then, in a second or so, became 100 percent vaporous. After a few moments, the vapor was gone.

The MIB implied that he could do exactly the same thing to Hopkins' heart. Hopkins got the message. The MIB shuffled his curious way to the door and vanished—as in *literally vanished*—into the chilled night. The strange and enigmatic alchemists of old had the ability to morph metals and regularly demonstrated such skills to amazed individuals. We would be hard pressed to deny they sound amazingly like centuries-old equivalents of Dr. Herbert Hopkins' very own manipulator, or in this case destroyer, of metal.

And, on this very point, there is one important thing I have left until last, something which further amplifies the connection between Herbert Hopkins' MIB and the alchemists of times long gone. According to Hopkins, at one point, the MIB touched his finger to his lips—deliberately, for effect, it seems. Although the man's face and hands were utterly white, his lips were bright red. When the MIB removed his finger from his lips, it was stained red. This led Hopkins to suspect that the man, rather oddly and unsettlingly, was wearing lipstick.

On the other hand, it's worth noting that way back in the seventeenth century, one Wenzel Seiler's exposure to the domain of alchemy occurred when he ran his finger across a large, oak table in the monastery in which he worked and found it coated in a bright red substance. It was, supposedly, the enigmatic Philosopher's Stone (none other than the mysterious red substance that could supposedly allow for the priceless alchemical transformation to take place). It was almost as if Herbert Hopkins' MIB was playing some strange, trickster-like mind game with Hopkins, one in which he dropped a few significant clues and hints to his—the MIB's—linkage to alchemy.

MICROBIOLOGIST DEATHS

If the New World Order really is bent on wiping out billions of people—as a part of its plan to create a new society—then it might be to the advantage of the NWO to take careful and secret steps to wipe out those who might be able to combat, and save us all from, agonizing deaths from deadly viruses. Ominously, that is exactly what we see happening.

From the final months of 2001 to mid-2005, numerous people employed in the elite field of microbiology—which is defined as the study of organisms that are too small to be seen with the naked eye, such as bacteria and viruses—died under circumstances that some within the media and government came to view as highly suspicious and deeply disturbing in nature. It would be impossible to list all of the deaths in a single article. However, a summary of a number of cases will let you see what was afoot.

The controversy largely began in November 2001, when Dr. Benito Que, a cell biologist working on infectious diseases, including HIV, was found dead outside of his laboratory at the Miami Medical School, Florida. The *Miami Herald* stated that his death occurred as he headed for his car, a white Ford Explorer, parked on Northwest 10th Avenue. Police said that he was possibly the victim of muggers.

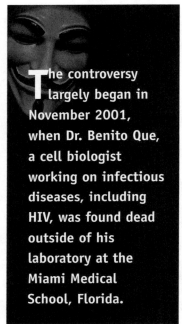

The controversy largely began in November 2001, when Dr. Benito Que, a cell biologist working on infectious diseases, including HIV, was found dead outside of his laboratory at the Miami Medical School, Florida.

Then, on November 21, Dr. Vladimir Pasechnik, a former microbiologist for Biopreparat, a bioweapons production facility that existed in Russia prior to the collapse of the Soviet Union, was found dead near his home in the county of Wiltshire, England. His defection to Britain, in 1989, revealed to the West for the very first time the incredible scale of the Soviet Union's clandestine biological warfare program. Pasechnik's revelations about the scale of the Soviet Union's production of biological agents, including anthrax, plague, tularemia, and smallpox, provided an inside account of one of the best-kept secrets of the Cold War. According to British Intelligence, Pasechnik passed away from the effects of a massive stroke and nothing more.

Three days later, the FBI announced it was monitoring an investigation into the disappearance of a Harvard biologist because of "his research into potentially lethal viruses," including Ebola. Dr. Don C. Wiley, 57, had last been seen in Memphis, Tennessee, where he attended the annual meeting of the Scientific Advisory Board of the St. Jude Children's Research Hospital. His rented car was found on November 16 on a bridge over the Mississippi River with a full fuel tank and the key still in the ignition. His body was eventually discovered near a hydroelectric plant in the Mississippi River.

Still, controversial deaths continued to occur, this time in Russia. On January 28, 2002, a microbiologist and a member of the Russian Academy of Science, Alexi Brushlinski, died as the result of what was blamed on a "bandit attack" in Moscow. Then, two weeks later, Victor Korshunov, 56, also a noted microbiologist, was hit over the head and killed at the entrance of his home in Moscow, Russia. He just happened to be the head of the microbiology sub-faculty at the Russian State Medical University.

The list, unfortunately, goes on and on.

Although the vast majority of controversial deaths in the field of microbiology occurred between 2001 and 2005, they still continue. *Healthy Protocols* noted in 2013 that "the death of Andrew Moulden is shrouded in mystery. Some sources say he had a heart attack and others say he committed suicide. A colleague of Dr. Moulden who wishes to remain anonymous reported to Health Impact News that he/she had contact with him two weeks before he died in 2013. Dr. Moulden told our source and a small number of trusted colleagues in October of 2013 that he was about to break his silence and would be releasing new information that would be a major challenge to the vaccine business of big pharma. He was ready to come back. Even though he had been silent, he had never stopped his research. Then, two weeks later, Dr. Moulden suddenly died. Dr. Moulden was about to release a body of research and treatments, which could have destroyed the vaccine model of disease management, destroyed a major source of funding for the pharmaceutical industry, and at the same time seriously damaged the foundation of the germ theory of disease."

In 2014, *The Telegraph* reported: "A Cambridge Professor has made the astonishing claim that three scientists investigating the melting of Arctic ice may have been assassinated within the space of a few months. Professor Peter Wadhams said he feared being labelled a 'looney' over his suspicion that the deaths of the scientists were more than just an 'extraordinary' coincidence. But he insisted the trio could have been murdered and hinted that the oil industry or else sinister government forces might be implicated. The three scientists he identified—Seymour Laxon and Katherine Giles, both climate change scientists at University College London, and Tim Boyd of the Scottish Association for Marine Science—all died within the space of a few months in early 2013. Professor Laxon fell down a flight of stairs at a New Year's Eve party at a house in Essex, while Dr Giles died when she was in collision with a lorry when cycling to work in London. Dr Boyd is thought to have been struck by lightning while walking in Scotland. Prof Wadhams said that in the weeks after Prof Laxon's death he believed he was targeted by a lorry which tried to force him off the road. He reported the incident to the police."

The three scientists—Seymour Laxon, Katherine Giles, and Tim Boyd—were all studying microbes and the melting of ice in the Arctic when they met their mysterious deaths.

Interestingly, microbial matters at the Arctic were areas that all three were working on.

IWB, in August 2014, revealed the following: "Glenn Thomas, a leading consultant in Geneva, an expert in AIDS and, above all, Ebola Virus, was on board the Boeing 777 Malaysia Airlines cut down on the border between Ukraine and Russia. Glenn Thomas was also the coordinator of the media and was involved in the investigations that were bringing to light the issue of trial operations of Ebola virus in the laboratory of biological weapons at the hospital in Kenema. Now that this workshop was closed by order of the government of Sierra Leone, more details emerge about the interests that are hidden behind its management. Bill and Melinda Gates have connections with biological weapons labs located in Kenema, the epicenter of the epidemic of Ebola developed from the hospital where they were doing clinical trials in humans for the development of its vaccine, and now, following the opening of an informal survey, it appears the name of George Soros, through its Foundation, is funding the laboratory of biological weapons."

Steve Quayle, who has carefully studied the mysterious wave of deaths that has occurred in the last decade and a half, posted this in 2015, a breaking story on yet another death: "Alberto Behar, Robotics expert at NASA at the JPL died instantly when his single-engine plane nosedived shortly after take-off Friday from Van Nuys Airport. He worked on two Mars missions and spent years researching how robots work in harsh environments like volcanoes and underwater. As part of the NASA team exploring Mars with the Curiosity rover, Behar was responsible for a device that detected hydrogen on the planet's surface as the rover moved.

"Forty-seven-year old NASA Scientist Alberto Behar helped to prove that there had once been water on Mars according to the *Daily Mail* story published to announce his recent death in a plane crash that happened on Friday in LA, California. While plane crashes do happen and scientists do die, Behar's name has now been added to a very long list of scientists and astronomers who have met their untimely ends prematurely, leading us to ask, did Behar know something that 'they' don't want the rest of society to find out?"

MICROCHIPS

One of the staple parts of the theory that we will very soon all be enslaved under the control of a dangerous New World Order suggests each and every one of us will be microchipped—effectively, to monitor and track our every movement, whether at work, at home, on vacation, and pretty much everywhere else, too. If you think that such an Orwellian-like thing could never happen, you are very wrong. *It has already begun.*

In May 2002, it was revealed that American doctors had successfully implanted, into the arms of an entire Florida family, chips that contained their complete medical histories. The Jacobs family—husband and wife, Jeffrey and Leslie, and their son, Derek—agreed to undergo the controversial procedure that, rather chillingly, their doctors stated they hoped would soon become "standard practice" all across the United States. Collectively, it took less than forty seconds—in a Boca Raton, Florida, clinic—to transform father, mother, and son into walking, talking human barcodes. It was all "thanks" to the VeriChip, the brainchild of a Florida-based company: Applied Digital Solutions.

Certain elements of the world's corporate media praised this groundbreaking procedure. They cited the fact that such implants would do away with the need for medical-alert bracelets, would prove to be vital in terms of identifying diseases and conditions when time was of the essence and would allow for continual updating of a person's medical history as and when was deemed necessary.

Other elements of the media were less than enamored by this creepy, creeping technology, including the BBC, who noted when the story surfaced: "The chips could also be used to contain personal information and even a global positioning device which could track a person's whereabouts, leading to fears the chip could be used for more sinister purposes."

Two years later, in 2006, the pros and cons of the microchipping technology were still being hotly debated. And it was still the VeriChip that was under the microscope, so to speak. Champions of the chips noted that crucial data—on such issues as blood type and potentially life-threatening allergies—could be stored and accessed by medical professionals, and lives would be saved as a direct result. Applied Digital Solutions expressed their hopes that, in terms of sales of the chip, it would be a case of today the United States and tomorrow the United Kingdom. After that was anyone's guess or their bad dream.

Also in 2006, the British media waded in on the controversy, noting that in the near future: "Human beings may be forced to be 'micro-chipped' like pet dogs, a shocking official report into the rise of the Big Brother state has warned."

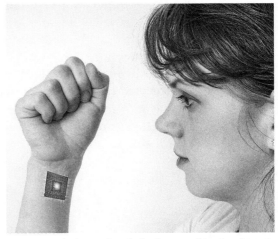

Some people have already had microchips implanted in them that include their medical histories. Could this become standard practice?

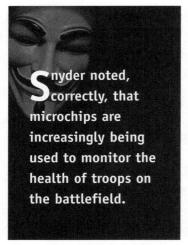

Snyder noted, correctly, that microchips are increasingly being used to monitor the health of troops on the battlefield.

The report to which the press was referring was edited by two highly respected sources: Dr. David Murakami Wood, the managing editor of the journal *Surveillance and Society*, and Dr. Kirstie Ball, who was an Open University lecturer in organization studies. Their report made the shocking claim that, by 2016, "our almost every movement, purchase and communication could be monitored by a complex network of interlinking surveillance technologies."

It was a report written by noted academics and for the specific attention of the UK's information commissioner, Richard Thomas. The media warned its readers that the chips "could be used by companies who want to keep tabs on an employee's movements or by governments who want a foolproof way of identifying their citizens—and storing information about them."

Moving on to 2012, Michael Snyder, of *The American Dream*, asked, on May 9, two important, yet very disturbing, questions: "What would you do if someday the government made it mandatory for everyone to receive an implantable microchip for identification purposes? Would you take it?"

Snyder noted, correctly, that microchips are increasingly being used to monitor the health of troops on the battlefield. It was something that led him to pose another question: "Once the government has microchips implanted in all of our soldiers, how long will it be before they want to put a microchip in all government employees for the sake of national security? Once the government has microchips in all government employees, how long will it be before they want to put a microchip in you?"

He foresaw a situation where the technology would not be forced on us overnight by jackbooted minions of the New World Order. Rather, it would work its way into our lives, bit by bit, piece by piece: "For now, it will creep into our lives at an incremental pace. But after enough people have voluntarily accepted the 'benefits' of implantable microchips, it will only be a matter of time before they become mandatory. Are you ready for that?"

The answer is: No, we are not ready for it. And we should all strive to ensure that it never, ever happens.

MILITARIZATION OF THE POLICE

No one doubts that the police have a difficult and dangerous job, a job that often places them in situations where making sudden, and potentially life-changing, decisions becomes almost routine. That said, there is no doubt that the last few years have seen a distinct change in how the police operate, with a significant movement toward, effectively, militarization. Indeed, it has become an all-too-common situation—one which is played out on mainstream media on a regular basis.

Investigative reporter Radley Balko addressed the issue of a militarized police force in his book *Rise of the Warrior Cop*. Giving the issue a historical perspective, Balko goes back to the Revolutionary period, when Americans had a healthy distrust of a militarized police force. Moving forward to the 1960s and the countercultural revolution, he discusses the inception of the SWAT unit, the first militarized force.

This approach to law enforcement grew worse with each administration: Richard Nixon's War on Drugs, Ronald Reagan's War on Poverty, Bill Clinton's COPS program, and, finally, the anti-terrorism programs resulting from the 9/11 attacks that have been put in place by George W. Bush and Barack Obama. As the police force became more powerful, civil liberties have suffered.

That attitude has changed dramatically in recent decades. America's police force increasingly looks like an occupying military detail. In his book, Balko asserts that the Fourth Amendment has been compromised, making people feel less secure at home. Furthermore, American citizens are made to feel more like they are the enemy, and police seem increasingly hostile toward them.

In June 2014, Alex Kane at *Alternet* reported: "A recent *New York Times* article by Matt Apuzzor reported that in the Obama era, 'police departments have received tens of thousands of machine guns; nearly 200,000 ammunition magazines; thousands of pieces of camouflage and night-vision equipment; and hundreds of silencers, armored cars and aircraft.' The result is that police agencies around the nation possess military-grade equipment, turning officers who are supposed to fight crime and protect communities into what look like invading forces from an army. And military-style police raids have increased in recent years, with one count putting the number at 80,000 such raids last year."

To his credit, in 2015, President Obama not only recognized this growing militarization of the police but also sought to do something about it. On May 18, the president said, before the Salvation Army Ray and Joan Kroc Corps Community Center, Camden, New Jersey: "We've seen how militarized gear can sometimes give people a feeling like there's an occupying force, as opposed to a force that's part of the community that's protecting them and serving them. It can alienate and intimidate local residents, and send the wrong message. So we're going to prohibit some equipment made for the battlefield that is not appropriate for local police departments.

"There is other equipment that may be needed in certain cases, but only with proper training. So we're going to ensure that departments have what they need, but also that they have the training to use it."

Having police forces that look more and more like the U.S. military has had the effect of eroding trust between civilians and those who are supposed to protect them.

It was a statement made by the president that had the support of Hillary Clinton, as the *Huffington Post* highlighted: "President Barack Obama's executive order banning the federal government from transferring certain types of military-style equipment to police forces would remain in place if Hillary Clinton wins the presidency in 2016. Clinton is 'supportive of the recommendations and of the need for reform,' a spokesperson for the Democratic candidate said Monday after Obama announced in Camden, New Jersey, that the transfer of certain military gear to police would be sharply curtailed."

Clinton said: "We can start by making sure that federal funds for state and local law enforcement are used to bolster best practices, rather than to buy weapons of war that have no place on our streets. President Obama's task force on policing gives us a good place to start. Its recommendations offer a roadmap for reform, from training to technology, guided by more and better data."

Will we see a continued growth in a trend that rightly disturbs many? Or, will we pull back from the brink of becoming a society in which the world of law enforcement becomes fully militarized? No doubt, the powerful figures behind the growing New World Order are aiming for the latter.

MIND CONTROL

If there is one sure-fire way that the New World Order will be able to control the masses—and particularly the dissenting ones—it's via mind manipulation, perhaps, better known as mind control. There exists a long and controversial history of research into how, and to what extent, the human mind can be harnessed—to the point where we might even find ourselves as zombie-like slaves, all as a result of being subjected to mind-numbing technologies.

Although the U.S. intelligence community, military, and government has undertaken countless official (and off the record, too) projects pertaining to both mind control and mind manipulation, without any doubt whatsoever, the most notorious of all was Project MKUltra: a clandestine operation that operated out of the CIA's Office of Scientific Intelligence and that had its beginnings in the Cold War era of the early 1950s.

The date of the project's actual termination is somewhat hazy; however, it is known that it was definitely in operation in the latter part of the 1960s—and, not surprisingly and regretfully, has since been replaced by far more controversial and deeply hidden projects.

To demonstrate the level of secrecy that surrounded Project MKUltra, even though it had kicked off at the dawn of the fifties, its existence was largely unknown outside of the intelligence world until 1975—when the Church Committee and the Rockefeller Commission began making their own investigations of the CIA's mind control-related activities—in part to determine if (a) the CIA had engaged in illegal activity; (b) the personal rights of citizens were violated; and (c) if the projects at issue had resulted in fatalities—which they most assuredly and unfortunately did.

Rather conveniently, and highly suspiciously, too, it was asserted at the height of the inquires in 1975 that two years earlier, in 1973, then CIA director Richard Helms had ordered the destruction of the agency's MKUltra files. Fortunately, this did not stop the Church Committee or the Rockefeller Commission—both of which had the courage and tenacity to forge ahead with their investigations, relying on sworn testimony from players in MKUltra, where documentation was no longer available for scrutiny, study, and evaluation.

The story that unfolded was both dark and disturbing—in equal degrees. Indeed, the scope of the project—and allied operations, too—was spelled out in an August 1977 document titled "The Senate MK-Ultra Hearings" that was prepared by the Senate Select Committee on Intelligence and the Committee on Human Resources as a result of its probing into the secret world of the CIA.

As the document explained: "Research and development programs to find materials which could be used to alter human behavior were initiated in the late 1940s and early 1950s. These experimental programs originally included testing of drugs involving witting human subjects, and culminated in tests using unwitting, non-volunteer human subjects. These tests were designed to determine the potential effects of chemical or biological agents when used operationally against individuals unaware that they had received a drug."

The Committee then turned its attention to the overwhelming secrecy that surrounded these early 1940s and 1950s projects: "The testing programs were considered highly sensitive by the intelligence agencies administering them. Few people, even within the agencies, knew of the programs and there is no evidence that either the Executive Branch or Congress were ever informed of them.

"The highly compartmented nature of these programs may be explained in part by an observation made by the CIA Inspector General that, 'the knowledge that the Agency is engaging in unethical and illicit activities would have serious repercussions in political and diplomatic circles and would be detrimental to the accomplishment of its missions.'"

The research and development programs, and particularly the covert testing programs, resulted in massive abridgments of the rights of American citizens, sometimes with tragic consequences. For example, the Committee uncovered details on the deaths of two Americans that were firmly attributed to the programs at issue while other participants in the testing programs were said to still be suffering from the residual effects of the tests as late as the mid-1970s.

As the Committee starkly noted: "While some controlled testing of these substances might be defended, the nature of the tests, their scale, and the fact that they were continued for years after the danger of surreptitious administration of LSD to unwitting individuals was known, demonstrate a fundamental disregard for the value of human life."

MIND MANIPULATION

There was far more to come: the Select Committee's investigation of the testing and use of chemical and biological agents also raised serious questions about the adequacy of command and control procedures within the Central Intelligence Agency and military intelligence and also about the nature of the relationships among the intelligence agencies, other governmental agencies, and private institutions and individuals that were also allied to the early mind-control studies.

For example, the Committee was highly disturbed to learn that with respect to the mind-control and mind-manipulation projects, the CIA's normal administrative controls were controversially—and completely—waived for programs involving chemical and biological agents—supposedly to protect their security, but more likely to protect those CIA personnel who knew they were verging upon (if not outright surpassing) breaking the law.

But it is perhaps the following statement from the Committee that demonstrates the level of controversy that surrounded—and that still surrounds—the issue of mind-control-based projects: "The decision to institute one of the Army's LSD field testing projects had been based, at least in part, on the finding that no long-term residual effects had ever resulted from the drug's administration. The CIA's failure to inform the Army of a death which resulted from the surreptitious administration of LSD to unwitting Americans, may well have resulted in the institution of an unnecessary and potentially lethal program."

The Committee added: "The development, testing, and use of chemical and biological agents by intelligence agencies raises serious questions about the relationship between the intelligence community and foreign governments, other agencies of the federal government, and other institutions and individuals.

"The questions raised range from the legitimacy of American complicity in actions abroad which violate American and foreign laws to the possible compromise of the integrity of public and private institutions used as cover by intelligence agencies."

While MKUltra was certainly the most infamous of all the CIA-initiated mind-control programs, it was very far from being an isolated one. Indeed, numerous subprojects, postprojects and operations initiated by other agencies were brought to the Committee's

LSD is usually placed on the tongue using a blotter stamp. The government, however, used surreptitious methods to dose unwitting Americans with the drug.

attention. One was Project Chatter, which the Committee described thus: "Project Chatter was a Navy program that began in the fall of 1947. Responding to reports of amazing results achieved by the Soviets in using truth drugs, the program focused on the identification and the testing of such drugs for use in interrogations and in the recruitment of agents. The research included laboratory experiments on animals and human subjects involving Anabasis aphylla, scopolamine, and mescaline in order to determine their speech-inducing qualities. Overseas experiments were conducted as part of the project. The project expanded substantially during the Korean War and ended shortly after the war in 1953."

Then there were Projects Bluebird and Artichoke. Again, the Committee dug deep and uncovered some controversial and eye-opening data and testimony: "The earliest of the CIA's major programs involving the use of chemical and biological agents, Project Bluebird, was approved by the Director in 1950. Its objectives were: (a) discovering means of conditioning personnel to prevent unauthorized extraction of information from them by known means, (b) investigating the possibility of control of an individual by application of special interrogation techniques, (c) memory enhancement, and (d) establishing defensive means for preventing hostile control of Agency personnel."

The Committee added with respect to Bluebird: "As a result of interrogations conducted overseas during the project, another goal was added—the evaluation of offensive uses of unconventional interrogation techniques, including hypnosis and drugs. In August 1951, the project was renamed Artichoke. Project Artichoke included in-house experiments on interrogation techniques, conducted 'under medical and security controls which would ensure that no damage was done to individuals who volunteer for the experiments. Overseas interrogations utilizing a combination of sodium pentothal and hypnosis after physical and psychiatric examinations of the subjects were also part of Artichoke."

Interestingly, the Committee noted that "information about Project Artichoke after the fall of 1953 is scarce. The CIA maintains that the project ended in 1956, but evidence suggests that Office of Security and Office of Medical Services use of 'special interrogation' techniques continued for several years thereafter."

MKDELTA

A special procedure, designated MKDelta, was established to govern the use of MKUltra materials when specifically utilized in overseas operations. Such materials were used on a number of occasions. According to the Committee: "Because MKUltra records were destroyed, it is impossible to reconstruct the operational use of MKUltra materials by the CIA overseas; it has been determined that the use of these materials abroad began in 1953, and possibly as early as 1950."

The Committee expanded further: "Drugs were used primarily as an aid to interrogations, but MKUltra/MKDelta materials were also used for harassment, discrediting, or disabling purposes. According to an Inspector General Survey of the Technical Services Division of the CIA in 1957—an inspection which did not discover the MKUltra project involving the surreptitious administration of LSD to unwitting, non-volunteer subjects—the CIA had developed six drugs for operational use and they had been used in six different operations on a total of thirty-three subjects. By 1963 the number of operations and subjects had increased substantially."

Aside from the CIA, the Committee learned that the Army was up to its neck in mind control-related projects too. In its 1977 report, the Committee wrote: "There were three major phases in the Army's testing of LSD. In the first, LSD was administered to more than 1,000 American soldiers who volunteered to be subjects in chemical warfare experiments. In the second phase, Material Testing Program EA 1729, 95 volunteers received LSD in clinical experiments designed to evaluate potential intelligence uses of the drug. In the third phase, Projects Third Chance and Derby Hat, 16 unwitting non-volunteer subjects were interrogated after receiving LSD as part of operational field tests."

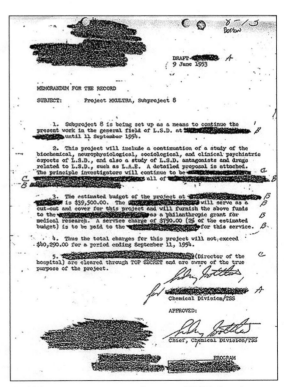

But what of the post-MKUltra era: Did the official world really cease its operations and destroy its files en masse, in 1973 as had been alleged? Probably not: In a 1977 interview, fourteen-year CIA veteran Victor Marchetti stated that the CIA's claim that MKUltra was abandoned was nothing more than a "cover story."

The possibility that we might see such mind-manipulating technologies used against us when the New World Order really hits us hard cannot be dismissed. In fact, it's all but certain that it will be used on a massive scale.

A CIA memo approving the use of LSD for the MKUltra project.

MKNaomi

MKNaomi was another major CIA program related to mind control, and whose work could easily be resurrected by the New World Order. In 1967, the CIA summarized the purposes of MKNaomi thus: "(a) To provide for a covert support base to meet clandestine operational requirements. (b) To stockpile severely incapacitating and lethal materials for the specific use of TSD [Technical Services Division]. (c) To maintain in operational readiness special and unique items for the dissemination of biological and chemical materials. (d) To provide for the required surveillance, testing, upgrading, and evaluation of materials and items in order to assure absence of defects and complete predictability of results to be expected under operational conditions."

Under an agreement reached with the Army in 1952, the Special Operations Division (SOD) at Fort Detrick was to assist the CIA in developing, testing, and maintaining biological agents and delivery systems—some of

Israeli soldiers are shown here preparing for biological and chemical war attacks, the thrust of the MKNaomi program.

which were directly related to mind-control experimentation. By this agreement, the CIA finally acquired the knowledge, skill, and facilities of the Army to develop biological weapons specifically suited for CIA use.

The Committee also noted: "SOD developed darts coated with biological agents and pills containing several different biological agents which could remain potent for weeks or months. SOD developed a special gun for firing darts coated with a chemical which could allow CIA agents to incapacitate a guard dog, enter an installation secretly, and return the dog to consciousness when leaving. SOD scientists were unable to develop a similar incapacitant [sic] for humans. SOD also physically transferred to CIA personnel biological agents in 'bulk' form, and delivery devices, including some containing biological agents."

In addition to the CIA's interest in using biological weapons and mind control against humans, it also asked SOD to study use of biological agents against crops and animals. In its 1967 memorandum, the CIA stated: "Three methods and systems for carrying out a covert attack against crops and causing severe crop loss have been developed and evaluated under field conditions. This was accomplished in anticipation of a requirement which was later developed but was subsequently scrubbed just prior to putting into action."

The Committee concluded with respect to MKNaomi that the project was "terminated in 1970. On November 25, 1969, President Nixon renounced the use of any form of biological weapons that kill or incapacitate and ordered the disposal of existing stocks of bacteriological weapons. On February 14, 1970, the President clarified the extent of his earlier order and indicated that toxins—chemicals that are not living organisms but are produced by living organisms—were considered biological weapons subject to his previous directive and were to be destroyed. Although instructed to relinquish control of material held for the CIA by SOD, a CIA scientist acquired approximately 11 grams of shellfish toxin from SOD personnel at Fort Detrick which were stored in a little-used CIA laboratory where it went undetected for five years."

Might such biological weapons—and worse—still exist today? Could they be used against the public when the New World Order goes global? Yes, indeed.

MONATOMIC GOLD POWDER

Longstanding rumors suggest that the senior figures within the New World Order are seeking to achieve something we all would like to achieve: physical immortality. It is believed that the New World Order is focusing its efforts on what is known as monatomic gold powder. More than four decades ago, David Hudson, an Arizona-based farmer whose income was derived from cotton, developed a keen interest in what is now known as the aforementioned monatomic gold powder, or, the aforementioned white powder gold. Although Hudson worked in the field of farming, he spent a great deal of his spare time focusing on the theme of alien immortality. As his work and research progressed, Hudson gave a name to the mystery he uncovered and, finally, understood. He termed it Orbitally Rearranged Monoatomic Elements, or ORME, which also just happens to be the ancient Hebrew term for nothing less than the Tree of Life, which is just about the most appropriate and relevant terminology of all.

Many of Hudson's investigations led him down a pathway toward the mysteries of the atom and to very surprising results concerning what is termed nucleus deformation. In simple terminology, during such deformation, the nuclei—the core—of monatomic matter performed in a decidedly strange fashion, and its configuration was altered. Hudson found that this specifically occurred in what are termed precious metals. Within this particular class are silver, palladium, rhodium, ruthenium, osmium, iridium, platinum … *and gold*. Dan Sewell Ward says of this issue: "Within the new configuration, the atoms interact in two dimensions, with the super-deformed nuclei reaching high spin, low energy states. In this state the elements become perfect superconductors, with their electrons combining in 'Cooper Pairs' and thus becoming photons of light."

Jim Marrs notes the most eye-opening aspect of this issue: "When reaching this state, the electrons turn to pure white light, and the individual atoms separate, producing a white monatomic powder."

Ward says that a careful study of all the data—ranging from the scientific to the folkloric—suggests Hudson tapped into something which has the ability to utterly transform the human body, making amazing and positive changes to DNA, and even reversing the ravages caused by the likes of cancer and other potentially fatal conditions and leading us toward the door marked "Immortality."

Ward is absolutely correct. A great deal of research—highly successful research, it is important to stress—has been undertaken that demonstrates that healing the body with gold is not as unlikely as it sounds. In fact, it works only too well. *ORO Gold* states: "Scientists now believe that they may have found a way to utilize gold and nanotechnology together, and may be able to treat cancer without any of the severe side effects."

At the forefront of this undeniably groundbreaking work is the staff of Rice University, Texas. Personnel at the university have seen great and astonishing success when those afflicted with cancer are injected with small spheres wrapped in gold. Nanoparticles exit the bloodstream and focus all of their attention upon the cancerous tumor. Infrared light is then "blasted" onto the tumor, something which allows the gold's nanoparticles to change the light into heat and effectively causing the obliteration of the tumor.

In a June 1, 2014, press release, Rice University explained that its work demonstrated the process would kill off cells that were cancerous but would not harm noncancerous cells or organs—which is one of the unfortunate side effects of more conventional ways of trying to combat cancer. In fact, it was reported that Rice's methods had proved to be around seventeen times more successful than those procedures that relied upon regular chemotherapy-based treatment and particularly so regarding cancers in the head and the neck.

Rice University staff continue that one particular "component" in the process of defeating cancer involves "an injectable solution of nontoxic gold colloids, tiny spheres of gold that are thousands of times smaller than a living cell. Quadrapeutics represents a new use of colloidal gold."

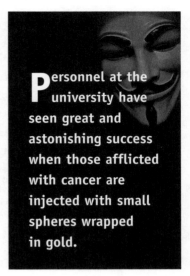

Personnel at the university have seen great and astonishing success when those afflicted with cancer are injected with small spheres wrapped in gold.

Things get even more controversial: it was Hudson's conclusion that when the powdered gold is ingested—in Orbitally Rearranged Monoatomic Element (ORME) form—a person is essentially transformed into a new being, one which possesses the skills of biolocation (divining), levitation, telepathy, having the ability to influence the minds of others, and even bringing new life into the recently dead, the latter being something the Anunnaki, ancient Mesopotamian dieties, sometimes thought to be aliens, were allegedly highly adept at achieving.

It should be noted that others have somewhat different views concerning white powder gold, which brings us to the work of Anna Hayes. She says that this life-giving substance briefly fires up "the dormant codes in the higher dimensional DNA strand Templates, releasing bursts of higher frequency into the DNA template, creating temporary 'windows' to the higher dimensions and giving the physical body a temporary boost."

Immortality may just be around the corner, but whether we will all benefit from it—or just a certain, dangerous elite—very much remains to be seen.

MONROE, MARILYN

*I*lluminatiRex says: "According to Cathy O'Brien, in her book *Trance Formation of America*, in which she relays her experiences as a Monarch mind-controlled slave, Marilyn Monroe was 'the first Presidential Model' and was 'killed in front of the public eye.' Presidential Models are sex slaves created specifically to service American presidents."

IlluminatiRex suggests that it was the Illuminati—key figures in the program to remodel the Earth with a ruthless New World Order—that were possibly at the heart of the killing of the legendary star.

Despite extensive investigations, the passing of Marilyn Monroe remains the enigma it was back in 1962. The story begins on August 4, one day before the actress' death. The afternoon was taken up by a visit to Monroe's Brentwood, Los Angeles, home by her psychiatrist, Dr. Ralph Greenson. He was attempting to get Monroe out of her depressive state of mind. A few hours later, at around 7:00 P.M., Monroe chatted on the phone with Joe DiMaggio, Jr. (the son of her former husband, and baseball legend, Joe DiMaggio) and was, said DiMaggio, Jr., in a good frame of mind. Not long after that, the actor Peter Lawford invited Marilyn over to his house for dinner. She chose not to go. Lawford was reportedly concerned by Monroe's stoned, slurry tones and decided to call her again later. This is where things become confusing—and potentially conspiratorial.

Movie star Marilyn Monroe dies under mysterious circumstances. Some have said that she was sexually serving President John F. Kennedy at the time of her death.

The story goes that Lawford tried to reach Monroe several times again that night—all to no avail. He was, however, able to speak with her housekeeper, Eunice Murray, who assured Lawford that all was well. He was not so sure. Murray would later state that at roughly 10:00 P.M. she saw a light coming from Monroe's bedroom but heard nothing and assumed the actress had fallen asleep and left the light on.

Around half an hour later, rumors were circulating that Marilyn had overdosed, something confirmed by Monroe's lawyer, Mickey Rudin, and her publicist, Arthur P. Jacobs. The nail in the coffin came at approximately 1:00 A.M. when Peter Lawford got a call from Rudin, stating the star was dead. That is somewhat curious, however, as at 3:00 A.M.—two hours later—Eunice Murray reportedly tried to wake Monroe by knocking on the bedroom door and the French windows.

Dr. Greenson was soon on the scene again, having been phoned by Murray; he quickly smashed the windows to gain entry. Sure enough, the world's most famous blonde was no more. The police arrived at a scene filled with confusion and suspicious activity. Murray was hastily washing the bedsheets when the investigating officers descended on Marilyn's home. Both Greenson and Murray made changes to their stories, specifically in regard to who called who and when and in relation to the particular time at which they believed she died—around 4:00 A.M. This was completely at odds with the conclusion of the undertaker, Guy Hockett, who put the time of death at around 9:30 P.M., a significant number of hours earlier. On top of that, the pathologist, Dr. Thomas Noguchi, was suspicious of the fact that even if Monroe had taken an overdose—of what was deemed to be Nembutal—she had not swallowed it, for example, via a glass of water. A study of her intestines demonstrated that. How the drugs got into the system of the actress remained a puzzle. Actually, everything remained a puzzle—and it pretty much still does.

Marilyn Monroe was laid to rest on August 8, 1962, at the Los Angeles, California-based Westwood Village Memorial Park Cemetery.

MOOD-ALTERING DRUGS

Global Research makes a very good point: "Here in the early stages of the twenty-first century, a ruling elite has manipulated our planet of seven billion people into a global economic system of feudalism. Through pillaging and plundering the earth, setting up a cleverly deceptive financial system that controls the production and flow of fiat paper money using the US dollar as the standard international currency, they have turned the world's citizens and nations into indentured servants, hopelessly in debt due to their grand theft planet. With Russia and China spearheading a shift away from the US dollar and petrodollar, and many smaller nations following their lead, a major shift in the balance of power is underway between Western and Eastern oligarchs. Thus, by design escalating calamity and crises are in overdrive at the start of 2015. By examining one aspect of this grand theft planet through the story of Big Pharma, one can accurately recognize and assess Big Pharma's success in its momentum-gathering power grab. Its story serves as a microcosm perfectly illustrating and paralleling the macrocosm that is today's oligarch engineered, highly successful New World Order nightmare coming true right before our eyes that we're all now up against."

This is not, however, just about money. It's the nature of the pharmaceuticals that we also need to focus on. In 2013, the *New York Times* noted something shocking: "Over the past two decades, the use of antidepressants has skyrocketed. One in 10 Americans now takes an antidepressant medication; among women in their 40s and 50s, the figure is one in four. Experts have offered numerous reasons. Depression is common, and economic struggles have added to our stress and anxiety. Television ads promote antidepressants, and insurance plans usually cover them, even while limiting talk therapy. But a recent study suggests another explanation: that the condition is being over-diagnosed on a remarkable scale."

One year later, *Scientific American* told its readers: "Antidepressant use among Americans is skyrocketing. Adults in the U.S. consumed four times more antidepressants in the late 2000s than they did in the early 1990s. As the third most frequently taken medication in the U.S., researchers estimate that 8 to 10 percent of the population is taking an antidepressant."

Healthline reveals disturbing statistics: "Opioids are a class of drugs known for their ability to produce a euphoric high, as well a debilitating addiction. They are strictly regulated for these reasons and should only be prescribed to treat chronic pain resulting from a disease, surgery, or injury, according to the Center for Addiction and Mental Health. Opioids—codeine, oxycodone, and hydrocodone—are increasingly popular recreational drugs that have been both celebrated and condemned in popular culture. There is a high potential for fatal opioid overdoses, made evident by the fact that 60 percent of the 38,329 people who died of a drug overdose in the U.S. in 2010—including comedian Greg Giraldo—died taking prescription drugs. Three out of four of those deaths were caused by opioid analgesics, according to CDC estimates."

Forbes notes that decades after Xanax was first placed on the market in 1981, "America is still a Xanax nation. It remains the most popular psychiatric drug, topping more recently introduced medicines like the sleeping pill Ambien (No. 2) and the antidepressant Lexapro (No. 3). Doctors write nearly 50 million prescriptions for Xanax or alprazolam (the cheap, generic equivalent) every year—that's more than one Xanax prescription every second. Upjohn vanished in a series of mergers—it's buried somewhere inside Pfizer now—but the decision its executives made still echoes through our culture, and through the bodies of psychiatric patients."

Americans are taking more and more antidepressants these days. A number of reasons might explain this, including economic stress and even the influence of TV advertisements.

While mood-altering drugs most assuredly help to combat anxiety-driven conditions, they are often so powerful that they create a near-zombified state in the user. For the New World Order, it's a double whammy: NWO cronies in the pharmaceutical industry reap in billions in profits, and the population becomes more and more hooked on their drugs of choice and less and less likely—in their medicated states—to stand up to those who want to take away our freedoms.

MR. ROBOT

The USA Network says of its hit television show, Mr. Robot, that it "follows Elliot (Rami Malek, 'The Pacific'), a young programmer who works as a cyber-security engineer by day and as a vigilante hacker by night. Elliot finds himself at a crossroads when the mysterious leader (Christian Slater, 'The Adderall Diaries') of an underground hacker group recruits him to destroy the firm he is paid to protect. Compelled by his personal beliefs, Elliot struggles to resist the chance to take down the multinational CEOs he believes are running (and ruining) the world. The series also stars Portia Doubleday ('Her'), Carly Chaikin ('Suburgatory') and Martin Wallström ('Simple Simon'). *Mr. Robot* is produced by Universal Cable Productions, this contemporary and culturally resonant drama is executive produced by Sam Esmail ('Comet') and Anonymous Content's Steve Golin ('True Detective') and Chad Hamilton ('Breakup at a Wedding')."

Although *Mr. Robot* is a work of thought-provoking, on-screen entertainment, it gets to the very heart of what is afoot in the world today, namely, powerful figures who manipulate society and who wish to take control of the planet and ensure that just about everyone lines up and accepts the New World Order.

In a September 2015 article titled "Mr. Robot and the New World Order," Jon Herrera wrote: "The Big Boys of the banking world, Citibank, Chase, Bank of America, etc. were all trading for around a quarter a share. The reason for this was they were, and mostly still are, run by greedy, selfish, cheating bastards. Our fine government stepped forward and said these Institutions were too big to fail. Everyone who owed them money was more than happy to see them fail. No more bank, no more debt. Which brings us to *Mr. Robot*, an often brilliant show from the USA Network. The main idea here is that a small group of hackers want to bring down the single largest financial mega-corporation on earth. The company is constantly referred to as Evil Corp and it could easily be a stand-in for your bank of choice. This is the fantasy fulfillment for everyone who wanted all the Gordon Gekkos of the world to end up homeless or dead."

In the same month, *The Daily Beast* ran an article titled "Mr. Robot Speaks." It began: "The day before USA Network was supposed to air the first season finale of its mind-bending mystery-thriller *Mr. Robot*, Christian Slater, who plays the titular character, reflected on the show's surreal timeliness. 'It's terrifying. The television show is supposed to represent this dystopian universe,' he told me. 'Is this the world that we want to be mirroring?'"

The star of the show, actor Rami Malek, who plays hacker Elliot Alderson, says: "*Mr. Robot* resonates because we're all concerned about what's happening in the world right now—the sense that it's just undulating right beneath our feet. At the same time, Sam's making all these points about hyper consumerism and the way we use technology. We spend all our time connecting by typing on devices or viewing the world through lenses. There is something inauthentic about that. So much of how we live is manufactured rather than real.

"I've always been concerned with where we're going and this show's only made me more so. The world is chaotic at the moment and we're shining a light on that. This show is asking exactly what effect this chaos might have on all of us. Do we all ultimately feel as uncomfortable as Elliot?"

The Guardian says of the hit show: "*Mr. Robot* is an addictive journey into the dark heart of modern America. Full of twists, the show follows reclusive hacker Elliot Alderson in his attempt to bring down corporate giant E Corp, which Elliot simply calls Evil Corp. In his now-iconic black hoodie, he stalks the streets of New York, shoulders hunched and eyes wild as his hacks cause mayhem."

Mayhem for the New World Order but a light at the end of the tunnel for the rest of us.

NATO

In an article titled "NATO and the New World Order," Sean Gabb says: "In 1815, at the end of the wars connected with the French Revolution, the conservative powers of Europe (Austria, Russia, Royalist France, and so forth) created the Holy Alliance. The purpose of this was to commit all its members to the suppression of liberal ideas wherever in any one member state they might take hold. We can see NATO and the European Union as the modern counterparts to this Holy Alliance. This explains the crisis Brexit has brought through much of the West. One core member state is withdrawing from the New World Order. Others may follow—the Dutch, for example. Meanwhile, the countries of Central Europe are increasingly semi-detached from the European institutions."

What, exactly, is NATO? Let's see. According to NATO itself: "NATO's essential purpose is to safeguard the freedom and security of its members through political and military means. NATO promotes democratic values and encourages consultation and cooperation on defence and security issues to build trust and, in the long run, prevent conflict. NATO is committed to the peaceful resolution of disputes. If diplomatic efforts fail, it has the military capacity needed to undertake crisis-management operations. These are carried out under Article 5 of the Washington Treaty—NATO's founding treaty—or under a UN mandate, alone or in cooperation with other countries and international organizations."

How, exactly, does NATO play a role in the New World Order? *Three World Wars* states: "The corporate portion of the NWO is dominated by international bankers, oil barons and pharmaceutical cartels, as well as other major multinational corporations. The Royal Family of England, namely Queen Elizabeth II and the House of Windsor, (who are, in fact, descendants of the German arm of European Royalty—the Saxe-Coburg-Gotha family—changed the name to Windsor in 1914), are high level players in the oligarchy which controls the upper strata of the NWO. The decision making nerve centers of this effort are in London (especially the City of London), Basel Switzerland, *and Brussels (NATO headquarters)*."

Sholto Byrnes' May 2016 article, "Why We Need a New World Order," provides these words: "When a former deputy commander of NATO warns that the West is on course for armed conflict with Russia within the next year, and China's vice foreign minister announces that should the United States 'stir up any conflict' his country is ready for a 'replay' of the Korean and Vietnam wars, one thing should be very clear: the world urgently needs a new security architecture.

"Across the continents, from the quagmire of competing and often contradictory participants in Syria and Iraq, to the Baltic states and to the seas of the Asia Pacific, the potential for conflict and escalation is rising dangerously. As well as the scenario outlined by Gen Sir Richard Shirreff—nuclear war in the event of a Russian invasion of Latvia—Nato has been drawn perilously close to the brink with Russia because of Turkey. The two countries actively support different sides in the Syrian conflict, and Turkish forces shot down a Russian warplane last November.

"The paradox—and the fear—is that the alliance, whose credibility rests on an attack on one being considered an attack on all, could be tested by a state that under its current leader and trajectory would probably never have been invited to join in the first place. One might have thought this was a time for Nato to take a step back, consolidate and think what its *raison d'être* is today. Instead it is going full steam ahead and inviting Montenegro to join—another move that, given its historic leadership of the Slavic nations, infuriates Russia."

Kurt Gritsch, the author of *The War for Kosovo*, says that the war in question was "the beginning of a new world order." He expands: "Kosovo was at the beginning, as a war in which NATO authorized itself to act outside the borders of the members of the Alliance. Kosovo is at the beginning of new wars, followed by other interventions abroad, Macedonia, the war in Afghanistan, Iraq—in which not all NATO members participated, then 2011, Libya, and in the meantime the eastern enlargement of NATO, which has been developing since the 1990s to the present day and has led to a rival relationship with Russia. Some say that this revived the Cold War. But at the beginning of everything was the Kosovo war."

A group photo of world leaders during a NATO meeting in Warsaw, Poland.

Richard Norton-Taylor, in September 2014 in *The Guardian*, offered the following in an article titled "UK, EU, and NATO all in need of a 'new world order?'"

"More than 50 years ago, Henry Kissinger, America's best known political scientist, hugely controversial diplomat and national security adviser, wrote his first book. *A World Restored* is a study, a celebration really, of how Count Metternich, the Austrian chancellor, brilliantly managed the international order, balancing power through a maze of alliances, in the early nineteenth century....

"Later this week, Kissinger publishes his latest work, *World Order: Reflections on the Character of Nations and the Course of History* (Allen Lane). He compares the Middle East today with Europe's 17th century wars of religion. 'Domestic and international conflicts reinforce each other. Political, sectarian, tribal, territorial, ideological, and traditional national-interest disputes merge,' he wrote in an extract for the *Sunday Times*. If order cannot be established, 'vast areas risk being opened to anarchy and to forms of extremism that will spread organically into other regions.' The world, says Kissinger, awaits 'the distillation of a new regional order by America and other countries in a position to take a global view.'"

Kissinger sees NATO as playing a key role in that new world.

NEW WORLD ORDER IN THE 1990S

Writing in the *Wall Street Journal* in September 1990, Richard Gephardt wrote: "We can see beyond the present shadows of war in the Middle East to a new world order where the strong work together to deter and stop aggression. This was precisely Franklin Roosevelt's and Winston Churchill's vision for peace for the post-war period."

"If we do not follow the dictates of our inner moral compass and stand up for human life, then his lawlessness will threaten the peace and democracy of the emerging new world order we now see, this long dreamed-of vision we've all worked toward for so long." Those are the January 1991 words of President George H.W. Bush.

> But it became clear as time went on that in Mr. Bush's mind the New World Order was founded on a convergence of goals and interests between the U.S. and the Soviet Union....

Also in January 1991, A. M. Rosenthal, in the *New York Times*, provided this: "But it became clear as time went on that in Mr. Bush's mind the New World Order was founded on a convergence of goals and interests between the U.S. and the Soviet Union, so strong and permanent that they would work as a team through the U.N. Security Council."

"I would support a Presidential candidate who pledged to take the following steps: At the end of the war in the Persian Gulf, press for a comprehensive Middle East settlement and for a 'new world order' based not on Pax Americana but on peace through law with a stronger U.N. and World Court," said George McGovern, who was quoted in the *New York Times* in February 1991.

"It's Bush's baby, even if he shares its popularization with Gorbachev. Forget the Hitler 'new order' root; F. D. R. used the phrase earlier," said William Safire, in the *New York Times* in the same month that McGovern made his statement. A senator at the time, Vice President Joe Biden wrote an article for the *Wall Street Journal* in April 1992 with the eye-opening title of "How I Learned to Love the New World Order."

"The Final Act of the Uruguay Round, marking the conclusion of the most ambitious trade negotiation of our century, will give birth—in Morocco—to the World Trade Organization, the third pillar of the New World Order, along with the United Nations and the International Monetary Fund." This was the text of a one-page ad—paid for by the Moroccan government—which was splashed across the *New York Times* in April 1994.

"The new world order that is in the making must focus on the creation of a world of democracy, peace and prosperity for all," the late Nelson Mandela was quoted in the *Philadelphia Inquirer* in October 1994.

President Hosni Mubarak of Egypt was quoted in an April 1995 issue of the *New York Times* as saying with regard to the renewal of the nonproliferation treaty, it was hugely important for "the welfare of the whole world and the new world order."

Finally, Arthur Schlesinger offered this gem in August 1995: "We are not going to achieve a new world order without paying for it in blood as well as in words and money."

9/11

September 11, 2001, will go down as one of the worst days in the history of the United States of America, if not *the* worst. In terms of tragedy and outrage, it is equaled only by the terrible events of December 7, 1941, when Japanese forces attacked Pearl Harbor, Hawaii, killing nearly two and a half thousand Americans in the process.

In shockingly quick progression—and with equally shocking ease—nineteen al-Qaeda terrorists seized control of four large passenger planes and, essentially, turned them into the equivalents of missiles. On the morning of September 11, United Airlines Flight 175 and American Airlines Flight 11 slammed, respectively, into the South and North towers of New York's World Trade Center. Another American Airlines plane, Flight 77, hit the Pentagon, and United Airlines Flight 93 hurtled to the ground outside of Shanksville, Pennsylvania, when a number of passengers attempted to wrestle control of the plane from the hijackers. Some suspected that the plan of the hijackers was to target none other than the White House itself. Before the day was over, a nation was stunned to its core, and almost three thousand people had lost their lives.

Steve Alten is a best-selling author, probably most widely known for his controversial novel *The Shell Game*, a 2009 story that tells of the next 9/11-style event on U.S. soil. Alten makes no bones about the fact that he has major suspicions that we have not been told the real story of what happened on September 11, 2001. In a foreword to his novel, Alten notes that on the morning of 9/11, then-Vice President Dick Cheney oversaw a series of war games which, in Alten's opinion, "purposefully diverted all of our jet fighters away from the Northeastern Air Defense Sector (NEADS) where the four

9/11 Memorial Park in Manhattan will forever mark the spot where the Twin Towers stood ... and fell.

hijackings took place, sending them over Alaska, Greenland, Iceland, and Canada."

Alten also significantly noted: "One of these exercises, *Vigilant Guardian*, was a hijack drill designed to mirror the actual events taking place, inserting twenty-two false radar blips on the FAA's radar screens so that flight controllers had no idea which blips were the hijacked aircraft and which were the war game blips."

The result: mass confusion over what was real and what was not and a lack of adequate military defense at the time when the Twin Towers were struck.

Let's not forget about certain highly suspicious stock trading that went on in the days immediately before the attacks, something which led to vocal assertions from the conspiracy minded that those engaged in the trading secretly knew what was about to hit the United States. Most of the activity revolved around the very two airlines whose planes were used in the attacks: American Airlines and United Airlines.

Allen M. Poteshman, of the *Journal of Business*, said of this curious state of affairs: "A measure of abnormal long put volume was also examined and seen to be at abnormally high levels in the days leading up to the attacks. Consequently, the paper concludes that there is evidence of unusual option market activity in the days leading up to September 11 that is consistent with investors trading on advance knowledge of the attacks."

It wasn't just airlines that were experiencing abnormal stock-based activity right before 9/11. The world of insurance did, too. Both Morgan Stanley and Citigroup Inc. experienced massive increases in trading from September 8 right up until the time of the attacks. Indeed, Citigroup Inc.'s trading was in excess of *forty times* its normal level. Citigroup stood to pay out millions in insurance claims from the World Trade Center attacks. Morgan Stanley had their offices *within* the World Trade Center. One of the United States' leading defense companies, Raytheon, saw trading leap more than five times its normal approximate level on September 10.

Then there is the theory that, as per the claims surrounding the December 7, 1941, attack on Pearl Harbor, 9/11 was allowed to happen in order to justify an invasion of the Middle East and the ushering in of a secretly planned New World Order. Michael Meacher was the British government's environment minister from 1997 to 2003. His words, as a senior official of the government, did not go by unnoticed. They were picked up widely: "It is clear the US authorities did little or nothing to pre-empt the events of 9/11. It is known that at least 11 countries provided advance warning to the US of the 9/11 attacks. Two senior Mossad experts were sent to Washington in August 2001 to alert the CIA and FBI to a cell of 200 terrorists said to be preparing a big operation. The list they provided included the names of four of the 9/11 hijackers, none of whom was arrested.

"It had been known as early as 1996 that there were plans to hit Washington targets with airplanes. Then in 1999 a US national intelligence council report noted that 'al-Qaida suicide bombers could crash-land an aircraft packed with high explosives into the Pentagon, the headquarters of the CIA, or the White House.'

"Fifteen of the 9/11 hijackers obtained their visas in Saudi Arabia. Michael Springman, the former head of the American visa bureau in Jeddah, has stated that since 1987 the CIA had been illicitly issuing visas to unqualified applicants from the Middle East and bringing them to the US for training in terrorism for the Afghan war in collaboration with Bin Laden. It seems this operation continued after the Afghan war for other purposes. It is also reported that five of the hijackers received training at secure US military installations in the 1990s."

A terrible event, one that was allowed to happen since it worked in favor of the long-term goals of the New World Order? Don't bet against it.

1984

There is no doubt that when it comes to fictionalized scenarios of a New World Order nature, the one that stands out more than any other is George Orwell's *Nineteen Eighty-Four*, alternately and more popularly known as *1984*. Orwell's book was published in 1949 and paints an overwhelmingly dark and foreboding 1984. Given the current state of the world today, many would argue—and with a great deal of justification—that Orwell was only off by a couple of decades when it comes to the matter of spying on the population, ever-intrusive technology, and increasing ways to take away our civil liberties and freedoms.

A good indication of life in Orwell's world can be found at *SparkNotes*: "Winston Smith is a low-ranking member of the ruling Party in London, in the nation of Oceania. Everywhere Winston goes, even his own home, the Party watches him through telescreens; everywhere he looks he sees the face of the Party's seemingly omniscient leader, a figure known only as Big Brother. The

Party controls everything in Oceania, even the people's history and language. Currently, the Party is forcing the implementation of an invented language called Newspeak, which attempts to prevent political rebellion by eliminating all words related to it. Even thinking rebellious thoughts is illegal. Such thought crime is, in fact, the worst of all crimes."

Such is the power of Orwell's *1984*, it has become the definitive warning sign for the real equivalent, which is getting closer and closer. Michael Payne, at *OpEd News,* makes this observation perfectly: "In this novel, published in 1949, Oceania is depicted as a nation of perpetual war, pervasive government, public mind control and the voiding of civil rights. Could that description fit America today? Well, one thing is certain; if America has not yet arrived at that point, we seem to be heading in that very direction.

"No, America does not have a Ministry of Truth, a Ministry of Peace (in '1984' war was considered peace), a Ministry of Plenty, or a Ministry of love (meaning love for only Big Brother and the Party), at least, not yet. But, examine Orwell's depiction of a world of perpetual war, pervasive government, public mind control and the voiding of civil rights and see how it relates to the America of today. Then ask this question; is America evolving into the living example of Orwell's journalistic masterpiece? Perpetual War that should be a no-brainer; since the end of World War II, the U.S. has conducted wars and military actions in the Korean War, the Vietnam War, Grenada, Panama, Bosnia, Somalia, Iraq, Afghanistan, and Pakistan. If that is not perpetual war, then what is it?"

Payne concludes: "When America arrives at the point that the laws of the nation allow government agencies to listen to cell phone, e-mail, text messaging, Facebook or any other form of communication of its citizens, then we have entered the era of 'Big Brother.' And we will have become the living proof of Orwell's prophetic visions. 'Big Brother is watching' used to be a joke; well, it's no longer a joke, it is becoming a reality in America. So, when you state your opinions on e-mails, cell phones, Facebook, or when you text, watch what you say because someone out there is listening and may be taking notes."

Born Eric Arthur Blair, author George Orwell was a staunch critic of totalitarianism and social injustice, positions famously expressed in his dystopian novel *1984.*

On this very same issue, *WND* provided the following in May 2014: "Written by Orwell in the late 1940s, the dystopian date of *1984* is now 30 years passed. But that doesn't mean the nightmarish world of complete state control is gone. Now, on May 27, a new voice will appear to warn Americans the Orwellian image of a boot stamping forever on the human face is inching closer. Cheryl Chumley's 'Police State USA: How Orwell's Nightmare is Becoming Our Reality' marshals the terrifying evidence to show the world of Big Brother is much closer than Americans want to admit.

"Chumley, a full-time reporter for the *Washington Times*, writes about politics and government for various newspapers, Internet news sites and think tanks. She is a journalism fellow with the Phillips Foundation, a prestigious organization in Washington, D.C., where she spent a year researching and writing about private property rights.

"From traffic light cameras to phone tapping, from militarized police forces to huge purchase orders by departments of the federal government for billions of rounds of ammunition, the government is increasing its control over individual lives. 'Police State USA' chronicles how America got to the point of being a de facto police state, what led to it and how citizens might overcome it and recapture the freedoms envisioned by the Founding Fathers."

The foreword to Chumley's book was penned by Representative Louie Gohmert of Texas, who said: "'What has been will be again, what has been done will be done again; there is nothing new under the sun.' This was Solomon's observation as the wisest of all kings. How does it apply here? Cheryl Chumley lays out clearly what is happening in this country now has happened to countries in the past, and the consequences are clear. People have liberty; people take liberty for granted; people become apathetic; people lose their liberty. We are on that track, but detouring back to the freedom road is still possible. Though there has never been a country in world history whose citizens have enjoyed the individual liberties found in the United States today, there have been countries whose citizens went from enjoying individual liberties to being oppressed by increasingly totalitarian rulers. Drawing from available information around us, Cheryl points out the shocking usurpations of our freedoms."

What all of the above demonstrates to us is that, as horrific as it sounds, we are rapidly entering a stage where the old ways may soon be gone. In their place will be a harsh and intrusive dystopia, that is unless, of course, humanity stands together and pushes back against the New World Order hordes.

See also the entries "Orwellian" and "Perpetual War."

NONE DARE CALL IT CONSPIRACY

News of Interest TV says of Gary Allen's controversial—but lauded in conspiracy circles—book, *None Dare Call It Conspiracy*: "'None Dare Call It Conspiracy' by Gary Allen and Larry Abraham is a book of great importance, having upset the ruling Western political Establishment by exposing much of their secretive underlying history and agendas that control the political processes of the United States and much of the rest of the world. The book was light-years ahead of its time when it was published in 1971. The information in this book is surprising and can even seem far-fetched to the uninitiated; however, the information is accurate and well documented.

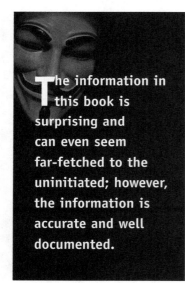

The information in this book is surprising and can even seem far-fetched to the uninitiated; however, the information is accurate and well documented.

"The first few chapters of the book contain preparatory information meant to acclimate uninitiated readers, followed by delving deeply into historical information explaining agendas of the little-known global Elite. Surprisingly to many, the book shows how this group of Establishment insiders has historically been responsible for secretively establishing and then supporting the totalitarian Communist regimes in Russia, China, and much of the rest of the world, and it is explained how globalist philosophies which are currently being implemented call for a similar uniform system of government to eventually be imposed on the entire populace of the planet in a totalitarian 'New World Order.'"

They continue: "Parts of the book criticize 'Liberals' in favor of 'Conservatives,' however the definition of 'Conservative' as used in this book should be interpreted to mean what today would be called 'Libertarian'—and not what today's common perception of 'Conservative' is as being represented by such individuals as Dick Cheney, Sarah Palin, Anne Colter, etc.—who the authors of this book would not like."

Lundbaek says of Gary Allen's New World Order-themed book: "'None Dare Call It Conspiracy' by Gary Allen, is one of the books recommended by then Apostle Ezra Taft Benson while speaking during the April 1972 Church General Conference. As an endorsement, he wrote: 'I wish that every citizen of every country in the free world and every slave behind the Iron Curtain might read this book.' If anything more need be said it might be that this book is, according to Dan Smoot, an FBI agent during WW2, an assistant to J. Edgar Hoover, and close colleague of W. Cleon Skousen, 'an admirable job of amassing information to prove that communism is socialism and socialism (a plot to enslave the world) is not a movement of the downtrodden but a scheme supported and directed by the wealthiest of people.'"

Allen's book was made notable by the fact that the introduction to the book was penned by U.S. Congressman John G. Schmitz—who was also a member of the controversial John Birch Society. Schmitz' words actually appeared shortly before the publication of *None Dare Call It Conspiracy* in the form of a paper that Scmitz planned on circulating himself as well as sharing it with Allen for his book. That paper reads as follows: "The story you are about to read is true. The names have not been changed to protect the guilty. This book may have the effect of changing your life. After reading this book, you will never look at national and world events in the same way again.

"*None Dare Call It Conspiracy* will be a very controversial book. At first it will receive little publicity and those whose plans are exposed in it will try to kill it by the silent treatment. For reasons that become obvious as you read this book, it will not be reviewed in all the 'proper' places or be available on your local bookstand. However, there is nothing these people can do to stop a grass roots book distributing system. Eventually it will be necessary for the people and organizations named in this book to try to blunt its effect by attacking it or the author. They have a tremendous vested interest in keeping you from discovering what they are doing. And they have the big guns of the mass media at their disposal to fire the barrages at *None Dare Call It Conspiracy*.

"By sheer volume, the 'experts' will try to ridicule you out of investigating for yourself as to whether or not the information in this book is true. They will ignore the fact that the author is about to conjecture. They will find a typographical error or argue some point that is open to debate. If necessary they will lie in order to protect themselves by smearing this book. I believe those who pooh-pooh the information herein because Psychologically many people would prefer to believe we are because we all like to ignore bad news. We do so at our own peril.

"Having been a college instructor, a State Senator and now a Congressman I have had experience with real professionals at putting up smokescreens to cover up their own actions by trying to destroy the accuser. I hope that you will read the book carefully, draw your own conclusions and not accept the opinions of those who of necessity must attempt to discredit the book. Your future may depend upon it."

As for Allen himself, he said the following in his 1971 book, "Most of us believe socialism is what the socialists want us to believe it is—a share-the-wealth program. That is the theory. But is that how it works? Let us examine the only Socialist countries—according to the Socialist definition of the word—extant in the world today. These are the Communist countries. The Communists themselves refer to these as Socialist countries, as in the Union of Soviet Socialist Republics. Here in the reality of socialism you have a tiny oligarchial clique at the top, usually numbering no more than three percent of the total population, controlling the total wealth, total production and the very lives of the other ninety-seven percent.

"If one understands that socialism is not a share-the-wealth program, but is in reality a method to consolidate and control the wealth, then the seeming paradox of superrich men promoting socialism becomes no paradox at all. Instead it becomes the logical, even the perfect tool of power-seeking megalo-maniacs. Communism, or more accurately, socialism, is not a movement of the downtrodden masses, but of the economic elite.

"If you wanted to control the nation's manufacturing, commerce, finance, transportation and natural resources, you would need only to control the apex, the power pinnacle, of an all-powerful socialist government. Then you would have a monopoly and could squeeze out all your competitors. If you wanted a national monopoly, you must control a national socialist govern-ment. If you want—a worldwide monopoly, you must control a world socialist government. That is what the game is all about. "Communism" is not a move-ment of the downtrodden masses but is a movement created, manipulated and used by power-seeking billionaires in order to gain control over the world . . . first by establishing socialist governments in the various nations and then con-solidating them all through a 'Great Merger,' into an all-powerful world, socialist super-state."

As Allen saw it, the New World Order is hovering over us, in menacing fashion, right now. He died in 1986 at the age of fifty. *None Dare Call It Con-spiracy* continues to sell to this very day.

NUCLEAR WINTER

This book shows that there are deranged figures within the New World Order who believe that a nuclear war—World War Three—is the way to create a new society, one which will be radically reduced in number as a result of the terrible destruction wrought by the world's massive atomic arsenal. But how, exactly, would the world look after a NWO-driven nuclear war?

In 2000, Mikhail Gorbachev, the former Soviet premier—who, thirty years ago, and along with the United States' President Ronald Reagan, sought to bring the Cold War to a close—said: "In the 1980s, you warned about the unprecedented dangers of nuclear weapons and took very daring steps to reverse the arms race. Models made by Russian and American scientists showed that a nuclear war would result in a nuclear winter that would be

A nuclear winter would be caused if nations exploded numerous nuclear warheads. The explosions would kick up so much dust into the planet's atmosphere that it would block out the sun for years, causing temperatures to plummet and resulting in an agricultural disaster that would starve millions.

extremely destructive to all life on Earth; the knowledge of that was a great stimulus to us, to people of honor and morality, to act in that situation."

So, what, exactly, is a nuclear winter, and what might be its connection to ancient atomic warfare fought by extraterrestrials? Let's see. We'll begin with the aforementioned decade of the 1980s, which was when the concept—and the doom-filled implications—of a nuclear winter really began to take shape on a large scale.

Today's atomic weapons have the ability to obliterate entire cities and millions of people in seconds. Compared to atomic weapons of the twenty-first century, the bombs dropped on Hiroshima and Nagasaki are mere toys. Bringing worldwide civilization to an end is something that is all too easily within our grasp, should we be so foolish to one day go down that nightmarish path. But, it's not just the immediate effects of an atomic war that we have to be concerned about. There are the long-term effects, too. Yes, trying to protect oneself from both the initial blast and the soon-to-be-everywhere deadly radiation would be absolutely paramount to one's survival. There is, however, something else to be aware of.

Such would be the massive scale of destruction in an atomic war, millions upon millions of tons of dust, dirt, soot, and the ashlike remains of probably five or six billion people, buildings, and more would be sucked into the huge, great firestorms erupting all across the quickly shattering globe. In no time at all, the dense, cloudy, worldwide masses would quickly reach the stratosphere, which is situated around six to eight miles above the planet's surface, and that's when the poor, irradiated, and burned survivors of the war would have something else to deal with, as if billions dead and killer radiation weren't enough to have on one's plate.

Such would be the almost unfathomable amount of sooty materials quickly overwhelming the planet's entire stratosphere, we would see a sudden and devastating change in temperatures. We're not talking about the temperature merely dropping. We're talking about it *plummeting*, as in almost off the scale, as the rays and heat of the sun become systematically blocked out, all as a result of our stupidity and recklessness.

In 1985, the National Research Council published a groundbreaking report titled "The Effects on the Atmosphere of a Major Nuclear Exchange" Its conclusions—which were prepared by the Committee on the Atmospheric Effects of Nuclear Explosions—were chilling and included the following words: "The realization that a nuclear exchange would be accompanied by the deposition into the atmosphere of particulate matter is not new. However, the suggestion that the associated attenuation of sunlight might be so extensive as to cause severe drops in surface air temperatures and other major climatic effects in areas that are far removed from target zones is of rather recent origin."

The committee also noted that "the massive species extinctions of 65 million years ago were part of the aftermath of the lofting of massive quantities of particulates resulting from the collision of a large meteor with the earth." A clear warning that by engaging in atomic warfare on a planetary scale, we risk going the same way as the dinosaurs—all as a result of significant changes to the planet's temperature.

We also have this from the committee: "The consequences of any such changes in atmospheric state would have to be added to the already sobering list of relatively well-understood consequences of nuclear war.... Long-term atmospheric consequences imply additional problems that are not easily mitigated by prior preparedness and that are not in harmony with any notion of rapid postwar restoration of social structure. They also create an entirely new threat to populations far removed from target areas, and suggest the possibility of additional major risks for any nation that itself initiates use of nuclear weapons, even if nuclear retaliation should somehow be limited."

In light of all the above, to what extent would the Earth's temperature be lowered? A chilling—no pun intended—statement comes from Dr. Alan

Robock, a professor of climatology in the Department of Environmental Sciences at Rutgers University. He says: "A minor nuclear war (such as between India and Pakistan or in the Middle East), with each country using 50 Hiroshima-sized atom bombs as airbursts on urban areas, could produce climate change unprecedented in recorded human history. This is only 0.03% of the explosive power of the current global arsenal."

Consider Dr. Robock's words carefully. He makes it very clear that the survivors of an atomic war would experience "climate change unprecedented in recorded human history," and all this with only 0.03 percent of the world's atomic weapons being used. Imagine, then, the effects if *all* of the remaining, *massive* percentage was used—and not just in the India-Pakistan area or in the Middle East but just about everywhere. It's not at all inconceivable that we would see our world plunged into nothing less than a full-blown Ice Age, never mind just a nuclear winter.

If this is the future the New World Order really wants, then they are clearly more dangerous and insane than most of us imagine.

OBESITY

Is it feasible that the New World Order is seeking to keep the population in check, and under control, by actively but secretly promoting obesity in the American population? The answer is almost certainly "Yes." Statistics from the U.S. Department of Health and Human Services paint a disturbing picture: "Data from the National Health and Nutrition Examination Survey, 2009–2010: More than 2 in 3 adults are considered to be overweight or obese. More than 1 in 3 adults are considered to be obese. More than 1 in 20 adults are considered to have extreme obesity. About one-third of children and adolescents ages 6 to 19 are considered to be overweight or obese. More than 1 in 6 children and adolescents ages 6 to 19 are considered to be obese. By 2010, the percentage of adults considered overweight, obese, or extremely obese had climbed to about 75. About 33 percent were considered overweight, about 36 percent were considered obese, and about 6 percent were considered extremely obese.

"In 2011, 4.5% of the Defense Department's active-duty forces were diagnosed as overweight or obese. In five years that number became 7.8%, a 73% increase across all age groups. The report notes that the statistic has gained as more healthcare providers now diagnose weight gain as a medical problem."

As for the severe health effects that obesity has on the average person, the Centers for Disease Control and Prevention reveals: "People who are obese, compared to those with a normal or healthy weight, are at increased risk for many serious diseases and health conditions, including the following: All-causes of death (mortality) High blood pressure (Hypertension), High LDL cholesterol, low HDL cholesterol, or high levels of triglycerides (Dyslipidemia), Type 2 diabetes, Coronary heart disease, Stroke, Gallbladder disease, Osteoarthritis (a breakdown of cartilage and bone within a joint), Sleep apnea and breathing problems, Some cancers (endometrial, breast, colon, kidney, gallbladder, and liver), Low quality of life, Mental illness such as clinical depression, anxiety, and other mental disorders, Body pain and difficulty with physical functioning."

The side effects of obesity lead to a greater reliance upon drugs and medicines to control such conditions as high blood pressure, diabetes, and heart disease. This permits the NWO-connected pharmaceutical companies to reap billions upon billions of dollars every year from people who are being encouraged to quite literally eat themselves to death.

There is another aspect to this: an obese nation is also one that, physically, is limited in what it can achieve. Even the U.S. military is noticing that, as *Sputnik News* makes abundantly clear: "Obesity in the U.S. military has become an issue following a 73% spike in the number of overweight service

Is the obesity epidemic in America actually an intentional phenomenon meant to keep citizens dependent on expensive medications?

members in just five years. Increasing numbers of overweight people among the US population has been a trend in the past few years, according to a report issued by the Defense Health Agency. A National Health and Nutrition Examination Survey recently estimated that 32% of men and 37% of women under the age of 40 in America are overweight or obese. Although the military's combined overweight and obesity rates are not as striking as those of the general US population, the number of military service applicants at risk of being labeled 'medically unfit' has risen significantly."

As more and more people become obese, and as more and more become "medically unfit," the less likely it is that they will be in good enough physical shape to do anything about it when the New World Order launches its takeover.

OCTOPUS

August 9, 1991, was the date on which a man named Danny Casolaro was found dead in the shower of room 517 of the Sheraton Inn in Martinsburg, West Virginia. It appeared that Casolaro had committed suicide: both of his wrists were slashed and there was a suicide note left for his family. But, was it really as tragically straightforward as it seemed? Not for the field of conspiracy theorizing, it wasn't. At the time of his death, Casolaro—an investigative journalist—was chasing down a powerful, secret society that he termed the Octopus—on account of the fact that it appeared to have powerful and influential tentacles that extended across just about the entire planet.

For Casolaro, it all began around a year and a half before his death. That was when he started digging into the saga of a man named William Hamilton, formerly of the National Security Agency, and an acknowledged leading figure in the world of computer software. Hamilton had come up with a highly sophisticated program for the Department of Justice (DoJ), one which would significantly help the DoJ to track and locate wanted criminals. When the DoJ claimed that Hamilton was overcharging them, a long and complicated legal battle began—Hamilton was the loser. But it wasn't the end for Hamilton's program—which was called PROMIS.

Shadowy figures in the intelligence community were making their own versions of Hamilton's program but with one big difference: the new versions contained a deeply buried "back door" that would allow U.S. Intelligence to spy on just about anyone and everyone that used the program—which included Israel and Iran. And the operation could all be traced back to the mysterious Octopus.

The further Casolaro dug, the more complicated the story got: the Octopus was composed of numerous powerful people in the world of big business, politics, the military, and the intelligence community. They were somewhat loose-knit and fluid, but they had the power and muscle to influence world events on a massive scale. As Casolaro headed ever deeper into the rabbit hole, he found that the Octopus had played key roles in the 1962 Cuban missile crisis (which brought the world to the brink of nuclear war), the Watergate scandal, which brought down President Richard M. Nixon, and the December 1988 destruction of a Boeing 747 jumbo jet aircraft over Lockerbie, Scotland. Then things got really weird.

The Octopus, Casolaro discovered, had a significant presence at the world's most famous secret base: Area 51, Nevada. The Octopus was reportedly funding research to create deadly viruses at both Area 51 and at an underground facility in northern New Mexico. Casolaro also made a connection between the Octopus and Majestic 12—the alleged secret group which oversees the secrecy surrounding what happened in Roswell, New Mexico, in early July 1947. Things took a strange turn when Casolaro met with a man named Michael Riconosciuto, who had worked in the field of spies, espionage, and intelligence for years and who advised Casolaro that many assumed UFOs were actually highly advanced, unusual aircraft of the military.

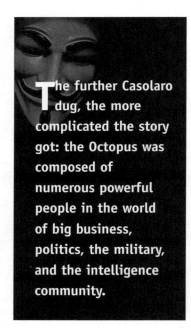

The further Casolaro dug, the more complicated the story got: the Octopus was composed of numerous powerful people in the world of big business, politics, the military, and the intelligence community.

Casolaro's research continued at a phenomenal rate to the point where he came to see the presence—and manipulative skills—of the Octopus in just about each and every major world event since the end of World War II. Of course, it all came crashing down for Casolaro when he was found dead in the tub, but was his death really just a suicide? Many within the field of conspiracy cried "No!" They pointed to the fact that less than a day before his death, Casolaro had a relaxing time hanging out with a man named William Turner, who was one of Casolaro's sources in the defense industry. Casolaro was apparently enthused and excited about where his research was taking him. Police investigators discovered that Casolaro had a chat with the man in the adjacent hotel room about his Octopus-based work; the man said Casolaro didn't appear depressed, down, or anxious. Quite the opposite. Nevertheless, the official verdict was suicide. There were, however, problems with the verdict, the main one being that both wrists were deeply cut. While it would have been easy for Casolaro to have inflicted the deep wounds to one wrist, doing so to the other—when it was already viciously hacked into—would have been much more difficult, some said.

In 1996, authors Jim Keith and Kenn Thomas wrote a book on the affair and Casolaro's suspiciously timed death. Its title? What else? *The Octopus*.

Keith soon found that his computer was hacked and that someone was reading his every written word. Then, in 1999, Keith died in a Reno hospital—under questionable circumstances—after falling off a stage and fracturing his tibia at the annual Burning Man festival in Nevada's Black Rock Desert. Then, in 2001, Ron Bonds—the publisher of *The Octopus*—died under equally controversial circumstances. The Octopus, it seems, is determined to ensure that no one gets too close to the truth of its world-manipulating activities—no matter what the cost.

OFF THE GRID

As more and more people seek to find ways to stay far away from the prying eyes of Big Brother and the New World Order, we are seeing a large increase in the number of people living "off the grid," as the phrase has become popularly known. In effect, it means staying offline, being self-sufficient, and not being a slave to "the man." While many might find such a lifestyle daunting and difficult to maintain in the long term, the off-the-grid community is growing and growing—and is growing ever quicker as the New World Order works toward its end-game strategy.

Survival Mastery says: "The term off-grid refers to being, rid of any dependency for existence. Literally put, it means anyone living off the grid of government provided electricity. In brief, it refers to families that survive on their own without depending on the society, government or public for any means of survival.

"This is a cloud term to include that independent house, which has its own endless supply of water, electricity, gas, food and fabric. During an apocalyptic situation, such a house or family has no fluctuations in its energy supply, food or fabric production. To make your own unlimited electricity, fuel, water and food requires a long stretch of productive hard work. In the course of time, man has started to misinterpret the purpose of life with getting employment or doing a job. To be a cogwheel under another's bums is what the world preaches each one to be alive, healthy. A steady 5-day week for 50 years and your insurances insure you to be cleverly, packaged before rotting! That, perhaps is the gist of such a life lived being dependent on someone else."

There are potential dangers to living off the grid, although when faced with the jackbooted thugs of the New World Order, the risk is worth taking. *Offgrid Survival* highlights those dangers: "Government officials from around the world have been systematically targeting those who choose to live an off the grid lifestyle. From targeting self-reliant homeowners with antiquated zoning laws and regulations to forming special zoning boards that are designed to force people back onto the grid, there seems to be a war against self-reliance, and sadly it seems like the government is winning.

"Throughout the country government agencies are forming so-called 'nuisance abatement teams' designed to intimidate and force Off Grid home-owners into giving up their land or abandoning their lifestyle. Believe it or not, people are actually being fined and jailed for choosing to live an off-grid existence. From Costilla County, Colorado trying to ban people from building off-grid homes or camping on their own land, to the federal government actually trying to make it illegal to live in a tiny home or off-the-grid RV, there are a growing number of government agencies attempting to regulate this lifestyle out of existence."

On the matter of Costilla County, Colorado, Jay Syrmopoulos at *The Free Thought* reveals: "Across the U.S., local zoning officials are making it increasingly difficult for people to go off the grid, in some instances threatening people with jail time for collecting rainwater or not hooking into local utilities. As zoning laws have increasingly targeted the off-grid lifestyle, many have moved to the Southwestern U.S. as an escape from overzealous zoning officials.

"In Costilla County, Colorado, there has been a major influx of off-grid residents to the San Luis Valley. The combination of lax zoning regulations, cheap property, and an already thriving community of self-reliant off-grid homesteaders has led to many new residents.

"The off-grid lifestyle, enjoyed by an estimated 800 people, is now being threatened as county officials have recently made moves to essentially regulate and license the lifestyle into oblivion.

Advances in technology and materials are making it easier for people to live off the grid, finding ways to build homes out of recycled materials, generate power from wind and solar energy, and collect and purify water.

"Tensions boiled over during a county commissioners' meeting in San Louis, Colorado, devolving into a shouting match between homesteaders and police. One of the major points of contention is the county's attempt to ban camping on your own property, in an effort to force the off-grid homesteaders back onto the grid."

Yes, in today's world you really can be banned from camping out on your very own land. *Counter Current News* explains the mind-boggling and outrageous situation: "For many it's a lifelong dream to get 'off the grid' and live self-sufficiently. But unplugging from municipal services has been ruled illegal by a court in Cape Coral, Florida. Special Magistrate Harold S. Eskin ruled that Robin Speronis is not allowed to live on her own private property without being hooked up to the city's water system.

"He admitted that she had the right to live without utility power, but said that her alternative power sources must always first be approved by the city. Speronis has been taking a stand for years against the city of Cape Coral. Back in November of 2013 a code enforcement officer attempted to evict her for 'living without utilities.'

"The city's argument is that the International Property Maintenance Code was 'violated' by her reliance on rain water rather than paying the city for water. The IPMC also would make it a crime for her to use solar panels instead of being tied into the electric grid. 'It was a mental fistfight,' Todd Allen, Speronis' attorney said regarding Eskin's review of the case. 'There's an inherent conflict in the code.' Allen says that at this point the argument is just that Speronis must 'hook up' to the grid, even if she doesn't use utilities from it."

The New World Order grip is getting ever tighter.

ONE-WORLD CURRENCY

If there is one thing that unites everyone on the planet, it's the need for money. Without it, none of us can survive. For the New World Order, however, the plan is to create a global, one-world currency—a currency that will be the veritable hallmark of the NWO. In 2015, the BBC informed its audience of the following: "When you look back, you'll remember it as the day the Chinese yuan began its journey to become one of the world's most important currencies. The International Monetary Fund (IMF) has announced that the yuan is now part of an elite basket of currencies that until now included only the US dollar, the Japanese yen, the euro and the British pound. The yuan won't actually start being a part of the basket until September 2016—so this move won't have any immediate impact on financial markets. But don't kid yourself. This largely symbolic gesture is an historic one—and a sign that China is rising ever faster and further on the global financial stage. So what does that mean for the rest of us? *Well, by some accounts it's the start of a whole new world order.* Nomura Securities predicts that by 2030 the yuan will become one of the top three major international currencies—'a peer to the US dollar and the euro as the most used currencies in the world.'"

ABC News has also taken keen notice of how China—a key player in the New World Order—is practically insisting on a new currency: "China is calling for a global currency to replace the dominant dollar, showing a growing assertiveness on revamping the world economy ahead of next week's London summit on the financial crisis. The surprise proposal by Beijing's central bank governor reflects unease about its vast holdings of U.S. government bonds and adds to Chinese pressure to overhaul a global financial system dominated by the dollar and Western governments. Both the United States and the European Union brushed off the idea.

"The world economic crisis shows the 'inherent vulnerabilities and systemic risks in the existing international monetary system,' Gov. Zhou Xiaochuan said in an essay released Monday by the bank. He recommended creating a currency made up of a basket of global currencies and controlled by the International Monetary Fund and said it would help 'to achieve the objective of safeguarding global economic and financial stability.' Zhou did not mention the dollar by name. But in an unusual step, the essay was published in both Chinese and English, making clear it was meant for a foreign audience."

In a report titled "Adapting the International Monetary System to Face 21st Century Challenges," the United Nations demands: "More intense debate on and reforms to the international monetary system imply that the current system is unable to respond appropriately and adequately to challenges that have appeared, or become more acute, in recent years. This paper focuses on four such challenges: ensuring an orderly exit from global imbalances, facilitating more complementary adjustments between surplus and deficit countries without recessionary impacts, better supporting international trade by reducing currency volatility and better providing development

The euro entered everyday markets in 2002, when coins and paper money became available to the public. Euros are the currency for all the European Union states.

and climate finance. After describing them, it proposes reforms to enable the international monetary system to better respond to these challenges."

At *Occupy Corporatism*, Susanne Posel states on this issue above: "They recommend movement toward a global currency that will replace all current currencies. Revaluation will be accessed and the worth of money would redistribute with oversight of the IMF, WTO and ultimately the UN. This would be the beginning of the UN's securitization of the world's monetary value and ability to trade for goods and services. Whether a country prospered or collapsed would be in the decisive right of the UN. A sort of economic terrorism by effectively controlling the flow."

ORIGINS OF THE NEW WORLD ORDER

Although the term "New World Order" is part and parcel of our world today, it is rarely noted that its origins are not just years but decades old. On November 27, 1915, Nicholas Murray Butler, while speaking for the Union League of Philadelphia, said: "The old world order changed when this warstorm broke. The old international order passed away as suddenly, as unexpectedly, and as completely as if it had been wiped out by a gigantic flood, by a great tempest, or by a volcanic eruption. The old world order died with the setting of that day's sun and a new world order is being born while I speak, with birth-pangs so terrible that it seems almost incredible."

M. C. Alexander, who was the executive secretary of the American Association for International Conciliation, stated four years after Nicholas Murray Butler: "The peace conference has assembled. It will make the most momentous decisions in history, and upon these decisions will rest the stability of the new world order and the future peace of the world."

Dr. Augusto O. Thomas, the president of the World Federation of Education Associations, made the following statement in a 1931 book, *International Understanding: Agencies Educating for a New World*: "If there are those who think we are to jump immediately into a new world order, actuated by complete understanding and brotherly love, they are doomed to disappointment. If we are ever to approach that time, it will be after patient and persistent effort of long duration. The present international situation of mistrust and fear can only be corrected by a formula of equal status, continuously applied, to every phase of international contacts, until the cobwebs of the old order are brushed out of the minds of the people of all lands."

In October 1940, these words were spoken at the House of Bishops and the House of Clerical and Lay Deputies of the Protestant Episcopal Church in their General Convention: "The term Internationalism has been popularized in recent years to cover an interlocking financial, political, and economic world force for the purpose of establishing a World Government. Today Internationalism is heralded from pulpit and platform as a 'League of Nations' or a 'Federated Union' to which the United States must surrender a definite part of its National Sovereignty. The World Government plan is being advocated under such alluring names as the 'New International Order,' 'The New World Order,' 'World Union Now,' 'World Commonwealth of Nations,' 'World Community,' etc. All the terms have the same objective; however, the line of approach may be religious or political according to the taste or training of the individual."

Also in October 1940, the *New York Times* ran an article titled "New World Order Pledged to Jews." In part, the article stated: "In the first public declaration on the Jewish question since the outbreak of the war, Arthur Greenwood, member without portfolio in the British War Cabinet, assured the Jews of the United States that when victory was achieved an effort would be made to found a new world order based on the ideals of 'justice and peace.'"

The Declaration of the Federation of the World, which was issued by the Congress on World Federation, noted: "If totalitarianism wins this conflict, the world will be ruled by tyrants, and individuals will be slaves. If democracy wins, the nations of the earth will be united in a commonwealth of free peoples, and individuals, wherever found, will be the sovereign units of the new world order."

One year later, specifically in June 1942, the *Philadelphia Enquirer* wrote: "Undersecretary of State Sumner Welles tonight called for the early creation of an international organization of anti-Axis nations to control the world during the period between the armistice at the end of the present war and the setting up of a new world order on a permanent basis."

A December 1942 *New York Times* article, on the American Institute of Judaism, said: "The statement went on to say that the spiritual teachings of religion must become the foundation for the new world order and that national sovereignty must be subordinate to the higher moral law of God."

"There are some plain common-sense considerations applicable to all these attempts at world planning. They can be briefly stated: To talk of blueprints for the future or building a world order is, if properly understood, suggestive, but it is also dangerous. Societies grow far more truly than they are built. A constitution for a new world order is never like a blueprint for a skyscraper," wrote Norman Thomas in his 1944 book, *What is Our Destiny?*

"He [John Foster Dulles] stated directly to me that he had every reason to believe that the Governor [Thomas E. Dewey of New York] accepts his point of view and that he is personally convinced that this is the policy that he would promote with great vigor if elected. So it is fair to say that on the first round the Sphinx of Albany has established himself as a prima facie champion of a strong and definite new world order." Those were the words of Ralph W. Page in the May 1944 edition of the *Philadelphia Bulletin*.

As all of the above shows, in decades long gone, the term "New World Order" meant many things to many people. Very few are in any doubt as to what it means today.

ORWELLIAN

One word, more than any other, which gets bandied around when it comes to the matter of the New World Order, and that's "Orwellian." The word is derived from George Orwell, whose 1949 novel *Nineteen Eighty-Four* (or *1984*) plunges the reader into a terrible future, one in which the human race is kept in check by a ruthless ruling elite, but what exactly does "Orwellian" mean? An adjective based on Orwell's last name, it is an adjective describing a society in which the citizens are completely dominated by an all-powerful government that uses constant surveillance, police brutality, propaganda, alteration of history, and misinformation.

When it comes to that term, Orwellian, Sam Jordison of *The Guardian* says: "A telling example comes up during a fascinating talk about Orwell from Christopher Hitchens. In this podcast from the rightwing American organization the Library of Economics and Liberty, the interviewer tries to suggest that Hitchens is a good Orwellian for supporting the war in Iraq. This makes an odd kind of sense. Hitchens, in his mind at least, was both standing up to fascism and refusing to be cowed by leftwing popular opinion, just as Orwell fought Franco in the Spanish Civil War, but also risked ostracism—not to mention quite a few publishing deals—by proclaiming the truth about Stalin.

"But plenty would argue that the anti-imperialist socialist Orwell would never have supported George W. Bush's vision of American empire. Clearly, the term is used selectively and subjectively. If you say that someone is Orwellian in character, the chances are that this person is on your side and jolly good too. Just as—to move on to the second strand of meaning—saying anything else is 'Orwellian' means it is something that you dislike."

Tom Head, an expert in the field of civil liberties, provides this: "In Orwell's novel, all citizens of Oceania are monitored by cameras, are fed fabricated news stories by the government, are forced to worship a mythical government leader called Big Brother, are indoctrinated to believe nonsense statements (the mantra 'WAR IS PEACE, SLAVERY IS FREEDOM, IGNO-

Part of an Orwellian future involves living in a society in which your every move is watched by omnipresent cameras, much like these in London, England, a city noted for street cameras.

RANCE IS STRENGTH'), and are subject to torture and execution if they question the order of things.

"The word is sometimes used to describe a particularly anti-libertarian government policy, but it is also sometimes used to describe the peculiar, nonsensical thought process behind Oceania's social structure—a thought process in which ideas that are obviously self-contradictory are accepted as true based on the fact that an authority figure is asserting them.

"The Bush administration's No Child Left Behind program (which is unfunded and therefore technically leaves children behind) and Clear Skies Initiative (which weakens anti-pollution regulations and therefore technically makes skies less clear) are often cited as examples of Orwellian policies, but so are London's omnipresent surveillance cameras and North Korea's patriotism indoctrination camps."

In an article titled "Orwellian Nightmare Unleashed on Schoolkids," Leo Hohmann says: "Parents and students have been 'opting out' of high-stakes testing in record numbers over the past year, saying the standardized tests waste valuable instruction time, cause undue stress and often measure 'skills' that have nothing to do with academic knowledge. Rather than merely asking for a right or wrong answer to a math, history or science question, the new assessment industry is capable of boring into a child's attitudes, values, opinions and beliefs, all of which parents and privacy advocates say is no business of the government's. The pushback has led some state education systems to recommend a reduction in the amount of high-stakes testing in public schools."

Orwellian: so, now you know.

See also the entries "1984" and "Perpetual War."

OVERPOPULATION

That planet Earth cannot adequately house an ever-growing population indefinitely is not a matter of any doubt. That the world's weather is changing—

in ways that are both hostile and suspicious—has given rise to the likelihood that global warming is the culprit. Humankind's ever-growing need for dwindling fossil fuels, combined with its near-exponentially increasing pollution of the planet's ecosystem, has almost irreversibly altered our future and has raised fears that our most precious commodity—water—will soon become scarce.

In 2012, Britain's *Guardian* newspaper reported: "Fresh water is crucial to human society—not just for drinking, but also for farming, washing and many other activities. It is expected to become increasingly scarce in the future, and this is partly due to climate change." It was added: "Especially little is known about future declines in regional groundwater resources because of lack of research on this topic, even though around 50% of global domestic water supply comes from groundwater. Although scientists are making progress in reducing uncertainty about fresh water scarcity, these kinds of unknowns mean that water supply strategies must be adaptable so that they can be effective under different scenarios."

In May 2013, Melanie McDonagh of the *Spectator* noted that the Royal Society had published a paper by Paul and Anne Ehrlich. Its title: "Can a Collapse of Global Civilization Be Avoided?"

A crowded street in Kyoto, Japan, is one of any number of examples of how cramped our planet has become, which could lead to global war and the collapse of civilization.

Of the question that the title of the report asked, McDonagh said: "No, is the short answer, unless we adopt 'dramatic cultural change.'"

The Ehrlichs noted: "Today, for the first time, humanity's global civilization … is threatened with collapse by an array of environmental problems. Humankind finds itself engaged in what Prince Charles described as 'an act of suicide on a grand scale.' The human predicament is driven by overpopulation, overconsumption of natural resources and the use of unnecessarily environmentally damaging technologies."

McDonagh added: "The authors assume an increase in population to 9.5 billion by 2050. Result: 'global collapse.'"

It could be argued that a radically smaller worldwide population would help allay—and perhaps even successfully keep at bay—dwindling water supplies, as noted by the *Guardian* in 2012. But there are other things that have certain people worried, such as fuel. In 2014, *USA Today* reported that the planet's entire oil reserves may be gone by 2065. It was *USA Today*'s juddering and shuddering revelation that led *Gas 2* (champions of so-called "green cars") to state: "These estimates are actually 1.1% more than last year, thanks in part to growing estimates of American shale oil. Of course keep in mind that the oil industry is regularly growing or shrinking estimated energy reserves, with California's Monterey Shale having its reserves downgraded some 96%. There's also suspicion that countries like Saudi Arabia are outright lying about how much crude they actually have left. So yeah. Skepticism."

Gas 2 cautioned, however: "53 years sounds like awhile, right? Well not really, but the bigger problem is that, as humanity reaches the last of its oil reserves, without an adequate energy transition in place, some countries could be caught flat-footed."

"Flat-footed" may very well prove to be an understatement of mammoth proportions. Worldwide panic, chaos, anarchy, and disaster might be far closer to the truth of what awaits us. And it's this issue—of potential planetary collapse—that has led to dark and disturbing theories that powerful figures have decided the only way to save the future of humanity is to shrink it and to shrink it *soon*. Does evidence of such a nightmarish program exist? Astonishingly, yes, it does. Make no mistake, the issue of overpopulation—and how to deal with it—is a major issue.

The speed at which the human race is infesting the planet (which is not unjustified terminology) is as alarming as it is amazing. It was in the very earliest years of the nineteenth century that the world's population finally reached one billion. It was not until around 1930 that the population was doubled to two billion. By the dawning of the Sixties, three billion of us were on Earth, four billion by the mid-Seventies, and five billion by the late Eighties. As the twenty-first century began, the number was six billion. In 2013, we hit seven billion. You may not like—or even be prepared for—what is to come next. Current estimates are that 2124 will roughly be when the Earth finds itself buckling under the weight of eight billion people. By 2040, we'll be at nine.

The New World Order is actively seeking ways to lower the population to a much smaller—and easily controllable—level. We have to find a way to tackle this issue that doesn't take us down the mass-murder-based path that the New World Order is intent on following.

PATRIOT ACT

The events of September 11, 2001—coupled with the anthrax attacks that occurred shortly afterward—provoked terror, fear, and feelings of deep paranoia and angst within the American population. They also provoked something else: the rapid passing of what became known as the Patriot Act. It was—and to this very day remains—without doubt one of the most controversial pieces of legislation ever put into place by government officials. Very few people doubted that, post-9/11, America needed to create new policies and programs to combat terror-driven attacks on the nation and its people. For many, however, the controversial content of the Patriot Act was way over the top and something that had the excessive ability to take away the rights, freedoms, and everyday existence of American citizens—and to do so with shocking speed if it was so deemed necessary.

It was on October 24, 2001—only a month and a half after 9/11 forever changed the United States—that Congress passed the act. It was not an act that everyone in government was happy about, however. The vote was 357 to 66 in the House. Twenty-four hours later, in the Senate, things were very different: 98 to a dissenting 1. Like it or like it not, the Patriot Act was now a reality and one that was here to stay.

Given that the Patriot Act was designed to help lessen the potential for terror attacks on the United States and its overseas interests, why did it so quickly

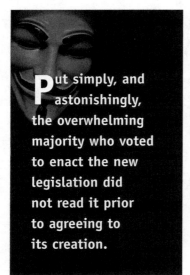

Put simply, and astonishingly, the overwhelming majority who voted to enact the new legislation did not read it prior to agreeing to its creation.

become the target of critics? The answer is as simple as it is disturbing: the act allowed for widespread monitoring of U.S. citizens in ways that had never been used before. It allowed for extreme measures to be taken—all in the name of national security—to keep the nation safe, and, said the critics, could be enforced to try to turn America into a nation of Orwellian proportions. One does not have to be a conspiracy theorist to see how such a sorry state of affairs could, one day, come to pass.

Included in the Patriot Act are clauses that allow government agencies and personnel to (a) access someone's home without their permission or even their knowledge; (b) hold individuals, in prison-style facilities, indefinitely; and (c) dig through emails, phone calls, and personal bank records—and all without any need for permission from a court or a judge.

Particularly chilling: The Patriot Act gives the government carte blanche access to the reading habits of each and every U.S. citizen and resident. It does so by allowing government agencies to record the title of every single book taken out of a library, to note who is borrowing the book, and to store their physical address in relevant data banks. It should be noted that while many—even within government and in the court system, have argued loudly and soundly that all of this is outrageously unconstitutional, it has not made a single bit of difference.

Although certain changes were made to the legislation in 2005, the Patriot Act continues to stand as an example of the kind of thing that would have given the likes of the aforementioned George Orwell nightmares. As for the New World Order, however, it is exactly what they want, and need, to ensure its goal of total, unending surveillance of the nation.

Only eight days after the attacks on the World Trade Center and the Pentagon, new legislation was presented to Congress by the Department of Justice. It was a bill entitled the Anti-Terrorism Act. It was also a bill that introduced Congress to the Patriot Act. It's an act whose very title has meaning. "Patriot" stands for *Provide Appropriate Tools Required to Intercept and Obstruct Terrorism*. In one sense, that was all well and good since the act would clearly help in the fight against those who wish to do us harm. It was, however, the negative impact that the tools used in the fight could have on American society that concerned so many. Indeed, the Anti-Terrorism Act swept aside preexisting acts designed to protect the rights of each and every U.S. citizen, including the Bank Secrecy Act, the Electronic Communications Privacy Act, the Money Laundering Control Act, and the Foreign Intelligence Surveillance Act.

One of the most outrageous aspects of the story of the Patriot Act is how it came to be so easily passed and why did only one person oppose it, Senator

Russell Feingold, of Wisconsin. Put simply, and astonishingly, the overwhelming majority who voted to enact the new legislation did not read it prior to agreeing to its creation. Worse still, there are solid indications that it was deliberately made difficult for senators to see the bill before passing it.

Alex Jones wrote: "Congressman Ron Paul (R-Tex) told the *Washington Times* that no member of Congress was allowed to read the first Patriot Act that was passed by the House on October 27, 2001. The first Patriot Act was universally decried by civil libertarians and Constitutional scholars from across the political spectrum." Jones also noted that William Safire, writing for the *New York Times*, detailed the first Patriot Act's powers by saying that "President Bush was seizing dictatorial control."

Jones continued: "The secretive tactics being used by the White House and Speaker Hastert to keep even the existence of this legislation secret would be more at home in Communist China than in the United States. The fact that Dick Cheney publicly managed the steamroller passage of the first Patriot Act, ensuring that no one was allowed to read it and publicly threatening members of Congress that if they didn't vote in favor of it that they would be blamed for the next terrorist attack, is by the White House's own definition terrorism. The move to clandestinely craft and then bully passage of any legislation by the Executive Branch is clearly an impeachable offense."

This scenario was further noted by Michael Moore in his 2004 documentary *Fahrenheit 9/11*. Congressman John Conyers makes an incredible statement in the movie on the matter of those who did or did not read the act before passing it. In Conyer's very own words: "We don't read most of the bills: do you really know what that would entail if we read every bill that we passed?"

Faced with such an extraordinary and mind-numbing statement—that major congressional figures do not read the bills they may be asked to pass bills that can have significant bearing on the entire American population—it's hardly surprising that the Patriot Act made an almost effortless transition from concept to reality. The passing of the law did not, however, stop numerous attempts to have the act modified and curtailed. At the same time that critics of the act were trying to reign in its abilities, however, New World Order personnel were trying to make it even more powerful.

PEARL HARBOR AND THE NEW WORLD ORDER PARALLELS

Arguably, it would only take a catastrophic false flag affair—such as the detonation of a dirty bomb or an atomic bomb in a major U.S. city—to allow the New World Order to take control, but, could such a thing really happen? It may already have happened. Witness, for example, the December 1941 events at Pearl Harbor, Hawaii, that plunged the United States into World War II, which was raging since September 1939, when Adolf Hitler and his Nazi hordes and cronies invaded Poland. Is it possible that people may have allowed Pearl Harbor to happen in the same way that they may have permitted 9/11 to go ahead, specifically to allow for the invasion of much of the Middle East to occur? The unfortunate state of affairs suggests this is precisely what happened.

When Japanese forces launched a surprise attack on the U.S. naval base, it resulted in death on a scale near unimaginable. More than 350 Japanese aircraft—comprised of bombers, fighters, and planes equipped with torpedoes—targeted Pearl Harbor. It was an attack that killed 2,403 American citizens and residents. Nearly 200 American military planes were destroyed. Each and every battleship in the harbor was severely damaged, of which four sunk. As for the Japanese, their losses were the exact opposite: fewer than thirty aircraft, a handful of small submarines, and not even seventy personnel.

The USS *Shaw* sinks during the Japanese attack of Pearl Harbor in this photo.

In all of this carnage, chaos, and conflict, a disturbing rumor began to circulate, one which continues to circulate to this very day. It suggests that some people in the governments of the United States and the United Kingdom had secret, advance warning of the Pearl Harbor attack but specifically stayed quiet and allowed the terrible events to occur, thus justifying bringing America into the war. It is a seldom discussed fact, but such is the ongoing endurance of the allegations that the attack on Pearl Harbor was known about in advance that the U.S. government has initiated *ten* separate official inquiries to try to get to the bottom of the rumors. Of those ten, nine were undertaken in the 1940s, while the most recent was in 1995.

Within conspiracy circles, the theory that someone, deep within officialdom, knew the attack was going to occur and allowed it to happen still very much endures. One significant part of the theory revolves around the matter of code breaking. American code breakers had, *prior* to the attacks on Pearl Harbor, successfully cracked a significant number of the ciphers that the Japanese military used. Certainly, the U.S. Navy's Office of Naval Intelligence (ONI) had teams of people working day and night to crack the Japanese's codes. The Army's Signal Intelligence Service (SIS) was doing likewise. That at least some of the codes were broken is an established fact.

Much of the controversy surrounds *97-shiki ōbun inji-ki*—or what the U.S. government code-named *Purple*. It was a secure, diplomatic code used at the highest level of the Japanese government. Those who adhere to the conspiracy theories argue that since the attacks on Pearl Harbor were clearly planned in advance and were steeped in overwhelming secrecy, why is it that nothing of relevance was picked up from the widespread penetration of *Purple*? Their argument is that relevant data *was* obtained and decoded, but—as per the conspiracy theory—was ignored in favor of the attack being permitted to happen, and it wasn't just a few dozen people working to crack Japan's codes, something that might have led to crucial material being overlooked. Collectively, it was in excess of *seven hundred*—and not a single, solitary word relevant to the Pearl Harbor attacks was ever found and decoded?

A second area of concern revolves around the activities of a certain ship, the SS *Lurline*, a huge liner that had the capacity to hold more than seven hundred people and which was launched in 1932. An enduring story goes that as the SS *Lurline* was traveling from San Francisco to Hawaii, it picked up very unusual communications using a form of Morse code. Contrary to popular assumption, more than one kind of Morse code exists. In fact, more than a few exist. One is a Japanese variation. When the SS *Lurline's* chief expert in the field of Morse code, Leslie Grogan, heard the messages, he concluded they were Japanese. They were also, reportedly, emanating from the east and coming this way.

The Japanese denied they engaged in any kind of chatter or communication during the flight toward Pearl Harbor. Japanese military papers of 1942, now in the public domain, note: "In order to keep strict radio silence, steps such as taking off fuses in the circuit, and holding and sealing the keys were taken. During the operation, the strict radio silence was perfectly carried out. The Kido Butai used the radio instruments for the first time on the day of the attack since they had been fixed at the base approximately twenty days before and proved they worked well. Paper flaps had been inserted between key points of some transmitters on board Akagi to keep the strictest radio silence."

Of course, the entire matter could be resolved by carefully studying the documentation and data that was prepared by Leslie Grogan and which was provided to the 14th Naval District, Honolulu. Unfortunately, that same documentation and data cannot be found—*anywhere*.

Another bone of contention relates to a statement made by Vice Admiral Frank E. Beatty, who strongly suggested that a war between Japan and the United States was desired: "Prior to December 7, it was evident even to me that we were pushing Japan into a corner. I believed that it was the desire of President Roosevelt, and Prime Minister Churchill that we get into the war, as they felt the Allies could not win without us and all our efforts to cause the Germans to declare war on us failed; the conditions we imposed upon Japan—to get out of China, for example—were so severe that we knew that nation could not accept them. We were forcing her so severely that we could have known that she would react toward the United States. All her preparations in a military way—and we knew their over-all import—pointed that way."

On a similar path, on October 7, 1940, a document was prepared by ONI operative Lieutenant Commander Arthur H. McCollum. He listed a number of theoretical issues and scenarios that might provoke the Japanese military into attacking the United States. McCollum also said: "If by these means Japan could be led to commit an overt act of war, so much the better."

Even more telling are the words of a man named Jonathan Daniels. At the time Pearl Harbor occurred, he was President Roosevelt's administrative assistant. Daniels said of the events of December 7, 1941, and of Roosevelt's reaction to it: "The blow was heavier than he had hoped it would necessarily be. But the risks paid off; even the loss was worth the price."

PERPETUAL WAR

George Orwell's book *1984*, which was published in 1949, tells the story of a grim, New World Order-style society that rules the planet with an iron fist—as we have seen. There is one issue, in particular, that Orwell focuses on and which is becoming all too real in our world today is that of perpetual war. In Orwell's story, continuous, neverending war is fought between the three superpowers: Oceania, Eurasia, and Eastasia. Interestingly, Orwell sows the seeds of conspiracy with suggestions that, on occasion, the respective powers launch false flags on their own people—specifically to ensure that support for the wars remains high. The false flag issue, of course, comes into play in the 9/11 and 7/7 atrocities. But, why would any state, nation, or superpower wish to see its people in a constant state of conflict? Orwell himself, addressed this very point. He stated: "The war is not meant to be won, it is meant to be continuous. Hierarchical society is only possible on the basis of poverty and ignorance. This new version is the past and no different past can ever have existed. In principle the war effort is always planned to keep society on the brink of starvation. The war is waged by the ruling group against its own subjects and its object is not the victory over either Eurasia or East Asia, but to keep the very structure of society intact."

Orwell's words make it abundantly clear that perpetual war would work to the great advantage of the New World Order.

America has been fighting one war after another for almost its entire history. Perpetual war is a way for ruling elites to foster fear, patriotism, and control over a populace, as George Orwell has explained.

In 2003, when the invasion of Iraq loomed large, Darren K. Carlson, the government and politics editor at Gallup, wrote: "With tensions between the United States and Iraq rising and North Korea's nuclear ambition now squarely in the public eye, the prospect of war looms large over the American public. While the United States maintains by all accounts the world's greatest military force, many Americans (particularly younger males) may wonder if a war would bring about the return of the military draft in this country. Gallup polling conducted earlier this month shows that roughly a quarter of the population (27%) currently thinks the United States should return to the military draft, while the majority (69%) thinks it should not."

More than a quarter of the population taking the view that the draft should be returned is not insignificant, and calls for conscription to be reinstated are still being made today with North Korea, ISIS, and Russia all flexing their muscles. In February 2016 at *U.S. News*, Lawrence J. Korb and Eric Goepel said the following: "The time has come to draw down the active duty military and reinstate the draft. If the U.S. has an interest to protect, it should have to rely on calling on potentially all its citizens to serve. There is hope that when Americans have skin in the game once again, the choice to go to war will not be a foregone conclusion.

"We have seen what relying on a small percentage of our nation to fight our battles has accomplished: thousands dead, tens of thousands injured, trillions spent with billions more on the way, and a failure to accomplish even the most modest of objectives. Our leaders have proven unequal to the task of managing the conflicts they embroil us in. To shy away from our collective obligation to national defense is to assure that we will have war without end, with nothing to show for it but crushing debt and wasted lives."

It's apt—and chillingly so—that we end this section with another quote from George Orwell: "The war, therefore if we judge it by the standards of previous wars, is merely an imposture. It is like the battles between certain ruminant animals whose horns are incapable of hurting one another. But though it is unreal it is not meaningless. It eats up the surplus of consumable goods, and it helps to preserve the special mental atmosphere that the hierarchical society needs. War, it will be seen, is now a purely internal affair."

Orwell continued: "In the past, the ruling groups of all countries, although they might recognize their common interest and therefore limit the destructiveness of war, did fight against one another, and the victor always plundered the vanquished. In our own day they are not fighting against one another at all. The war is waged by each ruling group against its own subjects, and the object of the war is not to make or prevent conquests of territory, but to keep the structure of society intact. The very word "war," therefore, has become misleading. It would probably be accurate to say that by becoming continuous war has ceased to exist.

"The peculiar pressure that is exerted on human beings between the Neolithic Age and the early twentieth century has disappeared and has been replaced by something quite different. The effect would be much the same if the three superstates, instead of fighting one another, should agree to live in perpetual peace, each inviolate within its own boundaries. For in that case each would still be a self-contained universe, freed forever from the sobering influence of external danger. A peace that was truly permanent would be the same as a permanent war. This—although the vast majority of Party members understand it only in a shallower sense—is the inner meaning of the Party slogan: WAR IS PEACE."

Will *1984*'s state of perpetual war become the norm in the years—possible even the immediate years—ahead? If the New World Order has things its way, the answer is almost certainly "Yes!"

See also the entries "1984" and "Orwellian."

PINE GAP

While just about everyone has heard of the National Security Agency—largely as a result of the revelations made by Edward Snowden regarding massive, widespread surveillance of the U.S. population—far less is known about Australia's equivalent, which is known as Pine Gap. Bill Chalker, an author and researcher, says: "Pine Gap (code named 'Merino') located near Alice Springs and described as a 'Joint Defense Space Research Facility,' has long been a subject of concern and attracted some mystique, principally because of its clandestine role in intelligence gathering. Much is known about its sensitive role as a ground station for the US defense satellite program and its part in the NSA and CIA presence in Australia."

While very little data comes out of Pine Gap, there were some notable releases of material. In 1974, for example, in an article titled "Spying Around," which was published in *Nation Review*, William H. Martin revealed the following: "The Pine Gap research facility near Alice Springs has managed to keep secret, until now, one of the most unbelievable research projects in the world. The United States has been carrying out continuous research into electromagnetic propulsion (EMP for short) at Pine Gap since it was established in 1966.... I understand that last minute flaws in the design and operation of the EMP vehicles have probably put the completion date back by four years (to 1979). Research into electromagnetic propulsion began in the United States soon after world war two. After some successful results it became necessary to move the experimentation from populated areas to more remote spots. Security aspects of the EMP project have included hypnotic and post

An aerial photo of Pine Gap, the communications facility near Alice Springs, Australia, that is run by both the U.S. and Australian governments.

hypnotic keys implanted in personnel prior to their acceptance into the project."

Bringing matters far more up to date, in 2016, the U.K.'s *Daily Mail* newspaper did a major exposé on Pine Gap and stated: "Pine Gap is the single most important US intelligence facility outside of America, according to the Nautilus Institute and employs 1000 people. It collects data for US drones, signals intelligence and provides early warning on missile launches as well as providing information on armed forces in Afghanistan. It is understood that the US can control its spy satellites from Pine Gap and its antennas are used to 'listen to Asia.' It has three surveillance systems but its main purpose is to serve as the ground control station or geosynchronous signals intelligence (SIGINT) satellites developed by the CIA."

There is, however, another aspect to Pine Gap, one which may have a major bearing on matters relative to the New World Order. Dr. Jean Francois Gille is someone cited in Chris Verismo's *The Universal Seduction, Volume II*. Verismo states: "Dr. Gille tells us that Pine Gap has enormous computers connected to US, Krugersdorp South Africa, Guam, Canberra, Antarctica, US base counterparts, which collects information from these countries, about finance, technology, and everything about the average citizen.... Much furniture has been delivered by plane from the United States. The locals also say that an enormous amount of food is stocked in warehouses of what could well be a true multi-leveled underground city. Dr. Gille writes further that shares put on the market at the same time will cause a stock market crash of such magnitude that all the national economies of the West will collapse at the same time. Cash will be worthless, and the risks of a global confrontation (planned!) will be high. The purpose of Pine Gap and other underground bases will become obvious. If a global confrontation is going to break out, those bases will serve as a place of safety for the politicians and their staff, as well as the international financiers, their families and friends."

POPULATION CULLING

Is a nefarious, secret, and deadly group hard at work to reduce the world's population—and to reduce it quickly, drastically, and to levels that will amount to nothing less than full-blown decimation? Certainly, one only has to take a look at the case of Adolf Hitler. He waged a determined war of extermination against the Jews during World War II, and, as a result, and with phenomenal, horrific speed, an entire race of people came close to being systematically wiped off the face of the planet. Could such a thing, one day, happen again? If it does, will it be due to the actions of a future Hitler, a madman with lunatic delusions of grandeur? Maybe not: conspiracy theorists maintain that the death knell for not just millions, but for *billions*, might come from none other than a secret cabal within the heart of the United Nations.

Many conspiracy theorists believe that a plan to cull the human population began in 1974, specifically on December 10 of that year, when a highly controversial report was prepared for the U.S. National Security Council. It was a report, attendant project, and study overseen by one of the most powerful figures in global politics, Henry Kissinger, who held such positions as U.S. secretary of state and national security advisor to the presidential office. The report was titled "Implications of Worldwide Population Growth for U.S. Security and Overseas Interests."

As the authors noted, in those particular countries where growth and development were far from being on par with the rest of the planet—such as Thailand, Pakistan, Brazil, Ethiopia, Egypt, Turkey, and Nigeria—it was possible that with falling food supplies, dwindling water and fuel, and more and more people, demands from the relevant populations for action to combat famine would soon result in civil unrest and uncontrollable anarchy. Kissinger's people worried about another thing. If the economies of countries with exploding populations collapsed, the result might be that the United States would be unable to import from those same countries things that were essential to its own economy. In that scenario, everyone suffers, or, maybe not: Kissinger was determined that the United States would not fall, even if other nations did. It was up to the United Nations and the United States to solve the problem.

> If the economies of countries with exploding populations collapsed, the result might be that the United States would be unable to import from those same countries things that were essential to its own economy.

Clearly, as the following extracts show, a great deal of thought had gone into how the rise of populations in the underdeveloped world could possibly bring the United States to its knees: "The U.S. economy will require large and increasing amounts of minerals from abroad, especially from less developed countries. That fact gives the U.S. enhanced interest in the political, economic, and social stability of the supplying countries. Wherever a lessening of population pressures through reduced birth rates can increase the prospects for such stability, population policy becomes relevant to resource supplies and to the economic interests of the United States."

The document continues: "The location of known reserves of higher grade ores of most minerals favors increasing dependence of all industrialized regions on imports from less developed countries. The real problems of mineral supplies lie not in basic physical sufficiency, but in the politico-economic issues of access, terms for exploration and exploitation, and division of the benefits among producers, consumers, and host country governments."

The following anticipates how things could turn very bad for the United States: "Whether through government action, labor conflicts, sabotage, or civil disturbance, the smooth flow of needed materials will be jeopardized. Although population pressure is obviously not the only factor involved, these types of frustrations are much less likely under conditions of slow or zero population growth."

The brains behind the report then targeted the people themselves, their collective mindset, and how to get around increasing issues of concern. In a section titled "Populations with a High Proportion of Growth," it was noted: "The young people, who are in much higher proportions in many LDCs, are likely to be more volatile, unstable, prone to extremes, alienation and violence than an older population. These young people can more readily be persuaded to attack the legal institutions of the government or real property of the 'establishment,' 'imperialists,' multinational corporations, or other—often foreign—influences blamed for their troubles."

There were words of warning in the report, too: "We must take care that our activities should not give the appearance to the LDCs of an industrialized country policy directed against the LDCs. Caution must be taken that in any approaches in this field we support in the LDCs are ones we can support within this country. 'Third World' leaders should be in the forefront and obtain the credit for successful programs. In this context it is important to demonstrate to LDC leaders that such family planning programs have worked and can work within a reasonable period of time."

The authors of the report make an interesting statement: "In these sensitive relations, however, it is important in style as well as substance to avoid the appearance of coercion."

In other words, the report does not deny that nations might be coerced, only that there is a concerted effort to "avoid the appearance" of such.

So much for the 1970s—when the program of planetary extermination, on an obscene scale, is reported to have begun—but what of today? According to some, today it's downright out of control: "A reasonable estimate for an industrialized world society at the present North American material standard of living would be 1 billion. At the more frugal European standard of living, 2 to 3 billion would be possible," stated the United Nations' Global Diversity Assessment, in shockingly matter-of-fact fashion.

See also entry "United Nations Population Plot."

PRISM PROGRAM

On the matter of Edward Snowden and his many revelations concerning the massive, secret surveillance undertaken by the National Security Agency, the BBC provides the following: "The scandal broke in early June 2013 when the *Guardian* newspaper reported that the US National Security Agency (NSA) was collecting the telephone records of tens of millions of Americans. The paper published the secret court order directing telecommunications company Verizon to hand over all its telephone data to the NSA on an 'ongoing daily basis.' That report was followed by revelations in both the Washington Post and Guardian that the NSA tapped directly into the servers of nine Internet firms, including Facebook, Google, Microsoft and Yahoo, to track online communication in a surveillance program known as PRISM. Britain's electronic eavesdropping agency GCHQ was also accused of gathering information on the online companies via PRISM."

The *Guardian* newspaper, which was at the forefront of the Snowden disclosures, said in June 2013: "The National Security Agency has obtained direct access to the systems of Google, Facebook, Apple and other US Internet giants, according to a top secret document obtained by the *Guardian*. The NSA access is part of a previously undisclosed program called PRISM, which allows officials to collect material including search history, the content of emails, file transfers and live chats, the document says."

The *Guardian* added: "Although the presentation claims the program is run with the assistance of the companies, all those who responded to a Guardian request for comment on Thursday denied knowledge of any such program."

Indeed, Google, responding to the story, released the following statement: "Google cares deeply about the security of our users' data. We disclose user data to the government in accordance with the law, and we review all such requests carefully. From time to time, people allege that we have created a government 'back door' into our systems, but Google does not have a back door for the government to access private user data."

The *Guardian* also stated: "Several senior tech executives insisted that they had no knowledge of PRISM or of any similar scheme. They said they would never have been involved in such a program. 'If they are doing this, they are doing it without our knowledge,' one said. An Apple spokesman said it had 'never heard' of PRISM."

Nevertheless, the existence of the program is not a matter of any doubt. Plus, it has provoked a huge furor. In 2013, *The Verge* said of PRISM and

Edward Snowden: "There's the group of people most affected by PRISM and its sibling programs: the American public. On July 4th, 'Restore the Fourth' rallies in more than 100 US cities protested the government's surveillance programs, focusing on electronic privacy. It's not clear if public outrage will result in reform, but thanks to the dramatic actions of a young intelligence contractor, we now at least have the opportunity to discuss what the U.S. government has been hiding from the public in the name of national security."

See also the entry "Snowden, Edward."

PROJECT BLUE BEAM

Within the field of conspiracy theorizing, there are few greater controversies than Project Blue Beam. Allegedly, it is the brainchild of a secret group of powerful figures in, among many others, NASA, the United Nations, the Bilderbergers, the Trilateral Commission, and the Vatican. Project Blue Beam, so the story goes, will be at the forefront of a program to create a new society dominated by martial law and an iron-fisted world government.

This would come about by faking the Second Coming of Jesus Christ, specifically by using sophisticated, hologram-type technology to project huge images of the Son of God across the skies of the United States, Canada, Australia, and much of Europe. Other parts of the world will see massive images of Buddha, of Allah, of Krishna, of Mohammed, and of multiple other gods, depending on the regions, the people and their cultures, and the beliefs of the relevant nations.

In mere days, however, each and every one of those images will merge into one far more sinister and terrifying image: that of the Antichrist, who will inform the people of Earth that not a single one of the world's religions has the correct version of events. Only that of this nightmarish entity is the accurate version. As a result, the entire human race will be expected to bow down and worship the Antichrist.

Such a thing will result in worldwide chaos, disorder, and anarchy—which the people behind Project Blue Beam shrewdly know only all too well. With the world plunged into states of fear and mayhem, this terrible ruse will then allow the United Nations to coordinate a planetwide program to enslave the Earth's entire population.

The story is as fantastic as it is terrifying. But is it true?

The source of the Project Blue Beam story was Serge Monast, a journalist from Montreal, Quebec, Canada. Although Monast began in his career in regular journalism, by 1994, he was focused almost exclusively on conspiracy theories, including matters relative to Masonic-based conspiracy theories and matters relative to the one-world government scenario. It was at this time that Monast claimed to have uncovered massive amounts of secret information on Project Blue Beam and how it would be utilized to enslave all but that afore-mentioned elite. That Monast died in December 1996, of a heart attack, at the age of just fifty-one has led to suspicions that he was murdered by agents of this dangerous program. The reason: to prevent Monast from blowing the whistle, big-time, on the project.

The Watcher Files notes: "The infamous NASA Blue Beam Project has four different steps in order to implement the new age religion with the antichrist at its head. We must remember that the new age religion is the very foundation for the new world govern-ment, without which religion the dictatorship of the new world order is completely impossible. I'll repeat that: With-out a universal belief in the new age religion, the success of the new world order will be impossible! That is why the Blue Beam Project is so important to them, but has been so well hidden until now."

This would come about by faking the second coming of Jesus Christ, specifically by using sophisticated hologram-type technology to project huge images of the Son of God across the skies....

The Watcher Files adds that Project Blue Beam "involves a gigantic 'space show' with three-dimensional optical holo-grams and sounds, laser projection of multiple holographic images to different parts of the world, each receiving a dif-ferent image according to predominating regional national religious faith. This new 'god's' voice will be speaking in all languages."

David Openheimer, who has studied the Project Blue Beam claims, says: "The 'system' has already been tested. Holographic projections of the 'CHRIST IMAGE' have already been seen in some remote desert areas. These have only been reported in tabloid papers, so they are instantly rendered moot. They can also project images of alien craft, aliens, monsters, angels—you name it. Computers will coordinate the satellites and software will run the show-and-tell.

"Holography is based on very nearly identical signals combining to pro-duce and image, or hologram, with depth perception. This is equally applica-ble to acoustic (ELF, VLF, LF) waves as it is to optical phenomena.

"Specifically, the 'show' will consist of laser projections of multiple holo-graphic images to different parts of the planet, each receiving different images according to the predominating regional religious faith. Not a single area will be excluded. With computer animation and sound effects appearing to come from the depths of space, astonished followers of the various creeds will witness their own returned Messiah in spectacularly convincing lifelike realness."

Time may tell if Project Blue Beam plays a role in the looming New World Order. Let us sincerely hope it does not.

PROJECT FOR THE NEW AMERICAN CENTURY

A controversial body of powerful people, the Project for the New American Century (PNAC) was launched in 1997 and, according to their website, "is a non-profit, educational organization whose goal is to promote American global leadership. The Project is an initiative of the New Citizenship Project; the New Citizenship Project's chairman is William Kristol and its president is Gary Schmitt."

The organization's "Statement of Principles" reads as follows: "American foreign and defense policy is adrift. Conservatives have criticized the incoherent policies of the Clinton Administration. They have also resisted isolationist impulses from within their own ranks. But conservatives have not confidently advanced a strategic vision of America's role in the world. They have not set forth guiding principles for American foreign policy. They have allowed differences over tactics to obscure potential agreement on strategic objectives. And they have not fought for a defense budget that would maintain American security and advance American interests in the new century.

"We aim to change this. We aim to make the case and rally support for American global leadership. As the 20th century draws to a close, the United States stands as the world's preeminent power. Having led the West to victory in the Cold War, America faces an opportunity and a challenge: Does the United States have the vision to build upon the achievements of past decades? Does the United States have the resolve to shape a new century favorable to American principles and interests?

"We are in danger of squandering the opportunity and failing the challenge. We are living off the capital—both the military investments and the foreign policy achievements—built up by past administrations. Cuts in foreign affairs and defense spending, inattention to the tools of statecraft, and inconstant leadership are making it increasingly difficult to sustain American influence around the world. And the promise of short-term commercial benefits threatens to override strategic considerations. As a consequence, we are jeopardizing the nation's ability to meet present threats and to deal with potentially greater challenges that lie ahead.

"We seem to have forgotten the essential elements of the Reagan Administration's success: a military that is strong and ready to meet both present and future challenges; a foreign policy that boldly and purposefully promotes American principles abroad; and national leadership that accepts the United States' global responsibilities.

"Of course, the United States must be prudent in how it exercises its power. But we cannot safely avoid the responsibilities of global leadership or the costs that are associated with its exercise. America has a vital role in maintaining peace and security in Europe, Asia, and the Middle East. If we shirk our responsibilities, we invite challenges to our fundamental interests. The history of the 20th century should have taught us that it is important to shape circumstances before crises emerge, and to meet threats before they become dire. The history of this century should have taught us to embrace the cause of American leadership."

Felicity Arbuthnot at *Global Research* offered her views on the PNAC: "The PNAC was founded under the Chairmanship of William Kristol, former Chief of Staff to Vice President Dan Quale during the Presidency of George Bush Snr. Kristol's father, Irving Kristol has been described as the 'Godfather of Neoconservatism.' The organization was: 'dedicated to a few fundamental propositions: That American leadership is good for America and the world.' Projects were devised '… to explain what American world leadership entails. Consulting 'the world' about the mind-numbing concept of a US planetary take-over was not a consideration.

"Little time was wasted in advancing this new world order. On 29th May 1998 the PNAC sent a letter (ii) to the then Speaker of the House of Representatives, Newt Gingrich and to Senate Majority Leader, Trent Lott. It referred to a letter sent to President Clinton four months earlier 'expressing our concern' that U.S. policy of 'containment of Saddam Hussein was failing.' Thus: 'the vital interests of the United States and its allies in the Middle East would soon be facing a threat as severe as any we had known since the end of the Cold War.

"Therefore a strategy should be implemented to '… protect the United States and its allies from the threat of weapons of mass destruction (and) put in place policies' that would topple the Iraqi leadership. Signatories, a veritable 'Who's Who' of neo-cons, included John Bolton, Donald Rumsfeld, Richard Perle, Paul Wolfowitz, Robert Kagan, James Wolsey, Zalmay Khalizad and PNAC co-founder Robert Kagan."

So, we see a situation involving the NWO, key New World Order figures, and the PNAC all involved in one of the key New World Order programs of the first decade of the twenty-first century: the invasion of Iraq.

PUTIN, TRUMP, AND THE NEW WORLD ORDER

Just a couple of days after the Brexit affair—a referendum in which the people of the UK voted to leave the European Union, a historic event that had the New World Order reeling—the media reported on how none other than Russian Premier Vladimir Putin sent a warning to none other than Donald Trump, warning him that the NWO was gunning for him and that a "secret cabal" within the New World Order had Trump "in their crosshairs," which was an ominous choice of words, to say the least.

Putin's specific words to Trump were: "There is a secret cabal above the elected rulers of your country, they have very clear goals for the next couple of years. They do not want you to be President, and they are conspiring against you."

Your News Wire had much to say about Putin's warning-filled statement: "President Putin hasn't endorsed Trump, but any enemy of the New World Order is a friend of the Russian President's, and he had a few words of warning to share with Trump when they spoke on the phone on Friday." Putin is said to have told Trump to expect "dirty tricks like we've already seen, and much worse." Putin added, *Your News Wire* revealed, that "the elites will do whatever it takes to stop you from thwarting them. The elites have chosen Hillary [and] the whole world has seen in her emails that the Democrats chose her as their nominee over a year ago and the election over Sanders was a farce."

Your News Wire was far from done: "In an annual press conference with his countrymen last April, Putin expressed skepticism about the American electoral process, which he believes is corrupt—elite family clans taking turns occupying the White House. He also hinted how he personally saw Hillary Clinton. 'First there was Bush senior in power, then Bush junior. [Bill] Clinton was [U.S. President] two times in a row, now his wife has ambitions. Again, the family might stay in power. As they say in Russia, a husband and a wife are the same Satan.' Neither side of the political establishment want Trump anywhere near the

One report says that Russian Premier Vladimir Putin warned President Donald Trump that the New World Order was out to get him.

White House. The mainstream media are vilifying him. In short, the sock puppets of the New World Order are united against him. They have a lot to lose if somebody who isn't playing by their rules takes control."

Finally, this is also from *Your News Wire*: "In Russia there is an old saying that roughly translates as 'If you don't understand the past, you won't be able to understand the present, or shape the future.' Putin lives by this saying. According to sources he has been studying the history of the New World Order so he can understand their plans and destroy the invasive organization before its roots and branches spread too far and wide around the world and it becomes too late."

R

RABIES

Is the NWO planning on releasing a nightmarish virus, one which might take out millions of people via an airborne "version" of rabies? It sounds unlikely. It may not be. The story suggests that, right now, classified research of a highly controversial nature is being undertaken to try to create a terrible cocktail. It is claimed to be one based around a mutated version of the rabies virus, one that will, in the near future, be unleashed upon enemy forces and cause them to attack each other in violent, homicidal fashion. They won't be literally dead, but trying to tell the difference between the real-life infected and those of television and cinema will be no easy task.

Could it be true? Are dark forces really at work, trying to create a virus that will mimic—as closely as conceivably possible—the effects of a real zombie apocalypse? If so, who are the perpetrators? In true, tried, and tested conspiratorial fashion, vague references to "them" and "they" are all that we get from those slightly (and occasionally significantly) unusual characters who are absolutely chomping at the bit to see a *real* zombie apocalypse erupt all around us.

Certainly, rabies radically transforms the character and actions of an infected individual to a radical degree. Its name is highly apt, too: it is a Latin term meaning nothing less than "madness." Rabies spreads from animal to animal via bites that penetrate the skin and provokes inflammation in the brain, as Ozzy Osbourne almost learned to his cost when he *very* unwisely bit the head off a bat at a Des Moines, Iowa, gig in 1982.

Left untreated, disturbing characteristics develop anywhere from weeks to months after infection, including violent outbursts, manic behavior, aggression, and a fear of water. Death usually occurs within forty-eight hours to two weeks after the first symptoms surface. Despite the assumption that rabies is on the way out, this is far from the case. Tens of thousands of people still die from this terrible condition every year, chiefly in Africa and Asia.

Disturbingly, most animals on the planet can fall victim to infection, too. Fortunately, vaccinations and care have kept levels of rabies to a minimum in the western world. Indeed, between 1996 and 2013, only forty-five cases of human infection occurred in the United States. All of the victims were bitten overseas prior to their return to the United States. Rumors among conspiracy theorists suggest that a rage-instilling, highly infectious, *airborne* version of rabies is, right now, being developed. It will not quickly kill the infected individuals, however. Instead, their lives will be prolonged, albeit in violent, murderous, rage-filled states. That might seem like an ideal weapon to release on enemy troops, then sit back and watch as they tear each other to pieces.

But what happens when the wind blows hard and weaponized, airborne rabies—mutated into something even more nightmarish—begins to spread far and wide outside of the confines of the battlefield? Will we be faced with a veritable army of rabid, infected killers, indiscriminately murdering and infecting everyone that crosses their paths? Maybe that is exactly what the New World Order wants.

RAND CORPORATION

When it comes to the matter of government interest in paranormal phenomena, certainly one of the most controversial aspects of the entire issue revolves around the ways and means by which official agencies have exploited—or have tried to exploit—religious iconography as a weapon of war, deception, and manipulation.

The story goes today that darkly ambitious plans are afoot to unleash upon the entire planet a monstrous and malignant holographic hoax relative to the so-called Second Coming. Known to the wilder elements of conspiracy theorizing as Project Blue Beam, it is said to be an operation designed to usher in a definitive New World Order-type society in which the populace—duped into believing by a series of aerial holograms that the final battle between good and evil is taking place in the skies above—will give up their freedoms and allow a secret society of powerful figures to rule them with an iron fist born out of Old Testament/wrath of God-style teachings.

Could such an astonishing scenario actually be true? Are there really coldhearted people, buried deep within the corridors of power, who see the religious teachings and beliefs of the ancients as being viable ways of keeping all of us living in a state of neverending, hell-driven terror and martial law? True or not, we do see prime evidence of official manipulation of religious iconography for military and psychological warfare purposes.

One of the most important, relevant, and earliest contributions to this particular debate is an April 14, 1950, publication of the RAND Corporation titled *The Exploitation of Superstitions for Purposes of Psychological Warfare*. Written by a RAND employee named Jean M. Hungerford and prepared for the attention of intelligence personnel within the U.S. Air Force, the thirty-seven-page document is an extremely interesting one and delves into some highly unusual areas, one of which has a direct bearing upon the extraordinary data contained within this particular article.

Before we get to the matter of the document itself, a bit of background on the RAND group is required. Although not a secret society, RAND is an organization that has fingers in numerous worldwide pies—as its very own website confirms: "The RAND Corporation is a nonprofit institution that helps improve policy and decision making through research and analysis. For more than six decades, RAND has used rigorous, fact-based research and analysis to help individuals, families, and communities throughout the world be safer and more secure, healthier and more prosperous. Our research spans the issues that matter most, such as energy, education, health, justice, the environment, and international and military affairs.

"As a nonpartisan organization, RAND is widely respected for operating independent of political and commercial pressures. Quality and objectivity are our two core values.

"RAND's research is commissioned by a global clientele that includes government agencies, foundations, and private-sector firms. Philanthropic contributions, combined with earnings from RAND's endowment and operations, make possible the RAND-Initiated Research program, which supports innovative research on issues that are crucial to the policy debate but that reach beyond the boundaries of traditional client funding."

All of which brings us back to the matter of RAND and religious manipulation.

Jean Hungerford stated: "Recently a series of religious 'miracles' has been reported from Czechoslovakian villages. In one instance the cross on the altar of a parish church was reported to have bowed right and left and finally, symbolically, to the West; the 'miracle' so impressed the Czechs that pilgrims began to converge on the village from miles around until Communist officials closed the church and turned the pilgrims away from approaching roads."

The RAND Corporation's headquarters is in Santa Monica, California; from here, the nonprofit global policy think tank has tendrils grabbing political and business interests all over the world.

On another occasion, noted Hungerford, the Virgin Mary herself was said to have materialized—in a vision—and to have given a communist a resounding slap that knocked him unconscious! And then there was a story from western Bohemia that made its way into Hungerford's report, which asserted locals had seen the Virgin Mary parading along the streets of a small town—with the American flag in her hand, no less—as U.S. troops and tanks followed dutifully behind.

Of course, the overriding message behind these particular visitations of the Marian kind, and the attendant, reported miracles, was acutely clear: God was (a) right behind Uncle Sam; and (b) hardly a noted supporter of communism. Whether or not this was all provoked by some top-secret hand of the U.S. government—of which RAND had no personal awareness—is unknown.

But, as RAND noted in its report to the Air Force, the U.S. government had carefully, and secretly, monitored Moscow- and Czech-based radio broadcasts that discussed the claimed miracles in great depth. Most notably of all, the Russians and the Czechs exhibited deep, on-air anger and annoyance that the rumors in question were essentially casting a major slur on the entire Soviet Bloc and the communist way of life.

Hungerford noted something else that clearly demonstrated the large-scale extent to which American agents were dutifully monitoring this particular situation: "According to the Foreign Broadcast Information Services' daily reports of Soviet and Eastern European radio broadcasts, there were nine broadcasts concerning the 'miracles' between February 28 and March 19, seven from Czech transmitters and two from Moscow (including a review of a *New Times* article on the subject)."

Every response and reaction by the Soviets, it appears, was being carefully watched and analyzed by the U.S. government.

In closing on this particular matter, Hungerford detailed that the Soviets had their deep suspicions that this was all some sort of religious ruse perpetrated on them by intelligence agents of the United States. Concerning the report of the Virgin Mary waving the stars and stripes, a Prague-based radio broadcaster, whose words were transcribed and translated by the CIA, said:

"It is obvious at first sight that this apparition bears the mark made in the United States. These despicable machinations only help to unmask the high clergy as executors of the plans of the imperialist warmongers communicated to them by the Vatican through its agents."

It is this affair, and, perhaps, this particular RAND-originated document of 1950, that galvanized America, and RAND itself, to further explore how, and under what particular circumstances, religion could be used as a tool of warfare, psychological manipulation, and control.

REAGAN'S VIEW OF A WORLD UNITED BY UFOs

One of the most notable, but often overlooked, aspects of the presidency of the late Ronald Reagan was his obsession with the UFO phenomenon—not just the mystery itself but how it might provoke a unified world. It was in November 1985 that President Reagan first went public with his views on this particular matter. The location was the Geneva Summit—a historic event in which Reagan and the then Soviet Union's General Secretary Mikhail Gorbachev paved the way for the end of the Cold War. A now declassified U.S. Department of State document details the relevant portion of what went down at the summit: "Reagan said that while the General Secretary was speaking, he had been thinking of various problems being discussed at the talks. He said that previous to the General Secretary's remarks, he had been telling Foreign Minister Shevardnadze (who was sitting to the President's right) that if the people of the world were to find out that there was some alien life form that

President Ronald Reagan once theorized that if Earth were invaded by aliens, the threat would necessarily unite all the countries on the planet.

was going to attack the Earth approaching on Halley's Comet, *then that knowledge would unite all the peoples of the world* [italics mine]. Further, the President observed that General Secretary Gorbachev had cited a Biblical quotation, and the President is also alluding to the Bible, pointed out that Acts 16 refers to the fact that 'we are all of one blood regardless of where we live on the Earth,' and we should never forget that."

One month later, specifically on December 4, 1985, President Reagan made a near-identical observation. The location was Fallston High School, Harford County, Maryland. The president told the audience: "I couldn't help but, when you stop to think that we're all God's children, wherever we live in the world, I couldn't help but say to [General Secretary Gorbachev] just how easy his task and mine might be if suddenly there was a threat to this world from some other species from another planet outside in the universe. We'd forget all the little local differences that we have between our countries and we would find out once and for all that we really are all human beings here on this Earth together. Well I guess we can wait for some alien race to come down and threaten us, but I think that between us we can bring about that realization."

Interestingly, Grant Cameron—a noted authority on the matter of presidential knowledge of the UFO phenomenon—said of the Fallston High School presentation that "a review of the speech writer files from the Fallston speech show that the 'alien invasion' reference was not in the drafts of the speech nor in the speech copy. Reagan had simply added his recollection of his 'alien invasion' comment to Gorbachev while he was speaking."

On February 16, 1987, at a conference at Grand Kremlin Palace in Moscow called the "Survival of Humanity," Gorbachev commented on Reagan's intriguing words: "At our meeting in Geneva, the U.S. President said that if the earth faced an invasion by extraterrestrials, the United States and the Soviet Union would join forces to repel such an invasion. I shall not dispute the hypothesis, although I think it's early yet to worry about such an intrusion. It is much more important to think about the problems that have entered in our common home."

Then, and as his speech came to a close at the forty-second General Assembly of the United Nations on September 21, 1987, Reagan said: "In our obsession with antagonisms of the moment, we often forget how much unites all the members of humanity. Perhaps we need some outside, universal threat to make us recognize this common bond. I occasionally think how quickly our differences worldwide would vanish if we were facing an alien threat from outside of this world. And yet I ask—is not an alien force already among us?"

And, finally, we have a statement made on May 4, 1988. It was a portion of a speech delivered by the president at the National Strategy Forum in the Chicago Palmer House Hotel. Reagan was asked the following question: "What do you consider to be the most important need in International Relations?" Reagan's reply both surprised and amazed many who were in attendance: "I've often wondered, what if all of us in the world discovered that we were threatened by an outer—a power from outer space, from another planet. Wouldn't we all of a sudden find that we didn't have any differences between us at all, we were all human beings, citizens of the world, and wouldn't we come together to fight that particular threat?"

Perhaps, during the course of eight years in office, President Ronald Reagan was secretly briefed on the matter of UFOs and of an alien presence on Earth, or, maybe—and even more controversially—he was subtly warning us of a ruthless cabal that wanted to create a New World Order by fabricating an alien invasion and, subsequently, taking control of the planet and its people.

RELIGION

That the New World Order has a mission to turn religion against religion and lead the planet into a future dominated by Old Testament-style "wrath of God" proportions is all but certain. One only has to look at the way in which such tactics have been used in the post-9/11 era.

In January 2010, the mainstream American media focused a wealth of attention on a startling and weird revelation: namely, that coded biblical messages were being inscribed on high-powered rifle sights designated for use by the U.S. military. The maker of the sights, a Michigan-based outfit called Trijicon, signed a $650 million, multiyear contract to provide up to 800,000 such sights to the Marine Corps. Trijicon was founded by one Glyn Bindon, a devout Christian who was killed in a plane crash in South Africa in 2003.

Although army regulations specifically and absolutely prohibit the proselytizing of any religion in Iraq and Afghanistan—specifically to lay to rest any claims that the U.S. military is on some sort of religious "crusade"—this did not stop the sights from being distributed and utilized. One of the citations on the gun sights read: "For God, who commanded the light to shine out of darkness, hath shined in our hearts, to give the light of the knowledge of the glory of God in the face of Jesus Christ." Very notably, other messages on the rifle sights come from the End Times-dominated Book of Revelation.

Michael Weinstein of the Military Religious Freedom Foundation (MRFF) said of the "Jesus Rifles": "It's literally pushing fundamentalist Christianity at the point of a gun against the people that we're fighting. We're emboldening an enemy." Rather disturbingly, U.S. military personnel told Weinstein that their commanders were referring to these weapons as "spiritually transformed firearm[s] of Jesus Christ."

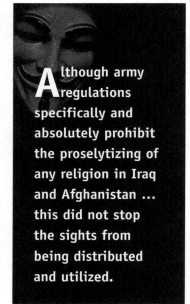

Although army regulations specifically and absolutely prohibit the proselytizing of any religion in Iraq and Afghanistan ... this did not stop the sights from being distributed and utilized.

As a result of the publicity and condemnation afforded the affair, Trijicon announced it would remove the messages from those weapons in its factory and would also "provide 100 modification kits to forces in the field to remove the reference on the already forward deployed optical sights." In response to this development, Haris Tarin, director of the Washington, D.C., office of the Muslim Public Affairs Council, said: "We must ensure that incidents like these are not repeated, so as not to give the impression that our country is involved in a religious crusade, which hurts America's image abroad and puts our soldiers in harm's way."

This is not the first time that religion and the U.S. military have crossed paths in the post-9/11 era. In 2003, intelligence briefings on the war in Iraq sent to the White House by the Pentagon were delivered with cover pages that quoted from the books of Psalms and Ephesians and the epistles of Peter. For example, the cover page of a report dated March 31, 2003, read: "Therefore put on the full armor of God, so that when the day of evil comes, you may be able to stand your ground, and after you have done everything, to stand."

Similarly, a Pentagon report of April 10, 2003, included this quote from Psalms on its front page: "Behold, the eye of the Lord is on those who fear Him.... to deliver their soul from death." It was accompanied by a photograph of a statue of Saddam Hussein being pulled to the ground in Baghdad, Iraq.

In response to these revelations, the Reverend Barry W. Lynn, executive director of Americans United for Separation of Church and State, said that American soldiers "are not Christian crusaders, and they ought not be depicted as such. Depicting the Iraq conflict as some sort of holy war is completely outrageous." Try telling that to the people who want us to believe that a holy war is exactly what is afoot.

The BBC noted—also in 2003—that when Lieutenant General William Boykin gave speeches at churches, and while in his uniform no less, that disparaged Islam and that defined the "War on Terror" in a specifically fundamentalist End Times scenario, he was not fired but promoted. In an unofficial acknowledgment of that view, "U.S. Defense Secretary Donald Rumsfeld," noted the BBC, "has declined to criticize a senior army officer who told audiences the war on terror is a battle with Satan."

Michael Weinstein of the Military Religious Freedom Foundation (MRFF) said: "There's an eschatology obsessed version of Christianity ... that is trying to make American foreign policy conterminous with their Biblical worldview," adding that there exists: "improper pressure within the military command structure to make members join them."

The MMRF also learned that, in 2007, an evangelical group called Operation Stand Up was preparing to mail "freedom packages" to soldiers in Iraq as part of an army program.

The MMRF also learned that, in 2007, an evangelical group called Operation Stand Up was preparing to mail "freedom packages" to soldiers in Iraq as part of an army program. Along with socks and snacks, the packages were set to include copies of an apocalyptic video game titled "Left Behind: Eternal Forces." Only when the details of the plan were publicized by those who saw such actions as fundamentally wrong did the Pentagon grudgingly announce that the operation would be shelved.

REPORT FROM IRON MOUNTAIN

Mercury Theatre on the Air performed Orson Welles' radio adaptation of H.G. Wells' classic sci-fi book *War of the Worlds* on October 30, 1938, specifically as a Halloween special. The program was broadcast from the twentieth floor of 485 Madison Avenue and was ingeniously presented in the form of a regular show that was repeatedly interrupted by a series of disturbing and escalating news stories detailing gigantic explosions on the planet Mars that were rapidly followed by frantic reports of the landing of an alien spacecraft near the town of Grover's Mill, New Jersey.

As the broadcast progresses, more Martian war machines land and proceed to wreak havoc throughout the continental United States. The secretary of the interior informs the pain-stricken populace of the grave nature of the ever-growing conflict, and the military launches a desperate counterattack against the burgeoning Martian assault. Frantic reports describe thousands of people fleeing urban areas as the unstoppable Martians head toward New York

City. "Isn't there anyone on the air?" pleads a desperate broadcaster in suitably dramatic and chilled tones.

Of course, Welles had merely intended the show to be an entertaining radio rendition of *War of the Worlds* and nothing more. However, those listeners who were unfortunate enough to have missed the beginning of the production—in which Welles was very careful to say that the broadcast was simply a piece of fictional entertainment and absolutely nothing else—really did believe that a Martian attack on the Earth had begun and that the end of civilization was possibly looming on the dark horizon.

Indeed, newspapers of the day stated that large-scale panic followed in the wake of the show. And although later studies suggested the hysteria was actually far less widespread than newspaper accounts initially suggested, many people were indeed caught up in the initial cosmic confusion.

It has been suggested by conspiracy theorists, such as the late William Cooper, that the *War of the Worlds* broadcast was actually a psychological warfare experiment secretly sponsored by a secret group within the U.S. government to try to accurately determine how the population might react to the presence of a hostile alien menace, albeit an entirely false and officially manufactured one, rather like a "War on Terror" for the *X-Files* generation.

Although the majority of those who have studied such claims have outright dismissed them, the scenario of government officials conspiring to unite (or, perhaps, enslave) humankind under one banner as a result of an intergalactic alien threat was discussed extensively in a controversial publication titled *Report from Iron Mountain*.

The late writer Philip Coppens states: "In 1967, a major publisher, The Dial Press, released *Report from Iron Mountain*. The book claimed to be a suppressed, secret government report, written by a commission of scholars, known as the 'Special Study Group,' set up in 1963, with the document itself leaked by one of its members. The Group met at an underground nuclear bunker called Iron Mountain and worked over a period of two and a half years, delivering the report in September 1966. The report was an investigation into the problems that the United States would need to face if and when 'world peace' should be established on a more or less permanent basis."

As the *Report* itself noted: "It is surely no exaggeration to say that a condition of general world peace would lead to changes in the social structures of the nations of the world of unparalleled and revolutionary magnitude. The economic impact of general disarmament, to name only the most obvious consequence of peace, would revise the production and distribution patterns of the globe to a degree that would make the changes of the past fifty years seem insignificant.

"Political, sociological, cultural, and ecological changes would be equally far-reaching. What has motivated our study of these contingencies has been the growing sense of thoughtful men in and out of government that the world is totally unprepared to meet the demands of such a situation."

Upon its first appearance in 1967, *Report from Iron Mountain* ignited immediate and widespread debate among journalists and scholars with its disturbingly convincing conclusion: namely, that a condition of "permanent peace" at the end of the Cold War would drastically threaten the United States' economic and social stability.

U pon its first appearance in 1967, *Report from Iron Mountain* ignited immediate and widespread debate among journalists and scholars....

Although subsequently identified as nothing more than an ingenious hoax written by Leonard Lewin, who had both conceived and launched the book with the help of a select body of players in the peace movement—including *Nation* editors Victor Navasky and Richard Lingeman, novelist E. L. Doctorow, and economist John Kenneth Galbraith—the controversy surrounding *Report from Iron Mountain* refuses to roll over and die.

Long out of print, the *Report* suddenly began to reappear in bootlegged editions more than twenty years after its original publication amid claims that its contents were all too real.

Colonel Fletcher Prouty, a national security aide in the Kennedy Administration (and the model for Donald Sutherland's character, "X," in Oliver Stone's hit movie *JFK*), continues to believe to this very day that the report is indeed authentic, and he specifically referred to it within the pages of his memoirs. Notably, in a 1992 preface to Prouty's memoirs, no less a person than Oliver Stone himself cited the *Report from Iron Mountain* as specifically raising "the key questions of our time."

After the book's initial publication, it was reported that then President Lyndon B. Johnson had deep suspicions that the late President John F. Kennedy had authorized the publication of the *Report*. Moreover, Johnson is famously alleged to have "hit the roof" upon learning of its publication.

In 1992, *Iron Mountain* author Lewin filed a lawsuit for copyright infringement against Willis Carto, a white supremacist, for allegedly publishing the now discontinued, bootleg editions of the book. Interestingly, Mark Lane, an author who has written extensively on the Kennedy assassination and who served as Carto's lawyer, stated that *Report from Iron Mountain* was indeed possibly a real government document and, therefore, could not be seen to have any bearing upon current U.S. copyright laws.

Similarly, a May 1995 front-page article in the *Wall Street Journal* reported that extreme-right fringe groups continued to quote *Report from Iron Moun-*

tain as "proof of a secret government plot to suppress personal liberties and usher in a New World Order dominated by the U.N."

REPTILIANS

There's no doubt that when it comes to the matter of conspiracy theories—and highly inflammatory conspiracy theories related to who really runs the New World Order—there is one controversial claim that just about beats all of the rest. It's the assertion that the British royal family are nothing less than deadly, bloodthirsty, shapeshifting monsters. "Bloodthirsty" is a very apt word to use since the royals are said to quaff on human blood just about as enthusiastically as the rest of the British population likes to knock back pints of beer in their local pub. They are shapeshifters with incredible power and influence. Here's where controversial becomes beyond controversial.

Welcome to the world of the Reptilians—eight-foot-tall, interdimensional monsters that masquerade as people but who are anything but. At least, that's how the story goes. There's one person to thank (if that's the correct term to use!) for bringing this strange and enduring claim to light. His name is David Icke. Once a well-known goalkeeper for Coventry City—an English soccer team—Icke is, today, a leading light in the shadowy domains where the conspiracy-minded and the paranoid hang out. His books include *The Biggest Secret* and *The David Icke Guide to the Global Conspiracy*.

Are the likes of Queen Elizabeth II, her husband Prince Philip (the Duke of Edinburgh), and the heir to the throne, Prince Charles, really monsters that are either (a) an ancient species that originate right here on Earth; or (b) extraterrestrials from a faraway world? We'll start with the first theory. According to those who adhere to this particular theory, the royal family is at the top of the pile when it comes to the matter of who owns the planet.

Forget presidents and prime ministers, the real, secret forces that control and manipulate our world are the Babylonian Brotherhood, an ancient race of dangerous shapeshifters that were responsible for ancient tales of the likes of Quetzalcoatl—whose name means "feathered serpent" and who was a significant, deity-like force in Mesoamerica and who first surfaced around 100 B.C.E. He is also said to have been an entity that brought science, farming, and culture of that era and area. Although, given the apparent hatred that the Reptilians have for us, the likelihood is that Quetzalcoatl's actions were very likely self-serving and were designed to keep people in their place and under his firm and cold-hearted control and sway.

It's intriguing to note that almost three thousand years ago, the ancient people of Mexico had other serpent-based gods—all of which has helped to nurture the idea that yesterday's Reptilian gods are still among us and are just about as widespread as they were way back when. Today, however, their influence is not just in Mesoamerica but all across the world, even in the domain of politics, too. That's right: it's not just the British royal family who the conspiracy-minded believe are monsters.

Leading Reptilians (so the likes of David Icke assure and warn us) include the Clintons (Bill and Hillary), Henry Kissinger—a former U.S. secretary of state and a national security advisor—and President George W. Bush. Oh, and lest we forget, the late Hollywood legend, Bob Hope, too. Yes, really. Or not.

One of those who helped to bring this matter to the attention of the conspiracy-obsessed—and, in quick time, to both the

Reptilians are eight-foot-tall, interdimensional creatures that disguise themselves as human beings and infiltrate our society.

media and popular culture, too—was a Californian woman named Arizona Wilder, who claims to have been mind-controlled and manipulated by the likes of the world's most infamous secret society, the dreaded and feared Illuminati. Wilder's claims get even, ahem, wilder. She maintains she has witnessed diabolical human sacrifice at the hands of the Rockefellers, the Rothchilds, members of the Bush family (yes, those Bushes), and at least one Pope. As for Queen Elizabeth II, well.

Certainly, Arizona Wilder's most graphic and controversy-filled claim is that she witnessed the Queen partake in such sacrifices and saw her eat the flesh, and drink the blood, of her unfortunate human victims. On one occasion, says Wilder, Queen Elizabeth was so fired up that she practically tore out a poor soul's throat, drinking it down as it spewed forth. According to Wilder, in her Reptilian form, the queen has skin that is a pale, sickly color. Her face, meanwhile, changes into something that closely resembles a beak.

Adding even more to this story is Wilder's claim that, back in 1981, she met with then-Lady Diana, soon to become Diana, Princess of Wales. According to Wilder, the Princess was forced to take part in an ancient and secret ritual, one which involved the Queen, Prince Philip, Prince Charles, and his lover and now wife, Camilla Parker-Bowles. Placed into a drugged-out state,

Are the numerous people who make up the British royal family shapeshifting reptiles with origins that date back millennia?

Diana was told that there was one reason, and one reason only, for the marriage: to ensure that the royal/Reptilian bloodline continued. When Diana was tragically killed in Paris, France, in 1997—admittedly, an incident still shrouded in mystery and intrigue years later—Icke weaved her untimely death into his Reptilian scenario.

Conspiracy theorists who fully believed the Reptilian scenario practically foamed at the mouth when Mohammed Al-Fayed—the father of Dodi Fayed, who was Diana's boyfriend at the time of her death and who died with her in the terrible car crash that took three lives—referred to Camilla Parker-Bowles as Prince Charles' "crocodile wife." Then, when Fayed labeled the entire royal family as the "Dracula Family," it only added to the idea that the royals were copious drinkers of human blood. Was Mohammed Al-Fayed—in a slightly less than subtle fashion—trying to warn people of the growing Reptilian threat in the midst of just about everyone?

Today, the so-called Reptilian agenda terrifies, intrigues, and entertains near-endless numbers of people. And it's a phenomenon that clearly isn't going away anytime soon. Are the numerous people who make up the British royal family shapeshifting reptiles with origins that date back millennia? Is the entire issue nothing but the likes of fabrication, lies, pranks, and jokes? Or does it hazily lie somewhere in between? It all depends on who you ask—as is the case with practically all conspiracy theories of a highly bizarre nature. There is, however, another aspect to this saga—one which focuses on the matter of so-called alien abductions, as we'll now see.

REPTILIANS AND SEX

It was on June 24, 1947, that the so-called modern era of ufology began with pilot Kenneth Arnold's encounter with a squadron of flying saucers over the Cascade Mountains, Washington state. It wasn't until the early years of the 1950s, however, that people began reporting encounters with alleged alien entities. That was the period in which, all across the United States, reports came pouring in of encounters with what became known as the Space Brothers. They were reported as being incredibly human looking and sported heads of long, blond hair. Typically, they would warn witnesses of the perils of atomic war and expressed concerns about our violent, warlike ways.

As the 1960s began, reports started to surface of so-called alien abductions, which really took off big time in the 1970s and continued to be big news in the 1980s and 1990s. It was also in the 1980s that there was another development in the matter of human-alien interaction. And it all revolved around the aforementioned Reptilians. Not content with ruling the planet—under the shapeshifted guises of world leaders and royalty—the Reptilians have also surfaced prominently in the issue of alien abductions.

Stories told by abductees, in relation to the Reptilian aspect, are just as controversial as matters concerning the British royal family. But, for very different reasons. Predominantly, but not exclusively, the Reptilians are present during abductions aboard alleged alien spacecraft which involve women. They're not looking for DNA, cells, or our blood, however. It's sex that these appearance-changing stud muffins are after. And, apparently, more than a few women were very satisfied by the experiences. One of them is Pamela Stonebrooke, a writer and jazz music performer/vocalist who makes no bones about the fact that, from her perspective, getting nailed aboard a UFO by the closest thing one can imagine to something that appears half human and half crocodile, is not a bad thing. Not everyone agrees, however.

Many people who have experienced sex at the hands of the Reptilians are, quite understandably, reluctant to go public with their experiences—at least, not with their full names. One of those is "Audrey," a thirty-eight-year-old woman who claims seven *very* close encounters with male Reptilians between 2001 and 2007. A resident of Sedona, Arizona—a place renowned for a wide range of paranormal phenomena—Audrey was first abducted by what she later recalled, in somewhat of a drugged, hypnotized state, was a group of military personnel in black fatigues late one night on the edge of town.

As she drove home after visiting a friend in Flagstaff, Audrey caught sight of a black van following her, one which loomed out of the shadows and ran her off the road. The next thing she remembered was being manhandled into that same van. After that, it was lights out. She later woke up to find herself strapped down to a table in a brightly lit, circular room. In front of her were three men in those same fatigues. For a while, at least. As Audrey craned to sit up, she watched in terror as all three men suddenly shimmered—as if caught in something akin to a heat haze. In no more than around six or seven seconds, they were replaced by a trio of approximately eight-foot-tall, green-colored monsters that looked like Godzilla's younger and smaller brothers.

Audrey states that the aliens moved toward the table, unstrapped her, and, one by one, had sex with her. She was somewhat embarrassed to admit that the encounter was exciting, if fraught. She was, however, unable to shake off the taboo of what she described as having sex with animals. If that's what they really were. According to Audrey, all of the other experiences occurred in her own home—again, late at night—and sex was the only thing that went down, so to speak.

Perhaps the most disturbing encounter was the fourth one, in which two men dressed in black suits, white shirts, and red ties, and with near-identical slicked-back hair, materialized in her bedroom as she lay in bed, listening to music on her iPod. As with the previous encounter, the men transformed into what looked like, and as she described it, giant lizards. Once again, Audrey had a swinging time—but was again eaten up by guilt, as she was on each and every subsequent occasion.

However, one unforeseen side effect of all this was that for around almost a year after the final encounter occurred, and whenever a man would look or stare at her, Audrey would have shivers go up and down her spine. She was fearful of the possibility that they, too, were shapeshifters that could take on human form but whose real form was that of a dangerous Reptilian. If a man looked at her for more than a second or two in a bar or in a restaurant, she would get the chills. If, while walking around Sedona, a man gave her a friendly nod, it meant he was a Reptilian. Realizing that she was plunging into a state of near-mental illness, Audrey eventually pulled herself back from the brink of complete and utter paranoia and moved on with her life, as did, apparently, the Reptilians.

Perhaps the most disturbing encounter was the fourth one, in which two men dressed in black suits ... materialized in her bedroom as she lay in bed, listening to music on her iPod.

It should be noted that there are numerous such reports on record—or, on far more occasions, off the record—display uncannily similar aspects. This has led even some quite conservative alien abduction researchers to take the matter of shapeshifting sex very seriously. And there is one final thing worth pondering: if these stories are not the result of wild fantasies and erotic dreams, then perhaps there really is an alien, Reptilian agenda on our planet. It's one thing to talk about sex with scaly ETs with forked tongues and thrashing tails who use women for sex. It's quite another, however, to suggest they're running the entire planet. Unless, of course, you have encountered the Reptilians yourself. Sometimes, truth really is stranger than fiction. But, on this particular issue, exactly how strange is still a matter of furious debate.

RESTORE THE FOURTH

In their own words: "Restore the Fourth is a nonpartisan 501(c)(4) nonprofit corporation, dedicated to robust enforcement of the Fourth Amendment to the U.S. Constitution. In the wake of the Snowden revelations of June 2013, and initially on Reddit, groups began meeting across the United States, under the banner of 'Restore The Fourth.' Under our first National Chair (Anna Wilmesher, summer 2013), we coordinated protests for July 4 and for Orwell Day. Under our second National Chair (Ben Doernberg, fall 2013), we helped organize the nationwide Stopwatching.us protests, culminating in a rally of thousands in Washington DC. Under Alex Marthews (2014–), our focus has shifted more towards legislative advocacy and public education, particularly around sunsetting the legal authorities underlying mass government surveillance."

As the New World Order seeks to take away our rights on an ever-increasing basis and as spying on our everyday activities and on our social media preferences become more and more widespread, more and more bodies like Restore the Fourth are doing their utmost to reverse the situation.

In 2013, the UK's *Guardian* newspaper gave Restore the Fourth significant page space. On July 5, *Guardian* journalist Rebecca Bowe wrote: "Protests took place across the U.S. on Thursday to demonstrate opposition to sweeping National Security Agency surveillance programs. The events were organized by a newly hatched organization called Restore the Fourth, named after the constitutionally guaranteed protection against illegal search and seizure under the Fourth Amendment. Rallies and marches took place in San Francisco, Los Angeles, Dallas, New York City, Washington DC and dozens of other US cities."

Bowe added: "Ryan Brown, a regional leader for the San Francisco Bay protests who has been coordinating with national organizers, said his participation in Restore the Fourth stemmed from concern over excessive governmental power implied by the spying programs. 'I see it as ethically disgusting that the government has both the opportunity and the ability ... to collect the data on us individually, without a given reason other than quote-unquote 'protecting our freedoms,' he said."

Among those who spoke at the event were representatives from the Electronic Frontier Foundation. In a spirited statement, they said: "Hello everybody, and thank you for coming out here today to stand up for all of our Fourth Amendment rights. At EFF, we've been engaged in lawsuits about these secret and unconstitutional NSA programs for the better part of a decade, and we need the government to see that the American people are outraged.

"Because nearly 250 years ago today, our founding fathers refused to live under tyranny and declared independence from their ruling government. The king, they wrote in the Declaration of Independence, had made it impossible to live under a rule of law.

"A few years later they wrote the document that established the United States of America, our Constitution, and with it they published our Bill of Rights to protect the basic rights that every person in this country is entitled to."

The EFF continued: "The actions of the National Security Agency spying on Americans, revealed by a series of whistleblowers driven by conscience, represents a break from that tradition. And it's our duty not to allow that break. It's our duty as human beings, entitled to dignity and privacy, and it's our duty as Americans, protecting those rights not just for ourselves but for everybody who follows in our steps. The Founders wrote the Fourth Amendment deliberately, with a specific purpose: to ensure that so-called 'general warrants' were illegal. These general warrants were broad and unreasonable dragnets, requiring anyone targeted to forfeit their information to the government.

"No, under the Fourth Amendment, a warrant needs to be specific. You need a particular target and probable cause. Compare that with what we know the NSA is doing, and has been doing for years. Even now we can't know the full scope of what the government is doing when it claims to act in our names...."

REVELATIONS

There are those who believe that none other than the Bible's Book of Revelations reveals a great deal about the history and agenda of the New World Order. Irvin Baxter, of *End Time Ministries*, says: "The prophesied one-world government is being formed on earth at this very time. The Bible prophesies that the Antichrist will ultimately reign over this world government for three-and-one-half years just prior to the Second Coming of Jesus to establish His own world government.

"Control of the coming endtime government will be consolidated into the totalitarian hands of the Antichrist. The dragon, which is the devil, gives this world governmental system its seat, power, and great authority (Revelation 13:2). We will all feel the oppression of this world government structure because it is satanically inspired, and it is forming right now.

"Revelation 13:7 states that power will be given to the Antichrist over 'all kindreds, and tongues, and nations.' Verse 3 says, 'And all the world wondered after the beast.' Daniel 7:23 tells of a world governmental system ruled by the Antichrist, 'The fourth beast shall be the fourth kingdom upon earth, which shall be diverse from all kingdoms, and shall devour the whole earth, and shall tread it down, and break it in pieces.' The prophecy then states that this world government will rule the world until the Second Coming."

Beginning and End has its own views on this undeniably controversial issue, too: "There are many details of this coming One World Order throughout the Bible but the most detailed description can be found in the book of the Revelation, Chapter 13. Revelation, the final book of the Bible, was written between 65–86 A.D. and is a description of the last years of the Earth leading up to the Second Coming of Jesus Christ. Revelation 13 is the primary chapter where see a description of society under the rule of The Beast, also known as The Antichrist. The vivid description of the antichrist is symbolic of his power structure. The animal parts and horns are all indicative of the government in which he will rule. We can know this because we get a description of what the vision John the Revelator has means in Revelation."

> **T**here are many details of this coming One World Order throughout the Bible but the most detailed description can be found in the book of the Revelation, Chapter 13

Beginning and End adds and asks a question: "So as we see a 'New World Order' approaching, what do we do? If we are concerned, instead of fighting it or grabbing or planning a resistance movement, we need to first understand that this is spiritual. Satan wants a One World Order and to deceive the world into making that happen. The antichrist is not going to come into power by force. He is going to be wanted, marveled at and beloved. This is the great deception. And the one counter to it is having Jesus Christ as your Savior. Because although there will be an Antichrist and a False Prophet and a One World Order, they are all defeated by Jesus Christ. In the end everyone takes a stand for Jesus or Satan. Do not be deceived. Having knowledge is not enough. Resisting is not enough. If the time comes that a Mark or implant of some sort is being required under penalty of death, just having foreknowledge will not save you. But having Jesus Christ as your Savior will. The Bible is dead on with this prediction. No other faith even attempts such a detailed description of a One world political, religious and economic system. God gave us these prophecies to know He is real and His word is true. But most importantly so that we can be forgiven for our sins through Jesus Christ and not suffer the fate of those who are deceived by Satan and his false Messiah. The time for repentance is now."

Of course, interpreting words put down thousands of years ago—words that were translated, interpreted, and reinterpreted on numerous occasions—is a highly controversial issue. All we can say for sure is that the scenario contained in the Book of Revelations about the New World Order has a sizeable number of adherents and followers.

REX 84

To see how disturbingly easy it would be for a powerful New World Order force to take over the United States, one only has to take a look at the matter of what was termed Readiness Exercise 1984, or REX 84. If you haven't heard of it and you are wondering what it's all about, read on. In all probability, you will not like what you learn, not at all. Diana Reynolds outlines matters perfectly on the *Constitution Society* website: "The Rex-84 Alpha Explan (Readiness Exercise 1984, Exercise Plan; otherwise known as a continuity of government plan), indicates that FEMA in association with 34 other federal civil departments and agencies, along with other NATO nations, conducted a civil readiness exercise during April 5–13, 1984. It was conducted in coordination and simultaneously with a Joint Chiefs exercise, Night Train 84, a worldwide military command post exercise (including Continental U.S. Forces or CONUS) based on multi-emergency scenarios operating both abroad and at home.

Details concerning the highly classified exercise first publicly surfaced, to an extensive degree, at least, on July 5, 1987.

"In the combined exercise, Rex-84 Bravo, FEMA and DOD led the other federal agencies and departments, including the Central Intelligence Agency, the Secret Service, the Treasury, the Federal Bureau of Investigation, and the Veterans Administration through a gaming exercise to test military assistance in civil defense.

"The exercise anticipated civil disturbances, major demonstrations and strikes that would affect continuity of government and/or resource mobilization. To fight subversive activities, there was authorization for the military to implement government ordered movements of civilian populations at state and regional levels, the arrest of certain unidentified segments of the population, and the imposition of martial law."

Details concerning the highly classified exercise first publicly surfaced, to an extensive degree, at least, on July 5, 1987. That was the day on which a journalist named Alfonso Chardy published an article on the controversy in the pages of the *Miami Herald*. It was, however, referenced to a limited degree in a 1984 issue of *Spotlight*, which was published by the now defunct Liberty Lobby. Its article had the eye-opening title of "Reagan Orders Concentration Camps."

Further data on this dangerous program surfaced in the massive numbers of pages of documentation concerning the so-called Iran–Contra affair and the actions of Lieutenant Colonel Oliver North, U.S. Marine Corps. One such extract reads as follows:

Congressman Jack Brooks: "Colonel North, in your work at the N.S.C. were you not assigned, at one time, to work on plans for the continuity of government in the event of a major disaster?"

Brendan Sullivan [North's counsel]: "Mr. Chairman?"

Senator Daniel Inouye: "I believe that question touches upon a highly sensitive and classified area so may I request that you not touch upon that?"

Congressman Jack Brooks: "I was particularly concerned, Mr. Chairman, because I read in Miami papers, and several others, that there had been a plan developed, by that same agency, a contingency plan in the event of emergency that would suspend the American constitution. And I was deeply concerned about it and wondered if that was an area in which he had worked. I believe that it was and I wanted to get his confirmation."

Senator Daniel Inouye: "May I most respectfully request that that matter not be touched upon at this stage. If we wish to get into this, I'm certain arrangements can be made for an executive session."

Clearly, Congressman Brooks had stumbled on something significant and of a national security nature.

An article titled "FEMA and the REX 84 Program" reveals: "There [are] over 600 prison camps in the United States, all fully operational and ready to receive prisoners. They are all staffed and even surrounded by full-time guards, but they are all empty. These camps are to be operated by FEMA (Federal Emergency Management Agency) should Martial Law need to be implemented in the United States. The Rex 84 Program was established on the reasoning that if a mass exodus of illegal aliens crossed the Mexican/US border, they would be quickly rounded up and detained in detention centers by FEMA. Rex 84 allowed many military bases to be closed down and to be turned into prisons.

"Operation Cable Splicer and Garden Plot are the two sub programs which will be implemented once the Rex 84 program is initiated for its proper purpose. Garden Plot is the program to control the population. Cable Splicer is the program for an orderly takeover of the state and local governments by the federal government. FEMA is the executive arm of the coming police state and thus will head up all operations. The Presidential Executive Orders already listed on the Federal Register also are part of the legal framework for this operation.

"The camps all have railroad facilities as well as roads leading to and from the detention facilities. Many also have an airport nearby. The majority of the camps can house a population of 20,000 prisoners. Currently, the largest of these facilities is just outside of Fairbanks, Alaska. The Alaskan facility is a massive mental health facility and can hold approximately 2 million people."

In 2008, Ted Twietmeyer wrote: "In May 2007, Bush signed executive new orders NSDP51 and HSDP20 to replace REX84. The older order REX84 was an older directive to establish martial law in the event of a national emergency. Everything done in government is done for a reason, and these two new orders are no exception. These new directives surprised and alarmed many real conservatives and true patriots at the time. These two orders established that the White House administration would take over all local governments under a national state of emergency, instead of Homeland Security."

Such legislation—which would be massively beneficial to the New World Order and its ever-expanding, militarized police force—still exists to this day.

RH NEGATIVES

Within UFO research circles, there is a wide belief that a small percentage of the human race, born with what is termed Rh negative blood, owe their curious lineage to the Anunnaki—Mesopotamian gods that many UFO adherents believe were really ancient astronauts who genetically altered early, primitive humans. Interestingly, we see the Rh negative factor running through the veins of numerous, powerful, elite figures—something which has led to an extraordinary theory: namely, that the New World Order is comprised largely of Rh negatives, continuing to keep afloat the ancient alien bloodline in powerful, worldwide form: the NWO.

The human race possesses four primary types of blood. They are A, B, AB, and O. The classifications are derived from the antigens of a person's blood cells—antigens being proteins that are found on the surface of the cells and which are designed to combat bacteria and viruses. Most of the human population have such proteins on their cells. They are the Rh positive percentage of the Earth's people. Within the United States, current estimates suggest that around 85 percent of all Caucasians, roughly 90 percent of African Americans, and approximately 98 percent of Asian Americans are Rh positive.

The small percentage of the U.S. population (and that of the rest of the world, too, it should be noted) that does not exhibit the relevant proteins falls into a very different category, that of the Rh negatives. There is, however, another, third group of people, the Basques of central Spain and the western parts of France, whose percentage of RH negatives is incredibly high: close to an amazing 40 percent. On top of that, and at the opposite end of the spectrum, the Basques almost completely lack individuals with B and AB blood.

Coincidence or not, Rh negative blood abounds among the powerful, the famous, and the infamous. President John F. Kennedy's alleged assassin, Lee Harvey Oswald, was Rh negative, as is his Russian wife, Marina. *The Investigation of the Assassination of President John F. Kennedy* (more familiarly known as the "Warren Commission") quotes Marina as saying, after she became pregnant to Lee: "The doctors told me that I might lose the baby since I had Rh negative blood. Lee was very upset by this, but when he had his own blood checked, it turned out that he was also Rh negative. Only a very small percentage have Rh negative blood, and this very unusual coincidence—in which both husband and wife were Rh negative—pleased us very much."

Rather amazingly, JFK himself was Rh negative, and specifically AB negative. And Kennedy was far from being a solitary negative in the White House. President Dwight D. Eisenhower was O negative, as was President Richard Milhous Nixon. President Bill Clinton is AB negative, and President George Bush, Sr., is A negative.

Then there is the matter of the British royal family, which has a notable connection to the history of the U.S. presidential office, as David Icke observed: "If it really is the Land of the Free and if, as is claimed, anyone really can become the president, you would fairly expect that the 43 presidents from George Washington to George W. Bush would express that genetic diversity. You're having a laugh. The presidents of the United States are as much a royal dynasty as anything in Europe, from whence their bloodlines came."

• O (I) Rh (+)	• B (III) Rh (+)
• O (I) Rh (−)	• B (III) Rh (−)
• A (II) Rh (+)	• AB (IV) Rh (+)
• A (II) Rh (−)	• AB (IV) Rh (−)

Rh Factor Set

In addition to the different blood types in humans—A, B, AB, and O—blood is either Rh negative or positive. Rh negative blood seems to be prevalent among the rich, famous, and powerful.

And still on the issue of the British royal bloodline: Queen Elizabeth II, Prince Charles, and even William and Kate are all Rh negative. What we have here, then, is a situation where some of the most powerful, influential, and famous figures in recent history are born out of the alien bloodline. Is this a case of the Anunnaki—no longer around on the scale they were hundreds of thousands of years ago—still ruling the Earth but via a form of distant proxy? The proxy being the New World Order. That may be exactly the situation.

One of the most fascinating—but also disturbing—aspects of the Rh negative phenomenon is that those with this particular blood group display certain physical characteristics that, while they are certainly not unique to these particular people alone, are most certainly more prevalent than they are in the rest of the population.

In terms of brainpower and intelligence, Rh negative individuals were shown to have significantly greater than average IQ levels. It's not at all unlikely (in fact, it's highly likely) that this stems from their connection to the Cro-

Magnons and the fact that Cro-Magnon man had a brain approximately 10 percent greater in size than any other human who has ever existed—and that includes us, *Homo sapiens*. To put that into its correct and understandable context, Cro-Magnon man's brain exceeded the size of a modern-day human brain by somewhere in the region of a tennis ball, as incredible as that might sound.

From the days when the earliest humans walked the earth, and including the timeframe in which Cro-Magnons dominated much of western Europe, the human brain grew progressively larger. It may surprise many to learn that this is not the case now. University of Wisconsin anthropologist John Hawks has commented on this issue. He says of how the human brain expanded in size as the millennia passed by: "That was true for two million of our evolution. But there has been a reversal. And it's also clear the brain has been shrinking."

Indeed, in the last 20,000 years or thereabouts, the average human brain has shrunk in size from 1,500 cubic centimeters to 1,350 cc. Whether or not this is an indication of the overall dumbing down of society, and humankind in general, is a matter of debate, the reason being that within the field of anthropology there is no solid consensus as to why our brains are shrinking, but what we *can* say for sure is that even if human brain mass is on a decline (irreversibly or not), the Rh negatives appear to have retained their Cro-Magnon-style brainpower.

Then there is the matter of the Rh negatives' inability to tolerate strong sunlight and high temperatures. Specifically, Rh negatives report problems that fall under the category of what is termed photosensitivity. In simple terms, it's a condition prompted by sunlight that affects the human immune system. The results can range from the mild to the alarming: nausea, vertigo, light-headedness, elevated heart rates, and dizziness are typical. Those affected by photosensitivity can also develop rashes, inflammation, and hives, which may range from small and localized to large and widespread, and that can result in mild irritation to intense itchiness.

Somewhat intriguingly, it's almost as if the immunity systems of the Rh negatives are not designed to be exposed to the power and heat of our own sun. This begs a thought-provoking question: Whose sun, exactly, *were* they designed to operate under? That of ancient, visiting extraterrestrials, perhaps? Given what we know from the time frame of the Cro-Magnons to the present era, such a question is hardly the stretch that some might assume it to be.

ROBERTSON, PAT

Born in 1930, Pat Robertson is a former Southern Baptist minister turned media mogul. He chairs the Christian Broadcasting Network and is the host of *The 700 Club*. In addition, he is a founder of the Christian Coalition, Regent University, the International Family Entertainment Inc. (ABC Family Channel), CBN Asia, Operation Blessing International Relief and Development Corporation, the American Center for Law & Justice (ACLJ), and other business concerns. Robertson campaigned for the office of president in 1988 but failed to gain the Republican nomination, and because of his political involvement, he can no longer have an official role in a church. His media interests and considerable fortune have, however, made him a well-known voice for Christian conservatives.

The son of U.S. Senator A. Willis Robertson, Robertson is a Southern Baptist and was active as an ordained minister with that denomination for many years, but holds to a charismatic theology not traditionally common among Southern Baptists. He unsuccessfully campaigned to become the Republican Party's nominee in the 1988 presidential election. As a result of his seeking political office, he no longer serves in an official role for any church. His media and financial resources make him a recognized, influential, and controversial public voice for conservative Christianity in the United States.

In 1991 Robertson's novel, *The New World Order*, was published. It went on to become a *New York Times* bestseller. It is, as one might expect, a book that contains all of the key ingredients of the New World Order, namely the involvement of the Illuminati, the Freemasons, the Trilateral Commission, and the Council on Foreign Relations—sections on each are also contained in this book.

The plot of Robertson's story revolves around a "behind-the-scenes Establishment" which has one key goal in mind: "the establishment of a one-world government where the control of money is in the hands of one or more privately owned but government-chartered central banks."

There is, however, far more than that to Robertson's *The New World Order*. Although it sold well, the book got patchy reviews.

Michael Lind said in 1995: "In its February 2 issue, *The New York Review* published my article on Pat Robertson's 1991 book, *The New World Order*. In it, I showed that the founder and the leader of the Christian Coalition proposes that modern world history has been largely determined by a two-centuries-old conspiracy by Bavarian Illuminati, Freemasons, Communists, and Wall Street financiers. Central to the conspiracy has been a succession of Jews, ranging from eighteenth-century Rothschilds in Frankfurt to Moses Hess and the American banker Paul Warburg.

"Instead of responding immediately, the Christian Coalition initially remained silent, perhaps in order to avoid drawing further attention to my exposure of its leader's bizarre views. I was attacked at once, however, by my former colleagues in conservative publications. The editors of *National Review*,

Christian televangelist Pat Robertson is the author of the novel *The New World Order.*

in the February 6 issue, alleged that 'the liberal establishment,' upset by the November election results, got me 'to do a hit on Pat Robertson.' (For the record, I submitted my first draft as an unsolicited article to this magazine last summer, before anyone envisioned a Republican sweep of Congress; I had had no contact with its editors until that point.)"

Frederick Clarkson, in an essay titled "What is Christian Reconstructionism?" wrote: "Pat Robertson claims Masonic conspiracies are out to destroy Christianity and thwart Christian rule. Throughout *The New World Order* Robertson refers to freemasonry as a Satanic conspiracy, along with the New Age movement. The distortion of reality that can follow from such views is well represented by Robertson's assertion that former Presidents Woodrow Wilson, Jimmy Carter, and George Bush are unwitting agents of Satan because they supported international groups of nations such as the United Nations."

Was his novel simply that, a novel to entertain and provoke thought? Or, was it a warning to the world? A warning that he, Robertson, was determined to share with the world. There is no doubt that Robertson believes that some form of New World Order is looming. Let's see what Robertson says about the New World Order outside of the world of fiction.

On December 23, 2007, Robertson said, on CNN, of President Obama: "I am remarkably pleased with Obama. I had grave misgivings about him. But so help me, he's come in forcefully, intelligently. He's picked a middle of the road cabinet. And so far, if he continues down this course, he has the makings of a great president."

ROSWELL

U p until the time of his death in 2009, author Mac Tonnies was researching the theory that the UFO phenomenon was not extraterrestrial in origin but has its origins in a very ancient, elite offshoot of the human race that

Tonnies referred to as the cryptoterrestrials—*Homo sapiens*-related beings that, millennia ago, were perceived as gods but who ultimately chose to move deep below ground when we began to grow in numbers.

Of the many reasons why Tonnies thrust the entire issue of ancient humans into the modern era, one in particular was his take on a certain event which occurred in early July 1947 on the Foster Ranch, Lincoln County, New Mexico. We're talking about the alleged crash of a UFO a couple of hours' drive from the famous town of Roswell.

Regardless of what UFO proponents might say, the fact of the matter is that none of us really knows what happened back in 1947 when something came down on the Foster Ranch, Lincoln County, New Mexico. So, Tonnies saw nothing wrong with addressing, and contemplating on, the merits—or the lack of merits—of the many and varied theories. Tonnies speculated on the possibility that the Roswell craft was built, flown, and ultimately disastrously crashed by ancient cryptoterrestrials that lurk in the depths of the planet. Controversial? Definitely. But Tonnies made some interesting observations on this possibility. In his own words: "The device that crashed near Roswell in the summer of 1947, whatever it was, featured properties at least superficially like the high-altitude balloon trains ultimately cited as an explanation by the Air Force. Debunkers have, of course, seized on the lack of revealingly 'high-tech' components found among the debris to dismiss the possibility that the crash was anything but a case of misidentification; not even Maj. Jesse Marcel, the intelligence officer who advocated an ET origin for the unusual foil and structural beams, mentioned anything remotely resembling an engine or power-plant."

Tonnies continued, in a fashion that emphasized the cryptoterrestrials may not be—today—as scientifically and technologically advanced as they might prefer us to think they are or were in the past: "The cryptoterrestrial hypothesis offers a speculative alternative: maybe the Roswell device wasn't high-tech. It could indeed have been a balloon-borne surveillance device brought down in a storm, but it doesn't logically follow that is was one of our own" (Ibid.).

Tonnies concluded on the matter of Roswell: "Upon happening across such a troubling find, the Air Force's excessive secrecy begins to make sense."

Despite what you, I, or indeed any number of the well-known Roswell researchers—such as Bill Moore, Kevin Randle, Stan Friedman, or Don Schmitt—might think or conclude, the fact is that Tonnies' cryptoterrestrial theory is probably the only one that allows for the Roswell crash site to have been comprised of (a) beings that lived outside of human society; and (b) incredibly simplistic technology. The alien theory should, of course, require highly advanced technology to have been recovered—yet, we hear very little on this matter, aside from talk of fields full of foil-like material with curious

The UFO Museum in Roswell, New Mexico, which offers evidence of extraterrestrials, but what if these aliens actually came from inside our planet as Mac Tonnies speculated?

properties. Accounts of the military coming across alien-created "power plants" and "engines"—as Tonnies described them—are curiously absent from the Roswell affair. It's that aforementioned foil and not much else. A sturdy reconnaissance balloon built by radiation-blighted cryptoterrestrials?

Mac Tonnies was not alone in talking about this particular theory. Walter Bosley, formerly of both the U.S. Air Force Office of Special Investigations and the Federal Bureau of Investigation (FBI), has revealed an interesting and notable story told to him by his very own father. Like Walter, he too served in the U.S. Force, in the late 1950s, on matters relative to the U.S. space program. Significantly, during the period of his employment with the military, Bosley Sr., received at Wright-Patterson Air Force Base, Dayton, Ohio, a highly classified briefing relative to the reported UFO crash near Roswell, New Mexico, in the summer of 1947.

Bosley said that by the time of his father's briefing, the U.S. Air Force had come to a startling and worrying conclusion: Neither the strange aerial device nor the bodies found in the desert outside of Roswell at the time in question had alien origins. Very significantly, Bosley revealed, his father told him the entities and their craft come from *inside* our planet. Their civilization supposedly resides within a huge, underground system of caverns and tunnels beneath the southwest portion of the United States (shades of the Death Valley rumors, perhaps?). Not only that, they are a civilization that once resided on the surface of the Earth but that, thousands of years ago, relocated their entire society deep underground. To escape the effects of the atomic weapons launched on them by their enemies? Quite possibly so.

Bosley was additionally told by his father: "They are human in appearance, so much so that they can move among us with ease with just a little effort. If you get a close look, you'd notice something odd, but not if the person just passed you on the street."

Today, some people believe the New World Order secretly knows all about Mac Tonnies' cryptoterrestrials, and the two—one an ancient elite and the other a modern-day one—are engaged in an uneasy truce over who rules the planet vs. who should rule it. To keep the down-to-earth secret hidden from the media, governments, and the public, the New World Order hides the truth of the cryptoterrestrials behind a massive smokescreen made up of bogus tales of alien abductors, extraterrestrial visitations, and flying saucers from other worlds.

SANDERS, BERNIE

Bernie Sanders was seen by many as the ideal candidate to ensure a Democratic Party victory in the 2016 presidential election, but not everyone agreed. Indeed, and incredibly, there were those who suspected that Sanders was nothing but a tool of the New World Order—whether wittingly or unwittingly is very much a case of speculation. *State of the Nation* said on this specific, thorny issue:

"Bernie Sanders is making lots of promises he will not be able to keep! His appeal to America's youth is understandable considering the failure of our current leaders as well as the nature of the expectations his policies create. But, the historical record of socialism is dismal. And the dire financial condition of the country will not support his ambitious plans. Taxing Wall Street and the rich sounds good but is likely to destroy jobs while providing only modest increases in revenue for the government. And, by failing to be aggressive in challenging the Military-Industrial Complex that supports America's imperial foreign policy, *Sanders implicitly embraces the true agenda of the 1% that has done more to destroy this country than anything else* [italics added]."

Allen L. Roland, Ph.D., said to *Veterans Today* in 2015: "There is a reason that Bernie Sanders has surged ahead in the Presidential Primary Polls and that Britain's Jeremy Corbyn has done the same thing in the UK—it's people power and it won't be stopped. The honesty of Bernie Sanders is a lifeboat in a sea of political deception and lost hope and soon he will be joined by the UK's Jeremy

Corbyn as a worldwide counter balance to corporate power and the elite 1 percent as well as a genuine reflection of a new world order based on people power."

7/7

On the morning of July 7, 2005, the United Kingdom's capital city of London was plunged into a state of overwhelming chaos, the likes of which had not been seen since the 1970s and 1980s when the Irish Republican Army (IRA) regularly launched cowardly terrorist attacks on British soil. It was a morning that began just like any other in the bustling city but which ended with fifty-six people dead, including four individuals believed to have been the crazed and deluded masterminds behind the attack. On top of that, over 700 people received injuries that ranged from minor to severe. It was an event that quickly became known as 7/7. It's also an event that has since become steeped in conspiracy theories.

The perpetrators chose their locations and times coldly, calculatingly, and carefully: the busy streets and packed London Underground rail system at the height of the early morning rush hour. Not only that, the date of the attacks was just one day after the UK had secured the contract to host the 2012 Olympic Games. Clearly, creating terror and intimidation—at a time that was supposed to be one of overriding celebration and national pride—was the name of the deadly game.

The British government did not look to the Middle East for the answers to who was responsible for the nightmarish events of July 7, 2005. Certainly, in the aftermath of 9/11, Britain's MI5 and MI6—the UK's equivalents of the FBI and the CIA—began to fear and suspect that any similar attack on mainland Britain would likely be undertaken by homegrown terrorists rather than those operating out of a cave in the mountains of Afghanistan. They appear to have been correct.

It did not take long for officialdom to identify the guilty parties. Careful and widespread study of literally hundreds of closed-circuit cameras across London, coupled with intelligence-based leads, revealed the chief suspects as Germaine Lindsay, Mohammed Sidique Khan, Hasib Hussain, and Shehzad Tanweer. Hussain, Tanweer, and Khan lived in the English city of Leeds, while Lindsay was from the Buckinghamshire town of Aylesbury.

All four men were recorded on CCTV cameras—together, as a group—at Luton Station on the morning of the attacks. They were also variously filmed on the London Underground or as they made their way toward it.

Explosives were found in Tanweer's vehicle, which was parked at Luton Railway Station. Lindsay, Tanweer, and Khan died in the underground explosions, while Hussain met his end on the double-decker.

Khan and Tanweer had made videorecordings that leave no room for doubt when it came to their mindset. "We are at war and I am a soldier," said Khan as he targeted his rage against the West. In a prerecorded statement, Janweer chillingly stated: "What you have witnessed now is only the beginning."

In addition, leads that developed from digging into the lives and backgrounds of all four men allowed both the police and the security services to make a number of arrests and also uncover quantities of explosives at a variety of locations across the country. In other words, there seems to be little doubt regarding who was responsible for the shocking events: home-grown terrorists who felt the need to take out their deranged fury on the people of London. So, with that being the case, why have so many questioned the official version of events? Let's take a look.

In an article titled "Coincidence of Bomb Exercises?"—which was prepared for Britain's Channel 4—writer Nicholas Glass wrote of the conspiracy theories surrounding 7/7: "It began when Peter Power, one time high ranking employee of Scotland Yard and member of its Anti-Terrorist Branch, reported in two major UK media outlets that his company Visor Consulting had on the morning of 7th of July been conducting 'crisis exercises' whose scenarios uncannily mirrored those of the actual attack."

Glass also noted that during the course of interviews with elements of the British media—specifically *Radio 5 Live* and *ITV News*—Power "appeared" to assert that the exercises in question involved "a thousand people," along with "a dedicated crisis team," one whose total number was never revealed. More astonishing, as Glass noted, Power described "the simulation of 'simultaneous attacks on an underground and mainline station' and 'bombs going off *precisely* at the railway stations' at which the actual bombings occurred."

Part of the exercise involved Visor Consulting planning to practice switching from a "slow-time thinking" to a "quick-time thinking" of the kind required by a situation dominated by crisis. As it transpired, said Glass, "they were forced to do so for real." And the story is not quite over.

Glass continued: "Three days after the London bombings, Power was in Toronto for the fifteenth 'World Conference on Disaster Management.' There, he took part in a discussion panel for the Canadian Broadcasting Corporation's news discussion program *CBS: Sunday Night*, in which he was quizzed again about what the host called the 'extraordinary' conjunction of his company's planned scenarios and the actual events. Power dismissed this as 'spooky coincidence.'

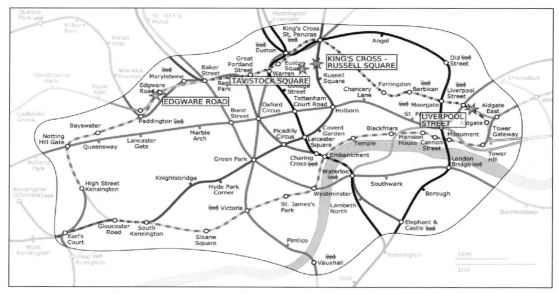

A map showing the locations of the three bombings of the London Underground on July 7, 2005.

Power added: "Our scenario was very similar, but it wasn't totally identical. It was based on bombs going off—the time, the locations, all this sort of stuff."

In response, Glass wrote that this undeniably odd development was "ignored by the mainstream media. Online publishers stepped in to add fuel to the fires of indignation. Colman Jones, an associate producer on *CBS: Sunday Night*, claimed in his blog that, while escorting participants from the building, he enquired of Power 'why there had not been more media coverage of this.' 'They were trying to keep it quiet,' Power purportedly responded, with what Jones called 'a knowing smile.'"

As Channel 4 also demonstrated, the world of conspiracy theorizing quickly sat up and took notice of this odd state of affairs. Particularly quick off the mark was the website *Prison Planet*. In an article titled "London Underground Bombing 'Exercises' Took Place at Same Time as Real Attack," they noted: "Whether Mr. Power and Visor Consultants were 'in on the bombing' is not that important," their report stated. "The British government or one of their private company offshoots could have hired Visor to run the exercise for a number of purposes. This is precisely what happened on the morning of September 11th 2001 with the CIA conducting drills of flying hijacked planes into the WTC and Pentagon at 8:30 in the morning."

In the same way that 9/11 allowed the U.S. government to justify placing the U.S. population under ever-increasing New World Order-style surveillance, so the 7/7 affair allowed the British government to do exactly likewise.

THE SINGULARITY AND ARTIFICIAL EVOLUTION

It may sound like wild, over-the-top science fiction, but it's not. The day may come when we find ourselves, as a species, radically and physically altered, specifically as a result of incredible advances in technology. They just might be advances that will lead to the world that Aldous Huxley feared so much, namely, a human society that did not stand up against the New World Order of Huxley's *Brave New World* for one particular reason: they didn't care. Pleasure and mind-altering substances were all that mattered. Could we, one day, find ourselves in a similar situation, one in which technology changes us so much that rising up against our leaders plays no role in a hedonistic, pleasure-driven future? Let us take a look at what might be on the horizon.

"It is nonsensical and counter-intuitive to believe that complex life was created only to end after a set period of time. An intelligent, complex being should be able to live indefinitely, or to put it in another way, it should not be allowed to die through aging. Otherwise, what is the point of its creation in the first place? However, it is clear that our current, naive attempts at dramatically increasing life-span are doomed to failure. An alternative approach could be based upon completely different and entirely un-indoctrinated ways of thinking. There is an evolutionary impetus to achieve higher complexity in the quickest way possible. Finding ways to enhance this process in humans, will lead to indefinite lifespans."

Those are the words of Marios Kyriazis, a medical doctor and someone who, in 1992, established the British Longevity Society. While Kyriazis believes that major breakthroughs in life extension are likely to be a reality one day, he doesn't believe it's on the immediate horizon: "What is there we can do in order to live longer? Do a bit of exercise, don't smoke, take a few supplements and what else? There is nothing else. We have to wait for new research to come through, stem cells, nanotechnology or other developments, so that we could take it in tablet or injection form and influence our aging. Apart from the ordinary things we have been talking about 20, 30 years ago, even 40 years ago (don't smoke, exercise, fresh air) what else is there in practical terms? Yes, there is a lot of research, and a lot of work done, but this is still in the laboratory. There is very little that can be applied now to the people in the street so that they can extend their lives."

Others disagree with Kyriazis—including those who believe that the answer to immortality will come via the splicing of human and machine: real-life equivalents of *Robocop* and *The Six Million Dollar Man* and even the uploading of one's memories and life experiences into highly advanced computers.

The idea of the "singularity" is that, one day, humans will be able to transfer their consciousnesses into machines and, thus, become immortal.

When it comes to the issue of the human race being radically altered in the future—and perhaps even in the astonishingly near future—and possibly even becoming immortal, few can rival Ray Kurzweil in the controversy stakes. The director of engineering at Google and a computer scientist, Kurzweil has made some jaw-dropping predictions for what may be in store by, perhaps, no later than 2045. It's his prediction that as computer technology develops at an exponential rate, and as nanotechnology becomes ever more advanced, we'll reach a tipping point which Kurzweil terms the Singularity.

That will be the moment when we become digitally immortal. Our minds will be uploaded into computers. We may even be able to live in both a physical and digital state, jumping from one to the other as we see fit. And, while we're in our physical states, we'll likely see our bodily organs increasingly replaced by sophisticated technology that will effectively transform us into cyborgs.

Although Kurzweil has made such predictions for a long time, it was his presentation at the 2013 New York-based "Global Futures 20145 International Congress" that really caught the attention of both the media and the public. It was a conference funded and organized by a Russian multimillionaire, Dmitry Itskov. Kurzweil's words were powerful and, for some, more than a bit daunting: "We're going to become increasingly non-biological to the point where the non-biological part dominates and the biological part is not important any more. In fact the non-biological part—the machine part—will be so powerful it can completely model and understand the biological part. So even if that biological part went away it wouldn't make any difference."

Expanding on this, Kurzweil added: "We'll also have non-biological bodies—we can create bodies with nanotechnology, we can create virtual bodies and virtual reality in which the virtual reality will be as realistic as the actual reality. The virtual bodies will be as detailed and convincing as real bodies. We do need a body, our intelligence is directed towards a body, but it doesn't have to be this frail, biological body that is subject to all kinds of failure modes. But I think we'll have a choice of bodies. We'll certainly be routinely changing our parent body through virtual reality and today you can have a different body in something like Second Life, but it's just a picture on the screen. Research has shown that people actually begin to subjectively identify with their avatar."

And, on the matter of the immortality that Kurzweil believes is getting ever closer, he offers the following observation: "If we had radical life extension only we would get profoundly bored and we would run out of things to do and new ideas. In addition to radical life extension, we're going to need radical life expansion."

A brave new world, or a grave new world? Perhaps, in just a few decades, we will have the answer to that question.

SKULL AND BONES

One of the most mysterious of all secret societies—and one which is shrouded in intrigue and filled with influential figures—is Skull and Bones. Although its origins date back to 1701, the society was formed in 1832 at Yale University, New Haven, Connecticut. The founders of Skull and Bones were William Huntingdon Russell, a powerful businessman and a notable figure in the history of the Republican Party, and Alphonso Taft, who—under U.S. President Ulysses S. Grant—held the positions of both secretary of war and attorney general. As a result of significant differences between various debating groups at Yale, Taft and Russell elected to create their very own, elite group. Skull and Bones, of course.

Kris Millegan, the editor of the Conspiracy Theory Research List, says: "According to information acquired from a break-in to the 'tomb' (the Skull and Bones meeting hall) in 1876, 'Bones is a chapter of a corps in a German University ... General Russell, its founder, was in Germany before his Senior Year and formed a warm friendship with a leading member of a German society. He brought back with him to college, authority to found a chapter here.' So class valedictorian William H. Russell, along with fourteen others, became the founding members of 'The Order of Scull and Bones,' later changed to 'The Order of Skull and Bones.'"

As a demonstration of how Skull and Bones developed a reputation as a powerful and shadowy order, we have the following from the October 1873 premier edition of *The Iconoclast*. Its staff held nothing back when it came to the matter of warning people of the power and influence that Skull and Bones wielded and on an ever-growing basis, too: "Out of every class Skull and Bones takes its men. They have gone out into the world and have become, in many instances, leaders in society. They have obtained control of Yale. Its business is performed by them. Money paid to the college must pass into their hands, and be subject to their will. No doubt they are worthy men in themselves, but the many, whom they looked down upon while in college, cannot so far forget as to give money freely into their hands. Men in Wall Street complain that the college comes straight to them for help, instead of asking each graduate for his share. The reason is found in a remark made by one of Yale's and America's first men: 'Few will give but Bones men and they care far more for their society than they do for the college....'"

The logo of the Skull and Bones. The first two numerals in 322 indicate the founding year of the society being 1832, and the 2 at the end indicates that this is the second chapter of the Bavarian Illuminati. Another theory is that 322 is the year of the Greek statesman Demosthenes' death, which is when the society begins its calendar.

The Iconoclast added: "Year by year the deadly evil is growing. The society was never as obnoxious to the college as it is today, and it is just this ill-feeling that shuts the pockets of non-members. Never before has it shown such arrogance and self-fancied superiority. It grasps the College Press and endeavors to rule it all. It does not deign to show its credentials, but clutches at power with the silence of conscious guilt."

Anthony C. Sutton is the author of a very revealing book, *America's Secret Establishment*. In its pages, Sutton says of Skull and Bones, "The order is not just another Greek letter fraternal society with passwords and handgrips common to most campuses. Chapter 322 is a secret society whose members are sworn to silence. It only exists on the Yale campus (that we know about). It has rules. It has ceremonial rites. It is not at all happy with prying, probing citizens—known among initiates as 'outsiders' or 'vandals.' Its members always deny membership (or are supposed to deny membership) and in checking hundreds of autobiographical listings for members we found only half a dozen who cited an affiliation with Skull & Bones. The rest were silent."

The membership of Skull and Bones is both illustrious and controversial and has included such noteworthy figures as former presidents of the United States William Howard Taft, George H.W. Bush, George W. Bush, and U.S. Secretary of State John Kerry. *Time* magazine says of Skull and Bones that "Bonesmen have, at one time, controlled the fortunes of the Carnegie, Rockefeller and Ford families, as well as posts in the Central Intelligence Agency, the American Psychological Association, the Council on Foreign Relations and some of the most powerful law firms in the world."

Within the field of conspiracy theorizing, Skull and Bones is said to have played major roles in the November 22, 1963, assassination of President John F. Kennedy, the Iran–Contra scandal of the 1980s, and the "rigging" of the 2000 U.S. presidential election.

SMART TV SPIES

In February 2015, a strange and controversial story erupted throughout the media. It was news picked up by many who have concerns about public privacy and secret, NWO-style meddling in our lives, including Clark Howard, who said: "You've heard of the government spying on you and even businesses spying on you. But have you heard of your TV spying on you?! If you're not familiar with 'smart TVs,' they are modern flat-screen TVs with built-in apps allowing you to access online content like Netflix, Hulu Plus, or Amazon Prime much more easily than you would access traditional broadcast content."

Howard continued: "Samsung is getting a lot of heat for smart TVs that can spy on you. In fact, their terms of service says they will spy on you: 'Please be aware that if your spoken words include personal or other sensitive information, that information will be among the data captured and transmitted to a third party through your use of Voice Recognition.' So at least they're telling you! But Samsung's response to the criticism they're now facing? 'Samsung takes consumer privacy very seriously.' Yeah, right!"

Digital Trends was far more skeptical of the situation and provided its readers this with regard to the "data captured" angle referred to by Clark Howard: "Granted, that sounds pretty nefarious, especially when taken out of context. Unfortunately, Samsung's overly succinct description is missing some critical context. Namely, it doesn't say when the spoken words are captured,

The technology used to give us smart TVs can be exploited in order to spy on people.

under what conditions data is transmitted to a third party, or who that third party is. We asked Samsung to clear up all of these questions, and frankly, the conspiracy theorists might be giving these 'smart' TVs too much credit. The suggestion that Samsung Smart TVs are 'always listening' is a misnomer, and at the core of all the scuttlebutt. The fact is, Samsung's Smart TVs are asleep on the job 99 percent of the time. They're programmed to 'wake up' when they detect a pre-programmed phrase such as 'Hi TV,' but—and this is critical—until that phrase is spoken, they aren't 'paying attention' to anything you say, nor are they storing or reporting anything."

But things don't end there. *Betanews* revealed there was a great deal more to the story: "The company had publicly acknowledged that it was indeed logging users' activity and voice commands (do note—in the company's defense, the privacy policy is also publicly available). The company also noted that 'these functions [voice tapping] are enabled only when users agree to the separate Samsung Privacy Policy and Terms of Use regarding this function when initially setting up the TV.' The company further noted that users' data was fully encrypted as part of the industry-standard measures it takes.

"But now we're learning that the data which Samsung gleans from its Smart TVs is not encrypted. Ken Munro and David Lodge, from the London-based Pen Test Partners tested one of Samsung's smart TVs to discover that the TV was uploading audio files in an unencrypted form. The finding further reveals that a transcribed copy of what had been said when beamed back to the TV (letting the TV act on the commands) was also in an unencrypted form for any hacker to decode."

Hackers in the employ of the New World Order? It would make perfect sense.

SNOWDEN, EDWARD

Nineteen Eighty-Four, as we have seen, is a satirical, political novel written by George Orwell in 1949. The story takes place in a nightmarish, then future, New World Order-style society where not only does the state demand one hundred percent conformity via indoctrination, punishment, fear, and propaganda, it also intrudes into the lives of one and all via constant surveillance and spying. Such a thing couldn't happen in the real world, could it? Wake up, world: it already has. Welcome to the revelations of the planet's most notorious whistleblower since Watergate's Deep Throat. We're talking about Edward Snowden. Up until the summer of 2013, he was a man unknown to just about everyone except his family, friends, and work colleagues. After the summer of 2013, practically everyone knew his name.

It was not so much who Snowden was that caught the world's attention but what he had to say. As an employee of the National Security Agency (NSA), Snowden blew the whistle just about as loudly as he possibly could on the alarming and near-unbelievable extent to which the NSA was spying not just on foreign nations but on U.S. citizens too—as in just about each and every one of them. Landlines, cell phones, email, Facebook, Twitter, and Skype: they had all been penetrated by the NSA, very often with the witting, subservient, and unforgivable help of those same companies. The data collection process was so mind-bogglingly huge that it would likely have had even George Orwell himself shaking his head in disbelief, except for just one thing: this was all too real.

To some, Snowden is an outright national hero, one who succeeded in demonstrating to the world that the NSA is an agency-run riot in its goal to place the entire United States under electronic surveillance. To others, he is a man who has jeopardized U.S. national security and placed our troops in danger. To many people, Snowden falls somewhere between both.

The U.S. government took immediate steps to try to curtail Snowden's actions: he faced a three-decades-long jail term for violating the Espionage

Protestors in Washington, D.C., march for privacy, one holding a placard with a photo of Snowden on it.

Act, and his passport was revoked. Snowden was very quickly a man on the run. Where, exactly, he ran to—or, rather, flew to—was Moscow, Russia's Sheremetyevo International Airport. Despite initial concerns on Snowden's part that he would not be allowed to stay—because of certain visa issues—his fears were soon eased when he was given a 365-day period of asylum. That has since been extended to a three-year period of asylum. At the time of this writing, Snowden remains in Russia, living in secret, and doing his utmost to be allowed to live out his life somewhere in Europe.

So, what was it that caused so much consternation for the U.S. government, and specifically for the NSA? A great deal, that's what.

Without doubt the biggest and most shocking revelations centered upon something that is called PRISM. Essentially, PRISM is a program that both collects and stores electronic data—and on a massive scale. We have to "thank" President George W. Bush for pushing PRISM through via the terms of (a) the Protect America Act of 2007, which was implemented on August 5, 2007; and (b) the FISA Amendments Act of 2008—FISA stands for Foreign Intelligence Surveillance Act. Collectively, the acts permit the gathering of electronic data from countless sources—and, in the process, protect those same sources from prosecution.

What outraged so many was who, precisely, the sources were that Snowden knew of and blew the whistle on. They included corporations such as Sprint, Yahoo, AT&T, Facebook, YouTube, Verizon, Google, Skype, Microsoft, Apple, and Paltalk—and that was just the top of the long list. In no time at all, the world realized the implications of all this: the National Security Agency had carte blanche to wade through the emails, photos, instant messages, Skype conversations (both audio and video), texts, file transfers, voice mail messages, and live conversations by phone and over the Internet of every U.S. citizen and resident—and without hardly a concern for the law or matters relative to personal privacy.

If all the NSA was doing was carefully watching the activities of potential or known terrorists, others that wish to do us harm, and those who are possible threats to the security of the nation, very few people would likely have any complaints. But, as the Snowden revelations showed, that's not what was, or still is, going on. Hospitals, universities, private corporations, and even libraries were targeted, as were bank records, doctor–patient files, and more.

Glenn Greenwald, an American journalist who significantly contributed to the publishing of the Edward Snowden revelations, said that the NSA's employees "listen to whatever emails they want, whatever telephone calls, browsing histories, Microsoft Word documents. And it's all done with no need to go to a court, with no need to even get supervisor approval on the part of the analyst."

See also the entry on "PRISM Project."

SOCIAL SECURITY ADMINISTRATION ARMS PURCHASES

It was a very weird story that got New World Order researchers worried. In 2012, to the amazement and puzzlement of many, it was revealed that none other than the U.S. Social Security Administration (SSA) had secretly, and at that time recently, purchased almost a quarter of a million rounds of ammunition. When the story broke, the SSA was quick to play down the entire thing as a matter of little consequence. Some conspiracy-minded figures suggested the agency was perhaps just a bit too quick to lay matters to rest. It may come as a surprise to a majority of people to learn that the SSA has its very own independent police force. The SSA assured everyone that the bullets were simply bought for target practice, as a means to train its personnel on the latest tactics and trends in the world of law enforcement. Uh-huh. Of course, what else? Well, maybe, quite a lot else.

Not everyone, unsurprisingly, was buying into the SSA's version of events. In fact, it's correct to say that hardly anyone bought into it. Certainly, the news provoked understandable suggestions that the SSA—along with other agencies and those orchestrating the New World Order—was preparing for a near-future period of nationwide civil uprising, possibly from the effects of a complete collapse of the entire U.S. economy.

What would the Social Security Administration want with bullets? In 2012 it was revealed that the agency had bought a quarter million rounds of ammunition.

In those online domains where the conspiratorial like to hang out, even bleaker rumors were quickly taking shape. One of the most controversial theories presented suggested that, to avoid complete economic collapse, plans were afoot to secretly, and drastically, lower the population level of the United States. This, we were told, would be achieved by switching on a dormant virus that was deliberately inserted into the flu vaccine. All of the tens of millions of people who regularly get flu jabs would suddenly fall sick and die. The military would handle the disaster, along with other agencies and bodies of government, including the SSA. With tens of millions dead—maybe more than one hundred million, the theory went, the economic strain would be gone, or, at least, significantly lifted.

Of course, it's all paranoid nonsense and couldn't really happen. Could it? Maybe we won't know the answer to that question until it is way too late to do anything about it—aside from not getting a flu shot, perhaps.

SPANISH FLU PANDEMIC

Some people scoff at the idea that the New World Order might unleash a deadly virus, one designed to wipe out not just millions, but billions, of people. The reason: to make it much easier to control the survivors, who may number perhaps around one billion, rather than the approximately seven billion people who are alive today. For those who think such a thing is simply not possible, we only have to look at the early twentieth-century outbreak of the Spanish Flu. Although not unleashed deliberately, it serves to show how quickly—and disastrously—such a NWO-created virus could wreak havoc on a worldwide scale.

In 1914, World War I began and led to millions of deaths all across Europe. The carnage finally came to an end in 1918 when Germany was defeated by Allied forces. Since, however, the first wave of infection began in early 1918—when the war was still being fought—its scale, and its attendant implications for the human race, went by largely unnoticed. That is, until it was all too late.

As is often the case in zombie-themed TV shows and movies, the origin and the eruption of the outbreak are matters of deep controversy and mystery. Such was the case with the Spanish Flu. Interestingly, and also paralleling established zombie lore, there were suspicions on the part of Allied soldiers that it was all the work of dark and secret experimentation. There was an undercurrent of belief that the Germans had created a deadly virus and then, using carefully placed agents all across the planet, unleashed it to wipe out any and all enemy nations.

And there is another zombie-based angle, too: when infection from the Spanish Flu set in, its effects could be seen in mere hours. Profuse bleeding from the mouth and nose was typical. A raging fever and pneumonia-like symptoms soon overwhelmed the infected. Death was not far behind. In fact, just about the only thing missing was nightmarish reanimation.

What is known for sure about the outbreak is that military personnel in training camps in the state of Kansas were among the very first victims. This has led to a theory that the Spanish Flu had its origins in the Kansas-based Fort Riley, where chickens and pigs were bred by the military for food. It is suspected in some quarters that a form of avian flu, present in the chickens, may have "jumped" to the human race, thus resulting in the chaos that followed.

Certainly, it would not be long at all before the rest of the world was in the icy grip of the deadly virus: parts of South America, Asia, Europe, the United States, and Africa were soon overwhelmed. One might think that such a powerful, mutated form of the flu virus would chiefly take its toll on the old and the sickly. Not so: most of the victims were under the age of thirty-five.

Incredibly, at the height of the epidemic, no less than 25 percent of the *entire* U.S. population was infected, as was around 18–20 percent of the rest of the planet. To put it in perspective, that collectively amounted to around 500

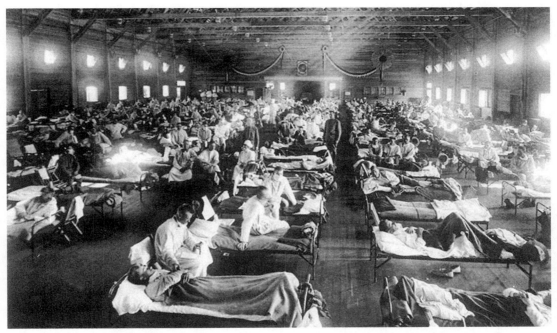

A ward in Kansas's Camp Funston tends to Spanish Flu patients in this 1918 photograph. Over fifty million people would die of the pandemic between 1918 and 1920.

million people worldwide. It's hardly surprising, then, that the Spanish Flu ultimately took the lives of around *fifty million people*.

In late 1918, and for reasons that remain unclear to this very day, the death toll began to drop at a significant rate and to the point where, by 1919, the epidemic was on its last legs. By the time that the outbreak was declared over, it had killed more people than had the hostilities of the entire World War I.

It happened in 1918. It could happen again today—albeit in ruthless, orchestrated, NWO-driven fashion.

SPRAYING CITIES

The idea that the minions of the New World Order might target for termination millions of city-dwelling Americans with dangerous toxins, viruses, and mind-altering substances—as they seek to take control—is not at all far-fetched. In some fashion, it has already occurred.

Among the many and controversial assignments given to Dr. Sydney Gottlieb by CIA chief Allen Dulles was the charge to create a method of producing large-scale aberrant mental states on an unsuspecting population. A substance was sought that could be used by the U.S. military when engaging an enemy that they could spray over a city and render both civilians and military opponents relatively helpless and unable to resist. The substance should be able to cause illogical thinking, produce disablement, such as paralysis of the legs, or cause mental confusion.

It would have been awkward at the time to experiment on foreign populations, so MKUltra created the appropriately named Operation Big City. CIA agents modified a 1953 Mercury so that its exhaust pipe extended eighteen inches beyond its normal length. A gas concocted to cause hallucinations was then emitted through the car's exhaust as the agents drove the Mercury for eighty miles around New York City, making careful note of the effects on pedestrians. In another test, operatives equipped with nasal filters boarded the New York subway with battery-powered emissions equipment fitted into suitcases to test the effects of LSD on people in confined areas.

An ambitious project was undertaken in 1957 when CIA personnel released a biological effect gas on the Golden Gate Bridge in San Francisco. The intent of the experiment was to blanket the entire city with the gas and then monitor how powerfully the disorienting properties of the substance would affect the population. The agents were dismayed when a sudden wind arose and blew the gas away before it could do any harm.

It should also be noted that in an experiment to determine how susceptible an American city would be to biological attack, the U.S. Navy sprayed a cloud of bacteria from ships over San Francisco in 1950. Many residents became ill with pneumonia and other illnesses. In 1951, the U.S. Department of Defense began open-air tests over many American cities, using disease-producing bacteria and viruses. Senate hearings on health and scientific tesearch in 1977 confirmed that 230 populated areas were contaminated with biological agents between 1949 and 1969. The list of cities included San Francisco, Key West, Panama City, Minneapolis, and St. Louis.

With such technology—and disregard for the lives of Americans—in place back in the 1950s, it's not at all implausible that agents of the New World Order will do likewise when Zero Hour comes around.

SUPERVIRUSES

If the New World Order is planning on unleashing deadly viruses to massively lower world population levels, they may have taken inspiration from *The Andromeda Strain*, a thought-provoking 1961 novel written by the late Michael Crichton of *Jurassic Park* fame. Two years later, *The Andromeda Strain* was turned into a movie of the same name.

An American space probe—as it returns to planet Earth and crashes in the wilds of Arizona—unleashes a lethal virus of extraterrestrial origins. Matters soon escalate in ominous, doomsday-like fashion: The U.S. government struggles to find an antidote. The virus threatens to wipe out the entire human race. And ... well, you get the apocalyptic picture.

While *The Andromeda Strain* is a highly entertaining story that is both disturbing and thought provoking, it does, rather incredibly, have its real-life counterparts. According to Article IX of "The Treaty on Principles Governing the Activities of States in the Exploration and Use of Outer Space, Including the Moon and Other Celestial Bodies" that was collectively signed in Washington, London, and Moscow on January 27, 1967, and that was entered into force on October 10 of that year: "In the exploration and use of outer space, including the Moon and other celestial bodies, States Parties to the Treaty shall be guided by the principle of co-operation and mutual assistance and shall conduct all their activities in outer space, including the Moon and other celestial bodies, with due regard to the corresponding interests of all other States Parties to the Treaty."

The document continues: "States Parties to the Treaty shall pursue studies of outer space, including the Moon and other celestial bodies, and conduct exploration of them so as to avoid their harmful contamination and also adverse changes in the environment of the Earth resulting from the introduction of extraterrestrial matter and, where necessary, shall adopt appropriate measures for this purpose."

It becomes very clear from studying the available data of that particular era that there was indeed official concern about a deadly—albeit admittedly theoretical—alien virus running wild on Earth and provoking a worldwide pandemic—one which just might escalate to the point where it could possibly wipe out each and every one of us.

Or, of course, we might see the New World Order try something similar but with a deadly, home-grown virus.

See also entry on "Viruses."

SURVIVALISTS

As more and more people fear that a New World Order is looming large on the horizon, there is an increasing focus on the survivalist movement. But, who are they? What is their agenda and approach to the New World Order? Let's see. *Newsweek* notes: "Survivalism is a movement of individuals or groups (called survivalists or preppers) who are actively preparing for emergencies, including possible disruptions in social or political order, on scales from local to international. The word prepper is derived from the word prepare. Survivalists often acquire emergency medical and self-defense training, stockpile food and water, prepare to become self-sufficient, and build structures (e.g., a survival retreat or an underground shelter) that may help them survive a catastrophe."

Off the Grid News offers its thoughts on the survivalist movement: "The prepping movement seems to be growing by leaps and bounds. While there are no accurate figures about how many people in the United States identify themselves as 'preppers,' estimates range right around 3 million people. A more accurate idea might come from looking at how many new prepping websites there are

A growing number of Americans fear their own government—or a world government—and have been arming themselves and living off the grid.

and how many new businesses which cater to those with a survivalist mentality. Why, even mainstream retail giants like Costco and Sam's Club are carrying prepackaged survival food.

"It's clear that the United States is preparing for something; although opinions vary considerably about what it is that we are preparing for. Some are looking no farther than a disastrous weather event, while others are predicting the end of life as we know it and a return to simpler times."

Henry Makow, Ph.D., brings religion into the equation when he states: "This isn't about storing silver coins or canned food or getting an AK-47. It's about saving your soul, not your skin. It's about the tendency to obsess on the New World Order, get depressed and become unbearable. The situation is depressing. A satanic cult controls the credit of the world and rules through myriad proxies. It is determined to destroy civilization and institute an Orwellian police state. You spend hours every day watching for new developments. Your face is pressed up against the top window of the world. You are 'externalized.' You can't go into the kitchen without switching on the radio. You try to squeeze your sustenance from the world. But much of what you imbibe is poisonous: depravity, corruption, duplicity and tragedy. (Is that the point of the mass media? To demoralize and brutalize?) Mankind is in the grip of a diabolical force that strives to legitimize itself through constant deception. You can't overcome this demon. But you still control your personal life. Ultimately, the battle is for the soul of humanity. Why not begin by defending your own soul? This means erecting a wall between the soul, and the world, and establishing a balance between the sacred and the profane. You need to shut out the world (the profane) for set periods of time and focus on what inspires you. That means turning off the TV, Internet and media in general."

TALBOTT, STROBE

Back in July 1999, the *Los Angeles Times* ran a feature titled "Strobe Talbott Leads toward One World." It noted that Talbott's—a former U.S. deputy secretary of state—work and beliefs reflect "a transformation in his own mind, from the Reaganism he was against, to the internationalism he was for. 'It has taken the events in our own wondrous and terrible century to clinch the case for world government,' he wrote that summer, when candidate Clinton already looked like a winner against George Bush. Talbott joined the State Department the next year.

"If nothing else, Talbott expressed himself plainly: 'All countries are basically social arrangements, accommodations to changing circumstances ... they are all artificial and temporary.' He pointed to the then-emerging European Union as a 'pioneer' of 'supranational' regional cohesion that could 'pave the way for globalism.'

"Talbott's vision of post-patriotic internationalism stands in sharp contrast to, for example, Abraham Lincoln's vision of this country as one united by 'mystic chords of memory, stretching from battlefield and patriot grave to every living heart and hearthstone all over this broad land,' but he's certainly in tune with our present-day NATO allies in the conflict with Serbia. As British Prime Minister Tony Blair put it, Operation Allied Force represents 'a new doctrine of international community.'"

Let's take a look at a few of Talbott's eye-opening quotes: "In the next century, nations as we know it will be obsolete; all states will recognize a single, global authority. National sovereignty wasn't such a great idea after all."

"Here is one optimists reason for believing unity will prevail ... within the next hundred years ... nationhood as we know it will be obsolete; all states will recognize a single, global authority. A phrase briefly fashionable in the mid-20th century—citizen of the world—will have assumed real meaning by the end of the 21st."

"Once again great minds thought alike: Einstein, Gandhi, Toynbee and Camus all favored giving primacy to interests higher than those of the nation. So, finally, did many statesmen. Each world war inspired the creation of an international organization, the League of Nations in the 1920s and the United Nations in the '40s."

"Globalization has also contributed to the spread of terrorism, drug trafficking, AIDS and environmental degradation. But because those threats are more than any one nation can cope with on its own, they constitute an incentive for international cooperation."

A former deputy secretary of state under President Bill Clinton, Strobe Talbott is currently a foreign policy analyst associated with the Brookings Institute.

Unity of the Polis says: "The ongoing WikiLeaks document dumps from the email account of John Podesta have drawn attention to a transcript of a speech by Rhodes Scholar and President of the Brookings Institution Strobe Talbott entitled 'Vladimir Putin vs. the 21st Century.' The transcript provides important context and foreshadowing on the current geopolitical tensions between the Anglo-American Establishment embodied in NATO and Putin's Russia. In this speech at Occidental College on April 22, 2014, Talbott details how Vladamir Putin and Russia represent the greatest threat that could 'jeopardize the progress the world has made in recent decades' toward the 'new world order.' In addition to holding a Rhodes Scholarship, Talbott has served as the Director of the Council on Foreign Relations and was also on the Executive Committee of the Trilateral Commission. Talbott is no stranger to writing on the concept and advocacy of the New World Order and has spent decades developing strategies to affect Global Governance. In addition to serving in the administration of his former college roommate President William Jefferson Clinton as Deputy Secretary of State, he is also known for his book *The Great Experiment* and his 1992 *Time Magazine* article 'The Birth of a Global Nation.'"

And, we'll close this entry with the words of *New World Order Today*: "The goal has never changed and there are globalists who are pushing towards world government. Strobe Talbott said it best in his article in Time magazine from 1992 when he said in the 21st century National sovereignty as we have known it will cease to exist and we will all answer to a single global authority. Strobe Talbott is the head of the Brookings Institution, probably the most influential think tank used by the U.S. government today.

"His protégé Susan Rice is now the US Ambassador to the United Nations. She was working under Strobe Talbott before she went to help Barrack Obama with his campaign and then ultimately was appointed as our Ambassador to the world governmental system, the United Nations. When Strobe Talbott said that National Sovereignty would cease to exist and that we would all answer to a single global authority it was quite a statement because to do so our Declaration of Independence must be negated, and the National Sovereignty of the United States must be suspended, and then we can be drafted onto a new world order, a one world government."

TELEVISION

Is it possible that the New World Order is using television to dumb us all down and turn us into a society of ignorant "sheeple"? It is far more than possible: The process of making us slaves to our televisions and ensuring that we toe the line are already in place. Take, for example, the words of Alex Ansary. He says: "One of the most common examples of mind control in our so-called free and civilized society is the advent and usage of the television set. This isn't to say that all things on TV are geared towards brainwashing you. They're not. But most of the programming on television today is run and programmed by the largest media corporations that have interests in defense contracts, such as Westinghouse (CBS), and General Electric (NBC). This makes perfect sense when you see how slanted and warped the news is today.

"Experiments conducted by researcher Herbert Krugman reveal that when a person watches television, brain activity switches from the left to the right hemisphere. The left hemisphere is the seat of logical thought. Here, information is broken down into its component parts and critically analyzed. The right brain, however, treats incoming data uncritically, processing infor-

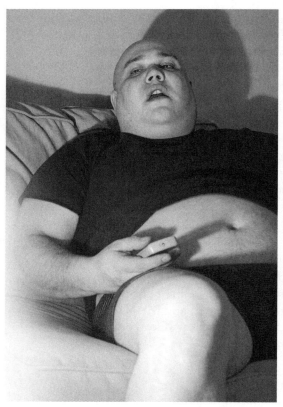

It's not called the "Boob Tube" for nothing. Many fear that television is being used to deliberately dumb down the population.

mation in wholes, leading to emotional, rather than logical responses. The shift from left to right brain activity also causes the release of endorphins, the body's own natural opiates—thus, it is possible to become physically addicted to watching television, a hypothesis borne out by numerous studies which have shown that very few people are able to kick the television habit. It's no longer an overstatement to note that the youth today that are raised and taught through network television are intellectually dead by their early teens."

Waking Times has done a praiseworthy job of keeping us informed of this issue, too: "Westerners spend four plus hours a day, the equivalent of two months a year, or nine years in a lifetime, being hypnotized by a television screen without being conscious of the effects this activity has on them. They have nearly stopped interacting with friends, neighbors, community, and even family. Their free time is spent in imaginary relationships with fictitious characters on the screen.

"A few US statistics will show us the extent of the phenomenon: 99% of households own at least one TV; there are 2.24 TVs per family; the television remains on 7 hours a day; 66% eat in front of their television sets. The addiction starts right after birth, since 30% of kids who are 0 to 1 year old and 47% of the 5 to 8 year-olds have televisions in their rooms. A typical US child spends 3.5 minutes per week in meaningful conversation with a parent, but 1,680 minutes per week in front of TV. Is this why television is called the 'one-eyed babysitter'? By the time they are 65, most people have seen 2,000,000 TV ads. This phenomenon is becoming global.

"The entire population of earth has become addicted to television. If one decides to quit the TV habit, they experience psychological withdrawal symptoms that can be as severe as those related to drug or alcohol abuse."

Hal Becker, an expert on the world of the media, made a statement that, in all probability, gets to the heart of the New World Order's agenda to control and manipulate us via the medium of television: "I know the secret of making the average American believe anything I want him to. Just let me control television.... You put something on the television and it becomes reality. If the world outside the TV set contradicts the images, people start trying to change the world to make it like the TV set images."

TOR PROJECT

Taking into consideration the sheer extent to which we are being secretly monitored by the ever-increasing New World Order, it is hardly surprising that many see the future from a pessimistic perspective. Is widespread surveillance an inevitable, neverending aspect of our future? Many within the NWO would dearly like that to be the case. Fortunately, there are those who are fighting back, specifically to ensure that our personal privacy does not go the way of the dinosaurs. Welcome to the world of the Tor Project, which was co-founded by Roger Dingledine, a computer scientist, and Nick Matthewson. If you are wondering what it might be, take a close look at the words of those behind the project posted on its website: "The Tor network is a group of volunteer-operated servers that allows people to improve their privacy and security on the Internet. Tor's users employ this network by connecting through a series of virtual tunnels rather than making a direct connection, thus allowing both organizations and individuals to share information over public networks without compromising their privacy.

"Along the same line, Tor is an effective censorship circumvention tool, allowing its users to reach otherwise blocked destinations or content. Tor can also be used as a building block for software developers to create new communication tools with built-in privacy features.

"Individuals use Tor to keep websites from tracking them and their family members, or to connect to news sites, instant messaging services, or the like when these are blocked by their local Internet providers. Tor's hidden services let users publish websites and other services without needing to reveal the location of the site. Individuals also use Tor for socially sensitive communication: chat rooms and web forums for rape and abuse survivors, or people with illnesses.

"Journalists use Tor to communicate more safely with whistleblowers and dissidents. Non-governmental organizations (NGOs) use Tor to allow their workers to connect to their home website while they're in a foreign country, without notifying everybody nearby that they're working with that organization."

In a dark world, in which more and more of our freedoms are being eradicated by the New World Order, the Tor Project is a welcome ray of sunshine.

TRACKING YOUR ONLINE PURCHASES

If you think that a New World Order won't follow your every move and action, you are very wrong. It has already begun. Take, for example, the way in which intelligence agencies are now actively monitoring the online purchases of millions of people. Orwellian? No: *beyond* Orwellian. Tim Chen, a contributor to *Forbes*, says: "If you thought having your body exposed by an airport screening scan was bad, how would you feel if I told you that the government might be watching your credit card purchases in real time as you make them? What about your airline reservations or even your Sam's Club Rewards Charge Card? If you think that it couldn't happen in America, don't be so sure. After 9/11 the government began prying into the privacy of Americans under the guise of protecting us from terrorists, but with their latest tactics exposed, many are questioning their motives."

Network World has revealed some startling and worrying information on this particular issue: "It should surprise very few to learn that federal law enforcement agencies track Americans without getting court orders, but this

The government is capable of tracking all Americans' online purchases without the need of a court order.

time the feds have been tracking U.S. residents using real-time surveillance of credit card transactions and travel reservations. Security researcher Christopher Soghoian obtained a 10 page document from the Justice Department about 'hotwatch' orders. 'As the document makes clear, Federal law enforcement agencies do not limit their surveillance of US residents to phone calls, emails and geo-location information. They are also interested in calling cards, credit cards, rental cars and airline reservations, as well as retail shopping clubs,' Soghoian explained."

In an article titled "Feds Warrantlessly Tracking Americans' Credit Cards in Real Time," Ryan Singel said in 2010: "Federal law enforcement agencies have been tracking Americans in real-time using credit cards, loyalty cards and travel reservations without getting a court order, a new document released under a government sunshine request shows. The document, obtained by security researcher Christopher Soghoian, explains how so-called 'Hotwatch' orders allow for real-time tracking of individuals in a criminal investigation via credit card companies, rental car agencies, calling cards, and even grocery store loyalty programs. The revelation sheds a little more light on the Justice Department's increasing power and willingness to surveil Americans with little to no judicial or Congressional oversight. For credit cards, agents can get real-time information on a person's purchases by writing their own subpoena, followed up by an order from a judge that the surveillance not be disclosed. Agents can also go the traditional route—going to a judge, proving probable cause and getting a search warrant—which means the target will eventually be notified they were spied on."

There is little doubt that as time and technology progresses, we may very well see a state of affairs in which the online purchases of everyone will be carefully monitored—and perhaps even regulated.

TRILATERAL COMMISSION

In its very own words, "The Trilateral Commission was formed in 1973 by private citizens of Japan, Europe (European Union countries), and North America (United States and Canada) to foster closer cooperation among these core industrialized areas of the world with shared leadership responsibilities in the wider international system. Originally established for three years, our work has been renewed for successive triennia (three-year periods), most recently for a triennium to be completed in 2015.

"When the first triennium of the Trilateral Commission was launched in 1973, the most immediate purpose was to draw together—at a time of consid-

This is the logo of the Trilateral Commission, a nongovernmental group founded by American banker David Rockefeller to foster relations between Europe, America, and Japan.

erable friction among governments—the highest-level unofficial group possible to look together at the key common problems facing our three areas. At a deeper level, there was a sense that the United States was no longer in such a singular leadership position as it had been in earlier post-World War II years, and that a more shared form of leadership—including Europe and Japan in particular—would be needed for the international system to navigate successfully the major challenges of the coming years."

A Trilateral Commission Task Force Report, presented at the 1975 meeting in Kyoto, Japan, titled "An Outline for Remaking World Trade and Finance," states: "Close Trilateral cooperation in keeping the peace, in managing the world economy, and in fostering economic development and in alleviating world poverty, will improve the chances of a smooth and peaceful evolution of the global system."

It is this "global system" issue which has led to claims and concerns that the Trilateral Commission is at the heart of a program to erode the idea of independent nations and usher in a single, planet-wide government.

Brad Steiger observes, "Conspiracy theorists estimate that the current membership of the Trilateral Commission includes approximately eighty Americans, ten Canadians, ninety Western Europeans, and seventy-five Japanese. Most conspiracists do not believe that the Trilateralists wish the destruction of the United States, but rather that it will surrender its independence and embrace the concept of a One World Government."

In 1990, Ron Paul (of the U.S. House of Representatives from 1997 to 2013) said: "For years now, it's been claimed by many, and there's pretty good evidence, that those who are involved in the Trilateral Commission and the Council on Foreign Relations usually end up in positions of power. And I believe this is true. If you look at the Federal Reserve, if you look at key positions at the World Bank or the IMF, they all come from these groups. If you have national television on, you might see a big debate about the Far East crisis, and you have Brzezinski and Kissinger talking about how to do it. One says don't invade today, invade tomorrow. And the other says, invade immediately. That's the only difference you find between the Rockefeller trilateralists."

TRUMP, DONALD

There are many who see Donald Trump as the one man, more than any other, who can bring the New World Order to its knees. Texe Marrs is one of them: "The Establishment is frightened and are in a panic. They can't believe it. Donald Trump is about to overturn their New World Order apple-cart. If he is elected President of the United States, all the carefully drafted plans of the Bilderbergers, the Council on Foreign Relations, the Council of the Americas, the World Economic Forum, the Skull and Bones Society, the Bohemian Grove and every other traitorous conspiratorial group will be smashed. The Jewish billionaires at the top are especially incensed and angry. How could this happen? For years they've wined and dined this extroverted braggadocio, Trump. They've groomed him and now, he is threatening their Jewish Utopia, the Plan of plans for global domination."

All News Pipeline said in 2016: "*The Economist* … tells us that Trump is thinking about getting the US out of the United Nations, great news for any-one paying attention to what the globalists have planned for America includ-ing disarmament and the gutting of the 2nd Amendment and global govern-ment with a loss of national sovereignty and rapidly dwindling rights for Americans with no Constitutional guarantees.

"As former Clinton aide Larry Nichols tells Greg Hunter in this new story on *USAWatchdog*, a 'silent coup' led by FEMA is beginning to take over America at this very moment that seeks to install Barack Obama as 'king.' With only a general election now standing in between Trump and the White House, what else does the 'new world order' have planned for America? What the global-ists call 'terrible news' is great news to most 'awake' Americans! Why the disconnect? It's now quite clear, only Donald Trump can stop their plans for a 'new world order.' What will they do to stop him? As Susan Duclos wrote in a recent story soon after Trump had seem-ingly guaranteed the nomination, do we real-ly expect the 'elite' to give up power as sim-ply as that?"

The election of New York businessman Donald Trump to the White House was a surprise to nearly everyone, whether they were ordinary citizens or political insiders.

Religious types are wading into the controversy, too. On March 17, 2016, *Charisma News* provided this: "Tuesday on *TruNews*, Pastor Rodney Howard-Browne, founder of Revival Ministries International, told host Rick Wiles he believes Donald Trump is the New World Order's 'worst nightmare.' Howard-Browne has endorsed the Republican Party front-runner. In discussing his choice, he said he believed the billionaire's candidacy has thrown 'the hold of the global agenda' out of sync. He then read from a statement he made Monday: 'Coming from outside America—and having become citizens of the USA—we see things a little differently. We see it from a global perspective; from what is happening globally. We know that the Bible tells us that the devil's end-time plan is a one-world religion, one-world money system and one-world government—a 'New World Order.' This is a plan that threatens every freedom we have and hold dear.

"Christianity and the Bible is a threat to this global plan. So is anyone who thinks for themselves. The American Constitution—the document that made America the great nation it is—stands in the way of this global agenda. This is why it has been under attack—from our own president, and others, on down. We realize that it is the New World Order's Agenda to destroy the United States."

On July 21, 2016, Dave Hodges of *The Common Sense Show* said: "The world is rejecting the New World Order like never before. The best and most recent example is Brexit in which the UK left the globalist organization known as the European Union. The French, the German and the Swedes are rejecting globalism as the protest against unrestrained illegal immigration into their countries. The Donald Trump movement is in full swing and is becoming a world-wide phenomenon. Nowhere was this movement more on display than at the GOP Convention on July 20th as Lying Ted Cruz attempted to engage in self-aggrandizement and his wife paid a heavy price for this would-be-couple's dream of occupying the White House. What happened last night is a feel good moment for long-time members of the Independent Media and Americans, in general, who love freedom."

TRUMP, DONALD, SPEECH

Donald Trump's victory speech after being elected president of the United States suggested that a new, revitalized future was on the cards for the nation. The fact that many saw President Trump as the man who can bring the agenda of the New World Order to a grinding halt was something that almost certainly ensured his place in the White House, as far as the voting public was concerned. It is important to note, however, that matters are not quite as straightforward and as black and white as they might seem. Let's take a look at key portions of Trump's speech: "Now it is time for America to bind the wounds of division, have to get together. To all Republicans and Democrats and independents across this nation, I say it is time for us to come together as one united people. It is time. I pledge to every citizen of our land that I will be President for all of Americans, and this is so important to me. For those who have chosen not to support me in the past, of which there were a few people, I'm reaching out to you for your guidance and your help so that we can work together and unify our great country.

"As I've said from the beginning, ours was not a campaign but rather an incredible and great movement, made up of millions of hard-working men and women who love their country and want a better, brighter future for themselves and for their family. It is a movement comprised of Americans from all races, religions, backgrounds, and beliefs, who want and expect our government to serve the people—and serve the people it will. Working together, we will begin the urgent task of rebuilding our nation and renewing the American dream. I've spent my entire life in business, looking at the untapped potential in projects and in people all over the world.

President Trump with his running mate, Mike Pence. In his victory speech, Trump said his election was a victory over the New World Order.

THE NEW WORLD ORDER BOOK

"That is now what I want to do for our country. Tremendous potential. I've gotten to know our country so well. Tremendous potential. It is going to be a beautiful thing. Every single American will have the opportunity to realize his or her fullest potential. The forgotten men and women of our country will be forgotten no longer.

"We are going to fix our inner cities and rebuild our highways, bridges, tunnels, airports, schools, hospitals. We're going to rebuild our infrastructure, which will become, by the way, second to none. And we will put millions of our people to work as we rebuild it. We will also finally take care of our great veterans who have been so loyal, and I've gotten to know so many over this 18-month journey. The time I've spent with them during this campaign has been among my greatest honors. Our veterans are incredible people.

"We will embark upon a project of national growth and renewal. I will harness the creative talents of our people, and we will call upon the best and brightest to leverage their tremendous talent for the benefit of all. It is going to happen. We have a great economic plan. We will double our growth and have the strongest economy anywhere in the world. At the same time, we will get along with all other nations willing to get along with us. We will be. We will have great relationships. We expect to have great, great relationships. No dream is too big, no challenge is too great. Nothing we want for our future is beyond our reach.

"America will no longer settle for anything less than the best. We must reclaim our country's destiny and dream big and bold and daring. We have to do that. We're going to dream of things for our country, and beautiful things and successful things once again. I want to tell the world community that while we will always put America's interests first, we will deal fairly with everyone, with everyone. All people and all other nations. We will seek common ground, not hostility; partnership, not conflict."

But will Trump make good on his promises? Or will he play into the agenda of the New World Order in unwitting fashion? In the following two entries, we will see what the future may bring.

TRUMP'S NEW WORLD ORDER

Although many see President Donald Trump as the man who can save civilization from the New World Order, ironically, Trump himself may initiate his very own New World Order. Indeed, one only has to take a look at some of the people who were groomed to come on board in the immediate aftermath of Trump's victory in the 2016 presidential election.

On November 14, 2016, in an article titled "Steve Bannon Accused of Having White Supremacist Views," Bethania Palmer at Snopes.com, said: "On 13 November 2016, President-elect Donald Trump tapped Steve Bannon, the head of the controversial, politically conservative website *Breitbart*, to serve as his White House chief strategist. The move was immediately condemned by many as evidence that Trump was welcoming support from white supremacists as he prepared to take office. Bannon took a leave of absence from *Breitbart* in August 2016 to lead Trump's ultimately victorious campaign."

Palmer expanded on this story: "The Southern Poverty Law Center, a civil rights advocacy organization, described *Breitbart* as having taken a shift in the year leading up to the 2016 election toward what has become known as the alternative right, or alt-right, 'a loose set of far-right ideologies at the core of which is a belief that "white identity" is under attack through policies prioritizing multiculturalism, political correctness and social justice and must be preserved, usually through white-identified online communities and physical ethno-states.'

"The hiring of Bannon was bound to elicit a strong response, as he is a controversial political figure even among conservatives. While *Daily Wire* editor-in-chief, former *Breitbart* editor, and vocal Bannon critic Ben Shapiro called the claims that Bannon is racist 'overstated,' he noted that Bannon has nonetheless courted the alt-right and the anti-Semitism and racism that go along with it, and he will do so as long as it serves his purposes."

Shapiro himself said of this controversial issue: "I have no evidence that Bannon's a racist or that he's an anti-Semite; the *Huffington Post's* blaring headline 'WHITE NATIONALIST IN THE WHITE HOUSE' is overstated, at the very least. With that said, as I wrote at *The Washington Post* in August, Bannon has openly embraced the racist and anti-Semitic alt-right—he called his *Breitbart* 'the platform of the alt-right.' Milo Yiannopoulos, the star writer at the site, is an alt-right popularizer, even as he continuously declares with a wink that he's not a member. The left's opposition to Trump, and their attempts to declare all Trump support the alt-right have obfuscated what the movement is. The movement isn't all Trump supporters. It's not conservatives unsatisfied with Paul Ryan, nor is it people angry at the media. Bannon knows that. He's a smart man, not an ignorant one. The alt-right, in a nutshell, believes that Western culture is inseparable from European ethnicity. I have no evidence Bannon believes that personally. But he's happy to pander to those people and make common cause with them in order to transform conservatism into European far-right nationalist populism. That means that the alt-right will cheer Bannon along as he marbles Trump's speeches with talk of 'globalism'—and that Bannon won't be pushing Trump to dump the racists and anti-Semites who support Trump anytime soon. After all, they love Bannon—actual white supremacists like Peter Brimelow called his August

White House Chief Strategist Steve Bannon (left) with White House Chief of Staff Reince Priebus. Bannon has been heavily criticized for his far-right views, as expressed in his role as chief executive of the *Breitbart News* website.

appointment 'great news,' and Richard Spencer explained, '*Breitbart* has elective affinities with the Alt Right, and the Alt Right has clearly influenced *Breitbart*. In this way, *Breitbart* has acted as a 'gateway' to Alt Right ideas and writers. I don't think it has done this deliberately; again, it's a matter of elective affinities.' That doesn't mean Bannon will push racist or anti-Semitic policy, or that he'll be anti-Israel himself—unless it serves his interests."

Mother Jones had this to say, just weeks before the election: "Trump 'may be the last hope for a president who would be good for white people,' remarked Jared Taylor, who runs a white nationalist website called *American Renaissance* and once founded a think tank dedicated to 'scientifically' proving white superiority. Taylor told us that Trump was the first presidential candidate from a major party ever to earn his support because Trump 'is talking about policies that would slow the dispossession of whites. That is something that is very important to me and to all racially conscious white people.'"

Mother Jones added: "But Trump did not become the object of white nationalist affection simply because his positions reflect their core concerns. Extremists made him their chosen candidate and now hail him as 'Emperor Trump' because he has amplified their message on social media—and, perhaps most importantly, has gone to great lengths to avoid distancing himself from the racist right. With the exception of Duke, Trump has not disavowed a single endorsement from the dozens of neo-Nazis, Klansmen, white nationalists, and militia supporters who have backed him. The GOP nominee, along with his family members, staffers, and surrogates, has instead provided an unprecedented platform for the ideas and rhetoric of far-right extremists, extending their reach. And when challenged on it by the press, Trump has stalled, feigned ignorance, or deflected—but has never specifically rejected any of these other extremists or their ideas."

The *Independent* reported on Bernie Sanders' deep concerns about how a Trump White House may turn America into, in effect, a one-party nation: "Sanders was keen not to dilute the stark reality of the consequences of the Republican's victory, suggesting the President-elect's team would monopolise power and make it increasingly difficult for US citizens to participate in

Democracy. 'The worst case, if not Trump himself, people around Trump are saying, hmm, let's see, we've got the House, the Senate, we've got the White House, we're going to have the Supreme Court, we're going to change the rules of the game so we don't lose anymore. [If they can] unleash billionaires to buy elections, make it hard for millions of people to participate, they think they can control this government indefinitely."

Controlling the world of government indefinitely also happens to be on the agenda of the NWO. Are we in a position where we have traded in one New World Order for another? The former filled with powerful figures from the worlds of politics, the military, and secret societies, and the latter comprised of right-wing extremists determined to ensure the Democratic Party never again stands a chance of getting back into power.

TRUMP'S WALL

There can be no doubt at all that one of Donald Trump's biggest selling points in the 2016 election was his plan to erect a huge wall, effectively isolating the United States from Mexico. Despite Trump's loud and repeated claims that such a massive task could be achieved, not everyone is quite so sure that it's in any way feasible. The BBC says of Trump's vision of a walled-in U.S. population: "The US–Mexico border is about 1,900 miles (3,100 km) long and traverses all sorts of terrain from empty, dusty desert to the lush and rugged surroundings of the Rio Grande. Some 650 miles of the border is covered already by a confused and non-continuous series of fences, concrete slabs and other structures. Mr. Trump says his wall will cover 1,000 miles and natural obstacles will take care of the rest. This is a wall we are talking about, not a fence—on that Mr. Trump has been clear ('a wall is better than fencing and it's much more powerful'). That rules out relatively cheap options like tall iron fence posts or wire mesh. Mr. Trump claims the total cost of the wall will be $10 (£7.5) billion to $12 billion. But estimates from fact checkers and engineers seem to be universally higher. The 650 miles of fencing already put up has cost the government more than $7 billion, and none of it could be described, even charitably, as impenetrable, physical, tall, powerful, or beautiful. Mr. Trump insists, emphatically, that Mexico will pay. Mexico's president, Enrique Pena Nieto, insists they won't. Former Mexican president Vicente Fox said: 'I'm not going to pay for that fucking wall,' using a somewhat unpresidential word to make his feelings on the matter clear. Asked by US journalists how he could force Mexico to pay, Mr. Trump suggested he could ransom the country by blocking undocumented immigrants from sending money home, using a provision of the US Patriot Act designed to stop funding for terrorism."

Newsweek is as doubtful as the BBC that Trump can support his claims that the building of such a huge wall is feasible. As John Dean notes: "Trump's wall typifies his governing ideas and tactics. He has simply tossed out a thought without carefully thinking it through. As a result, it is unrealistic and unworkable. It would likely cause more harm than good. No informed person with whom I have spoken believes any good could come from such a wall, although there is no shortage of bad things that could occur. Nor is there public clamor for such a draconian sealing of our southern border. According to the latest Pew Research Poll, only about a third of Americans support the idea of a wall, with Republicans predominantly favoring it. Pew reports, 'By nearly two-to-one (63 percent to 33 percent), Republicans and GOP leaners favor building a wall along the entire U.S.–Mexico border. By contrast, just 13 percent of Democrats favor building a border wall, while 84 percent are opposed.'"

Fortune makes a very good point, one which would have a huge, and disturbing, impact on the U.S. population, should such a wall one day be constructed: "Trump's initial proposal as to how Mexico will be forced to 'pay for the wall' was unwise, unworkable, and displayed an astonishing lack of understanding of how global finance actually works, as I have written in detail before. His proposal, which relies on vague legal authority to force banks to cut off their customers' access to move their own money around the world, assumes that American banks have the ability to cut off payments from any non-citizen or lawful visitor: they don't. His plan, if implemented, would essentially shut off the ability for most Americans to send funds to anyone in the world because Trump's proposal requires them to prove citizenship or legal status to their bank."

In other words, Trump's goal will play right into the New World Order types who are intent on ensuring that access to our own personal money is increasingly restricted.

See also entry on "Border Closings."

2016 PRESIDENTIAL ELECTION STOLEN

If the New World Order is to have its way—namely, enslaving the planet and dictating how we live—it may do so not by brute force but by far more cunning and sly methods. One of those very same methods may involve rigging—and even stealing—elections from under our very noses, the voters. Too brazen to be true? Nothing is too brazen for the New World Order.

Paul Craig Roberts said just days before the 2016 presidential election that "there are disturbing signs that a digital 9/11 false flag terror attack is being readied for election day in the US to ensure that Donald Trump does not win. Such an attack—involving widespread Internet and power outage—would have nothing to do with Russia or any other foreign state. It would be furnished by agencies of the US Department of State in a classic 'false flag' covert manner. But the resulting chaos and 'assault on American democracy' will be conveniently blamed on Russia.

"That presents a double benefit. Russia would be further demonized as a foreign aggressor 'justifying' even harsher counter measures by America and its European allies against Moscow.

"Secondly, a digital attack on America's presidential election day this week, would allow the Washington establishment to pronounce a Trump win invalid due to 'Russian cyber subversion.' Invalidation is a prepared option if the ballot results show Republican candidate Donald Trump as the imminent victor.

"Democrat rival Hillary Clinton is the clear choice for the White House among the Washington establishment. She has the backing of Wall Street finance capital, the corporate media, the military-industrial complex and the Deep State agencies of the Pentagon and CIA. The fix has been in for months to get her elected by the powers-that-be owing to her well-groomed obedience to American imperialist interests."

Judi McLeod at *Canada Free Press* said on November 6, 2016—just two days before the election: "America seems headed for a real life 'Ruby Tuesday' on November 8. The events of Friday and Saturday should be sending chills down the spines of average citizens IF, as US Intelligence is warning, al Qaeda strikes with terrorist attacks in three states tomorrow and ISIS follows through on its threats to slaughter voters going to the polls on Tuesday. Last night, Austyn Daniel Crites, 33, of Reno, Nevada self-identified as a member of 'Republicans against Trump' in an incident that saw Secret Service agents hustling the 'Make America Great Again' candidate off the stage, in what many see as a dry-run for his assassination. On Friday, President Barack Hussein Obama seemed to use a Republican veteran plant to go after Donald J. Trump as the wrong president to have his finger on America's nuclear button. If these Hillary Clinton suspected stunts are happening two days before Election 2016, and the Democrats are playing the role of the Great Pretenders, who knows what is coming next?"

The established elite clearly favored former Secretary of State Hillary Clinton over Senator Bernie Sanders to win the Democrat nomination and then the presidential election.

McLeod concluded: "So about tomorrow's possible terrorist attacks in three states? And ISIS striking to kill voters on Tuesday? How far would Obama go to hang onto the power of a third term in the Oval Office through the election of Hillary Clinton? Only time will tell."

One month before the election, *The Political Insider* warned of voter fraud in Illinois—such shenanigans being of great benefit to the New World Order: "The Kankakee County State's Attorney's office says it is investigating possible voting fraud after the clerk's office reported three complaints from people who said they were offered bribes for votes. In a news release issued late Tuesday afternoon, Jamie Boyd, the state's attorney, also said 'several' vote-by-mail applications seem to have come from people living outside of Kankakee County.

"'This unprecedented action was taken in response to reports of individuals from Chicago offering gifts to potential voters in exchange for a vote for Kate Cloonen, Hillary Clinton and others,' Boyd said in the news release. 'Our office takes seriously the obligation to protect the rights of citizens to vote for the candidate of their choice, and to do so without undue influence from special interest groups. The investigation will also focus on the authenticity of vote by mail requests. Several applications have been filed with the election authority that appear to be fraudulently executed.'

"Late last week, Kankakee County Clerk Bruce Clark said potential voters were being brought to the clerk's office to vote early. 'Whoever it is should not be doing this,' he said. 'People should be allowed to come in here and vote without being harassed.'"

Try telling that to the New World Order.

2030 AGENDA

On September 25, 2015, the United Nations revealed a plan of action titled "Transforming our World: The 2030 Agenda for Sustainable Development." The United Nations states: "On 25 September, the United Nations General Assembly unanimously adopted the Resolution 70/1, Transforming our World: the 2030 Agenda for Sustainable Development. This historic document lays out the 17 Sustainable Development Goals, which aim to mobilize global efforts to end poverty, foster peace, safeguard the rights and dignity of all people, and protect the planet."

The resolution begins with a declaration that states: "On behalf of the peoples we serve, we have adopted a historic decision on a comprehensive, far-reaching and people-centered set of universal and transformative Goals and targets. We commit ourselves to working tirelessly for the full implementation of this Agenda by 2030. We recognize that eradicating poverty in all its forms and dimensions, including extreme poverty, is the greatest global challenge and an indispensable requirement for sustainable development. We are committed to achieving sustainable development in its three dimensions—economic, social and environmental—in a balanced and integrated manner. We will also build upon the achievements of the Millennium Development Goals and seek to address their unfinished business.

"We resolve, between now and 2030, to end poverty and hunger everywhere; to combat inequalities within and among countries; to build peaceful, just and inclusive societies; to protect human rights and promote gender equality and the empowerment of women and girls; and to ensure the lasting protection of the planet and its natural resources. We resolve also to create conditions for sustainable, inclusive and sustained economic growth, shared prosperity and decent work for all, taking into account different levels of national development and capacities.

"As we embark on this great collective journey, we pledge that no one will be left behind. Recognizing that the dignity of the human person is fundamental, we wish to see the Goals and targets met for all nations and peoples and for all segments of society. And we will endeavour to reach the furthest behind first.

"This is an Agenda of unprecedented scope and significance. It is accepted by all countries and is applicable to all, taking into account different national realities, capacities and levels of development and respecting national policies and priorities. These are universal goals and targets which involve the entire world, developed and developing countries alike. They are integrated and indivisible and balance the three dimensions of sustainable development.

"The Goals and targets are the result of over two years of intensive public consultation and engagement with civil society and other stakeholders around the world, which paid particular attention to the voices of the poorest and most vulnerable. This consultation included valuable work done by the Open Working Group of the General Assembly on Sustainable Development Goals and by the United Nations, whose Secretary-General provided a synthesis report in December 2014."

It should be noted that despite the seemingly positive nature of this plan for the world by 2030, not everyone is happy with it. Some are downright concerned and worried. Particularly disturbed by all this is *The New American*: "The Agenda 2030 agreement makes the audacity of the scheme clear, too. 'This is an Agenda of unprecedented scope and significance,' boasts the document. 'Never before have world leaders pledged common action and endeavor across such a broad and universal policy agenda,' the agreement continues.

'What we are announcing today—an Agenda for global action for the next fifteen years—is a charter for people and planet in the twenty-first century."

The New American adds: "Perhaps the single most striking feature of Agenda 2030 is the practically undisguised roadmap to global socialism and corporatism/fascism, as countless analysts have pointed out. To begin with, consider the agenda's Goal 10, which calls on the UN, national governments, and every person on Earth to 'reduce inequality within and among countries.' To do that, the agreement continues, will 'only be possible if wealth is shared and income inequality is addressed.'"

As the UN document also makes clear, national socialism to "combat inequality" domestically is not enough—international socialism is needed to battle inequality even "among" countries. "By 2030, ensure that all men and women, in particular the poor and the vulnerable, have equal rights to economic resources,'" the document demands. "In simpler terms, Western taxpayers should prepare to be fleeced so that their wealth can be redistributed internationally as their own economies are cut down to size by Big Government.'

Natural News comes straight to the point: "This document describes nothing less than a global government takeover of every nation across the planet. The 'goals' of this document are nothing more than code words for a corporate-government fascist agenda that will imprison humanity in a devastating cycle of poverty while enriching the world's most powerful globalist corporations like Monsanto and DuPont."

Charisma News reports this: "The U.N. has stated that these new 'global goals' represent a 'new universal Agenda' for humanity. Virtually every nation on the planet has willingly signed on to this new agenda, and you are expected to participate whether you like it or not."

Ufologists and Spying

As we have seen, the issue of UFOs is one that deeply interests the New World Order. With that in mind, it would make sense for the NWO to keep a secret and careful watch on those who investigate the subject. Indeed, there are numerous examples of this. For our purposes, one classic example will suffice.

On September 3, 1999, author (of the acclaimed *Project Beta*), researcher, and radio host Greg Bishop stated the following in an email exchange with Jim Keith—an author of numerous books on UFOs and conspiracy theories who died under circumstances that some still see as highly suspicious only four days after he and Greg exchanged emails: "I turned on my computer about midweek last week (the last week of August, 1999) and found that all of my article and work in progress files had been deleted. Luckily, I had backed them up. What was weird was the fact that the articles were not only 'trashed,' but were also deleted from the trash AND erased from the trash sector of the hard drive, making them unrecoverable. This takes a few steps of which I would have most likely been aware, and certainly don't remember, if indeed I was the culprit. There are a few possibilities: I was hacked through the modem, I was given a virus that only affects my article folder and no other Word files, or someone broke in the house and deleted them. I guess I'll believe the story that makes me feel best."

And this odd and slightly unsettling affair was far from being a singular event as Bishop astutely noted when he referred to yet another curious series of circumstances in which he found himself well and truly immersed: "Mail tampering is the darling of clinical paranoids, but nearly every piece of mail that the late researcher/abductee Karla Turner sent to [my] PO Box looked like it had been tampered with or opened. Since this is easy to do without having to be obvious, we figured someone was interested in her work enough to make it clear that she was being monitored. She took to putting a piece of transparent tape over the flap and writing 'sealed by sender' on it."

Bishop continued with the story: "Karla pretty much took it for granted after awhile, and suggested I do likewise. The same mail problems later cropped up with a cattle mutilation researcher. Our postal and even e-mail exchanges were often a marvel of missed and misrouted communications. He recently suggested that we back off our discussions for awhile for reasons he would not talk about. Then there were the endless hang-up calls. '*69' never worked with any of them. These came in sometimes five to ten times (or more) a day. If we picked up the receiver, there was static or silence."

And Bishop has still more to say on this matter of official, secret attention by, well, someone. This time, it's with regard to Bishop's self-published magazine of the 1990s, *The Excluded Middle*, that sought to uncover the many and varied intricacies of the UFO puzzle and a whole range of conspiracies and secrets: "Is a silly little UFO zine worth any attention? Well, maybe. Just think of all the wasted effort and money that our government puts out to justify a salary or political peccadillo. With unlimited cash flow plus idle hands and an intel operative's pet paranoia in charge, we begin to see why this might not be so far-fetched."

UFOs in Ottawa

Midway through November 1989, a document—prepared by a still unknown source—was circulated to a number of researchers within the field of ufology, including Leonard Stringfield. It detailed the alleged landing—or crash landing—of a UFO in the Canadian town of Carp, which is located near Ottawa. Although there was talk of the entire issue being a hoax, Stringfield felt the case was either (a) genuine; or (b) "an orchestrated disinformation ploy, designed to muddy the waters." Pertinent parts of the document are detailed below: "Canadian and American Security Agencies are engaged in a conspiracy of silence to withhold from the world the alien vessel seized in the swamps of Corkery Road, Carp, in 1989. UFO sightings in the Ontario region had intensified in the 1980's, specifically around nuclear power generating stations. On November 4, 1989 at 20:00 hrs., Canadian Defense Department radars picked up a globe shaped object traveling at a phenomenal speed over Carp, Ontario. The UFO abruptly stopped, and dropped like a stone.

"Canadian and American Security Agencies were immediately notified of the landing. Monitoring satellites traced the movements of the aliens to a triangular area, off Old Almonte and Corkery Roads. The ship had landed in deep swamp near Corkery Road. Two AJ-64 Apaches and a UH-60 Blackhawk headed for the area the following night. The helicopters carried full weapon loads. They were part of a covert American unit that specialized in the recovery of alien craft.

"Flying low over Ontario pine trees, the Apache attack choppers soon spotted a glowing, blue, 20 meter in diameter sphere. As targeting lasers locked-on, both gunships unleashed their full weapon loads of eight missiles each. All sixteen were exploded in proximity bursts ten meters downwind from the ship. The missiles were carrying VEXXON, a deadly neuroactive gas which kills on contact. Exposed to air, the gas breaks down quickly into inert components. Immediately after having completed their mission, the gunships turned around, and headed back across the border.

"Now the Blackhawk landed, as men exploded from its open doors. In seconds, the six-man strike-team had entered the UFO through a seven meter hatchless, oval, portal. No resistance was encountered. At the controls, three dead crewmen were found. With the ship captured, the United States Air Force, Pentagon, and Office of Naval Intelligence were notified. Through the night, a special team of technicians had shut down and disassembled the sphere. Early the next morning, November 6, 1989, construction equipment and trucks were brought into the swamp. The UFO parts were transported to a secret facility in Kanata, Ontario.

"As a cover story, the locals were informed that a road was being built through the swamp. No smokescreen was needed for the military activity as Canadian forces regularly train in the area. Although someone anonymously turned in a 35mm roll of film, it was received by the National Research Council of Canada, in Ottawa. The film contained several clear shots of an entity holding a light. At this time, the photographer is still unidentified.

"The humanoids were packed in ice and sent to an isolation chamber at the University of Ottawa. CIA specialists performed

In 1989, a UFO reportedly crashed near the town of Carp, Ottawa, Canada.

the autopsies. Three reptilian, fetus-headed beings, were listed as CLASS 1 NTE's (Non-Terrestrial Entities). Like others recovered in previous operations, they were muscular, grey-white skinned humanoids.

"The ship was partially reassembled at the underground facility in Kanata. Unlike previous recoveries, this one is pure military. Built as a 'Starfighter,' it is heavily armed and armored. In design, no rivets, bolts, or welds were used in fastening, yet when reconstructed, there are no seams. The UFO itself is made up of a matrixed dielectric magnesium alloy."

The report continues in a controversial fashion and in some respects mirrors certain scenarios involving the New World Order and its plans. For example, it contains references to (a) aliens allegedly pledging some kind of allegiance to China; (b) a looming nuclear war in the Middle East; and (c) countless people implanted with alien "mind-control" devices, people who, at some point, will be used to attack the rest of the human race as the aliens seize control of the planet. True, hoax, or—as Leonard Stringfield suspected—disinformation? The jury is still out.

UFOs OF THE NEW WORLD ORDER

There is no doubt that one of the most thought-provoking theories concerning how, exactly, the New World Order will seek to take control is that which suggests it will come about as a result of a faked alien invasion. Could the world's population be taken in by a brilliant ruse, one which will see NWO-created UFOs presented as an alien menace? Perhaps the UFO phenomenon is being carefully and secretly groomed for the day when flying saucers of a terrestrial—rather than extraterrestrial—nature will take to the skies of our world and have us all believe we are under attack by ETs. If such a thing does happen, it will almost certainly lead to the very things that the New World Order needs to achieve its dangerous goals, such as martial law, detainment camps, constant surveillance of the public, and new and draconian laws. As amazing as all this sounds, there is evidence that such a plan is underway. Certainly, as we have already seen, Kenneth Goff uncovered relevant material on this very issue back in the 1950s. Indeed, as we shall now see, it was in the 1950s that the first seeds were sown in this plan to enslave us all via a nonexistent alien threat.

On December 2, 1952, the CIA's Assistant Director H. Marshall Chadwell noted in a classified report on UFO activity in American airspace: "Sightings of unexplained objects at great altitudes and traveling at high speeds in the vicinity of major U.S. defense installations are of such nature that they are not attributable to natural phenomena or known types of aerial vehicles."

Believing that something might really be afoot in the skies of America, Chadwell prepared a list of saucer-themed recommendations for the National Security Council:

1. The director of central intelligence shall formulate and carry out a program of intelligence and research activities as required to solve the problem of instant positive identification of unidentified flying objects.

2. Upon call of the director of central intelligence, government departments and agencies shall provide assistance in this program of intelligence and research to the extent of their capacity provided, however, that the DCI shall avoid duplication of activities presently directed toward the solution of this problem.

3. This effort shall be coordinated with the military services and the Research and Development Board of the Department of Defense, with the Psychological Board and other governmental agencies as appropriate.

4. The director of central intelligence shall disseminate information concerning the program of intelligence and research activities in this field to the various departments and agencies which have authorized interest therein.

Forty-eight hours later, the Intelligence Advisory Committee concurred with Chadwell and recommended that "the services of selected scientists to review and appraise the available evidence in the light of pertinent scientific theories" should be the order of the day. Thus was born the Robertson Panel, so named after the man chosen to head the inquiry: Howard Percy Robertson, a consultant to the agency, a renowned physicist, and the director of the Defense Department Weapons Evaluation Group.

Chadwell was tasked with putting together a crack team of experts in various science, technical, intelligence, and military disciplines and have them carefully study the data on flying saucers currently held by not just the CIA but the Air Force too—who obligingly agree to hand over all their UFO files for the CIA's scrutiny, or, at least, the Air Force *said* it was all they had.

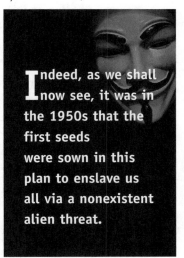

Indeed, as we shall now see, it was in the 1950s that the first seeds were sown in this plan to enslave us all via a nonexistent alien threat.

Whatever the truth of the matter regarding the extent to which the USAF shared its files with Chadwell's team, the fact that there was a significant body of data to work with was the main thing. And so the team—which included Luis Alvarez, physicist and radar expert (and later a Nobel Prize recipient); Frederick C. Durant, CIA officer, secretary to the panel, and missile expert; Samuel Abraham Goudsmit, Brookhaven National Laboratories nuclear physicist; and Thornton Page, astrophysicist, radar expert, and deputy director of Johns Hopkins Operations Research Office— quickly got to work.

The overall conclusion of the Robertson Panel was that while UFOs, *per se*, did not appear to have a bearing on national security or the defense of the United States, the way in which the subject could be used by unfriendly forces to manipulate the public mindset and disrupt the U.S. military infrastructure *did* have a bearing—and a major one, too—on matters of a security nature. According to the panel's members: "Although evidence of any direct threat from these sightings was wholly lacking, related dangers might well exist resulting from: A. Misidentification of actual enemy artifacts by defense personnel. B. Overloading of emergency reporting channels with 'false' information. C. *Subjectivity of public to mass hysteria and greater vulnerability to possible enemy psychological warfare.*"

There was also a recommendation that a number of the public UFO investigative groups that existed in the United States at the time, such as the Civilian Flying Saucer Investigators (CFSI) and the Aerial Phenomena Research Organization (APRO), should be "watched" carefully due to "the apparent irresponsibility and the possible use of such groups for subversive purposes."

The panel also concluded that "a public education campaign should be undertaken" on matters relative to UFOs. Specifically, agreed the members, such a program would "result in reduction in public interest in 'flying saucers' which today evokes a strong psychological reaction. This education could be accomplished by mass media such as television, motion pictures, and popular articles. Basis of such education would be actual case histories which had been puzzling at first but later explained. As in the case of conjuring tricks, there is much less stimulation if the 'secret' is known. Such a program should tend to reduce the current gullibility of the public and consequently their susceptibility to clever hostile propaganda.

"In this connection, Dr. Hadley Cantril (Princeton University) was suggested. Cantril authored 'Invasion from Mars' (a study in the psychology of panic, written about the famous Orson Welles radio broadcast in 1938) and has since performed advanced laboratory studies in the field of perception. The names of Don Marquis (University of Michigan) and Leo Roston were mentioned as possibly suitable consultant psychologists.

"Also, someone familiar with mass communications techniques, perhaps an advertising expert, would be helpful. Arthur Godfrey was mentioned as possibly a valuable channel of communication reaching a mass audience of certain levels. Dr. Berkner suggested the U.S. Navy (ONR) Special Devices Center, Sands Point, L. I., as a potentially valuable organization to assist in such an educational program. The teaching techniques used by this agency for aircraft identification during the past war [were] cited as an example of a similar educational task. The Jam Handy Co. which made World War II training films (motion picture and slide strips) was also suggested, as well as Walt Disney, Inc. animated cartoons."

Robbie Graham, a UFO researcher who has studied the many and varied intricacies of the Robertson Panel and its links to Disney and Ward Kimball, says: "The panel's singling-out of Disney made sense given the animation giant's then firmly established working relationship with the U.S. government: during World War II Disney made numerous propaganda shorts for the US military, and in the 1950s corporate and government sponsors helped the company produce films promoting President Eisenhower's 'Atoms for Peace' policy, as well as the retrospectively hilarious 'Duck and Cover' documentary, which depicted schoolchildren surviving an atomic attack by sheltering under their desks."

Graham continued: "That the Robertson Panel highlighted Disney is significant in that the Panel's general recommendation to debunk UFOs through media channels is known to have been acted upon in at least one instance: this being the CBS TV broadcast of *UFOs: Friend, Foe, or Fantasy?* (1966), an anti-UFO documentary narrated by Walter Cronkite. In a letter addressed to former Robertson Panel Secretary Frederick C. Durant, Dr Thornton Page confided that he 'helped organize the CBS TV show around the Robertson

The Walt Disney animation studios were contacted by the U.S. government to cooperate on various propaganda movies, as well as a documentary about UFOs.

Panel conclusions,' even though this was thirteen years after the Panel had first convened. In light of this case alone, it seems reasonable to assume that the government may at least have attempted to follow through on the Robertson Panel's Disney recommendation."

As for Ward Kimball, in 1979 he went public on certain aspects of Disney's links to the UFO conundrum and officialdom and stated that it wasn't just the CIA that Disney was working with when it came to UFOs. At some point during 1955 or 1956, Disney was contacted by representatives of the U.S. Air Force and was asked to secretly cooperate on a documentary about the UFO controversy. As part of the deal, the Air Force offered to supply actual UFO footage, which Disney was told they could include in their film.

According to Kimball, at that time, it wasn't at all unusual for either Walt Disney or his studio to go along with the government's wishes—or, perhaps, demands might be a far more accurate term to use. Kimball revealed how, during World War II, the military practically took over Disney's Burbank facilities, where dozens of hours of military training productions and war-effort films featuring Disney characters, like Donald Duck, were made.

The studio began work on the requested UFO documentary; animators were asked to imagine what an alien would look like while Walt Disney himself eagerly waited for the Air Force to deliver the promised film of actual UFOs. At the last moment, however, the Air Force mysteriously withdrew the offer of the footage, and the planned documentary was canceled.

What all this does demonstrate is that Disney had a link to UFOs, the CIA, and secret projects—and specifically, and collectively, in a fashion that revolved around manipulating and controlling public opinion on, and perception of, all things of the flying saucer variety.

In 1981, Ward Kimball made a stealthy, and somewhat tentative, approach to a man named Miles Axe Copeland, Jr., who, during World War II, served with the Strategic Services Unit (the remnants of the Office of Strategic Services) and later became a key and senior figure within the CIA. Kimball wanted to talk about the CIA's mind-control program MKUltra, flying saucers, and L. Ron Hubbard of Scientology fame, but why did Kimball seek out Copeland? Let's see.

Miles Copeland, as a senior CIA operative, knew a great deal about MKUltra. As far as his bosses were concerned, maybe way too much. And Copeland had nothing positive to say about the program, either. He went on record as stating that, in the buildup to the 1972 election, Democratic presidential candidate Edmund Muskie was secretly targeted by a CIA goon squad who knew far more than a few disturbing things about psychedelics and scrambled minds. The reason: Richard Nixon's people wanted the CIA to covertly but regularly slip Muskie LSD and provoke ongoing, increasingly erratic and emotional behavior in the man that, when seen by the public and commented upon by the media, would hopefully discredit him and push voters further toward Nixon. History has shown that Muskie did indeed suddenly begin to exhibit odd, over-the-top actions, and Nixon won the vote. Copeland also maintained that when the MKUltra program became public knowledge in the 1970s, the Church Committee got no more than the "barest glimpse" at what was really, and deeply, afoot behind closed doors at Langley and elsewhere.

In addition, Copeland had notable things to say about L. Ron Hubbard's Church of Scientology, which, Copeland asserted, was created with the helping hand of our old friends at the CIA. Investigative writer Daniel Brandt says of this matter: "Toward the end of his career, Hubbard was certainly a renegade, far beyond anyone's capacity to control him. But in the 1950s and early 1960s, it's probable that he had support from U.S. intelligence. His early expertise in mind control is curious, as well as his lifetime interest in intelligence tradecraft. Former CIA officer Miles Copeland claims that his CIA colleague Bob Mandlestam made 'arrangements' with Scientology and Moral Re-Armament [an organization established in 1938 that encouraged spiritual, multi-faith development and which was infiltrated and manipulated by the CIA] about this time."

Copeland also commented on the CIA's involvement in the UFO issue and confirmed that, while certain elements of the agency never actually ruled out the possibility of a small number of alien intrusions, far more pressing and intriguing to agency personnel was how the phenomenon could be manipulated and used as a tool of psychological warfare and propaganda. This is the exact area in which the CIA envisioned the Walt Disney Corporation, including Ward Kimball, playing a potential role. Thus, while we can never be 100 percent sure, it seems fairly safe to conclude that Kimball had heard of Copeland's combined comments relative to LSD, MKUltra, UFOs, and L. Ron Hubbard and sought him out for those specific reasons. And, it should be noted, Hubbard's Church of Scientology had a connection to Kenneth Goff (via its 1955 manual, "Brain-Washing: A Synthesis of the Russian Textbook on Psychopolitics"). What did Kimball have to say to Copeland? A great deal, actually, most of it pretty disturbing and whacked out.

> Copeland also commented on the CIA's involvement in the UFO issue and confirmed that ... far more pressing and intriguing to agency personnel was how the phenomenon could be manipulated and used as a tool of psychological warfare and propaganda.

In a lengthy, typed letter, Kimball claimed to Copeland that he was very disturbed by something that he had learned from longtime friends in the CIA as a result of the Church Committee's probing into MKUltra in the 1970s. After outlining to Copeland his work with Disney, the CIA, a mid-1950s post-Robertson Panel operation to confuse the Soviets on what the U.S. government knew about UFOs, and the manipulation by agency personnel of a number of UFO research groups across the country in the early years of the Cold War—all of which Kimball felt was fine, justified, and "not overstepping the mark"—Kimball then began spilling the beans on certain other "things" that, he stressed, he was not involved in but had merely "heard about" and which, if true, most assuredly *did* overstep the mark.

Those "things" included agency personnel using American citizens—members of the public, people in the UFO research arena, certain players in Scientology, patients in asylums, prisoners, and military personnel—in MKUltra-connected "experiments" to (a) "affect the public's views" on UFOs as a means to "seeing how far they [the CIA] could go" in terms of harnessing, controlling, and *altering human perception* and belief via potent chemical cocktails; (b) "*construct a UFO mythos*" behind which such experimentation could be carefully concealed; and, perhaps most worrying of all, (c) develop a long-term plan to understand how chemical and subliminal manipulation, as well as the creation of "new beliefs" and the modification of old ones, could be used to create a subservient, docile populace that was envisioned as being part *1984* and part *Brave New World*.

Perhaps eerily anticipating what we are seeing today with regard to the New World Order, more than three decades ago, Kimball told Copeland that these plans included long-term operations to ensure that more and more of the American population became hooked on addictive, mood-altering and mood-controlling drugs; attempts to drive U.S. culture away from outdoors/social activity and more toward lethargy and solely indoors-based activities, such as being glued to the television 24/7; the creation of "fear myths" to keep the populace in a perpetual state of terror born out of *nonexistent threats*; a slow but deliberate erosion of civil liberties; and even plans for a "*manufactured UFO threat*," one that might even take decades to carefully create, nurture, and instill in the minds of the people but which, in part, would include "MK techniques" with a "defined end."

Then, with a population pummeled and subdued by drugs, a significant lessening in outside excursions, mounting ill health of both a physical and psychological nature, and a growing number of spurious threats to national security—including, specifically, one of a flying saucer nature—it would be a case of nothing less than cold-hearted checkmate, after which a grave new world of a bleak, totalitarian nature would take the place of the old world.

UK INDEPENDENCE PARTY

When the Brexit affair of 2016 shook the New World Order to its absolute core, much of the anger-filled finger pointing from NWO figures were aimed at the UK Independence Party. But, what, exactly, is the UKIP? The BBC said in 2014: "The party was founded on 3 September 1993 at the London School of Economics by members of the Anti-Federalist League, which had been founded by Dr. Alan Sked in November 1991 with the aim of running candidates opposed to the Maastricht Treaty in the 1992 general election. UKIP's early days were overshadowed by the higher-profile and well-financed Referendum Party, led by Sir James Goldsmith, which was wound up soon after the 1997 election. The new party's initial successes were all in the proportional representation elections for the European Parliament— winning its first three seats in 1999 with 7% of the vote."

A former member of the Conservative Party, British broadcaster and political analyst Nigel Farage became head of the UK Independence Party.

Without doubt the one person, more than any other, who has been associated with the UKIP is Nigel Farage—and rightly so. UKIP says: "Nigel Farage is a UKIP MEP for the South East of England. Elected in 1999, he has used his experience of the EU to increase awareness of its activities back home in the United Kingdom. Nigel was re-elected Leader of the UK Independence Party in November 2010. A firm believer in Independence for the United Kingdom he is a proponent of free speech and has faced considerable hostility from his political opponents for speaking out in favor of free and fair referendums on the transfer of power from elected politicians to the EU."

When the results of the Brexit vote came in, there was worldwide coverage and comment. Joseph Murray, writing at *Breitbart* on June 23, 2016, reported: "Whether the protectors of the NWO admit it or not, the world is changing. Brexit won, the Scots—though defeated—will be rejuvenated in their quest for independence, Venice wants to break away from Italy, and Catalonia is giddy to secede from Spain. The old tribes of the West are getting together for a reunion. And, yes, America has Trump. Just last week Trump became the first major presidential candidate in decades to reject the NWO. Quoting Lincoln on tariffs and declaring he will place 'America First', Trump is making it known that under his watch America will be first, second, and third; NWO be damned. What does that mean? 2016 is the year the NWO comes crashing down."

See also entry on "Brexit."

UNITED NATIONS ARMY

If a takeover of the planet by the New World Order goes ahead, it is almost certainly the case that at the forefront of trying to ensure that we do not put up any resistance will be the United Nations army.

The United Nations states of its military arm: "United Nations military personnel are the Blue Helmets on the ground. Today, they consist of over 90,000 military personnel contributed by national armies from across the globe. Military personnel are the backbone and the most visible component of a peacekeeping operation. We work alongside UN Police and civilian colleagues to promote stability, security, and peace processes; we protect personnel and property; we work with the local community, the local military personnel, and other military entities in the area to promote lasting peace.

"In many missions, protection of civilians is at the heart of our mandate. Blue Helmets are protecting populations against threats and contributing to a secure environment.

"All military personnel working under the Blue Helmet are first and foremost members of their own national armies and are then seconded to work under the command and control of the UN. We have more than 95,000 UN uniformed personnel coming from over 120 countries. They come from nations large and small, rich and poor. They bring different cultures and experience to the job, but they are united in their determination to foster peace."

While all of that sounds entirely fine and in keeping with the UN's mandate to ensure that peace prevails around the world, in a fraught, unpredictable world—one in which the New World Order seeks to take control—the situation might be very different.

Back in 2009, the *Financial Times* ran an article titled "Why the world needs a United Nations army." In part, it stated:

"The idea of a 'UN army' remains deeply controversial. Critics can point to some horrendous peacekeeping failures. In the 1990s UN forces failed to prevent the Rwandan genocide and the Srebrenica massacre. More recently, UN-mandated troops were involved in sex crimes in the Congo. Like many international bureaucracies, the UN is often not a pretty sight when viewed from close quarters.

"Many nations also have understandable qualms about a permanent, multinational military force, intervening all over the world. The Americans do not put their forces under UN commanders. It often falls to poorer countries, such as Bangladesh, Pakistan and Indonesia, to provide most of the

Part of a UN force, these Turkish soldiers are seen patrolling Beirut, Lebanon, in 2006.

troops for UN operations. But they worry that setting up a permanent force would mean that they would lose the ability to pick and choose which missions they take part in.

Yet the demand for UN peacekeeping forces keeps going up. There are currently 116,000 UN peacekeepers deployed around the world in 17 different operations—an eightfold increase since 1999. Only the US has more troops deployed around the world than the UN."

In 2016, Kristan T. Harris of *American Intelligence Report* said: "United Nations military troops may soon arrive and see action on American soil following the United States' announcement of support for 'a set of principles that give a green light for U.N. peacekeeping troops and police to use force to protect civilians in armed conflicts,' *Military Times* reports. U.S. Ambassador Samantha Power told attendees at an important U.N. meeting that the United States was 'proud' and 'humbled' to be a included in the new agenda and promised to follow by the 18 pledges, *Fox News* reports. The arrival of the United Nations requires federalization of police in order to set a global standard of law enforcement. President Barack Obama has pounced on the opportunity to exploit recent shootings to push for the federalization of local police forces. More federalization of local police, collaborated with the arrival of the

United Nations military presence, could mean big trouble for liberty and freedom of speech in America."

Indeed, it could. Unless, of course, we all stand up against it.

UNITED NATIONS POPULATION PLOT

The United Nations has offered several different scenarios for what might be in store in the decades ahead of us in terms of how the New World Order is intent on killing billions of people to achieve its goal of total control. In a 2003 report titled "Long-range World Population Projections" (prepared by the Department of Economic and Social Affairs), various scenarios were detailed for the years to come. One such scenario was truly nightmarish. The DESA recorded: "If the fertility of major areas is kept constant at 1995 levels, the world population will soar to 256 billion by 2150."

To put that figure in an understandable context, we would be talking about a worldwide population of more than *thirty times* its current figure. Of course, all of this could be averted by encouraging smaller families via a greater promotion of birth control. The conspiracy rumor mill suggests this is not enough for the world's most powerful figures. They want the figures down sooner than later and by just about any means possible. We're talking wipeout. For all intents and purposes, we're talking *holocaust*, and it's something that dates back decades.

Many conspiracy theorists believe that things began in 1974, specifically on December 10 of that year, when a highly controversial report was prepared for the U.S. National Security Council. It was a report, attendant project, and study overseen by one of the most powerful figures in global politics, Henry Kissinger, who held such positions as U.S. secretary of state and national security advisor to the presidential office. The report was titled "Implications of Worldwide Population Growth for U.S. Security and Overseas Interests."

Rather disturbingly, while the document noted that a growing worldwide population was undeniably a problem—and one destined to only get worse—much of its attention was focused on targeting specific nations instead of the planet and its people as a whole. In other words, rather than encourage a united Earth to address the issue, the scenario envisioned lowering the population levels in the least advanced parts of the world. The countries that Kissinger's team felt posed the biggest "problems" were India, Bangladesh, Pakistan, Indonesia, Thailand, the Philippines, Turkey, Nigeria, Egypt, Ethiopia, Mexico, Colombia, and Brazil. It was estimated that these countries would account for close to fifty percent of the future increases in the world's population. And such increases, combined with the attendant, localized possibilities for societal collapse, should not be allowed to come to pass.

As the authors noted, in those countries—where growth and development were far from being on par with the rest of the planet—there was a distinct possibility that with falling food supplies, dwindling water and fuel, and more and more people, demands from the relevant populations for action to combat famine would soon become civil unrest and then uncontrollable anarchy. There was another worry for Kissinger's people. If the economies of countries with exploding populations collapsed, the result might be that the United States would be unable to import from those same countries things that were essential to its own economy. In that scenario, everyone suffers, or maybe not: Kissinger was determined that the United States would not fall, even if other nations did. It was up to the United Nations and the United States to solve the problem.

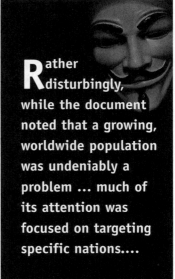

Rather disturbingly, while the document noted that a growing, worldwide population was undeniably a problem ... much of its attention was focused on targeting specific nations....

Clearly, as the following extracts show, a great deal of thought had gone into how the rise of populations in the underdeveloped world could possibly bring the United States to its knees: "The U.S. economy will require large and increasing amounts of minerals from abroad, especially from less developed countries. That fact gives the U.S. enhanced interest in the political, economic, and social stability of the supplying countries. Wherever a lessening of population pressures through reduced birth rates can increase the prospects for such stability, population policy becomes relevant to resource supplies and to the economic interests of the United States."

The document continues: "The location of known reserves of higher grade ores of most minerals favors increasing dependence of all industrialized regions on imports from less developed countries. The real problems of mineral supplies lie not in basic physical sufficiency, but in the politico-economic issues of access, terms for exploration and exploitation, and division of the benefits among producers, consumers, and host country governments."

Anticipating how things could turn very bad for the U.S., there is the following: "Whether through government action, labor conflicts, sabotage, or civil disturbance, the smooth flow of needed materials will be jeopardized. Although population pressure is obviously not the only factor involved, these types of frustrations are much less likely under conditions of slow or zero population growth."

The brains behind the report then targeted the people themselves, their collective mindset, and how to get around increasing issues of concern. In a

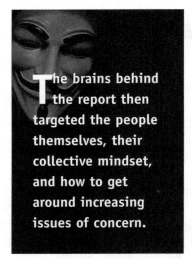

The brains behind the report then targeted the people themselves, their collective mindset, and how to get around increasing issues of concern.

section titled "Populations with a High Proportion of Growth," it was noted: "The young people, who are in much higher proportions in many LDCs, are likely to be more volatile, unstable, prone to extremes, alienation and violence than an older population. These young people can more readily be persuaded to attack the legal institutions of the government or real property of the 'establishment,' 'imperialists,' multinational corporations, or other—often foreign—influences blamed for their troubles."

There were words of warning in the report, too: "We must take care that our activities should not give the appearance to the LDCs of an industrialized country policy directed against the LDCs. Caution must be taken that in any approaches in this field we support in the LDCs are ones we can support within this country. 'Third World' leaders should be in the forefront and obtain the credit for successful programs. In this context it is important to demonstrate to LDC leaders that such family planning programs have worked and can work within a reasonable period of time."

The authors of the report make an interesting statement: "In these sensitive relations, however, it is important in style as well as substance to avoid the appearance of coercion." In other words, the report does not deny that nations might be coerced, only that there is a concerted effort to "avoid the appearance" of such.

See also entry on "Population Culling."

U.S. CONSTITUTION EROSION

The U.S. National Archives says: "The Declaration of Independence, Constitution and Bill of Rights, collectively known as the Charters of Freedom, have guaranteed the rights and freedoms of Americans for over 200 years."

One of the most important sections of the U.S. Constitution states: "We the people of the United States, in Order to form a more perfect Union, establish Justice, insure domestic Tranquility, provide for the common defense, promote the general Welfare, and secure the Blessings of Liberty to ourselves and our Posterity, do ordain and establish this Constitution for the United States of America."

Today, however, those who see New World Order figures seeking to take control believe that this same NWO is actively and deliberately eroding the

Constitution, possibly even to the point where it eventually becomes extinct—at which point the entire U.S. population will be at the mercy of NWO hordes.

Take, for example, *Reason.com*. In 2015, they stated: "The Patriot Act vastly expanded government power. And yet, for the NSA, it did not go far enough. It is helpful to have the Second Circuit slap the agency down, but the courts are not always so constraining. The Supreme Court certainly was not when, in a series of cases culminating with *Kelo v. New London* in 2005, it gradually unmoored the language of the Fifth Amendment from the purpose for which it was written.

"Under the Fifth Amendment, government can take private property only for 'public use.' In cases concerning blight and the breaking up of land oligopolies, 'public use' became 'public purpose.' Then, in *Kelo*, public purpose became public benefit, even in cases where the property taken went to another private party, rather than the public: So long as the government could assert that the seizure would, someday and however indirectly, redound to the common good, the taking qualified as one for public use."

Alternet has taken note of this disturbing erosion of rights, too: "It's still possible to remember, almost nostalgically, how the Fifth Amendment used to guarantee Americans due process. The key phrase was indeed that 'due process.' It meant the government could not take away your property or imprison or execute you without first allowing you a chance to defend yourself. You would have your day in court with a lawyer and a jury of your peers to make the final decision. This would all be quite public and the people involved would be held accountable for their actions. The Fifth was meant by those who wrote it as a check on the ultimate in government excess: the purposeful taking of citizens' lives. Today, it increasingly seems an artifact of a quaint past, as seemingly lost to history as the corded phone or manual typewriter."

U.S. MILITIA

In the final few days before the 2016 presidential election, the national media gave significant page and online space to the matter of the growing U.S. militia as it has become known; sizeable numbers of people who see that the only way to keep the New World Order at bay is by civil war and rising up those who are seen as New World Order orchestrators.

Reuters, on November 2, 2016, said: "As the most divisive presidential election in recent memory nears its conclusion, some armed militia groups are preparing for the possibility of a stolen election on Nov. 8 and civil unrest in the days following a victory by Democrat Hillary Clinton. They say they won't fire the first shot, but they're not planning to leave their guns at home, either. Trump's populist campaign has energized militia members ... who admire the Republican mogul's promise to deport illegal immigrants, stop Muslims from entering the country and build a wall along the Mexico border. Trump has repeatedly warned that the election may be 'rigged,' and has said he may not respect the results if he does not win. At least one paramilitary group, the Oath Keepers, has called on members to monitor voting sites for signs of fraud."

On the very same day, *Press TV* shared the following with its followers: "A militia group in the US state of Georgia is preparing for civil unrest should Democratic presidential nominee Hillary Clinton win in next week's election. Chris Hill, leader of the Three Percent Security Force militia, said if Clinton beats her Republican opponent Donald Trump on November 8, they would not remain silent, Reuters reported Wednesday. This is the last chance to save America from ruin. I'm surprised I was able to survive or suffer through eight years of [President Barack] Obama without literally going insane, but Hillary is going to be more of the same," said Hill, who goes by the name of 'Blood-agent.' In case of a fraudulent Clinton victory, Hill said the group will march on Washington to protect protesters and prevent the new president from taking their guns. I will be there to render assistance to my fellow countrymen, and prevent them from being disarmed, and I will fight and I will kill and I may die in the process,' said Hill."

V FOR VENDETTA

There is, perhaps, no better fictional example of how society might be when it is placed under the tyrannical grip of a power-mad leader who initiates harsh rules on the population than V *for Vendetta*. Starring Natalie Portman, Hugo Weaving, John Hurt, and Stephen Rea, this movie is based on Alan Moore and David Lloyd's 1988 comic book series of the same name. It is a story set several decades from now, when the United Kingdom is controlled by a ruthless dictator, his jackbooted minions, a police force similar to a Cold War-era Soviet Union, curfews, and constant surveillance. Entire swathes of movies and music are banned. Those who dare to oppose the oppressive regime mysteriously vanish. Except for one, however: "V" of the movie's title, played by Weaving.

Without giving away the plot, we see V—who wears a Guy Fawkes mask throughout the movie—and Portman's character, Evey, doing their utmost to return the U.K. to its pre-New World Order-like existence. It's notable that a great deal of attention was given to the movie when it was released in 2006, not just by movie reviewers, but also by the mainstream media and particularly so in relation to how the movie eerily mirrored the growing threat to our civil liberties in the real world.

The Guardian provides background on the story itself: "Imagine, if you will, the Britain of some 20 years hence as a kind of retro-futurist Orwellian police state with tatty, Blitz-era posters with creepy state slogans on decaying brick walls, but modern buildings like the Gherkin visible on the London sky-line, and in which there are portraits of John Hurt everywhere as a gauntly bearded, Leninist Big Brother. You will have to imagine it pretty hard, because this movie has not imagined it, at least in no more than in a 1980s pop video way. The British people are living in a state of resentful oppression and dental disrepair: and they are represented in various scenes by about a dozen or so Equity members, quaintly shown at the pub or in their prole front rooms, glum-ly watching the state television network on which propaganda is pumped out."

Peter Travers at *Rolling Stone* says of *V for Vendetta*: "Written by the Wachowskis—Andy and his transgender brother, Larry—and directed by first-timer James McTeigue, their assistant on *The Matrix*, the film flies on a rhythm all its own. There's nothing Neo about V, the masked avenger who uses bombs, daggers and his telegenic charisma to take down a regime that has left him a burned remnant of its ungodly experiments.

"The source material is the 1989 graphic novel illustrated by David Lloyd and written by Alan Moore, who wants no part of what the Wachowskis have wrought. Moore took his name off the film's credits. Moore's novel skewered the 1980s England of Margaret Thatcher. In the Wachowski update, England is a police state ruled by Chancellor Sutler (John Hurt), a fear-mongering, gay-bash-ing, Islam-hating dictator who strips citizens of their civil rights and religious freedoms in exchange for protection from bioweapons of mass destruction. Some see parallels here to Bushworld. Come on. The chancellor, as acted to the hilt by Hurt, can't be W—he's hyperarticulate."

A protestor in London, England, wears an Anonymous mask inspired by the film *V for Vendetta*.

Cinema Blend provides its view on *V for Vendetta*: "At times it almost feels like you're watching something forbidden, like you're seeing something you shouldn't be allowed to see. It's shocking that a movie like this, especially in these times, ever actually got made. It's even more unbelievable that it was made by a major Hollywood studio. It's fun to accuse Hollywood of liberal activism, but you don't expect this kind of real film-making bravery from corporate America or a company like Warner Bros."

Christopher Orr of *The Atlantic* offers his views, which include the following: "Moore's comic envisioned a fascist British government that had come to power in the wake of a nuclear war. The film, released on video today, updates this scenario for contemporary (and

American) audiences in two ways: First, the event that precipitated the descent into dictatorship was a biological attack on English soil; and second, though allegedly the work of terrorists, the attack was in fact conducted by the British government itself, as a pretext for exerting vast, police-state powers over the lives of its citizens. The resonance with critiques of the Bush administration's political use of the war on terror are hard to miss and entirely intentional."

For those who think that a New World Order stands no chance whatsoever of ever happening, *V for Vendetta* is a definitive wake-up call. Although a work of fiction—albeit with a nod or several in the direction of certain world-changing events of the early twenty-first century—the movie skillfully hits home how easily we could, almost overnight, descend into a state of *1984*-style proportions.

Veterans Today

On the matter of the nature of the New World Order, *Veterans Today* summarizes things as follows: "The New World Order is incoherent because it is implicitly and practically based on the principle that double standard and contradiction are logical. In a rational universe, A cannot be a non-A at the same time and in the same respect. But in the minds of New World Order agents, contradictory things are possible.

"So, the New World Order violates the law of non-contradiction, which is foundational to all reasonable interactions. Terrorism, in the New World Order, can be non-terrorism at the same time and in the same respect. For example, New World Order agents supported Osama bin Laden in the 1980s, but they later declared that bin Laden was a terrorist and therefore needed to be deposed. Why? Because bin Laden stopped working for them.

"In a similar vein, George W. Bush declared ad nauseam that he was fighting terrorism in the Middle East, but George W. Bush trained terrorist organizations such as the MEK in Nevada. NWO agents declare that they are spreading democracy in the Middle East, but they want to remove democratically elected officials such as Assad from power. That indeed is a contradiction, and no reasonable person will stand for this. What we are seeing again and again is that NWO agents seem to embrace John Milton's Satan, who says 'Evil, be thou my good.'

"In other words, NWO agents replace good with evil and evil with good. This principle is essentially diabolical and Talmudic. In short, NWO agents are replacing practical reason with Satanism and are desperately spreading this poison across the Middle East."

VIRUSES

There is no doubt that one of the primary goals of the New World Order is to lower the world's population levels and to lower them to levels that would result in billions of deaths. But how could such an abominable thing ever be achieved? Perhaps, theorists suggest, by unleashing lethal viruses that only the New World Order is immune to. Some theorists believe that the recent outbreaks of the Zika virus may represent a kind of "testing of the waters" when it comes to trying to determine how quickly and easily it might be possible to wipe out a significant portion of the world's population via a deadly virus. But, what is the Zika virus? To answer that question, we have to turn our attentions to the Centers for Disease Control and Prevention (CDC), which is a key player in the battle to keep the virus at bay.

The CDC says: "Zika virus was first discovered in 1947 and is named after the Zika Forest in Uganda. In 1952, the first human cases of Zika were detected and since then, outbreaks of Zika have been reported in tropical Africa, Southeast Asia, and the Pacific Islands. Zika outbreaks have probably occurred in many locations. Before 2007, at least 14 cases of Zika had been documented, although other cases were likely to have occurred and were not reported. Because the symptoms of Zika are similar to those of many other diseases, many cases may not have been recognized.

"Zika is spread mostly by the bite of an infected *Aedes* species mosquito (*Ae. aegypti* and *Ae. albopictus*). These mosquitoes bite during the day and night. Zika can be passed from a pregnant woman to her fetus. Infection during pregnancy can cause certain birth defects. There is no vaccine or medicine for Zika. Local mosquito-borne Zika virus transmission has been reported in the continental United States.

"Many people infected with Zika virus won't have symptoms or will only have mild symptoms. The most common symptoms of Zika are fever, rash, joint pain, conjunctivitis (red eyes). Other symptoms include: muscle pain, headache. Symptoms can last for several days to a week. People usually don't get sick enough to go to the hospital, and they very rarely die of Zika. Once a person has been infected with Zika, they are likely to be protected from future infections.

"Zika infection during pregnancy can cause a birth defect of the brain called microcephaly and other severe fetal brain defects. Other problems have been detected among fetuses and infants infected with Zika virus before birth, such as defects of the eye, hearing deficits, and impaired growth. There have also been increased reports of Guillain-Barré syndrome, an uncommon sickness of the nervous system, in areas affected by Zika.

"There is no vaccine to prevent Zika. The best way to prevent diseases spread by mosquitoes is to protect yourself and your family from mosquito bites."

Is it possible that the huge increase in cases of the Zika virus has sinister origins—all based around plans to lower the population? Certainly, some believe that to be the case. *The Independent's* Andrew Griffin acknowledges that there are multiple conspiracy theories that suggest this is indeed the case, but he suggests that such scenarios are unlikely. Griffin states: "The idea that Zika is being used to keep the number of people down slots neatly into a range of popular conspiracy theories. But it doesn't really make sense, even by its own logic. The Zika virus would be an incredibly inefficient way of wiping out populations, if that was the New World Order's aim.... It is likely that people in affected countries will have fewer children while the disease is raging, as a way of looking to stave off its effects on their babies. But that would be an incredibly inefficient way of keeping the population down.... The two big baddies of most conspiracy theories, many have claimed that the Rothschild family and/or the Rockefellers are responsible for the spread of the Zika virus. (It isn't clear why they would do this.) This the-

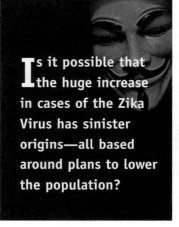

Is it possible that the huge increase in cases of the Zika Virus has sinister origins—all based around plans to lower the population?

ory is laid out on one conspiracy website, Collective Evolution. That site claims that the Rockefeller Foundation 'owns the patent on the virus,' and that is being sold throughout the world."

Griffin adds the following words: "One of the big claims of conspiracy theorists is that babies being born with microcephaly, or abnormally small heads, aren't related to Zika. Instead, they're caused by one of the many favorite ills of conspiracy theorists: chemtrails, vaccines, or even the pesticides that are being used to fumigate areas where people are at risk of mosquito bites. It's true that there has been no conclusive connection between Zika and microcephaly. The World Health Organization has said that 'a causal relationship between Zika infection during pregnancy and microcephaly is strongly suspected, though not yet scientifically proven.'"

See also entry on "Superviruses."

VOTING RESTRICTIONS

A *coup d'état* might be a very real way for a New World Order to take control of not just the United States but multiple nations too, but there is a far more subtle way for those powerful figures to seize control. Rather than install an NWO-driven government via brute force and threats of incarceration or even death for those who go against it, those pushing for a very dangerous change might resort to a far simpler way of influencing who gets elected into power and who doesn't. In fact, we are seeing evidence that this particular tactic is already in place. It's the issue of making it more and more difficult for people to vote.

Correct the Record comes straight to the point: "Almost fifty years after the Voting Rights Act was passed, the right to vote is still under attack. Today, Republican presidential hopefuls are attempting to hijack our democracy by restricting the voting rights of everyday Americans. In states across the country, Republicans are pushing for restrictive laws that disproportionately impact turnout among African Americans, Latinos, working Americans, seniors, and America's youth.

"Some of the top names in the Republican field, including Marco Rubio, Jeb Bush, and Chris Christie, support limiting early voting, while others like Scott Walker and Rick Perry have enacted strict voter ID laws that make it more difficult to vote. If we do nothing to combat these discriminatory laws, the voices of hundreds of thousands of voters will be silenced at the polls in 2016."

On this specific matter, the Brennan Center for Justice says: "In 2016, 14 states will have new voting restrictions in place for the first time in a presiden-

A long line at a school in Arlington, Virginia, greets people wanting to vote in the presidential election. Voting behavior has been altered by making voting more difficult for certain people—especially those who are poor. One way to do this is to limit the number of places one can vote, as well as having election day during the work week.

tial election. The new laws range from strict photo ID requirements to early voting cutbacks to registration restrictions. Those 14 states are: Alabama, Arizona, Indiana, Kansas, Mississippi, Nebraska, New Hampshire, Ohio, Rhode Island, South Carolina, Tennessee, Texas, Virginia, and Wisconsin.

"(This number decreased from 15 to 14 when the D.C. Circuit blocked a voter registration requirement in Alabama, Georgia, and Kansas on September 9, 2016. Georgia was removed, but Alabama and Kansas remain on the map because certain restrictions remain in place. Other recent court rulings have impacted the map: North Carolina and North Dakota were removed after courts blocked restrictive laws. Despite a recent court victory mitigating the impact of Texas's photo ID law, it is still included because the requirement is more restrictive than what was in place for the 2012 presidential election.)

"This is part of a broader movement to curtail voting rights, which began after the 2010 election, when state lawmakers nationwide started introducing hundreds of harsh measures making it harder to vote."

Public Radio International has had a great deal to say about this issue, too: "The two white scions of billionaire Donald J. [(Ivanka and Eric Trump)] and the black social activist daughter of Eric Garner, whose Staten Island choking death sparked national outrage, have virtually nothing in common. Until now. None of them could vote in last week's New York primary election. Add their names to the list of potentially millions of Americans who will be blocked by onerous voter registration laws, many of them new and deliberately discriminatory.

"Both Ivanka and Eric, registered independents, missed last October's deadline to register as Republicans, which was required for New York's closed primary. Their dad, Republican presidential candidate Trump, said the two siblings felt 'very, very guilty.' Erica Garner, one of Democrat presidential candidate Bernie Sanders' highest profile supporters, also missed the October deadline. She took to Facebook to express her frustration, 'If yr nt a Dem or GOP you can't vote???'

"Now, millions of Americans are facing voting barriers that go beyond what happened to Ivanka, Eric and Erica. These voters are running into new state laws limiting polling places, restricting election hours, and requiring special identification. In the recent Wisconsin primary, Dennis Hatten found out exactly what that meant. The Marine veteran struggled for months to get the official state issued ID. But, at the polls, he was turned away because the address didn't match his new polling place. Hatten had to go home, get a utility bill, and return. All told, it took him six months, two trips to the polls and an hour in line to cast his ballot."

WACKENHUT CORPORATION

G4S Secure Solutions (USA) is an American security services company and a wholly owned subsidiary of G4S plc. It was founded as the Wackenhut Corporation in 1954, in Coral Gables, Florida, by George Wackenhut and three partners (all of them former FBI agents). In 2002, the company was acquired for $570 million by Danish corporation Group 4 Falck (itself then merged to form a British company, G4S, in 2004). In 2010, G4S Wackenhut changed its name to G4S Secure Solutions (USA) to reflect the new business model. The G4S Americas Region headquarters is in Jupiter, Florida.

After early struggles (including a fistfight between George Wackenhut and one of his partners), Wackenhut took sole control of his company in 1958, then choosing to name it after himself. By 1964, he had contracts to guard the Kennedy Space Center and the U.S. Atomic Energy Commission's nuclear test site in Nevada, which included Area 51. The following year, Wackenhut took his company public. In the mid-1960s, Florida Governor Claude Kirk commissioned the Wackenhut Corporation to help fight a "war on organized crime," awarding the company a $500,000 contract. The commission lasted about a year but led to more than eighty criminal indictments, including many for local politicians and government employees. Following the murder of a British tourist at a rest stop in 1993, Florida contracted with Wackenhut to provide security at all state rest stops.

The company's work includes: permanent guarding service, security officers, manned security, disaster response, emergency services, control-room monitoring, armed security, unarmed security, special event security, security patrols, reception/concierge service, access control, emergency medical technician (EMT) service, and ambassador service. Like other security companies, G4S targets specific sectors: energy, utilities, chemical/petrochemical, financial institutions, government, hospitals and healthcare facilities, major corporations, construction, ports and airports, residential communities, retail and commercial real estate, and transit systems.

Having expanded into providing food services for U.S. prisons in the 1960s, Wackenhut—in 1984—launched a subsidiary to design and manage jails and detention centers for the burgeoning private prison market. Wackenhut then became the nation's second largest for-profit prison operator. In April 1999, the state of Louisiana took over the running of Wackenhut's fifteen-month-old juvenile prison after the U.S. Justice Department accused Wackenhut of subjecting its young inmates to "excessive abuse and neglect."

U.S. journalist Gregory Palast commented on the case: "New Mexico's privately operated prisons are filled with America's impoverished, violent outcasts—and those are the guards."

The GEO Group, Inc. now runs former Wackenhut facilities in fourteen states as well as in South Africa and Australia. Some facilities, such as the Wackenhut Corrections Centers in New York, retain the Wackenhut name, despite no longer having any open connection with the company.

Frequent rumors that the company was in the employ of the Central Intelligence Agency, particularly in the 1960s, were never substantiated; however, George Wackenhut, who was obsessive about high-tech security gadgets in his private life, never denied the rumors.

WALKING CORPSE SYNDROME

It may intrigue many to learn that there exists a medical condition called Walking Corpse Syndrome (WCS). For the sufferers, it's an absolute nightmare and no joke at all. WCS is officially known as Cotard's Syndrome. It's a condition steeped in mystery and intrigue. Very disturbingly, Cotard's Syndrome causes the victim to believe that he or she is dead or that their limbs are no longer living or even theirs. The condition takes its name from one Jules Cotard, a French neurologist who died in 1889 from diphtheria. He spent much of his career studying and cataloging cases of Walking Corpse Syndrome. Not only do those affected by WCS believe they are dead, they also fall into spirals of psychosis and fail to take care of their personal appearance. What does all of this have to do with the New World Order? Read on.

One of the most disturbing cases of Walking Corpse Syndrome surfaced out of the United Kingdom in May 2013. A man, referred to by the medical community only as "Graham," found himself descending into a deeply depressed state to the point where he ultimately came to believe he was literally a member of the walking dead club. As Graham's condition rapidly worsened, and as he actually spent his days and nights wandering around graveyards, his family was forced to seek medical treatment. For a while, Graham became convinced that his brain was clinically dead or was "missing" from his skull. Fortunately, treatment finally brought Graham back to the world of the living.

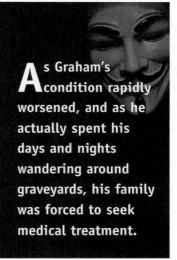

As Graham's condition rapidly worsened, and as he actually spent his days and nights wandering around graveyards, his family was forced to seek medical treatment.

New light was soon shed on the nature of Cotard's Syndrome as a result of a connection to Zovirax. It is generally used in the treatment of herpes-based conditions, such as cold sores. Although Zovirax is known for having a small number of side effects, studies revealed that approximately one percent of people prescribed Zovirax developed psychiatric conditions, including Cotard's Syndrome. Intriguingly, most of those taking Zovirax and who experienced Walking Corpse Syndrome were also suffering from renal failure at the time.

Studies undertaken by Anders Helldén, of the Stockholm, Sweden-based Karolinska University Hospital and Thomas Linden, based at the Sahlgrenska Academy in Gothenburg, Sweden, have uncovered remarkable, albeit unsettling, data on this curious phenomenon. Their case studies included that of a woman who was prescribed Zovirax after having a bout of shingles. When the drug took hold of the woman, who also happened to have renal failure, she began to act in a crazed and concerned fashion, believing—or suspecting—that she was dead. When given emergency dialysis to cope with the effects of kidney failure, her strange beliefs began to fade to the point where she finally came to accept that she was not dead, after all. For hours, however, she remained convinced that "my left arm is definitely not mine."

The Independent said of this strange saga: "The woman ran into a hospital in an extremely anxious state, author of the research Anders Helldén from the Karolinska University Hospital in Stockholm said. After receiving dialysis, the woman explained that she had felt anxious because she had been overwhelmed by a strong feeling that she was dead. Within a few hours her symptoms began to ease, until she felt that she was 'pretty sure' she wasn't dead, but remained adamant her left arm did not belong to her. After 24 hours, her symptoms had disappeared. Blood analysis later revealed that acyclovir, which can normally be broken down in the body before being flushed out by the kidneys, can leave low levels of breakdown product CMMG in the body. Blood tests of those who had Cotard's symptoms showed much higher levels of CMMG. All but one of those tested also had renal failure."

While the Zovirax–Cotard's connection is still not fully understood, administering the drug to those who are susceptible to it in such a strange fashion—and then medically treating those same patients to ensure their firm beliefs that they are dead are removed—may allow for Walking Corpse Syndrome to be turned on and off at will. Might this allow for an unscrupulous New World Order to create the closest thing possible to a mind-controlled, old-school zombie?

WALMART CONSPIRACY

A massive New World Order-driven conspiracy concerning Walmart? It sounds bizarre and outlandish. It may not be. In 2015, Jason Dias wrote: "Walmart closed five stores on short notice recently, supposedly due to plumbing problems. But Walmart conspiracy theories emerged right away. The best one: Walmart is teaming with FEMA and the federal government to turn some of its stores into concentration camps for American citizens—particularly scared, gun-toting conservative Libertarian citizens. And, anyway, Walmart is already a labor camp. It just pays the absolute minimum we will accept to transfer the maximum amount of that labor into wealth for shareholders, the minimum into wealth for workers. Also, Walmart suppresses wages and drives out competition. When it moves into a town, it does so after negotiating significant tax breaks and building code changes. It puts local businesses out of business and its workers are frequently former business owners from the community with no-place else to go. The conspiracy theory about Walmart joining FEMA and other feds to build nefarious labor camps does make sense in that light: What we're hearing really are metaphors for what is already taking place."

But are they really just metaphors? *Snopes* commented on the matter too, citing a number of theories, including this one: "The closed WalMart stores are being converted into giant entrance facilities for a network of underground tunnels that the U.S. military will use to link 'deep underground military bases' (DUMBs) and secretly transport troops across the U.S. But why risk public exposure by building all those entrances in existing WalMart stores when the federal government owns plenty of land all over the country? And unless the military only intends to move troops to and from a handful of states,

According to some conspiracy theorists, the owners of Walmart are renovating some stores to serve as concentration camps in the near future.

they'll need other entrances (and exits), so where are those other entrances going to be located, and how will the military cover their construction? For that matter, how is this massive underground tunnel complex across the U.S. going to be built in the first place?"

The Inquisitr had its views on all this, too: "Conspiracy theory speculations about the sudden 'mysterious' closures of at least five Wal-Mart stores in four states where Jade Helm military training exercises are scheduled to start got a boost in the last few days following release of footage purportedly showing police officers guarding loading docks and entrances at a 'closed' Wal-Mart under circumstances that many say are suspicious.

"Two 'exclusive' videos shot by one of the subscribers of the YouTube conspiracy theorist Dahboo777, inside the closed Pico Rivera Walmart super-center, California, according to some, show an attempt by police guards helping Walmart maintain security to hide sinister goings-on at the closed store.

"In the first footage, guards order the person filming to stop and shelves appeared to have been arranged to conceal goings on in an area inside the store. In the second footage, Walmart officials allegedly attempt to conceal what was happening in the store by covering up windows with plastic sheets.

"The speculations are diverse, but one line of speculation that has emerged prominently in conspiracy theory circles focuses on alleged underground tunnels constructed by Wal-Mart in collaboration with NSA and DHS, which will play a key role in the logistics of a rumored plan by the authorities to convert the Wal-Mart centers into operational and emergency staging areas for NSA and DHS operatives, once the anxiously anticipated martial law kicks in."

Walmart in league with the New World Order? Stranger things have happened. Maybe they are soon to get even stranger.

WATCH LISTS

In terms of the New World Order, the erosion of civil liberties, and increasing spying on the population of the planet, we hear more and more about what are known as Watch Lists. But what, exactly, are they? While Watch Lists can prove extremely helpful when it comes to the matter of people who wish to do us harm, on more than a few occasions, Watch Lists have proved to contain the names of people who have no place on them. *Wired* notes: "The Terrorist Screening Database was created in 2003 by order of a Homeland Security Presidential Directive. The database includes the names and aliases of anyone known to be, or reasonably suspected of being, involved in terrorism or assisting terrorists through financial aid or other ways. The federal Terrorist Screening Center maintains the database, and an array of government agencies nominate people to it through the National Counterterrorism Center."

As *Wired* also revealed, however: "'Instead of a watch list limited to actual, known terrorists, the government has built a vast system based on the unproven and flawed premise that it can predict if a person will commit a terrorist act in the future,' Hina Shamsi, head of the ACLU's National Security Project, told *The Intercept*. 'On that dangerous theory, the government is secretly blacklisting people as suspected terrorists and giving them the impossible task of proving themselves innocent of a threat they haven't carried out.'"

The American Civil Liberties Union says: "The U.S. government maintains a massive watchlist system that risks stigmatizing hundreds of thousands of people—including U.S. citizens—as terrorism suspects based on vague, overbroad, and often secret standards and evidence. The consequences of being placed on a government watchlist can be far-reaching. They can include questioning, harassment, or detention by authorities, or even an indefinite ban on air travel. And while the government keeps the evidence it uses to blacklist people in this manner secret, government watchdogs have found that as many as 35 percent of the nominations to the network of watchlists are outdated and tens of thousands of names were placed on lists without an adequate factual basis. To make matters worse, the government denies watchlisted individuals any meaningful way to correct errors and clear their names."

The ACLU concludes: "A bloated, opaque watchlisting system is neither fair nor effective. A system in which innocent people languish on blacklists indefinitely, with their rights curtailed and their names sullied, is at odds with our Constitution and values."

WATER CONTROL

If there is one thing that we, the human race, cannot live without, it is water. The Centers for Disease Control and Prevention says: "Getting enough water every day is important for your health. Healthy people meet their fluid needs by drinking when thirsty and drinking with meals. Most of your fluid needs are met through the water and beverages you drink. However, you can get some fluids through the foods that you eat. For example, broth soups and foods with high water content such as celery, tomatoes, or melons can contribute to fluid intake. Water helps your body: keep your temperature normal, lubricate and cushion joints, protect your spinal cord and other sensitive tissues, and get rid of wastes through urination, perspiration, and bowel movements. Your body needs more water when you are: in hot climates, more physically active, running a fever, or having diarrhea or vomiting."

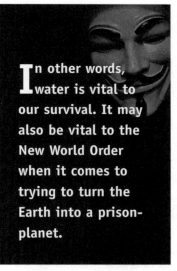

In other words, water is vital to our survival. It may also be vital to the New World Order when it comes to trying to turn the Earth into a prison-planet.

In other words, water is vital to our survival. It may also be vital to the New World Order when it comes to trying to turn the Earth into a prison-planet. After all, if we are denied water to significant degrees, then we will find ourselves in an extremely perilous position and highly vulnerable to a New World Order takeover. Could we see ourselves plunged into such a precarious state? The answer is yes, undoubtedly.

The United Nations notes how precarious the current state of affairs is, let alone tomorrow: "According to the Millennium Development Goals Report 2012, 783 million people, or 11 percent of the global population, remain without access to an improved source of drinking water. Such sources include household connections, public standpipes, boreholes, protected dug wells, protected springs and rainwater collections. The world has met the MDG drinking water target five years ahead of schedule but work is not yet completely done. We must not forget that since it is not yet possible to measure water quality globally, dimensions of safety, reliability and sustainability may actually be slowing progress. Furthermore, there are regions particularly delayed such as Sub-Saharan Africa where over 40 percent of all people without improved drinking water live.

"The United Nations has long been addressing the global crisis caused by insufficient water supply to satisfy basic human needs and growing demands on the world's water resources to meet human, commercial and agricultural needs. The United Nations Water Conference (1977), the International Drinking Water Supply and Sanitation Decade (1981–1990), the International Conference on Water and the Environment (1992) and the Earth Summit (1992)—all focused on this vital resource. The Decade, in particular, helped some 1.3 billion people in developing countries gain access to safe drinking water."

In 2012, Market Oracle and Global Research reported: "A disturbing trend in the water sector is accelerating worldwide. The new 'water barons'—the Wall Street banks and elitist multibillionaires—are buying up water all over the world at unprecedented pace.

"Familiar mega-banks and investing powerhouses such as Goldman Sachs, JP Morgan Chase, Citigroup, UBS, Deutsche Bank, Credit Suisse, Macquarie Bank, Barclays Bank, the Blackstone Group, Allianz, and HSBC Bank, among others, are consolidating their control over water. Wealthy tycoons

Fresh drinking water is increasingly coming under the control of governments and large companies. Having control over such a precious commodity is one way to hold power over any population.

such as T. Boone Pickens, former President George H.W. Bush and his family, Hong Kong's Li Ka-shing, Philippines' Manuel V. Pangilinan and other Filipino billionaires, and others are also buying thousands of acres of land with aquifers, lakes, water rights, water utilities, and shares in water engineering and technology companies all over the world."

In 2013 *Natural News* said: "Gun control may be a hot topic, but what about water control? Recent comments from Nestle CEO Peter Brabeck imply that the world's water will soon come under the control of corporations like his. Brabeck makes the astonishing claim that water is not a human right, but should be managed by business people and governing bodies. He wants water controlled, privatized, and delegated in a way that sustains the planet."

Natural News adds: "All of this means that Brabeck's future plans include monitoring and controlling the amount of water people use. One day, cities and towns may be forced by international law to limit each household to a set amount of water. People may have to obtain permits to dig wells or pay fines for collecting rainwater."

Time stated in 2015: "Global water resources may soon meet only 60% of the world's water demands, the United Nations warned in a dire new report. The World Water Development Report, issued ahead of World Water Day on Sunday, says demand for water around the world will increase by 55% over the next 15 years. With current supplies, that means only 60% of the world's water needs will be met in 2030."

What all of the above tells us is that our most precious commodity may one day be used against us—or denied us—as a means to keep us under a New World Order thumb.

WEAPONS OF MASS DESTRUCTION

There is absolutely no doubt, whatsoever, that one of the primary reasons why the war in Iraq went ahead when it did, and on the scale it did, is because of the claims that Saddam Hussein possessed weapons of mass destruction, or WMDs. We were told by our leaders that it was practically imperative that the WMDs be found, lest the entire western world might find itself in the midst of a near-Armageddon-like disaster.

On August 26, 2002, Vice President Dick Cheney said: "Simply stated, there is no doubt that Saddam Hussein now has weapons of mass destruction."

One month later, Senator Joseph Lieberman told the American people: "Every day Saddam remains in power with chemical weapons, biological

Vice President Dick Cheney declared there was no doubt that Iraq's Saddam Hussein had weapons of mass destruction. Later, he was proven completely wrong.

weapons, and the development of nuclear weapons is a day of danger for the United States."

In February 2003, Colin Powell stated: "We know that Saddam Hussein is determined to keep his weapons of mass destruction, is determined to make more."

Then, on March 18, 2003, President George Bush warned America: "Intelligence gathered by this and other governments leaves no doubt that the Iraq regime continues to possess and conceal some of the most lethal weapons ever devised."

That Saddam Hussein was a ruthless killer, one who had no qualms about using chemical weapons on the battlefield, is not a matter of any dispute at all. They were used by the Iraqi regime in the 1980s (when Iran was in Hussein's sights) and during the first Gulf War of 1990 against Kuwaiti forces. There is good evidence, too, that Hussein was doing his utmost to develop and build atomic weapons. Unlike the situation in the 2000s, United Nations weapons inspectors actually found weapons of mass destruction when they toured Iraq after the first Gulf War—and in mass numbers, too. They were carefully contained and then completely obliterated.

There was a sharp contrast between what happened after the first Gulf War of 1990 and the events that erupted in 2002–2003. In the wake of the former, the WMDs were found and destroyed. In the latter, the alleged existence of the weapons of mass destruction was all based on hazy, and hardly ever expanded on, references to "intelligence data" and "expert sources."

None of this was of any concern to President Bush, who took the proverbial bull by the proverbial horns: The war on Iraq began in earnest in March 2003. On the 19th of the month, Bush told the American people: "My fellow citizens. At this hour, American and coalition forces are in the early stages of military operations to disarm Iraq, to free its people and to defend the world from grave danger."

This was in sharp contrast to the words of a man named David Kay. The former head of the Iraq Survey Group, he told the BBC that "anyone out there holding—as I gather Prime Minister Blair has recently said—the prospect that, in fact, the Iraq Survey Group is going to unmask actual weapons of mass destruction, is really delusional."

A major, damning dent in the claim that the Iraqis were hiding WMDs surfaced in late May 2003 when the Iraq war was well underway. On the 27th of the month, analysts from the Defense Intelligence Agency (DIA) revealed to the White House that a pair of trailers that were captured by Kurdish military personnel, and which the then Secretary of State, Colin Powell, in the buildup to war had said were connected to Iraq's plans to deploy deadly chemical weaponry, were actually nothing of the sort.

In words that came back to haunt him, Powell said: "We have firsthand descriptions of biological weapons factories on wheels and on rails. We know what the fermenters look like. We know what the tanks, pumps, compressors and other parts look like."

Despite the fact that the DIA made it very clear that the trailers had a zero "connection to anything biological," the White House refused to acknowledge the fact, and the CIA continued to loudly assert that the trailers were being used in "mobile biological weapons production."

Despite the fact that the DIA made it very clear that the trailers had a zero "connection to anything biological," the White House refused to acknowledge the fact....

In February 2004—in the face of the criticism that the Iraq war was all for nothing and that people could have gotten rid of Hussein without a huge war, one that was costly in both lives and money—President Bush established a body, the Iraq Intelligence Commission, to address the huge errors, or as some saw it, deliberate mistakes, on the matter of Hussein's WMDs. Its conclusions mirrored those of what just about everyone else was saying.

Britain's Prime Minister, Tony Blair, said: "What you can say is that we received that intelligence about Saddam's programs and about his weapons that we acted on that, it's the case throughout the whole of the conflict.

"I remember having conversations with the chief of defense staff and other people were saying well, we think we might have potential WMD find here or there. Now these things didn't actually come to anything in the end, but I don't know is the answer. We expected, I expected to find actual usable, chemical or biological weapons after we entered Iraq.... And the problem is, I can apologize for the information that turned out to be wrong, but I can't, sincerely at least, apologize for removing Saddam. The world is a better place with Saddam in prison not in power. I can apologize for the information being wrong but I can never apologize, sincerely at least, for removing Saddam. The world is a better place with Saddam in prison."

Indeed, it is; however, it is entirely possible that the entire WMD issue was conjured up as a means to justify implementing the kind of change in the Middle East that the New World Order both requires and desires.

WEATHERMEN

In 2015, a strange and controversial story surfaced concerning the existence of a secret group known as the Weathermen. Their mandate is to clandestinely research, and ultimately perfect, weaponry that can provoke significant and drastic changes in the world's weather. The reason is to provoke extremes of weather that will ensure massive starvation, flooding, tornadoes, and earthquakes, all as a means to ensure one sinister reason: to depopulate human civilization until it can be effectively controlled and enslaved by a looming New World Order. If such a scenario sounds like science fiction, it's not. It's all too real.

April 28, 1997, was the date on which a startling statement was made by William S. Cohen—at the time the U.S. secretary of defense in the Clinton Administration. The location was the University of Georgia, which was playing host to "The Conference on Terrorism, Weapons of Mass Destruction, and U.S. Strategy." As a captivated audience listened intently, Cohen revealed something that was as remarkable as it was controversial.

Hostile groups—that Cohen, whether by design or not, did not name— were actively "engaging in an eco-type of terrorism whereby they can alter the climate, set off earthquakes and volcanoes remotely through the use of Electro-Magnetic waves. So there are plenty of ingenious minds out there that are at work finding ways in which they can wreak terror upon other nations. It's real."

Cohen was not wrong: in 1996 the U.S. Air Force unveiled to the public and the media an astonishing document. It read like science fiction. It was, however, nothing less than amazing, controversial, science fact. The title of the document was "USAF 2025." It was, basically, a study of where the Air Force hoped to be—technologically and militarily speaking—in 2025.

Researched and written by the 2025 Support Office at the Air University, Air Education and Training Command, and developed by the Air University Press, Educational Services Directorate, College of Aerospace Doctrine, Research, and Education, Maxwell Air Force Base, Alabama, the document was "designed to comply with a directive from the chief of staff of the Air Force to examine the concepts, capabilities, and technologies the United States will require to remain the dominant air and space force in the future."

Beyond any shadow of doubt, the most controversial section of the entire "USAF 2025" report was the section titled "Weather as a Force Multiplier: Owning the Weather in 2025." Forget missiles, bombs, bullets, troops, and aircraft. The future, very possibly, lies in defeating the enemy via global weather manipulation.

"In 2025, US aerospace forces can 'own the weather' by capitalizing on emerging technologies and focusing development of those technologies to war-fighting applications. While some segments of society will always be reluctant to examine controversial issues such as weather-modification, the tremendous military capabilities that could result from this field are ignored at our own peril. Weather-modification offers the war fighter a wide-range of possible options to defeat or coerce an adversary," the report stated.

The authors also noted: "The desirability to modify storms to support military objectives is the most aggressive and controversial type of weather-modification. While offensive weather-modification efforts would certainly be undertaken by U.S. forces with great caution and trepidation, it is clear that we cannot afford to allow an adversary to obtain an exclusive weather-modification capability."

Forget missiles, bombs, bullets, troops, and aircraft. The future, very possibly, lies in defeating the enemy via global, weather manipulation.

It's very clear that a great deal of thought had gone into the production of this particular section of the report. It begins by providing the reader with a theoretical scenario, one filled with conflict but which may very well be resolvable by turning the weather into a weapon: "Imagine that in 2025 the US is fighting a rich, but now consolidated, politically powerful drug cartel in South America. The cartel has purchased hundreds of Russian- and Chinese-built fighters that have successfully thwarted our attempts to attack their production facilities. With their local numerical superiority and interior lines, the cartel is launching more than 10 aircraft for every one of ours. In addition, the cartel is using the French *system probatoire d' observation de la terre* (SPOT) positioning and tracking imagery systems, which in 2025 are capable of transmitting near-real-time, multispectral imagery with 1 meter resolution. The US wishes to engage the enemy on an uneven playing field in order to exploit the full potential of our aircraft and munitions."

At this point, a decision is taken to focus carefully on making the local weather work for the United States and against the cartel: "Meteorological analysis reveals that equatorial South America typically has afternoon thunderstorms on a daily basis throughout the year. Our intelligence has confirmed that cartel pilots are reluctant to fly in or near thunderstorms. Therefore, our weather force support element (WFSE), which is a part of the commander in chief's (CINC) air operations center (AOC), is tasked to forecast storm paths and trigger or intensify thunderstorm cells over critical target areas that the enemy must defend with their aircraft. Since our aircraft in 2025 have all-weather capability, the thunderstorm threat is minimal to our forces, and we can effectively and decisively control the sky over the target."

The WFSE, the report notes, has the necessary sensor and communication capabilities to observe, detect, and act on weather-modification requirements to support U.S. military objectives. These capabilities, we are told, "are part of an advanced battle area system that supports the war-fighting CINC. In our scenario, the CINC tasks the WFSE to conduct storm intensification and concealment operations. The WFSE models the atmospheric conditions to forecast, with 90 percent confidence, the likelihood of successful modification using airborne cloud generation and seeding."

The countdown to Weather War One may soon begin.

WEBCAM SPYING

If, let's say, two decades ago, someone told you a New World Order-style government could spy on you, in your very own home and whenever they wanted to, you would very likely dismiss the entire matter as nothing but over-the-top paranoia. Unfortunately, in today's world—in which widespread surveillance of the population has reached extreme levels—such a situation has become a grim, outrageous reality. It is extremely easy for the NWO to spy on you and your activities by hacking into the camera on your laptop. To what extent it is taking place is quite another matter. Perhaps we are all being watched—which would be beyond disturbing if such a thing could be proved. So, with that all said, what evidence is there that this is actually taking place? The answer is dark: it is taking place here, there, and everywhere.

In December 2013, the U.K.'s *Daily Mail* newspaper shed extremely disturbing light on this Orwellian nightmare. The newspaper told its readers: "The U.S. government has been able to secretly spy on its citizens through their computer's webcams for several years, it has been revealed. The FBI has long been able to activate a computer's camera without triggering the 'recording light' to let the owner know the webcam is on, a former assistant director of its tech division has said. Their usage of remote administration tools (RATs) comes to light as the world's most powerful technology firms call on Barack Obama to curb government spying on Internet users."

The *Daily Mail* continued: "The FBI have been able to use the spyware technology for years and have put it in place in terrorism cases or the most serious criminal investigations, Marcus Thomas, former assistant director of the FBI's Operational Technology Division in Quantico, told the *Washington Post*. Although the FBI reportedly uses 'ratting' sparingly, they have rejected remotely activating video feeds on at least one occasion, in Houston, Texas, in December last year. The FBI were investigating a suspect in a bank fraud case,

Think your computer webcam offers a private line to other people? Think again. It is actually quite easy for hackers to access your cam and view whatever you are doing.

but the presiding judge ruled that the risk of accidentally obtaining information of innocent people was too great.

"Hacking into webcams using remote administration tools, also known as 'ratting,' to spy on women and 'enslave' them by controlling their computers and secretly filming and taking pictures is not a new phenomenon but has grown in the past year."

Then, in 2014, there was another troubling disclosure, this one from *Wired*: "The latest story from the Edward Snowden leaks yesterday drives home that the NSA and its spy partners possess specialized tools for doing exactly that. According to *The Intercept*, the NSA uses a plug-in called Gumfish to take over cameras on infected machines and snap photos. Another NSA plug-in called Captivatedaudience hijacks the microphone on targeted computers to record conversations. Intelligence agencies have been turning computers into listening devices for at least a decade, as evidenced by the Flame spy tool uncovered by Kaspersky Lab in 2012, which had the ability to surreptitiously turn on webcams and microphones and perform a host of other espionage operations. Researchers believe Flame has been around since 2007."

Two years later, in 2016, it was revealed that none other than FBI Director James Comey regularly places black tape over his laptop camera—and he suggests that the rest of us do likewise. *The Australian Financial Review* said of this matter in July 2016: "At a forum on cybersecurity this week in Washington, Assistant Attorney General John P. Carlin, who heads the national security division, said he was all for taping over webcams, given the prevalence of computer hacking. 'It does seem like a good idea,' Carlin said. FBI Director Comey admitted in a question-and-answer session April 6 at Kenyon College in Ohio that he saw a colleague with tape over his webcam and decided to follow suit."

Comey explained: "I have, obviously, a laptop, personal laptop. I put a piece of tape over the camera. Because I saw somebody smarter than I am had a piece of tape over their camera."

Also in 2016, the *Guardian* stated: "Covering cameras isn't new for those who know that the Internet is always watching. Eva Galperin, a policy analyst for the Electronic Frontier Foundation, says that since she bought her first laptop with a built-in camera on the screen, a MacBook Pro, in 2007, she's been covering them up. EFF started printing its own webcam stickers in 2013, as well as selling and handing out camera stickers that read: 'These removable stickers are an unhackable anti-surveillance technology.'

On this particular way of protecting yourself, *Digital Spy* says: "You've probably seen people in your local coffee shop with a bit of sticky tape, part of a Post-It® note or a plaster over their laptop's camera—heck, even Facebook founder and full-on billionaire Mark Zuckerberg does just that. Well, it turns out that's the most effective means of keeping secure, even if some new fangled hack manages to bypass your antiviral software. So what are you waiting for? Get sticking."

It's something that each and every one of us should be doing. Every little bit of action on our part helps to hinder the oppressive goals of the New World Order.

WEBSTER, NESTA HELEN

*M*etapedia: The Alternative Encyclopedia says of Nesta Helen Webster, a controversial woman who saw the rise of what today, we would call the New World Order (but who had disturbing views in relation to the Jewish people), that she "was a British author with an interest in topics such as the Illuminati, Freemasonry, and conspiracy theories involving Jews. She argued for a secret society which plotted world domination, using various common conspiracy theories as smokescreens. According to her, the international subversion included the French Revolution, the 1848 Revolution, the First World War, and the Bolshevik Revolution of 1917. In 1920, Webster was one of the contributing authors who published a series of articles in *The Morning Post* centered on *The Protocols of the Elders of Zion*. These articles were subsequently compiled and published in the same year, in book form under the title of *The Cause of World Unrest*. She had a wide readership, including Winston Churchill."

The Grand Lodge of British Columbia and Yukon says: "Webster's theory can be easily outlined. She believes that for the entire history of Christianity there has been a coordinated and continuous conspiracy of Jews to destroy Christianity and dominate the world. She has defined any stream of religious or philosophical thought that is not Trinitarian Christian as either Satanic or anti-Christian, and any political or economic theories that do not incorporate *laissez faire* capitalism as Communism, which, to her mind, is much the same thing. Having defined a broad spectrum of beliefs under the rubric of Satanic or anti-Christian, with a casual disregard for the many differences and a careful selection of superficial similarities, Webster believes she has discovered a history of conspiracy when she has only assembled a disparate collection of unrelated events and people.

"Denying any anti-Semitism, Webster takes every opportunity to imply or suggest that many of the persons mentioned in her books were Jews. Denying that British Freemasonry is at all implicated in her accusations against European 'Grand Orient' Masonry, she nonetheless makes constant references to 'Freemasonry' without distinguishing the two, or noting the many other streams in Masonry. While denying her belief in the historical validity of *The Protocols of the Elders of Zion*, she also makes several references to the *Protocols* as if it was not a fraud.

"With her lack of empirical proof, her demonstrated errors and her reliance on earlier published opinion, Mrs. Webster's arguments are easily identified, and discredited."

Indeed, while Webster was certainly on the right path, in terms of realizing that there exists a powerful cabal that wants to run the entire planet, her issues with the Jewish people and her acceptance of *The Protocols of the Elders of Zion* make her deeply, deeply flawed.

WELLS, H. G.

Back in 1940, H. G. Wells had a book published titled *The New World Order*. Wells was an optimist, someone who saw a New World Order as being good, even vital, for the human race—which is radically different from how many of us perceive it today. Wells said: "There will be no day of days then when a new world order comes into being. Step by step and here and there it will arrive, and even as it comes into being it will develop fresh perspectives, discover unsuspected problems and go on to new adventures. No man, no group of men, will ever be singled out as its father or founder. For its maker will be not this man nor that man nor any man but Man, that being who is in some measure in every one of us. World order will be, like science, like most inventions, a social product, an innumerable number of personalities will have lived fine lives, pouring their best into the collective achievement....

"A growing miscellany of people are saying—it is *getting about*—that 'World Pax is possible,' a World Pax in which men will be both united and free and creative. It is of no importance at all that nearly every man of fifty and over receives the idea with a pitying smile. Its chief dangers are the dogmatist and the would-be 'leader' who will try to suppress every collateral line of work which does not minister to his supremacy. This movement must be, and it must remain, many-headed. Suppose the world had decided that Santos

Dumont or Hiram Maxim was the heaven-sent Master of the Air, had given him the right to appoint a successor and subjected all experiments to his inspired control. We should probably have the Air Master now, with an applauding retinue of yes-men, following the hops of some clumsy, useless and extremely dangerous apparatus across the country with the utmost dignity and self-satisfaction. Yet that is precisely how we still set about our political and social problems.

"Bearing this essential fact in mind that the Peace of Man can only be attained, if it is attained at all, by an advance upon a long and various front, at varying speed and with diverse equipment, keeping direction only by a common faith in the triple need for collectivism, law and research, we realize the impossibility of drawing any picture of the new order as though it was as settled and stable as the old order imagined itself to be. The new order will be incessant; things will never stop happening, and so it defies any Utopian description. But we may nevertheless assemble a number of possibilities that will be increasingly realizable as the tide of disintegration ebbs and the new order is revealed."

Visionary author H. G. Wells was famous for such novels as *The Time Machine, The War of the Worlds,* and *The Island of Dr. Moreau,* and he also penned *The New World Order* in which he favors a world without borders.

While Wells saw good in the concept of a New World Order, for us today, it is these words of Wells that remain so relevant and chilling: "There will be no day of days then when a new world order comes into being. Step by step and here and there it will arrive."

Unless we stop it.

WIKILEAKS

There is no doubt at all that WikiLeaks played a significant role in the plan to derail Hillary Clinton's plans to become president of the United States—Clinton, of course, being a major player in the New World Order and its plans to radically alter society with its iron grip. To show the extent to which WikiLeaks and Assange were viewed as major threats by Clinton, we have to turn our attentions in the direction of the *New York Magazine*, which, in July 2016, reported: "Julian Assange, the founder and head of WikiLeaks, has laid his cards on the table: He views it as his mission to do what he can to prevent Hillary Clinton from becoming president of the United States of America. And his reasons aren't just political, as Charlie Savage wrote earlier this week in the *New York Times*: In an interview with Robert Peston of ITV on June 12, Savage wrote, Assange 'suggested that he not only opposed her candidacy on policy grounds, but also saw her as a personal foe.'

"Recently, the Internet rumor mill has been circulating an enticing possibility for those rooting for an Assange takedown of Clinton: Assange says that he has, in his possession, an email or emails that will offer 'enough evidence'—that's the simple, two-word quote that is repeated over and over and over, everywhere—for authorities to indict Clinton."

That Clinton saw Assange as not just an annoying obstacle but also as a threat to her plans for the presidency is clear—as *Infowars* noted. On October 3, 2016, Adan Salazar, writing for *Infowars*, stated: "Democrat presidential candidate Hillary Clinton once proposed using a military drone strike to extrajudicially assassinate WikiLeaks founder Julian Assange, a document published by the organization states. The screenshot tweeted Monday cites a report from TruePundit.com claiming in 2010 the State Department explored ways to suppress the trouble-making Assange before he could publish damaging information on 'conversations between State Dept. personnel and its foreign assets and allies.'

"'Can't we just drone this guy?' Clinton openly inquired, TruePundit.com reports. While WikiLeaks has not confirmed the veracity of the report, the *Washington Examiner* notes that during the same time the State Department was involved in discussions on what 'nonlegal' methods were available to subdue Assange.

"Emails previously released from Clinton's private server reveal Anne Marie Slaughter, a former director of policy planning at the State Department, sent an email on the same day in 2010 on the subject of possible 'nonlegal strategies' for dealing with WikiLeaks. That email also notes that a meeting was held that day to discuss WikiLeaks, reports the *Washington Examiner*."

In November 2016, in a feature titled "WikiLeaks email shows Clinton 'sealed her OWN FATE' in plot to make Donald Trump her rival," the UK's *Express* newspaper reported. The *Express's* Jon Austin told the story: "Hillary Clinton may have paved the way for Donald Trump's victory and sealed her own fate by trying to elevate the controversial business tycoon in the press in the hope it would damage the Republicans. A camp Clinton plot to try to harm the Republican campaign by getting more press coverage for the party's more conservative candidates was revealed in a email released by Julian Assange's WikiLeaks. The email was sent in April 2015—two months before Trump announced he was going to stand and is one of tens of thousands published by WikiLeaks from the apparently hacked gmail account of Clinton campaign boss John Podesta.

"The email from Marissa Astor, and assistant to Clinton campaign manager Robby Mook, to Mr. Podesta, and copied to the Democratic National Committee (DNC), suggests the campaign knew Mr. Trump was going to run for president, and believed by promoting him into the press, it could ultimately harm the Republicans. The email also suggests Hillary Clinton's team felt it would be good for Mrs. Clinton if she ran against someone like Mr. Trump,

WikiLeaks was founded for the expressed purpose of leaking secret information (government, corporate, etc.) to the public and to protect whistleblowers from prosecution.

as she would have more chance of success. The memo described Donald Trump, Senator Ted Cruz, and Ben Carson as 'Pied Piper candidates.'"

As for what, exactly, the memo stated, it reads as follows: "We need to be elevating the Pied Piper candidates so that they are leaders of the pack and tell the press to [treat] them seriously. Our hope is that the goal of a potential HRC campaign and the DNC would be one and the same: to make whomever the Republicans nominate unpalatable to a majority of the electorate. We have outlined three strategies to obtain our goal: 1) Force all Republican candidates to lock themselves into extreme conservative positions that will hurt them in a general election; 2) Undermine any credibility/trust Republican presidential candidates have to make inroads to our coalition or independents."

Under the heading "Pied Piper Candidates," the memo continued: "There are two ways to approach the strategies mentioned above. The first is to use the field as a whole to inflict damage on itself similar to what happened to Mitt Romney in 2012.

"The variety of candidates is a positive here, and many of the lesser known can serve as a cudgel to move the more established candidates further to the right. In this scenario, we don't want to marginalize the more extreme candidates, but make them more 'Pied Piper' candidates who actually represent the mainstream of the Republican Party. Pied Piper candidates include, but aren't limited to: Ted Cruz, Donald Trump and Ben Carson.

"Most of the more-established candidates will want to focus on building a winning general election coalition. The 'Pied Pipers' of the field will mitigate this to a degree, but more will need to be done on certain candidates to undermine their credibility among our coalition (communities of color, millennials, women) and independent voters. In this regard, the goal here would be to show that they are just the same as every other GOP candidate: extremely conservative on these issues."

As history and WikiLeaks have both shown, however, the plans of the New World Order to place Hillary Clinton in the White House failed.

WORLD BANK

Many researchers of the New World Order have warned against the concept of a so-called World Bank, one body controlling all of the world's finances. In a sense, we are already halfway there. A World Bank was created in the final stages of World War II. It states of its origins and agenda: "Since inception in 1944, the World Bank has expanded from a single institution to a closely associated group of five development institutions. Our mission evolved from the International Bank for Reconstruction and Development (IBRD) as facilitator of post-war reconstruction and development to the present-day mandate of worldwide poverty alleviation in close coordination with our affiliate, the International Development Association, and other members of the World Bank Group, the International Finance Corporation (IFC), the Multilateral Guarantee Agency (MIGA), and the International Center for the Settlement of Investment Disputes (ICSID).

"Once, we had a homogeneous staff of engineers and financial analysts, based solely in Washington, D.C. Today, we have a multidisciplinary and diverse staff that includes economists, public policy experts, sector experts and social scientists—and now more than a third of our staff is based in country offices. Reconstruction remains an important part of our work. However, at today's World Bank, poverty reduction through an inclusive and sustainable globalization remains the overarching goal of our work."

While there is no doubt that the World Bank has achieved great things, it is viewed with suspicion by many observers and researchers of the New World Order.

As for the precise nature of the work of the bank, there is this: "The World Bank Group has set two goals for the world to achieve by 2030: End extreme poverty by decreasing the percentage of people living on less than $1.90 a day to no more than 3% [and] promote shared prosperity by fostering the income growth of the bottom 40% for every country. The World Bank is a vital source of financial and technical assistance to developing countries around the world. We are not a bank in the ordinary sense but a unique partnership to reduce poverty and support development. The World Bank Group comprises five institutions managed by their member countries. Established in 1944, the World Bank Group is headquartered in Washington, D.C. We have more than 10,000 employees in more than 120 offices worldwide."

While there is no doubt that the World Bank has achieved great things, it is viewed with suspicion by many observers and researchers of the New World Order. They fear the creation of a very different World Bank, one which controls all of our finances—whether we like it or not. Ivan Fraser and Mark Beeston of *Truth Campaign* say of the World Bank that it "ends money to finance projects in the Third World to meet the needs of the multinationals. By financing projects which are totally irrelevant to the needs of the local people; the local economy is destroyed and rainforests are decimated. This conveniently adds to the environmental 'problem' (see later). Bill Clinton nominated the current president of the World Bank—James Wolfensohn from the Schroder Bank, Population Council, Bilderberg Steering Committee, CFR and business partner of the Rothschilds."

Of the International Monetary Fund, the pair say: "When poor countries get into Elite-engineered financial trouble, the IMF intervenes to offer more loans (thereby increasing the debt) on the condition that the Elite's policies are followed, e.g., giving up land, which should be used to grow crops to feed the country's population, to produce luxury cash crops instead, which are exported at cut down prices to the multinationals."

And they have this to say on the issue of the European Monetary Union: "The most obvious stepping stone to a global bank and currency is the move by the European Union towards a centralized bank and single currency. Despite the apparent debate, this has already been decided upon with the UK's supposed opt-out clause in the Maastricht Treaty being over-ruled by another. Also in the Maastricht Treaty are details of the control of the European currency and the reserves of each member state by six members of the Executive Board of the European Central Bank who, through their eight years of guaranteed security of tenure, 'may not seek or take instructions from Community institutions ... or any other body.'"

In 2009, Alex Jones said: "My belief in the existence of the New World Order centers around the activities, actions and writings of the members of the elite (mostly Anglo-American) inside the international banking cartel—which of course includes the Rockefeller and Rothschild families—over roughly the last century. (*See also the entry "Bretton Woods System"*)

"This cartel, through their financing of two World Wars; the revolutions of Lenin/Stalin and Hitler, among others; the creation of the IMF, World Bank and other private 'central banks' like the Federal Reserve and the Bank of England; as well as their backing of international organizations like the United Nations, World Health Organization, World Trade Organization has sought to control not only the purse strings of the governments of the world, but also the policies, laws and programs that those governments and agencies implement."

Jones also says: "Through their financing of both sides of wars (WWI and II, Cold War, War on Drugs, War on Terror, etc.); their manufacture of financial crisis (Great Depression, the coming Greater Depression) and financing of ideological movements (eugenics/population control, feminism, communism, fascism, global warming, etc.) the banking cartel has sought to undercut the political, economic and social sovereignty of nations around the world. As a result, their IMF, World Bank and other central bank proxies have managed to put nation after nation in massive debt to them. And as a result, they can further manipulate and control the governments (and citizens) of those nations to further enact their goal of a global government and banking system run—by them and for them—at the expense of all of humanity."

Gary Allen, the author of *None Dare Call It Conspiracy*—which sought to expose the New World Order's plans for us all—said: "The master planners devised the strategy of a merger—a Great Merger—among nations. But before such a merger can be consummated, and the United States becomes just another province in a New World Order, there must at least be the semblance of parity among the senior partners in the deal. How does one make the nations of the world more nearly equal? The Insiders determined that a two-prong approach was needed; use American money and know-how to build up your competitors, while at the same time use every devious strategy you can devise to weaken and impoverish this country. The goal is not to bankrupt the United States. Rather, it is to reduce our productive might, and therefore our standard of living, to the meager subsistence level of the socialized nations of the world.

"The plan is not to bring the standard of living in less developed countries up to our level, but to bring ours down to meet theirs coming up.... It is your standard of living which must be sacrificed on the altar of the New World Order."

Dean Henderson, the author of *Big Oil & Their Bankers In the Persian Gulf*, went on the record as stating: "Freidrich Hegel's Hegelian dialectic put forth a process whereby opposites 'thesis' and 'antithesis' are reconciled into 'synthesis.' The Rothschild's Business Roundtable that sponsored him saw in the dialectic a boon to their monopolies by presenting phony communism (antithesis) as bogeyman to capitalism (thesis).... By upholding Soviet state capitalism to all the world as an example of 'failed Communism,' the bankers could discredit this dangerous idea while producing their desired 'synthesis'—a New World Order ruled by the Illuminati banking families and Black Nobility monarchs, with *laissez faire* monopoly capitalism as their economic paradigm."

In *The Committee of 300*, Dr. John Coleman offered his findings on the New World Order and the banking community: "The Black Nobility are the oligarchic families of Venice and Genoa, who in the 12th century held privileged trading rights (monopolies). The first of three crusades, from 1063 to 1123, established the power of the Venetian Black Nobility and solidified the power of the wealthy ruling class. In 1204 the oligarchic families parceled out feudal enclaves to their members, and from this date, they built up power until government became a closed corporation of the leading Black Nobility families.

"The European Black Nobility is responsible for the insidious entanglements of numerous secret societies and organizations, which are backed with high finance and powerful political connections. Such organizations include: Trilateral Commission, Bilderberg Group, Council on Foreign Relations (CFR), United Nations, International Monetary Fund (IMF), World Bank, Bank of International Settlements (BIS), Club of Rome, Chatham House, and many others. Present day European Black Nobility families are connected with the House of Guelph, one of the original Black Nobility families of Venice from which the House of Windsor and thus the present Queen of the United Kingdom Elizabeth II descends."

Sholto Byrnes, of *The National Opinion*, said in March 2015, "The Obama administration, according to a recent report, has decided that institutions over which it has great influence, such as the World Bank, should work with China's proposed Asian Infrastructure Investment Bank (AIIB). Earlier this week, US Treasury under-secretary for international affairs Nathan Sheets said 'the US would welcome new multilateral institutions that strengthen the international financial architecture.'

"This only came after Washington had a very public hissy fit over the fact that in the past few weeks Britain, Germany, France and Italy declared that they wanted to join the AIIB as founding members (the deadline for that status is the end of this month). The White House let it be known via the American press that 'some of its closest allies' had ignored 'direct pleas' not to do so and that the move was a 'stinging rebuke.'"

Byrnes was not done: "The US Treasury's Mr. Sheets has also said that co-financing projects with existing institutions such as the World Bank or the Asian Development Bank 'will help ensure that high quality, time-tested standards are maintained.' That is code for what Washington has been warning all along: we don't trust a Chinese-led institution to meet those standards—and neither should you.

"But that is not entirely convincing. More realistic is the conclusion of one Australian commentator that the US fears that without proper governance procedures in place the bank could be used by China as a tool of foreign policy. Of course it will—precisely as the World Bank has been used as a tool of US policy.

"Ever since their inception at the Bretton Woods conference in 1944, the World Bank has traditionally been headed by an American and the IMF by a European. Both institutions are based in Washington. Their location and the geographical provenance of their leadership were reflective of the post-World War II order. But they are out of date. Continuing to privilege Europe and America in this way is indefensible...."

WORLD ORDER

On October 24, 2014, in Sochi, Russia, Russian President Vladimir Putin gave an eye-opening and notable speech that was greatly relevant to the matter of the New World Order. It was a presentation given before the Valdai

International Discussion Club XI Session. The specific theme of the event was "The World Order: New Rules or a Game without Rules?"

Putin stated: "The world is full of contradictions today. We need to be frank in asking each other if we have a reliable safety net in place. Sadly, there is no guarantee and no certainty that the current system of global and regional security is able to protect us from upheavals. The international and regional political, economic, and cultural cooperation organizations are also going through difficult times.

"The Cold War ended, but it did not end with the signing of a peace treaty with clear and transparent agreements on respecting existing rules or creating new rules and standards. This created the impression that the so-called 'victors' in the Cold War had decided to pressure events and reshape the world to suit their own needs and interests.

"In a situation where you had domination by one country and its allies, or its satellites rather, the search for global solutions often turned into an attempt to impose their own universal recipes. This group's ambitions grew so big that they started presenting the policies they put together in their corridors of power as the view of the entire international community. But this is not the case.

"A unilateral diktat and imposing one's own models produces the opposite result. Instead of settling conflicts it leads to their escalation, instead of sovereign and stable states we see the growing spread of chaos, and instead of democracy there is support for a very dubious public ranging from open neo-fascists to Islamic radicals.

"Today, we are seeing new efforts to fragment the world, draw new dividing lines, put together coalitions not built for something but directed against someone, anyone, create the image of an enemy as was the case during the Cold War years, and obtain the right to this leadership, or diktat if you wish.

"Sanctions are already undermining the foundations of world trade, the WTO rules and the principle of inviolability of private property. They are dealing a blow to a liberal model of globalization based on markets, freedom and competition, which is a model that has primarily benefited precisely the Western countries.

"You cannot mix politics and the economy, but this is what is happening now. I have always thought and still think today that politically motivated sanctions were a mistake that will harm everyone.

"Russia is a self-sufficient country. We will work within the foreign economic environment that has taken shape, develop domestic production and technology and act more decisively to carry out transformation. Pressure from outside, as has been the case on past occasions, will only consolidate our society.

"We have no intention of shutting ourselves off from anyone and choosing some kind of closed development road. We are always open to dialogue, including on normalizing our economic and political relations. We are counting here on the pragmatic approach and position of business communities in the leading countries.

"Russia is supposedly turning its back on Europe—such words were probably spoken already here too during the discussions—and is looking for new business partners, above all in Asia. Let me say that this is absolutely not the case. Our active policy in the Asian-Pacific region began not just yesterday and not in response to sanctions, but is a policy that we have been following for a good many years now. Like many other countries, including Western countries, we saw that Asia is playing an ever greater role in the world, in the economy.

"There is no doubt that humanitarian factors such as education, science, healthcare and culture are playing a greater role in global competition. This also has a big impact on international relations, including because this 'soft power' resource will depend to a great extent on real achievements in developing human capital rather than on sophisticated propaganda tricks.

"We are sliding into the times when, instead of the balance of interests and mutual guarantees, it is fear and the balance of mutual destruction that prevent nations from engaging in direct conflict.

"In absence of legal and political instruments, arms are once again becoming the focal point of the global agenda; they are used wherever and however, without any UN Security Council sanctions. And if the Security Council refuses to produce such decisions, then it is immediately declared to be an outdated and ineffective instrument.

"It is obvious that success and real results are only possible if key participants in international affairs can agree on harmonizing basic interests, on reasonable self-restraint, and set the example of positive and responsible leadership.

"International relations must be based on international law, which itself should rest on moral principles such as justice, equality and truth. Perhaps most important is respect for one's partners and their interests. This is an obvious formula, but simply following it could radically change the global situation.

"The work of integrated associations, the cooperation of regional structures, should be built on a transparent, clear basis; the Eurasian Economic Union's formation process is a good example of such transparency.

"Russia made its choice. Our priorities are further improving our democratic and open economy institutions, accelerated internal development, taking into account all the positive modern trends in the world, and consolidating society based on traditional values and patriotism.

"Russia does not need any kind of special, exclusive place in the world. While respecting the interests of others, we simply want for our own interests to be taken into account and for our position to be respected.

"Building a more stable world order is a difficult task. We were able to develop rules for interaction after World War II, and we were able to reach an agreement in Helsinki in the 1970s. Our common duty is to resolve this fundamental challenge at this new stage of development."

WORLD WAR III

Is it feasible that in its plans to depopulate the planet to manageable levels, crazed and powerful New World Order types might resort to deliberately orchestrating a third world war, one which will kill billions of people—all in the name of an insane agenda? It sounds outlandish and unthinkable. It may, however, already be on the way. In an article titled "NWO Plans To Depopulate the Earth," Steve Jones presents a nightmarish scenario, one which encompasses biological warfare, deadly viruses, and nuclear weapons: "Plans are underway now, implemented by the New World Order Elite, to depopulate the planet's 6–7 billion people to a manageable level of between 500 million and 2 billion. There are many means and methods of depopulation that are being employed today, the 3 primary of which include; unsustainable/exploitative international development, which leads to massive hunger, starvation and famine worldwide (at least 40 million deaths annually), the fomentation of war, hatred and military procurements throughout the nations leading to millions of deaths worldwide, and finally, the creation and spread of infectious diseases leading to global pandemic, plague and pestilence on an unprecedented scale.

"Other methods used include; the build-up and use of nuclear, chemical and biological agents, weapons and warfare, the poisoning and contamination of the planet's food and water supplies, the introduction and use of deadly pharmaceutical drugs in society, weather modification and the triggering of earthquakes, volcanic eruptions and tsunamis through electromagnetic psychotronic weapons both on Earth and in space, the promotion of homosexuality to limit population growth and spread the deadly AIDS virus, forced sterilization in countries such as China, forced vaccinations, abortion, euthanasia etc."

Global Research presents a similar, grim scenario: "This crumbling, predatory system of empiric imperialism is run by an elitist sub-species of evil psychopaths who for centuries were pathologically born devoid of any human heart, thereby never suffering even a tinge of guilty conscience for murdering in cold blood millions and billions of innocent humans over the millennium. Though braindead now, it has not stopped them from preparing for this fateful moment in time. They've utilized advancing technology to their full advantage in their broken corrupt system to squeeze what's left of the global masses' lifeblood in order to wield absolute power and authority in today's manifesting New World Order.

"With contingency plans for enduring and surviving even a nuclear holocaust on the earth's surface, underground bunkers, cities and cross continental tunnels have been secretly built during the post-World War II decades to accommodate continued survival of the elites comprising just .025% of the world's population—the controlling oligarchs along with their necessary errand boys and girls running the mega-corporations and national governments on the planet.

"For more than a century these globalists have been promoting their NWO eugenics plan for a sustainable earth population of about a half billion people. The UN Agenda 21 spells it all out in graphic detail. This means within the next several years they plan to kill 13 out of 14 of us 7.2 billion people currently living and breathing on this planet. For decades they've been busily deploying both slower, 'soft kill' methods as well as their faster, 'hard kill' methods to drastically reduce the world population. The hard kill scenario manifests through war and both manmade induced natural disasters as well as naturally

Should there actually be a third world war, the result would be the deaths of not *millions*, but BILLIONS of people. Civilization as we know it would end.... Is this what the New World Order wants?

occurring natural disasters with a recent noticeable crescendo of activity of all these cataclysmic events. Death, and the management of who lives and who dies, has become the central organizing principle of the 21st century."

Your News Wire brings Vladimir Putin into the equation: "Brave Vladimir Putin is determined to destroy the Illuminati, describing the destruction of the world's most elusive organization as the 'most important legacy' he could possibly leave behind, and according to Kremlin sources he understands the role of Islam in the Illuminati's plan to start World War 3. In Russia there is an old saying that roughly translates to 'If you don't understand the past, you won't be able to understand the present, or shape the future.' Putin lives by this saying. According to sources he has been studying the history of the Illuminati so he can understand their plans and destroy the invasive organization before its roots and branches spread too far and wide around the world and it becomes too late."

Could Putin save the planet and end the dark agenda of the New World Order? Let us see.

If the New World Order is really contemplating manipulating civilization with the intent of plunging us all into a World War Three of apocalyptic proportions, they may know that there is a chance for them to survive and start over anew—with a completely NWO-driven society for those who survived the war. How could they know? By carefully studying the past, that is how. Indeed, there is good evidence that our civilization is not the first to have developed atomic weapons.

The website *Message to Eagle* notes that, in the early 1950s, "archaeologists conducting excavations in Israel discovered a layer of fused green glass. The layer was a quarter of an inch thick and covered an area of several hundred square feet. It was made of fused quartz sand with green discoloration, similar in appearance to the layers of vitrified sand left after atomic tests in Nevada in the 1950s. Five years earlier a thin layer of the same glass, was dug up below the Neolithic, Sumerian and Babylonian strata in southern Iraq. To the south, the western Arabian desert is covered with black rocks that show evidence of having been subjected to intense radiation. These broken and burned stones are called 'harras' that are strewn over an area of 7,000 square miles."

Of these anomalies, Immanuel Velikovsky, the author of such books as *Worlds in Collision* and *Earth in Upheaval*, noted they were very similar to those found at the Trinity site in New Mexico in 1945: "Some single fields are one hundred miles in diameter and occupy an area of six or seven thousand square miles, stone lying next to stone so densely packed that passage through the field is almost impossible. The stones are sharp-edged and scorched black. No volcanic eruption would have cast scorched stones over fields as large as the harras. Neither would the stones from volcanoes have been so evenly spread.

The absence in most cases of lava (the stones lie free) also speaks against a volcanic origin for the stones."

Similarly, researcher Leonardo Vintini said: "In December 1932, Patrick Clayton, a surveyor from the Egyptian Geological Survey, drove between the dunes of the Great Sand Sea, close to the Saad Plateau in Egypt, when he heard crunching under the wheels. When he examined what was causing the sound, he found great chunks of glass in the sand."

Vintini continued: "The find caught the attention of geologists around the world and planted the seed for one of the biggest modern scientific enigmas. What phenomenon could be capable of raising the temperature of desert sand to at least 3,300 degrees Fahrenheit, casting it into great sheets of solid yellow-green glass?"

David Icke, who has studied reports of ancient atomic warfare in the Pakistan/India area, notes that the stories are supported by "an amazing find found in the prehistoric Indian cities of Mohenjo-daro and Harappa. On the street level were discovered skeletons, appearing to be fleeing, but death came too quick. They were found to be highly radioactive, on a level comparable to Hiroshima and Nagasaki. Yet there are absolutely no indications of volcanic activity, and it appears that both cities were destroyed at virtually the same time."

Micah Hanks, a noted authority on claims of ancient nuclear warfare, says of "places like Mohenjo-daro, a once prosperous ancient city in modern day Pakistan," that they appear to "bear trace evidence of some kind of cataclysmic event in its historic past that, even by today's standards, remains difficult to explain.

"Granted, if we are to utilize modern conventions available to us in the present day, a number of the peculiarities about this particular location can (and do) bear remarkable similarity to the aftermath of a nuclear explosion," Hanks offers. "The problem, of course, is to attempt to reconcile with the anomalies of places like Mohenjo-daro by asserting that nuclear explosions—the likes of which have been seen previously only at places like Hiroshima and Nagasaki during WWII—could have occurred thousands of years ago."

Hanks adds to his observations: "While I'm hesitant, as many probably should be, to say there is definitive proof of nuclear weapons being used in ancient or even prehistoric times, I don't think it can be argued that nuclear events of some variety—perhaps even naturally occurring—did occur in Earth's distant past."

Perhaps the New World Order knows this all too well and is planning on surviving a worldwide, radioactive cataclysm, after which they will surface from their underground bunkers to take control of whatever is left.

In the immediate wake of the 2016 U.S. presidential election, a great deal of media attention was focused on the words of Russian Premier Vladimir

Putin. On November 12, 2016, *The Independent* newspaper ran an article with the following eye-catching, and disturbing, title: "Donald Trump's victory averted World War Three, top Putin aide claims."

The Independent informed its readers: "One of Vladimir Putin's closest advisors has claimed Donald Trump's victory has averted a third world war. Speaking after Mr. Trump won a shock victory over Hillary Clinton on Tuesday, Kremlin advisor Sergei Glazyev said the Democrat politician was a 'symbol of war' and under Mr. Trump the US had 'a chance to change course.'

"He told Russian news wire RNS: 'Americans had two choices: World War Three or multilateral peace. Clinton was a symbol of war, and Trump has a chance to change this course.'"

The *Daily Mail* also reported on this particular issue of President Trump, Vladimir Putin, and a potential third world war: "The Russian President, who had a frosty relationship with President Obama and Hillary Clinton, contin-

ued: 'We are ready to do our part and do everything to return (US–Russian) relations to the trajectory of development. This would be in the interest of Russian and American people and would positively affect the general climate in international relations, considering the special responsibility of Russia and the US for ensuring global stability and security.' Russian State Duma Speaker Vyacheslav Volodin voiced hopes for more constructive US–Russian dialogue when the newly elected president takes office."

In Volodin's own words: "Current Russian–US relations cannot be called friendly. One would like to hope that a more constructive dialog between the two countries will be possible when the new president takes office."

As for Putin, he said, of the election results: "We have heard the pre-election statements by then-candidate Trump, which were directed at rebuilding relations between Russia and the US. We understand that this will not be an easy path considering the unfortunate degradation of relations. But Russia is ready and wants to restore full-fledged relations with the US."

Russian State Duma Speaker Vyacheslav Volodin has publicly spoken about the sorry state of relations between his country and the United States.

Of course, cordial relations between the United States and Russia is the very last thing the New World Order wants.

AntiWars says of this dangerous state of affairs: "Glazyev said many within the Russian government saw Hillary Clinton as a 'symbol of war,' and that the American voters' rejection of Clinton in favor of Trump showed a rejection of that level of hostility. Russian officials have also praised Trump, saying he appears to have the same foreign policy mindset as Vladimir Putin. All this talk of embracing Trump, however, may simply reflect Russia's happiness that Clinton didn't win, as Clinton campaigned heavily on being hostile toward Russia, accusing Russia of plotting against her campaign, and talking openly about military action in Syria designed to get 'military leverage' against Russia.

"Since the regime change in Ukraine saw the replacement of a long-time Russian ally with a pro-West government, NATO in general and the US in particular have been stepping up military deployments along Russia's border in Eastern Europe, with some 300,000 NATO troops deployed in the Baltic states for a battle with Russia.

"Clinton was positioning herself as a continuation of that anti-Russia buildup, and more hawkish, which makes it pretty clear that Russia would've seen her election as another step toward open warfare"—which is exactly what the New World Order wanted.

ZERO HOUR

If the day finally comes when the New World Order makes a play to ensure that the planet and its people are, in effect, enslaved under the dangerous control of an equally dangerous and powerful elite, there is a big question that needs answering: how will it all go down? There are numerous possibilities. One, however, stands out more than any other. In all probability, matters will kick off in the United States, possibly caused by the detonation of a so-called "dirty bomb." Worse still, we may see the complete and utter destruction of a major American city as a result of the detonation of a powerful, atomic bomb—one far more devastating than the two which were dropped on the Japanese cities of Nagasaki and Hiroshima in 1945. The event may be the work of terrorists, of another nation, or of a secret group within the government, a group which decides to take the false flag scenario to its ultimate, terrifying degree. Whoever may be behind the attack, however, it will still feed the New World Order's appetite for control.

In the wake of a massive attack on a U.S. city, and with several million killed and even more severely injured and suffering from the effects of potentially lethal radiation, martial law will quickly be imposed across the entire nation. Borders will be closed. Aircraft will be grounded. Curfews will be the order of the day—or, rather, of the night. Just about anyone and everyone who has ever spoken out loudly and vocally on matters relative to the likes of 9/11, the weapons of mass destruction fiasco, the New World Order, conspiracies, cover-ups, widespread surveillance of the public, and issues relative to the freedom of both the people and the press will be quickly rounded up and detained in camps and heavily guarded facilities. And who, exactly, will be rounding up all of the above? The answer is very simple: the police who, in the last few years, were groomed more and more to take on the role of a military force. You think all those police-owned tanks and military vehicles are simply there for show? No.

Immediately after the terrible event has occurred, emergency powers will be quickly passed, allowing the likes of the National Security Agency the unlimited ability to monitor everyone—and to an unending degree. Armored police and troops will patrol the streets of every city. Blogs, websites, and social media outlets that promote conspiracy-themed commentary and debate—as well as radio shows that cover similar topics—will be shut down. Certain books will very likely be taken off the shelves of bookstores. Checkpoints will be everywhere.

As for the situation overseas, in all probability, spurious stories will be spread by the New World Order to the effect that other major cities—perhaps London, Paris, Rome, Moscow, and Berlin—are rumored to be the targets of the next atomic. And the next. And the next. Grudgingly, those in overseas governments who are not a part of the New World Order will be forced to go ahead and introduce new, restrictive laws—all in the event that something earthshaking and terrible might happen. In a shockingly short period of time, we might see just about every major nation on the planet—and its people—reduced to the equivalent of a massive prison, one from which there is no escape.

In time, people will come to accept the new world of the NWO, secretly longing for the old days but too fearful to speak out against the iron-fisted state of the new days, and, as new generations are born and grow, the old world—the one we live in right now—will become nothing but a memory. The future will be George Orwell's *1984* meets *Harrison Bergeron* meets *Brave New World*. Only worse.

There is, of course, one way to prevent all this from taking place. It requires the seven billion—or thereabouts—people on the planet to all band together and fight the oppressive New World Order. Seven billion against an elite of probably several million—and its militarized minions—ensures us all a good chance of winning, even if the war is a long one. It can be won. All it needs is those seven billion to rise up and turn things around—if they are willing to do so. The alternative is neverending slavery. It's our choice.

Further Reading

"About CFR." http://www.cfr.org/about/. 2016.

"About DEN." http://www.flydenver.com/about. 2016.

"About Nigel." http://www.ukip.org/about_nigel. 2016.

"About the RAND Corporation." http://www.rand.org/about.html. 2016.

"About the Trilateral Commission." http://trilateral.org/page/3/about-trilateral. 2016.

Ackerman, Spencer. "There's a Secret Patriot Act, Senator Says." http://www.wired.com/2011/05/secret-patriot-act/. May 25, 2014.

Adachi, Ken. "Chemtrails." http://educate-yourself.org/ct/. 2014.

Adams, Mike. "The United Nations 2030 Agenda Decoded." http://www.naturalnews.com/051058_2030_Agenda_United_Nations_global_enslavement.html. September 4, 2015.

Adams, Scott. "Martial Law Coming?" http://blog.dilbert.com/post/147894069726/martial-law-coming. July 24, 2016.

Addley, Esther. "7/7 survivors end battle for public inquiry into bombings." http://www.theguardian.com/uk/2011/aug/01/7-july-bombings-public-inquiry. August 1, 2011.

"Adolf Hitler." http://vault.fbi.gov/adolf-hitler/. 2014.

"Adolf Hitler." FBI file. https://vault.fbi.gov/adolf-hitler/adolf-hitler-part-01-of-04/view. 2016.

"Adolf Hitler Biography." http://www.biography.com/people/adolf-hitler-9340144#death-and-legacy. 2014.

"Adolf Hitler Escaped to Argentina after the War." http://guardianlv.com/2014/02/adolf-hitler-escaped-to-argentina-after-the-war/. February 24, 2014.

Advisory Committee on Human Radiation Experiments. Pittsburgh, PA: U.S. Government Printing Office, 1995.

"Advisory Committee on Pesticides." http://www.publications.parliament.uk/pa/cm200506/cmhansrd/vo051108/text/51108w11.htm. November 8, 2005.

"AIDS as a Biological Weapon." http://iipdigital.usembassy.gov/st/english/texttrans/2005/01/20050114151424atlahtnevel8.222598e-02.html#axzz49rivnGUM. 2016.

"Air Force 2025—Final Report." http://www.bibliotecapleyades.net/sociopolitica/sociopol_weatherwar08.htm. 2014.

Alexis, Jonas E. "NATO Is Losing the War among Intellectuals; Russia Continues to Win; NWO Agents Are Deteriorating." http://www.veteranstoday.com/2016/06/03/nato-is-losing-the-war-among-intellectuals-russia-continues-to-win-nwo-agents-are-deteriorating/. June 3, 2016.

Allen, Gary. *None Dare Call It Conspiracy*. New York: Buccaneer Books, 1976.

Allen, Joseph. "The White God Quetzalcoatl." https://www.nephiproject.com/white_god_quetzalcoatl.htm. 2002.

American Civil Liberties Union. "Watchlists." https://www.aclu.org/issues/national-security/privacy-and-surveillance/watchlists. 2016.

"Amerithrax or Anthrax Investigation." http://www.fbi.gov/about-us/history/famous-cases/anthrax-amerithrax/amerithrax-investigation, 2011.

Anderson, Lorri. "United Nations Meet to Disarm American Citizens; Population Focused on 'ISIS Murderer.'" http://freedomoutpost.com/united-nations-meet-to-disarm-american-citizens-population-focused-on-isis-murderer/. June 14, 2016.

"Animal Mutilation." http://vault.fbi.gov/Animal%20Mutilation. 2014.

"Another Dead Scientist: Composite Released in Fatal Hit and Run." *Houston Chronicle*, December 12, 2003.

Ansary, Alex. "Mass Mind Control through Network Television." http://rense.com/general69/mass.htm. December 29, 2005.

"Anunnaki." http://www.halexandria.org/dward185.htm. February 5, 2009.

Arbuthnot, Felicity. "The Neocons' Project for the New American Century." http://www.globalresearch.ca/the-neocons-project-for-the-new-american-century-american-world-leadership-syria-next-to-pay-the-price/5305447?print=1. September 20, 2012.

"Arizona Wilder." http://ageoftruth.dk/arizona-wilder/. 2016.

"Assassination of Martin Luther King, Jr. (4 April 1968)." http://mlk-kpp01.stanford.edu/index.php/encyclopedia/encyclopedia/enc_kings_assassination_4_april_1968/. 2014.

Associated Press. *Biologist Disappears; FBI Interested*. November 28, 2001.

Associated Press. "Family Implanted with Computer Chips." http://usatoday30.usatoday.com/tech/news/2002/05/10/implantable-chip.htm. May 10, 2002.

Associated Press. "Wolfowitz Comments Revive Doubts Over Iraq's WMD." http://usatoday30.usatoday.com/news/world/iraq/2003-05-30-wolfowitz-iraq_x.htm. June 1, 2003.

"Attack at Pearl Harbor." http://www.eyewitnesstohistory.com/pearl.htm. 2014.

Austin, Jon. "WikiLeaks Email Shows Clinton 'Sealed Her Own Fate.'" http://www.express.co.uk/news/world/730459/Julian-Assange-WikiLeaks-Hillary-Clinton-Donald-Trump-pied-pipers. November 9, 2016.

Balko, Radley. *Rise of the Warrior Cop*. New York: Public Affairs Books, 2014.

Baraniuk, Chris. "The Disastrous Events That Would Break the Internet." http://www.bbc.com/future/story/20150310-how-to-break-the-internet. March 11, 2015.

"Barcode Everyone at Birth." http://www.bbc.com/future/story/20120522-barcode-everyone-at-birth. November 18, 2014.

Baulkman, Jaleesa. "Dead Alive." http://www.medicaldaily.com/walking-corpse-syndrome-cotards-syndrome-mental-illness-387623. May 25, 2016.

Baxter, Irvin. "The New World Order (NWO). "https://www.endtime.com/new-world-order/. 2016.

Beeston, Mark, and Ivan Fraser. "The Brotherhood, Part 3. Economic Control, Steps Towards a Global Bank." http://educate-yourself.org/nwo/brotherhoodpart3.shtml. 2016.

Bell, Rachel. "The Death of Marilyn." http://www.crimelibrary.com/notorious_murders/celebrity/marilyn_monroe/index.html. 2014.

"Benjamin Franklin True Patriot Act." https://en.wikipedia.org/wiki/Benjamin_Franklin_True_Patriot_Act. 2016.

Bennett, Jessica. "Rise of the Preppers: America's New Survivalists." http://www.newsweek.com/rise-preppers-americas-new-survivalists-75537. December 27, 2009.

Berwick, Jeff. "The US Closing Borders for Americans." https://dollarvigilante.com/blog/2015/12/15/the-us-closing-borders-for-americans.html. December 15, 2015.

"Bilderberg." http://www.sourcewatch.org/index.php/Bilderberg. 2016.

"Bin Laden Scenario Prelude to New War." http://www.presstv.com/detail/178272.html. May 4, 2011.

Bishop, Greg. *Project Beta*. New York: Paraview-Pocket Books, 2005.

Blair, Tony. Speech, January 6, 2003.

"Black Helicopters Exist." http://www.theforbiddenknowledge.com/hardtruth/black_helicopters_exist.htm. 2016.

"Body Carrying Missing Scientist's ID Found in Mississippi River." http://www.courttv.com. December 21, 2001.

Blumenfeld, Samuel. "Ethnic Cleansing—American Style." http://www.wnd.com/1999/06/100/. June 10, 1999.

Bogdanos, Michael. "The Casualties of War: The Truth about the Iraq Museum." *American Journal of Archaeology*. 2005.

———. *Thieves of Baghdad*. New York: Bloomsbury, 2005.

"Bohemian." http://www.worldwidewords.org/qa/qa-boh1.htm. 2016.

"Bohemian Grove." http://bohemiangroveexposed.com/. 2016.

Bowart, Walter. *Operation Mind Control*. New York: Dell Publishing, 1978.

Bowe, Rebecca. "NSA Surveillance." https://www.theguardian.com/world/2013/jul/04/restore-the-fourth-protesters-nsa-surveillance July 5, 2013.

Bowen, Alison. "Osama bin Laden: Conspiracy Theories Thrive on Lack of Proof." http://www.metro.us/newyork/news/international/2011/05/02/osama-bin-laden-conspiracy-theories-thrive-on-lack-of-proof/. May 2, 2011.

Bradshaw, Peter. "V for Vendetta." https://www.theguardian.com/culture/2006/mar/17/1. March 16, 2006.

"Brain Washing, Social Control and Programming—Why You Should Kill Your Television." http://www.wakingtimes.com/2014/02/26/brain-washing-social-control-programming-kill-your-television/. February 26, 2014.

Brewda, Joseph. "Kissinger's 1974 Plan for Food Control Genocide." http://www.larouchepub.com/other/1995/2249_kissinger_food.html. December 8, 1995.

Broden, L. "The Bob Lazar Story." http://www.ufoevidence.org/documents/doc1249.htm. 2014.

Brown, Larisa. "Military Unveils Insect-sized Spy Drone with Dragonfly-Like Wings." http://www.dailymail.co.uk/sciencetech/article-3734945/Now-bugged-Military-unveils-insect-sized-spy-drone-dragonfly-like-wings.html. August 11, 2016.

Brown, Nate. "The Elite Abolished the EU to Create a European Superstate New World OrderRising." https://christiantruther.com/end-times/nwo/elite-eu-european-superstate-new-world-order/. June 27, 2016.

Brown, Tim. "12 Holistic Doctors Have Now Died within a Little Over 90 Days." http://freedomoutpost.com/12-holistic-doctors-have-now-died-within-a-little-over-90-days/. October 13, 2015.

"Bush Declares War." http://www.cnn.com/2003/US/03/19/sprj.irq.int.bush.transcript/. March 19, 2003.

"Bush 'Disappointed' Data on Prewar Iraq Were Wrong." http://www.washingtontimes.com/news/2006/apr/6/20060406-112119-5897r/?page=all. April 6, 2006.

Bush, George H. W. Speech, September 11, 1990.

Bush, George H. W. Speech, January 29, 1991.

"Bush Wants Right to Use Military If Bird Flu Hits." http://www.freerepublic.com/focus/news/1497126/posts?page=152. 2014.

Byrnes, Sholto. "China's New Bank Is Proof There's a New World Order." http://www.thenational.ae/opinion/comment/chinas-new-bank-is-proof-theres-a-new-world-order. March 24, 2015.

———. "Why We Need a New World Order." http://www.thenational.ae/opinion/comment/why-we-need-a-new-world-order. May 24, 2016.

Caladan, T. S. "Are the Hunger Games Real?" http://blog.world-mysteries.com/guest_authors/doug-yurchey/are-the-hunger-games-real/. February 20, 2014.

Caliari, Aldo. "Adapting the International Monetary System to Face 21st Century Challenges. http://www.un.org/esa/desa/papers/2011/wp104_2011.pdf. May 2011.

Carlson, Darren K. "Conscription Opinions: Return of the Draft?" http://www.gallup.com/poll/7621/conscription-opinions-return-draft.aspx?ref=mn-clientservices#!mn-business. January 21, 2003.

Carrasco, David. *Quetzalcoatl and the Irony of Empire: Myths and Prophecies in the Aztec Tradition.* Boulder, CO: University Press of Colorado, 2001.

"Chemtrail Conspiracy Theory." http://moonconspiracy.wordpress.com/chemtrail-conspiracy-theory/. 2014.

"Chemtrails." http://www.sheepkillers.com/chemtrails.html. 2014.

"Chemtrails Killing Organic Crops, Monsanto's GMO Seeds Thrive." http://www.geoengineeringwatch.org/chemtrails-killing-organic-crops-monsantos-gmo-seeds-thrive/. May 23, 2014.

"Chemtrails—Spraying in Our Sky." http://www.holmestead.ca/chemtrails/response-en.html. 2014.

Cherif, Omar. "The Global Warming Hoax—A Convenient Excuse for a New World Order." http://consciouslifenews.com/global-warming-hoax-convenient-excuse-new-world-order-2/1158164/. June 4, 2013.

"China Internet: Xi Jinping Calls for 'Cyber Sovereignty." http://www.bbc.com/news/world-asia-china-35109453. December 16, 2015.

Chossudovsky, Michel. "Manufacturing Dissent." http://wakeup-world.com/2016/02/27/manufacturing-dissent-the-anti-globalization-movement-is-funded-by-the-corporate-elites/. February 27, 2016.

Chua, Philip. "Bar Code for Humans?" http://newsinfo.inquirer.net/543137/bar-code-for-humans. December 9, 2013.

Chumley, Cheryl K. *Police State USA*. Washington, DC: WND Books, 2014.

"CIA Killed Lennon." http://ciakilledlennon.blogspot.com/2005/12/q-who-killed-john-lennon-the-cia-or.html. 2005.

Clarkson, Frederick. "Christian Reconstructionism." http://www.publiceye.org/magazine/v08n1/chrisre3.html. March/June 1994.

"Climate Change: How Do We Know?" http://climate.nasa.gov/evidence/. 2016.

"Climate Change Is U.N.-Led Hoax to Create 'New World Order.'" https://www.rt.com/news/256861-climate-change-un-hoax/. May 8, 2015.

"Close the Border Petition." http://www.petition2congress.com/1860/close-border-petition. 2016.

"Closing the Borders." http://worldpress.org/Americas/382.cfm. 2016.

"Club of Rome." http://www.clubofrome.org/. 2016.

"The Club of Rome." http://www.jeremiahproject.com/newworldorder/club-of-rome.html. 2016.

Coleman, John. "'Committee of 300' aka … Olympians." http://www.bibliotecapleyades.net/sociopolitica/esp_sociopol_committee30011.htm. 2016.

Collins, Tony. *Open Verdict: An Account of 25 Mysterious Deaths in the Defense Industry*. London, U.K.: Sphere Books, 1990.

"Committee of 300." http://www.whale.to/b/300.html. 2016.

A Concise Compendium of the Warren Commission Report on the Assassination of John F. Kennedy. New York: Popular Library, 1964.

"Conspiracy Theory: NDP Deputy Leader Mulcair Doubts U.S. Has bin Laden Photos." http://www.thestar.com/news/canada/2011/05/04/conspiracy_theory_ndp_deputy_leader_mulcair_doubts_us_has_bin_laden_photos.html. May 4, 2011.

"Constitution." https://www.archives.gov/founding-docs. 2016.

Cope, Alec. "The Commercial That Shows What TV Does to Your Brain." http://www.collective-evolution.com/2014/11/19/this-is-what-tv-can-do-to-your-brain/. November 19, 2014.

Corbett, James. "Lone Gunmen Producer Questions Government on 9/11." http://www.corbettreport.com/articles/20080225_gunmen_911.htm. February 25, 2008.

"Council for National Policy." https://www.cfnp.org/. 2016.

"Council for National Policy." http://www.publiceye.org/ifas/cnp/. 2016.

"Council for National Policy." 2016. http://www.sourcewatch.org/index.php/Council_for_National_Policy

"The Council on Foreign Relations." http://www.jeremiahproject.com/newworldorder/nworder06.html. 2016.

"Count St. Germain." http://www.crystalinks.com/stgermain.html. 2016.

CounterPunch Wire. "Weapons of Mass Destruction: Who Said What When." http://www.counterpunch.org/2003/05/29/weapons-of-mass-destruction-who-said-what-when/. May 29, 2003.

"Coup d'etat." http://www.dictionary.com/browse/coup-d-etat. 2016.

Cowan, Alison Leigh. "Four Librarians Finally Break Silence in Records case." *New York Times*, May 31, 2006. http://www.nytimes.com/2006/05/31/nyregion/31 library.html?_r=0.

Crossley, Callie. "Is the US Making It Too Hard to Vote?" http://www.pri.org/stories/ 2016-04-26/are-we-making-it-too-hard-vote. April 26, 2016.

Dakss, Brian. "John Lennon Remembered." *CBS News*, December 8, 005. http://www .cbsnews.com/news/john-lennon-remembered-08-12-2005/.

"David Hudson." https://monatomic-orme.com/david-hudson/. 2016.

Davidson, Michael. "A Career in Microbiology Can Be Harmful to Your Health— Especially Since 9-11." http://www.rense.com/general20/car.htm. February 15, 2002.

Davidson, Michael, and Michael C. Ruppert. "Microbiologist Death Toll Mounts as Connections to Dynocorp, Hadron, Promis Software & Disease Research Emerge." http://www.rense.com/general20/mic.htm. March 3, 2002.

Dean, John. "Trump's Wall: Impractical, Impolitic, Impossible." http://www.news week.com/trump-wall-impractical-impolitic-impossible-459802. May 16, 2016.

"Defense Advanced Projects Research Agency." http://www.darpa.mil/. 2016.

DeMorro, Christopher. "BP Estimates the World Has Just 53. 3 Years of Oil Left." http://gas2.org/2014/07/03/bp-estimates-world-just-53-3-years-oil-left/. July 3, 2014.

Denison, Caleb. "Samsung Smart TVs Don't Spy on Owners." http://www.digital trends.com/home-theater/samsung-tvs-arent-spying-eavesdropping-listening/. February 9, 2015.

"Denver Airport Murals Explained by Dr. Leonard Horowitz." http://www.waronwethe people.com/denver-airport-murals-explained-dr-leonard-horowitz/. 2016.

Dias, Jason. "Why Walmart Conspiracy Theories Aren't Totally Nuts." http://anew domain.net/2015/08/03/walmart-conspiracy-theories-not-all-that-crazy-considering/. August 1, 2015.

"Dick Gephardt Quotes." http://www.azquotes.com/quote/696638. 2016.

Didymus, John Thomas. "Jade Helm, Wal-Mart Underground Tunnels Conspiracy Theory." http://www.inquisitr.com/2024232/jade-helm-wal-mart-underground- tunnels-conspiracy-theory-footage-inside-closed-walmart-what-are-cops-trying- to-hide/. April 19, 2015.

Ditz, Jason. "Putin Aide: Trump's Election May Avert World War III." http://news .antiwar.com/2016/11/11/putin-aide-trumps-election-may-avert-world-war-iii/. November 11, 2016.

Dmitry, Baxter. "New World Order Using Climate Change Agenda to Enslave Humanity." http://yournewswire.com/new-world-order-using-climate-change- agenda-to-enslave-humanity/. May 22, 2016.

———. "Putin: Illuminati Plans to Use Islam to Spark World War 3." http://yournews wire.com/putin-illuminati-plans-to-use-islam-to-spark-world-war-3/. April 22, 2016.

———. "Putin Warns Trump: 'New World Order out to Get You.'" http://yournews wire.com/putin-warns-trump-new-world-order-out-to-get-you/. June 19, 2016.

Dodd, Vikram, Ian Cobain, and Helen Carter. "7/7 Leader: More Evidence Reveals What Police Knew." *The Guardian*, May 2, 2007. http://www.theguardian.com /uk/2007/may/03/july7.topstories3.

Duffy, Jonathan. "Bilderberg: The Ultimate Conspiracy Theory." *BBC News*, June 3, 2004. http://news.bbc.co.uk/2/hi/uk_news/magazine/3773019.stm.

"Dugway Says Lockdown Caused by 'Serious Mishandling' of Nerve Agent." https://www.ksl.com/?sid=14157393. January 27, 2011.

Durante, Thomas. "Bin Laden WAS NOT Buried at Sea, but Flown to the U.S. for Cremation at Secret Location, Claims Intelligence Boss in Leaked Email." *Daily Mail*, March 7 2012. http://www.dailymail.co.uk/news/article-2111001/Osama-bin-Laden-WAS-NOT-buried-sea-flown-US-cremation-leaked-emails- reveal.html.

"Ebola (Ebola Virus Disease)." https://www.cdc.gov/vhf/ebola/. 2016.

"Ebola Virus Disease." http://www.who.int/mediacentre/factsheets/fs103/en/. January 2016.

"Economic and Monetary Union." http://ec.europa.eu/economy_finance/euro/emu/index_en.htm. 2016.

"Edward Snowden: Leaks That Exposed US Spy Program." http://www.bbc.com/news/world-us-canada-23123964. January 17, 2014.

"Edward Snowden: Timeline." http://www.bbc.com/news/world-us-canada-23768248. August 20, 2013.

Edwards, Anna. "New Book Claims THIS Picture Proves Hitler Escaped His Berlin Bunker and Died in South America in 1984 aged 95." *Daily Mail*, January 25, 2014. http://www.dailymail.co.uk/news/article-2545770/New-book-claims-THIS-picture-proves-Hitler-escaped-Berlin-bunker- died-South-America-1984-aged-95.html.

Elliott, Tony. "2016 Presidential Elections Showing New World Order is Alive and Kicking in Washington." *Freedom Outpost*, April 14, 2016. http://freedomoutpost.com/2016-presidential-elections-showing-new-world-order-is-alive-and-well-in-washington/.

Engler, Mark. "Defining the Anti-Globalization Movement." http://democracyuprising.com/2007/04/01/anti-globalization-movement/. April 1, 2007.

Enserink, Martin. "Scientists Brace for Media Storm around Controversial Flu Studies." *Science*, November 23, 2011. http://news.sciencemag.org/2011/11/scientists-brace-media-storm-around-controversial-flu-studies.

Eschliman, Bob. "Charismastic Pastor: Donald Trump Is the New World Order's Worst Nightmare." *Charisma News*, March 17, 2016. http://www.charismanews.com/politics/primaries/55914-charismatic-pastor-donald-trump-is-the-new-world-order-s-worst-nightmare.

"The EU in Brief." https://europa.eu/european-union/about-eu/eu-in-brief_en. 2016.

"The European Union in the New World Order." http://europa.eu/rapid/press-release_SPEECH-14-612_en.htm. September 21, 2014.

"Even If Iraq Managed to Hide These Weapons, What They Are Now Hiding Is Harmless Goo." *Guardian*, September 18, 2002. http://www.theguardian.com/world/2002/sep/19/iraq.features11.

"Everything You Need to Know about PRISM." http://www.theverge.com/2013/7/17/4517480/nsa-spying-prism-surveillance-cheat-sheet. July 17, 2013.

"The Evolution of a Conspiracy Theory." http://news.bbc.co.uk/2/mobile/uk_news/magazine/7488159.stm. July 4, 2008.

"Extreme Lifespans through Perpetual-equalizing Interventions (ELPIs)." http://www.elpistheory.info/. 2016.

"Federal Emergency Management Agency." http://www.fema.gov. 2016.

"Federalism." http://www.ushistory.org/gov/3.asp. 2016.

"FEMA: About the Agency." https://www.fema.gov/about-agency. 2016.

"FEMA The Department of Homeland Security." http://www.nwotoday.com/agenda/the-global-government-plans-for-america/fema-the-department-of-homeland-security. 2016.

"FEMA's First Concentration Camp Officially Opens in Arizona." http://nationalreport.net/femas-first-concentration-camp-officially-opens-arizona/. 2016.

Fisher, Max. "Chinese Army Colonel Says Avian Flu Is an American Plot against China." *Washington Post*, April 9, 2013. http://www.washingtonpost.com/blogs/worldviews/wp/2013/04/09/chinese-army-colonel-says-avian-flu-is-an-american-plot-against-china/.

"The Five Eyes." https://www.privacyinternational.org/node/51. 2016.

"FOIA: Frequently Asked Questions." https://www.foia.gov/faq.html. 2016.

Fontaine, Richard, and Mira Rapp-Hooper. "How China Sees World Order." http://nationalinterest.org/feature/how-china-sees-world-order-15846. April 20, 2016.

"Freemasonry." https://tshaonline.org/handbook/online/articles/vnf01. 2016.

Froelich, Amanda. "50 Holistic Doctors Have Mysteriously Died in the Last Year, But What's Being Done About It?" http://truththeory.com/2016/06/26/50-holistic-doctors-have-mysteriously-died-in-the-last-year-but-whats-being-done-about-it/. June 26, 2016.

Gabb, Sean. "NATO and the New World Order." https://thelibertarianalliance.com/2016/08/16/nato-and-the-new-world-order/. August 16, 2016.

Gallagher, Ryan, and Glenn Greenwald. "How the NSA Plans to Infect 'Millions' of Computers with Malware." https://firstlook.org/theintercept/2014/03/12/nsa-plans-infect-millions-computers-malware/. March 12, 2014.

Gabric, Toni. "On Escalation of Violence in the Middle East." *Croatian Feral Tribune*. March 12, 2013. https://chomsky.info/20020507/.

"Garden Plot & REX 84." http://www.constitution.org/abus/garden_plot/garden_plot.htm. 2016.

Gardner, Laurence. "The White Powder Gold of the Ancients." *Nexus Magazine*, June-July 2004.

Garrison, Jim. *On the Trail of the Assassins*. London: Penguin Books, 1988.

Gattuso, James L. "Internet Censorship Is Europe's Latest Export to America." http://www.heritage.org/research/reports/2015/08/europes-latest-export-to-america-internet-censorship. August 19, 2015.

"GCHQ: What We Do." https://www.gchq.gov.uk/what-we-do. 2016.

Geerhart, Bill. "Red Scare: The Best of Kenneth Goff." http://conelrad.blogspot.com/2010/09/red-scare-best-of-kenneth-goff.html. September 11, 2010.

Gibson, Dave. "Congress Has Already Given Obama the Power to Suspend the 2016 Election." http://ufpnews.com/2016/congress-already-given-obama-power-suspend-2016-election/. November 4, 2016.

Gidda, Mirren. "Edward Snowden and the NSA Files—Timeline." *Guardian*, July 25, 2013. http://www.theguardian.com/world/2013/jun/23/edward-snowden-nsa-files-timeline.

Glass, Nicholas. "Coincidence of Bomb Exercises?" http://www.channel4.com/news/articles/uk/coincidence+of+bomb+exercises/109010.html. July 17, 2005.

Global Research. "9/11 Theologian Says Controlled Demolition of World Trade Center Is Now a Fact, Not a Theory/" http://www.globalresearch.ca/9-11-theologian-says-controlled-demolition-of-world-trade-center-is-now-a-fact-not-a-theory/1129?print=1. October 21, 2005.

Goepel, Eric. and Lawrence J. Korb. "The Case for the Draft." *U.S. News & World Report,* February 11, 2016. http://www.usnews.com/opinion/blogs/world-report/articles/2016-02-11/reinstate-the-draft-dont-just-expand-selective-service-to-women.

Gorbachev, Mikhail. Speech, December 7, 1988.

Goss, Jennifer L. "Hitler Commits Suicide." http://history1900s.about.com/od/1940s/a/Hitler-Suicide.htm. 2014.

Gray, Michael. "Why Are So Many Bankers Committing Suicide?" *New York Post,* June 12, 2016. http://nypost.com/2016/06/12/why-are-so-many-bankers-committing-suicide/.

Greenberg, Andy. "How the NSA Could Bug Your Powered-Off iPhone, and How to Stop Them." *Wired,* June 3, 2014. https://www.wired.com/2014/06/nsa-bug-iphone/.

Gregory, Paul Roderick. "The Dirty Bomb: A Thwarted Putin False Flag Operation?" *Forbes,* August 11, 2015. http://www.forbes.com/sites/paulroderickgregory/2015/08/11/the-dirty-bomb-a-thwarted-putin-false-flag-operation/#d61fecd182d2.

Griffin, Andrew. "GCHQ Spying on British Citizens Was Unlawful, Secret Court Rules in Shock Decision." *Independent,* February 6, 2015. http://www.independent.co.uk/life-style/gadgets-and-tech/news/gchq-spying-on-british-citizens-was-unlawful-secret-court-rules-in-shock-decision-10028306.html.

———. "iPhone Has Secret Software That Can Be Remotely Activated to Spy on People, Says Snowden." *Independent,* January 21, 2015. http://www.independent.co.uk/life-style/gadgets-and-tech/news/iphone-has-secret-software-that-can-be-remotely-activated-to-spy-on-people-says-snowden-9991754.html.

———. "UK Surveillance Agencies Illegally Kept Data on British Citizens' Communications, Spying Court Finds." *Independent,* October 17, 2016. http://www.independent.co.uk/life-style/gadgets-and-tech/news/uk-spying-surveillance-investigatory-powers-bill-tribunal-gchq-intelligence-agencies-a7366386.html.

Grim, Ryan. "Hillary Clinton Backs Obama Plan to Reverse Police Militarization." *Huffington Post,* May 18, 2015. http://www.huffingtonpost.com/2015/05/18/hillary-clinton-police-militarization_n_7309296.html.

Gurney, Mark. "SARS Virus First Discovered in 1998." www.rense.com/general35/sarrs.htm. (Accessed June 1 2017).

Gurney, Ian. "The Mystery of the Dead Scientists: Coincidence or Conspiracy?" http://www.rense.com/general39/death.htm. July 20, 2003.

Hagopian, Joachim. "The Dumbing Down of America—By Design." http://www.globalresearch.ca/the-dumbing-down-of-america-by-design/5395928. August 14, 2014.

———. "The Evils of Big Pharma Exposed." http://www.globalresearch.ca/the-evils-of-big-pharma-exposed/5425382?print=1. March 7, 2016.

———. "The Globalists' New World Order: Soft and Hard Kill Methods. An Unknown and Uncertain Future." http://www.globalresearch.ca/the-globalists-new-world-order-soft-and-hard-kill-methods-an-unknown-and-uncertain-future/5451356?print=1. May 23, 2015.

Hanks, Micah. "Secrets of the Past: Early Evidence of Nuclear Weapons?" http://newpagebooks.blogspot.com/2012/03/secrets-of-past.html. March 26, 2012.

———. "The Ancient Nukes Question: Were There WMDs in Prehistoric Times?" http://mysteriousuniverse.org/2011/12/the-ancient-nukes-question-were-there-wmds-in-prehistoric-times/. December 19, 2011.

Harper, Mark J. "Dead Scientists and Microbiologists—Master List." http://rense.com/general62/list.htm. (Accessed June 1, 2017).

Harris, Kristan T. "United States Politicians Gleefully Approve of United Nations Invasion of America." http://www.alipac.us/f19/un-military-troops-allowed-us-soil-os-executive-order-335275/. July 23, 2016.

Harris, Tom. "How Dirty Bombs Work." http://science.howstuffworks.com/dirty-bomb.htm. 2016.

"Harrison Bergeron: Plot Overview." http://www.sparknotes.com/short-stories/harrison-bergeron/summary.html. 2016.

Hayakawa, Norio. "My Recollections of the Enigmatic Bob Lazar … Alleged Former Area 51 'Scientist.'" http://www.rense.com/general72/recoll.htm. July 8, 2006.

"The Health Effects of Overweight and Obesity." http://www.cdc.gov/healthyweight/effects/. 2016.

"Henry Kissinger Biography." http://www.biography.com/people/henry-kissinger-9366016. 2016.

Herper, Matthew. "America's Most Popular Mind Medicines." *Forbes*, September 17, 2010. http://www.forbes.com/2010/09/16/prozac-xanax-valium-business-healthcare-psychiatric-drugs.html.

Herrera, John. "Mr Robot and the New World Order." http://www.ifyouwriteit.com/mr-robot-and-the-new-world-order/. September 5, 2015.

Heyes, J.D. "US Internet Censorship Mirrors China's." http://www.naturalnews.com/049593_censorship_China_Internet.html. May 5, 2105.

Hicks, Frederick C. *The New World Order*. CreateSpace. 2015.

"Hidden History: Monoatomic Gold and Human Origins—Jim Marrs." http://www.zengardner.com/hidden-history-monoatomic-gold-and-human-origins-jim-marrs/. July 25, 2013.

Higgins, Parker. "EFF Addresses Protesters at San Francisco's 'Restore the Fourth' Protest." https://www.eff.org/deeplinks/2013/07/eff-rallies-protesters-restore-fourth. July 15, 2013.

Hinkle, A. Barton. "Big Government Continues Eroding the Constitution." *Reason*, May 18, 2015. https://reason.com/archives/2015/05/18/how-big-government-erodes-the-constituti/print.

Hodges, Dave. "Last Night the GOP Rejected the New World Order." http://www.thecommonsenseshow.com/2016/07/21/last-night-the-gop-rejected-the-new-world-order/. July 21, 2016.

———. "What Are Your Odds of Surviving in a FEMA Camp?" http://www.thecommonsenseshow.com/2016/08/18/odds-surviving-fema-camp/. August 18, 2016.

————. "Will Humanity Survive the Depopulation Agenda of the Global Elite?" http://www.thecommonsenseshow.com/2014/04/26/will-humanity-survive-the-depopulation-agenda-of-the-global-elite/. April 26, 2014.

————. "The Three Step Plan to Destroy America and Implement the New World Order." http://www.thecommonsenseshow.com/2016/05/21/the-three-step-plan-to-destroy-america-and-implement-the-new-world-order/. May 1, 2016.

Hohmann, Leo. "'Nervous' Jeb Defends Poppy Bush's 'New World Order.'" http://www.wnd.com/2016/02/nervous-jeb-defends-poppy-bushs-new-world-order/. February 4, 2016.

————. "Orwellian Nightmare Unleashed on Schoolkids." http://www.wnd.com/2015/03/orwellian-nightmare-unleashed-on-schoolkids/. March 15, 2015.

Holcombe, Jesse, Amy Mitchell, and Kristen Purcell. "Investigative Journalists and Digital Security." http://www.journalism.org/2015/02/05/investigative-journalists-and-digital-security/. February 5, 2015.

Holloway, April. "Archaeologists Discover 300 Burials in Ancient Merovingian Necropolis." http://www.ancient-origins.net/news-history-archaeology/archaeologists-discover-300-burials-ancient-merovingian-necropolis-001932. August 3, 2014.

"How Realistic is Donald Trump's Mexico Wall?" http://www.bbc.com/news/world-us-canada-37243269. September 1, 2016.

"How Will Climate Change Impact on Fresh Water Security?" *Guardian*, December 21, 2012. https://www.theguardian.com/environment/2012/nov/30/climate-change-water.

Howard, Clark. "Your Smart TV Could Be Spying on You." http://www.clark.com/your-smart-tv-spying-you. February 10, 2015.

Hughes, Sarah. "Mr Robot's Rami Malek." *Irish Times*, July 22, 2016. http://www.irishtimes.com/culture/tv-radio-web/mr-robot-s-rami-malek-so-much-of-how-we-live-is-manufactured-rather-than-real-1.2731002.

"'The Hunger Games': A Glimpse at the Future?" http://vigilantcitizen.com/moviesandtv/the-hunger-games-a-glimpse-at-the-new-world-order/. April 5, 2012.

Hunt, Alex: "UKIP: The Story of the UK Independence Party's Rise." http://www.bbc.com/news/uk-politics-21614073. November 21, 2014.

Hunt, Alex, and Brian Wheeler. "Brexit: All You Need to Know about the UK Leaving the EU." http://www.bbc.com/news/uk-politics-32810887. November 24, 2016.

Icke, David. "Flu Is Not the Biggest Danger.... It's the Vaccine!" http://www.bibliotecapleyades.net/ciencia/ciencia_influenza32.htm. (Accessed June 1, 2017.)

————. "Reptilian Agenda." https://www.davidicke.com/category/271/reptilian-agenda. 2016.

"If I Were Reincarnated I Would Wish to Be Returned to Earth as a Killer Virus to Lower Human Population Leves." http://beforeitsnews.com/politics/2014/08/if-i-were-reincarnated-i-would-wish-to-be-returned-to-earth-as-a-killer-virus-to-lower-human-population-levels-2643598.html. August 9, 2014.

"Illuminati: Order of the Illumined Wise Men." http://www.bibliotecapleyades.net/esp_sociopol_illuminati.htm. 2016.

"Illuminati Symbolism of Princess Diana's Death in Selena Gomez 'Slow Down' Video." http://illuminatiwatcher.com/illuminati-symbolism-of-princess-dianas-death-in-selena-gomez-slow-down-video/. July 22, 2013.

"In Quotes: Blair and Iraq Weapons." http://news.bbc.co.uk/2/hi/uk_news/politics/3054991.stm. September 29, 2004.

"The Influenza Pandemic of 1918." https://virus.stanford.edu/uda/. 2016.

"Internal DOJ Memo Confirms Obama's Plan For Gun Confiscation." http://www.truthandaction.org/internal-doj-memo-confirms-obamas-plan-gun-confiscation/. 2016.

"Internet Censorship: What You Need To Know." http://www.bbc.com/news/technology-17476788. March 22, 2012.

"Is the Government Tracking Your Credit Card Purchases?" *Forbes*, January 26, 2011. http://www.forbes.com/forbes/welcome/?toURL=http://www.forbes.com/sites/moneybuilder/2011/01/26/is-the-government-tracking-your-credit-card-purchases/.

"Israel Could Use Dirty Nuke in False Flag Attack in US: Ex-CIA Contractor." http://www.presstv.com/Detail/2015/07/23/421532/Israel-dirty-nuke-false-flag-attack/. July 23, 2015.

Jacobsen, Annie. *Area 51: An Uncensored History of America's Top Secret Military Base.* New York: Little, Brown, 2012.

"James Earl Ray Biography. Murderer (1928–1998)." http://www.biography.com/people/james-earl-ray-20903161. 2014.

"John Holdren, Obama"s Science Czar, Says: Forced Abortions and Mass Sterilization Needed to Save the Planet." http://zombietime.com/john_holdren/. 2014.

"The John Lennon FBI Files." http://www.lennonfbifiles.com/. 2014.

Johnson, Lance. "Nestle CEO Seeks to Control the World's Water Supply." http://www.naturalnews.com/040026_Nestle_water_supply_domination.html. April 22, 2013.

Johnson, Luke. "Can People Really Spy on Me through My Laptop's or Smartphone's Camera?" *Digital Spy*, September 29, 2016. http://www.digitalspy.com/tech/feature/a795242/can-people-spy-on-me-through-my-laptops-or-smartphones-camera/.

Johnson, Tim. "It's Not Paranoia: Hackers Can Use Your Webcam to Spy On You." http://www.afr.com/technology/web/security/its-not-paranoia-hackers-can-use-your-webcam-to-spy-on-you-20160701-gpwna6. July 1, 2016.

Jones, Alex. "The International Banking Cartel Is the New World Order." http://www.infowars.com/the-international-banking-cartel-is-the-new-world-order/. July 23, 2009.

Jones, Clarence B. "The 2016 'Dumbing Down' of America." *Huffington Post*, May 14, 2016. http://www.huffingtonpost.com/clarence-b-jones/the-2016-dumbing-down-of_b_9976278.html.

Jones, Steve. "NWO Plans to Depopulate the Earth." http://rense.com/general64/pordc.htm. April 13, 2005.

Jordison, Sam. "Do You Really Know What 'Orwellian' Means?" *Guardian*, September 18, 2008. https://www.theguardian.com/books/booksblog/2014/nov/11/reading-group-orwellian-1984.

"Judicial Watch Sues Department of Defense for Records of Communications Relating to May 2011 FOIA Request for bin Laden Death Photos." http://www.judicial watch.org/press-room/press-releases/judicial-watch-sues-department-defense-records-communications-relating-may-2011-foia-request-bin-laden-death-photos/. July 24, 2014.

Kane, Alex. "11 Shocking Facts about America's Militarized Police Forces." http://www.alternet.org/civil-liberties/11-shocking-facts-about-americas-militarized-police-forces. June 27, 2014.

Keith Jim. *Black Helicopters II*. Lilburn, GA: IllumiNet Press, 1997.

———. *Black Helicopters Over America*. Lilburn, GA: IllumiNet Press, 1994.

———. *Casebook on the Men in Black*. Lilburn, GA: IllumiNet Press, 1997.

———. *Mind Control, World Control*. Kempton, IL: Adventures Unlimited Press, 1998.

Kelly-Detwiler, Peter. "Failure to Protect U.S.Against Electromagnetic Pulse Could Make 9/11 Look Trivial Some Day." *Forbes*, July 31, 2014. http://www.forbes.com/sites/peterdetwiler/2014/07/31/protecting-the-u-s-against-the-electromagnetic-pulse-threat-a-continued-failure-of-leadership-could-make-911-look-trivial-someday/#7271c2797fcd.

"Kenneth Goff." Federal Bureau of Investigation file, declassified under the terms of the Freedom of Information Act.

"Key Facts about Avian Influenza (Bird Flu) and Highly Pathogenic Avian Influenza A (H5N1) Virus." http://www.cdc.gov/flu/avian/gen-info/facts.htm. 2014.

Kharpal, Arjun. "iPhone Encryption 'Petrified' NSA: Greenwald." http://www.cnbc.com/2015/03/18/iphone-encryption-petrified-nsa-greenwald.html. March 18, 2015.

"Kim Johnson's Chemtrail Analysis—Updated." http://www.nmsr.org/mkjrept.htm. October 31, 1999.

King, Jon. "Did the CIA Murder John Lennon?" http://www.consciousape.com/2012/10/08/did-the-cia-murder-john-lennon/. October 8, 2012.

Kingsley, Patrick, and Sam Jones. "Osama bin Laden Death: The Conspiracy Theories." *Guardian*, May 5, 2011. http://www.theguardian.com/world/2011/may/05/osama-bin-laden-conspiracy-theories.

Klein, Aaron. "Here's Why Donald Trump's Plan to Build a Wall Is Bogus." *Fortune*, September 1, 2016. http://fortune.com/2016/09/01/donald-trump-mexico-wall-2/.

Knox, Olivier. "Intelligence Chief Clapper: I Gave 'Least Untruthful' Answer on U.S. Spying." http://news.yahoo.com/blogs/the-ticket/intel-chief-clapper-gave-least-untruthful-answer-u-164742798.html. June 10, 2013.

Koebler, Jason. "Global Flu Pandemic 'Inevitable,' Expert Warns." *U.S. News & World Report*, December 24, 2012. http://www.usnews.com/news/articles/2012/12/24/global-flu-pandemic-inevitable-expert-warns.

Korkis, Jim. "Ward Kimball and UFOs." http://www.mouseplanet.com/9720/Ward_Kimball_and_UFOs. August 24, 2011.

Kosar. "Vote Fraud Happening in Illinois! Stealing the Election...." http://www.the politicalinsider.com/voter-fraud-illinois-happening-stealing-election/. October 6, 2016.

"Kosovo War Was Beginning of New World Order." http://www.b92.net/eng/news/world.php?yyyy=2016&mm=06&dd=09&nav_id=98268. June 9, 2016.

Krans, Brian. "With 70 Percent of Americans on Medication, Have We Become a Pill Culture?" http://www.healthline.com/health-news/policy-seventy-percent-of-americans-take-prescription-drugs-062113. June 21, 2013.

Lardinois, Frederic. "U.S. Government: Reports about PRISM Contain 'Numerous Inaccuracies.'" http://techcrunch.com/2013/06/06/u-s-government-reports-about-prism-contain-numerous-inaccuracies/. June 6, 2013.

Lashmar, Paul. "Pearl Harbor Conspiracy Is Bunk." *Independent*, August 24, 1998. http://www.independent.co.uk/news/pearl-harbor-conspiracy-is-bunk-1173728.html.

"Law and Order—Curfew America." http://dotconnectoruk.blogspot.com/2008/08/law-and-order-curfew-america.html. August 21, 2008.

Lawrence, Mark. "Electro Magnetic Pulse—Top 5 Dangerous Places to Be When an EMP Takes Place." http://www.secretsofsurvival.com/survival/emp.html. 2016.

"Lee Harvey Oswald." http://jfkassassination.net/russ/jfkinfo4/jfk12/defector.htm#OS WALD 2014.

Lee, Timothy B. "Here's Everything We Know about PRISM to Date." *Washington Post*, June 12, 2013. http://www.washingtonpost.com/blogs/wonkblog/wp/2013/06/12/heres-everything-we-know-about-prism-to-date/.

Lendman, Stephen. "'The True Story of the Bilderberg Group' and What They May Be Planning Now." http://www.globalresearch.ca/the-true-story-of-the-bilderberg-group-and-what-they-may-be-planning-now/13808. June 1, 2009.

Leon, Melissa. "Mr. Robot Speaks." *Daily Beast*, September 2, 2015. http://www.thedailybeast.com/articles/2015/09/02/mr-robot-speaks-christian-slater-on-mr-robot-s-shocking-roanoke-delayed-finale-and-season-2.html.

Lewin, Leonard. *Report grom Iron Mountain*. Carson City, NV: Bridger House Publishers, 2008.

Lind, Michael. "On Pat Robertson His Defenders." http://www.nybooks.com/articles/1995/04/20/on-pat-robertson-his-defenders/. April 20, 1995.

"Long-range World Population Projections." http://www.un.org/esa/population/publications/longrange/longrange.htm. 2014.

Lynn, Matthew. "Abolish Cash? You'd Be Losing a Crucial Part of Free Society." *Telegraph*, August 21, 2015. http://www.telegraph.co.uk/finance/newsbysector/banksandfinance/11835603/Abolish-cash-Youd-be-losing-a-crucial-part-of-free-society.html.

M. Rich. "The Modern Survivalist Movement: It's Really Not All That Modern." http://www.offthegridnews.com/extreme-survival/the-modern-survivalist-movement-its-really-not-all-that-modern/. 2016.

Maestri, Nicoletta. "Quetzalcoatl—Pan-Mesoamerican Deity." http://archaeology.about.com/od/Aztec-Religion/a/Queztalcoatl.htm. 2014.

Mako, Henry. "Surviving the New World Order." http://www.rense.com/general69/surv.htm. January 8, 2005.

Malm, Sara. "FBI Can Spy on You through Your Webcam." *Daily Mail*, December 9, 2013. http://www.dailymail.co.uk/news/article-2520707/FBI-spy-webcam-triggering-indicator-light.html.

Marcotte, Amanda. "The Clinton BS Files." *Salon*, October 31, 2016. http://www
.salon.com/2016/10/31/the-clinton-bs-files-hillary-is-not-building-a-new-world-
order-out-to-destroy-the-white-man/.

"Marines, Police Prep for Mock Zombie Invasion." http://www.foxnews.com/us/ 2012/
10/27/marines-police-prep-for-mock-zombie-invasion.html. October 27, 2012.

"Mark Chapman: The Assassination of John Lennon." http://www.crimeandinvestiga
tion.co.uk/crime-files/mark-chapman—the-assassination-of-john-lennon. 2014.

Marrs, Jim. *The Rise of the Fourth Reich*. New York: William Morrow, 2008.

Marrs, Texe. "Donald Trump, Slayer of New World Order Dragons." http://www.texe
marrs.com/042016/donald_trump.htm. April, 2016.

Martens, Pam, and Russ Martens, Russ. "Suspicious Deaths of Bankers Are Now
Classified as 'Trade Secrets' by Federal Regulator." *Wall Street on Parade*, April 28,
2014. http://wallstreetonparade.com/2014/04/suspicious-deaths-of-bankers-are-
now-classified-as-%E2%80%9Ctrade-secrets%E2%80%9D-by-federal-regulator/.

Martin, Patrick. "The Sacking of Iraq's Museums: US Wages War against Culture and
History." http://www.wsws.org/en/articles/2003/04/muse-a16.html. April 16, 2003.

"Mass Spying on UK Citizens 'Essential,' Say MPs in Landmark Report." https://
www.rt.com/uk/240017-spying-uk-mps-report/. March 12, 2015.

McClellan, Jason. "Bob Lazar Dtill Defends Area 51 UFO info 25 Years Later." http://
www.openminds.tv/bob-lazar-still-defends-area-51-ufo-info-25-years-later/27560.
May 14, 2014.

McDonald, Joe. "China Calls for New Global Currency." http://abcnews.go.com/Bus
iness/story?id=7168919. 2016.

McKay, Andrew. "How to Live Off the Grid." http://survival-mastery.com/basics/how-
to-live-off-the-grid.html. 2016.

McLeod, Judi. "How Far Will Dems Go to Steal Election 2016?" http://canadafree
press.com/article/how-far-will-dems-go-to-steal-election-2016. November 6,
2016.

Meacher, Michael. "This War on Terrorism Is Bogus." *Guardian*, September 6, 2003.
http://www.theguardian.com/politics/2003/sep/06/september11.iraq.

Meek, James Gordon. "FBI Was Told to Blame Anthrax Scare on Al Qaeda by White
House Officials." *Daily News*, August 2, 2008. www.nydailynews.com/news/
national/2008/08/02/2008-08-02_fbi_was_told_to_blame_anthrax_scare_on_a
.html.

Meghan, Neal. "Is a Human 'Barcode' on the Way?" *Daily News*, June 1, 2012. http://
www.nydailynews.com/news/national/human-barcode-society-organized-invades-
privacy-civil-liberties-article-1.1088129.

Mendo, Alberto. "Quetzalcoatl: Beyond the Feathered Serpent." http://www.aap.berk
eley.edu/journals/2003Journal/AMendo.html. 2014.

Merton, Reginald. "Comte Saint-Germain." http://www.alchemylab.com/count_saint
_germain.htm. 2016.

Message to Eagle. "Physical Evidence of Ancient Atomic Wars Can Be Found World-
Wide." http://www.messagetoeagle.com/nuclearwarsgods.php#.VClKhWOEeSo.
June 3, 2014.

"Microchip Mind Control, Implants And Cybernetics." http://www.rense.com/general
17/imp.htm. December 6, 2001.

"A Microchipped Population—David Said This Was Coming 12 Years Ago and Here It Is, Folks!" http://www.redicecreations.com/news/2004/microicke.html. October 23, 2004.

Mikkelson, David. "666 Barcode." http://www.snopes.com/business/alliance/barcode.asp. April 30, 2011.

———. "Walmartyrs to the Cause." *Snopes*, April 23, 2015. http://www.snopes.com/politics/conspiracy/walmartclosures.asp.

"Military." http://www.un.org/en/peacekeeping/issues/military/. 2016.

Miller Judith. "Russian Scientist Dies in Ebola Accident at Former Weapons Lab." *New York Times*, May 25, 2004.

Miranda, Charles. "Britain's New Plan to Tackle Terrorism Both Home and Abroad with Controversial Security Alliance." http://www.news.com.au/world/europe/britains-new-plan-to-tackle-terrorism-both-home-and-abroad-with-controversial-security-alliance/news-story/2ef64da03f39b977834e0214acd0ea05. February 17, 2016.

Mitchell, Alanna, Simon Cooper, and Carolyn Abraham. "Strange Cluster of Microbiologists' Deaths under the Microscope." *Globe and Mail*, May 4, 2002.

Mitchell, Justin, and Andy Sullivan. "U.S. Militia Girds for Trouble as Presidential Election Nears." http://www.reuters.com/article/us-usa-election-militia-idUSKBN12X11R. November 2, 2016.

Mortimer, Caroline. "Donald Trump's Victory Averted World War Three, Top Putin Aide Claims." *Independent,* November 11, 2016. http://www.independent.co.uk/news/world/americas/us-elections/world-war-three-donald-trump-president-averted-putin-aide-claims-a7412111.html.

"Mr. Robot: Cast and Info." http://www.usanetwork.com/mrrobot/cast. 2016.

Mungin, Lateef, and Michael Pearson. "Social Security Combats Bullet Rumors." http://www.cnn.com/2012/09/04/us/social-security-bullets/. September 5, 2012.

Murdock, D. M., and S. Acharya. "Who Are the Anunnaki?" http://www.truthbeknown.com/anunnaki.htm. September 2014.

Murray, Joseph. "Brexit Signals the End of the New World Order." http://www.breitbart.com/london/2016/06/23/brexit-signals-end-new-world-order/. June 23, 2016.

Nance, Rahkia. "James Earl Ray's Brother Claims Federal Government Killed Martin Luther King." *Birmingham News*, April 1, 2008.

National Research Council. *The Effects on the Atmosphere of a Major Nuclear Exchange.* Washington, DC: National Academies Press, 1985.

"Neil Postman Quotes." https://www.goodreads.com/author/quotes/41963.Neil_Postman. 2016.

"New Voting Restrictions in Place for 2016 Presidential Election." http://www.brennancenter.org/voting-restrictions-first-time-2016. September 12, 2016.

"New World Order: 37 Quotes on the New World Order, One-World Government and One-World Religion." https://endtimesprophecyreport.com/2013/06/05/new-world-order-37-quotes-on-the-new-world-order/. June 5, 2013.

"New World Order Definition." http://www.threeworldwars.com/new-world-order.htm. 2016.

"New World Order Quotes." http://www.theforbiddenknowledge.com/quotes/. 2016.

Newling, Dan. "Britons 'Could Be Microchipped Like Dogs in a Decade.'" *Daily Mail*, October 30, 2006. http://www.dailymail.co.uk/news/article-413345/Britons-microchipped-like-dogs-decade.html.

Newman, Alex. "Globalist Henry Kissinger Outlines 'New World Order.'" *New American*, September 1, 2014. http://www.thenewamerican.com/world-news/item/19030-globalist-henry-kissinger-outlines-new-world-order.

———. "Hosting G20, Communist China Touts 'Lead Role' in New World Order." *New American*, August 17, 2016. http://www.thenewamerican.com/world-news/asia/item/23879-hosting-g20-communist-china-touts-lead-role-in-new-world-order.

———. "UN Agenda 2030." *New American*, January 6, 2016. http://www.thenewamerican.com/tech/environment/item/22267-un-agenda-2030-a-recipe-for-global-socialism.

"News Gathering Is Illegal under New Patriot Act II." http://www.democraticunderground.com/discuss/duboard.php?az=view_all&address=104x4899596mber. September 27, 2005.

"9/11 Attacks." http://www.history.com/topics/9-11-attacks. 2014.

"1980: John Lennon Shot Dead." http://news.bbc.co.uk/onthisday/hi/dates/stories/december/8/newsid_2536000/2536321.stm. 2008.

"1984 Vision of '1984' Becoming a Reality." http://www.wnd.com/2014/05/1984-predictions-about-police-state-now-reality/. May 21, 2014.

"1977 Senate Hearings on MKULTRA." http://www.druglibrary.org/Schaffer/history/e1950/mkultra/index.htm/. 2014.

Nivola, Pietro S. "Does Federalism Have a Future?" https://www.brookings.edu/articles/does-federalism-have-a-future/. December 1, 2001.

"None Dare Call It Conspiracy." http://www.ldsfreedomforum.com/viewtopic.php?t=1390. December 21, 2005.

Norton-Taylor, Richard. "UK, EU, and NATO—All in Need of a 'New World Order.'" *Guardian*, September 2, 2014. https://www.theguardian.com/world/defence-and-security-blog/2014/sep/02/nato-isis.

"An Octopus Named Wackenhut." http://www.bibliotecapleyades.net/esp_sociopol_wackenhut.htm. 2016.

Oppenheim, Maya. "Bernie Sanders to Donald Trump." *Independent*, November 15, 2016. http://www.independent.co.uk/news/people/bernie-sanders-ray-of-hope-post-trump-victory-a7418201.html.

Oppenheimer, David. "What Is the Blue Beam Project?" http://www.bibliotecapleyades.net/sociopolitica/esp_sociopol_bluebeam04.htm. April 16, 2000.

Organic Consumers Association. "Food for Thought—Several Dozen Microbiologists & Scientists Dead under "Suspicious Circumstances." http://www.organicconsumers.org/corp/suspicious012805.cfm. January 27, 2005.

Orr, Christopher. "The Movie Review: 'V for Vendetta.'" *Atlantic*, August 1, 2006. http://www.theatlantic.com/entertainment/archive/2006/08/the-movie-review-v-for-vendetta/69609/.

"Overweight and Obesity Statistics." https://www.niddk.nih.gov/health-information/health-statistics/Pages/overweight-obesity-statistics.aspx. 2016.

"Overweight Military: Obesity Rates Rise for US Service Members." https://sputnik news.com/military/201609301045850862-us-military-obesity-rates/. September 30, 2016.

Palma, Bethania. "Steve Bannon Accused of Having White Supremacist Views." *Snopes,* November 14, 2016. http://www.snopes.com/2016/11/14/steve-bannon-accused-of-having-white-supremacist-views/.

Park, Alice. "The World's Water Supply Could Dip Sharply in 15 Years." *Time,* March 21, 2015. http://time.com/3753332/world-water-day-un-warning/.

Payne, Michael. "Orwell's 1984 Becoming a Reality in Modern-Day America." http://www.opednews.com/articles/Orwell-s-1984-becoming-a-by-michael-payne-100429-640.html. May 2, 2010.

Posner, Sarah, and David Neiwert. "How Trump Took Hate Groups Mainstream'" *Mother Jones,* October 14, 2016. http://www.motherjones.com/politics/2016/10/donald-trump-hate-groups-neo-nazi-white-supremacist-racism.

"Pearl Harbor, 7 December, 1941." http://bytesdaily.blogspot.com/2010/12/pearl-harbour-7-december-1941.html. December 6, 2010.

"Pearl Harbor Conspiracy." http://www.ancientmonks.com/mystical-order-of-neglected-knowledge/6th-degree-master-bishop-of-the-arcane-secret/pearl-harbor-conspiracy. 2014.

"Pearl Harbor, Oahu—The Attack: Facts and Information." https://www.pearlharboroahu.com/attack.htm. 2014.

Perloff, James. "Pearl Harbor: Hawaii Was Surprised; FDR Was Not." *New American,* December 7, 2013. http://www.thenewamerican.com/culture/history/item/4740-pearl-harbor-hawaii-was-surprised-fdr-was-not.

Pinkerton, James P. "Strobe Talbott Leads toward One World." *Los Angeles Times,* June 8, 1999. http://articles.latimes.com/1999/jun/08/local/me-45260.

Posel, Susanne. "UN Wants to Stable Global Economy with One World Currency." https://www.occupycorporatism.com/un-wants-to-stabilize-global-economy-with-one-world-currency/. April 10. 2013.

"President Obama's Speech on Osama bin Laden's Death." *Los Angeles Times,* May 2, 2011. http://articles.latimes.com/2011/may/02/nation/la-na-bin-laden-obama-text-20110502.

"Princess Diana's Death and Memorial: The Occult Meaning." http://vigilantcitizen.com/vigilantreport/princess-dianas-death-and-memorial-the-occult-meaning/. April 13, 2009.

"Prison Planet Forum." http://forum.prisonplanet.com/index.php?topic=64372.0. 2016.

"Profiting from Your Thirst as Global Elite Rush to Control Water Worldwide." http://www.marketoracle.co.uk/article38167.html. December 21, 2012.

"Project Blue Beam." http://www.thewatcherfiles.com/bluebeam.html. 2016.

"Project for the New American Century." http://www.sourcewatch.org/index.php/Project_for_the_New_American_Century. 2016.

Prothero, Donald. "Area 51: Myth and Reality." http://www.skepticblog.org/2014/01/08/area-51-myth-and-reality/. January 8, 2014.

Putin, Vladimir. Speech, October 24, 2014.

Quain, John R. "Big Brother? US Linked to New Wave of Censorship?" *Fox News*, February 27, 2013. http://www.foxnews.com/tech/2013/02/27/special-report-surveillance-and-censorship-america.html.

Quayle, Steve. "Dead Scientists 2004–2014." http://www.stevequayle.com/?s=146. 2014.

"Quetzalcoatl." http://www.azteccalendar.com/god/quetzalcoatl.html. 2014.

"Quetzalcoatl." http://www.crystalinks.com/quetzalcoatl.html. 2014.

Rabin, Roni Caryn. "A Glut of Antidepressants." http://well.blogs.nytimes.com/2013/08/12/a-glut-of-antidepressants/?_r=0 August 12, 2013.

Rachman, Gideon. "Why the World Needs a United Nations Army." https://www.ft.com/content/325b3c42-7558-11de-9ed5-00144feabdc0. July 20, 2009.

Radford, Benjamin. "Viral Video Claims to Prove 'Chemtrails' Conspiracy." http://news.discovery.com/human/psychology/viral-video-claims-to-prove-chemtrails-conspiracy-140501.htm. May 1, 2014.

Rayner, Gordon. "Investigative Journalism to Be 'Stopped Dead in Tracks' by 'Menacing' Laws after Leveson Inquiry." *Telegraph*, October 15, 2015. http://www.telegraph.co.uk/news/uknews/leveson-inquiry/11933515/Investigative-journalism-to-be-stopped-dead-in-tracks-by-menacing-laws-after-Leveson-Inquiry.html.

Redfern, Nick. *Bloodline of the Gods.* Wayne, NJ: New Page Books, 2015.

———. *Final Events.* San Antonio, TX: Anomalist Books, 2010.

———. *The Real Men in Black.* Wayne, NJ: New Page Books, 2011.

"Reform the Patriot Act." https://www.aclu.org/reform-patriot-act. 2014.

Reisinger, Don. "iPhones in Use in the US Rise to 94M, New Study Suggests." https://www.cnet.com/news/nearly-100m-iphones-in-use-in-the-us-new-study-shows/. May 15, 2015.

Rense, Jeff. "Cattle Mutilations Explained? End of the Beef Industry?" http://www.rense.com/general32/beef.htm. July 2, 2003.

"Report of the Commission to Assess the Threat to the United States From Electromagnetic Pulse (EMP) Attack." http://www.empcommission.org/docs/A2473-EMP_Commission-7MB.pdf. June 12, 2002.

"Report of the Select Committee on Assassinations of the U.S. House of Represent atives." http://www.archives.gov/research/jfk/select-committee-report/. 2014.

"Report of Scientific Advisory Panel on Unidentified Flying Objects Convened by Office of Scientific Intelligence, CIA. January 14–18, 1953." http://www.cufon.org/cufon/robert.htm. 2016.

"Reptilians and Aztec." http://arcturi.com/ReptilianArchives/AztecMythology.html. 2010.

"Restore the Fourth—Who We Are." https://restorethe4th.com/who-we-are/. December 8, 2015.

"Retired General 'Surprised' No WMD Found." http://www.abc.net.au/news/2004-08-16/retired-general-surprised-no-wmd-found/2026360. August 16, 2004.

"RFK Assassination Witness Nina Rhodes-Hughes Says Sirhan Sirhan Didn't Act Alone." *Huffington Post,* April 30, 2012. http://www.huffingtonpost.com/2012/04/30/rfk-assassination-nina-rhodes-hughes_n_1464439.html.

"Rhodes Scholar Strobe Talbott Blames Putin and Russia for Upsetting the 'New World Order.'" http://www.unityofthepolis.com/rhodes-scholar-strobe-talbott-blames-putin-and-russia-for-upsetting-the-new-world-order/. October 30, 2016.

Richardson, Robert. "Is Living Off the Grid Now a Crime?" http://offgridsurvival .com/livingoffthegridcrime/. 2011.

Richelson, Jeffrey T., ed. "The Secret History of the U-2—and Area 51." http:// www2.gwu.edu/~nsarchiv/NSAEBB/NSAEBB434/. August 15, 2013.

"The Robert Kennedy Assassination." https://www.maryferrell.org/wiki/index.php/ Robert_Kennedy_Assassination. 2014.

Roberts, Paul Craig. "How the Oligarchy Has Prepared the Groundwork for Stealing theElection." http://www.paulcraigroberts.org/2016/11/06/how-the-oligarchy-has-prepared-the-groundwork-for-stealing-the-election/. November 6, 2016.

Robock, Alan, and Owen Brian Toon. "Local Nuclear War, Global Suffering." http:// palgrave.nature.com/scientificamerican/journal/v302/n1/full/scientificamerican0 110-74.html. 2009.

Roddy, Dennis B. "Looting of Baghdad Treasures Shines Light on a 'Dirty Business.'" http://old.post-gazette.com/World/20030427lootingworld3p3.asp. April 27, 2003.

Roland, Allen L. "Bernie and Jeremy—A New World Order Based on People Power." http://www.veteranstoday.com/2015/10/08/bernie-and-jeremy-a-new-world-order-based-on-people-power/. October 8, 2015.

Roller, Emma. "This Is What Section 215 of the Patriot Act Does." *Slate*, June 7, 2013. http://www.slate.com/blogs/weigel/2013/06/07/nsa_prism_scandal_what_ patriot_act_section_215_does.html.

Root, Tik. "Life under Curfew for American Teens." *Guardian*, May 28, 2016. https://www.theguardian.com/us-news/2016/may/28/curfew-laws-san-diego.

Rosenberg, Jennifer. "Robert Kennedy Assassination." http://history1900s.about.com /od/1960s/a/Robert-Kennedy-Assassination.htm. 2014.

Ross, Chuck. "Sydney Blumenthal: 'Right Wing' FBI Agents Took Down Hillary in a Coup d'état." *Daily Caller*, November 11, 2016. http://dailycaller.com/2016/11/ 11/sidney-blumenthal-right-wing-fbi-agents-took-down-hillary-in-a-coup-detat-video/.

"Saddam Hussein's Weapons of Mass Destruction." http://www.pbs.org/wgbh/pages/ frontline/shows/gunning/etc/arsenal.html. 2014.

Salazar, Adan. "Wikilkeaks: Hillary Clinton Proposed Killing Assange with Drone Strike." http://www.infowars.com/wikileaks-hillary-clinton-proposed-killing-assange-with-drone-strike/. October 3, 2016.

Sans, Ricky, and Kari Koeppel. "8 Conspiracy Theories about the Denver Airport That'll Freak You Out." https://www.buzzfeed.com/rickysans/the-mysterious-conspiracy-theories-surrounding-the-denver-ai?utm_term=.tuYvAKEJD#.aiO 5D3BzV. April 12, 2016.

Scheck, Rick. "Is Bernie Sanders Merely the Pied Piper of the New World Order?" http://stateofthenation2012.com/?p=34789. March 31. 2016.

Schifferes, Steve. "How Bretton Woods Shaped the World." http://news.bbc.co.uk /2/hi/business/7725157.stm. November 14, 2008.

"Scottish Governor Sees Growing Number of Appeals." http://www.freedominfo .org/2012/09/scottish-commissioner-sees-growing-number-of-appeals/. September 20, 2012.

Shapiro, Ben. "Brexit Is the End of the New World Order, and I Feel Fine." *Daily Wire,* June 24, 2016. http://www.dailywire.com/news/6915/brexit-end-new-world-order-we-know-it-and-i-feel-ben-shapiro.

Sieff, Martin. "China Wants Its Own New World Order to Oppose US Version." http://rense.com/general19/oppo.htm. February 6, 2002.

Singal, Jesse. "Does Julian Assange Really Have an Email That Will Get Hillary Clinton Tossed in Prison?" *New York Magazine*, July 29, 2016. http://nymag.com/ daily/intelligencer/2016/07/will-a-wikileaks-email-get-clinton-imprisoned.html.

Singh, Manish. "Samsung Lied." http://betanews.com/2015/02/19/samsung-lied-its-smart-tv-is-indeed-spying-on-you-and-it-is-doing-nothing-to-stop-that/. February 19, 2015.

"Sinister Sites—The Denver International Airport." http://vigilantcitizen.com/ sinistersites/sinister-sites-the-denver-international-airport/. 2016.

"Sirhan Sirhan and His Account of Delta Programming Mind Control." http:// vigilantcitizen.com/latestnews/sirhan-sirhan-and-his-account-of-delta-program ming-mind-control/. May 5, 2011.

Snyder, Michael. "After the Government Microchips Our Soldiers, How Long Will It Be before They Want to Put a Microchip in YOU?" http://endoftheamerican dream.com/archives/after-the-government-microchips-our-soldiers-how-long-will-it-be-before- they-want-to-put-a-microchip-in-you. May 8, 2012.

———. "From 7 Billion People to 500 Million People—The Sick Population Control Agenda of the Global Elite." http://endoftheamericandream.com/archives/from-7-billion-people-to-500-million-people-the-sick-population-control-agenda-of-the-global-elite. October 27, 2011.

———. "Newly Discovered Eighth Grade Exam From 1912 Shows How Dumbed Down America Has Become." http://www.infowars.com/newly-discovered-eighth-grade-exam-from-1912-shows-how-dumbed-down-america-has-become/. August 13, 2013.

Soni, Darshna. "Survey: 'Government Hasn't Told Truth about 7/7.'" http://www .channel4.com/news/articles/society/religion/survey+government+hasnt+told+tr uth+about+77/545847.html. June 4, 2007.

Stanford, Stefan. "NWO Warns of Terrible News for America and the World." http://allnewspipeline.com/Illuminati_Trump_False_Flag_Warning_Till_Novem ber.php. May 16, 2016.

"State's Freedom of Information Being Eroded." http://www.dailygate.com/opinion/ article_0a282963-5c18-5a85-91f5-4b380b03b79e.html. April 22, 2010.

Stebner, Beth. "Bobby Kennedy Assassin Still Claims He Was 'Victim of Mind Control and His Gun Didn't Fire Fatal Shot' in New Appeal after Parole Is Denied." *Daily Mail*, December 15, 2011. http://www.dailymail.co.uk/news/ article-2066883/Robert-F-Kennedy-assassin-Sirhan-Sirhan-claims-victim-mind-control.html.

Steiger, Brad. "Ancient Secret Societies, UFOs, and the New World Order." http://www.bibliotecapleyades.net/sociopolitica/sociopol_brotherhoodss30.htm. January 29, 2008.

———. *Conspiracies and Secret Societies*. Detroit, MI: Visible Ink Press, 2013.

———. "Three Tricksters in Black." *Saga's UFO Report*, winter, 1974.

Steill, Ben. "Would a New 'Bretton-Woods' Save the Global Economy?" http://www.pbs.org/newshour/rundown/would-a-new-bretton-woods-save-the-global-economy/. May 15, 2013.

Stephey, M. J. "Bretton Woods System." http://content.time.com/time/business/article/0,8599,1852254,00.html. October 21, 2008.

Stinnett, Robert B. "The Pearl Harbor Deceit." http://worldwar2history.info/Pearl-Harbor/deceit.html. 2000.

Stringfield, Leonard. *UFO Crash/Retrievals: The Inner Sanctum*. Cincinnati, OH: privately printed, 1991.

Stuster, J. Dana. "Declassified: The CIA Secret History of Area 51." http://blog.foreignpolicy.com/posts/2013/08/15/declassified_the_cias_secret_history_of_area_51. August 15, 2013.

"A Summary of the Book 'None Dare Call It Conspiracy.'" http://www.newsofinterest.tv/politics/book_summaries/book_ndcc.php. 2016.

"Surveillance under the USA PATRIOT Act." https://www.aclu.org/national-security/surveillance-under-usa-patriot-act. December 10, 2010.

Syrmopoulos, Jay. "Camping on Your Own Land Is Now Illegal." http://thefreethoughtproject.com/camping-land-illegal-homesteading-regulated-existence/. October 2, 2015.

———. "Mainstream Media Finally Admits Mass Banker 'Suicides' Were Likely Murder." http://thefreethoughtproject.com/mainstream-media-finally-admits-mass-banker-suicides-2015-criminal-conspiracy/. June 16, 2016.

Szymanksi, Greg. "Plans to Microchip Every Newborn in US and Europe Newborn in US and Europe Medical Officer of Finland." http://www.rense.com/general71/under.htm. May 11. 2006.

Thomas, Gordon. "Microbiologists with Link to Race-Based Weapon Turning Up Dead." *American Free Press*. http://www.americanfreepress.net/08_09_03/Microbiologists_With/microbiologists_with.html. August 9, 2003.

———. "The Secret World of Dr. David Kelly." http://www.rumormillnews.com/cgi-bin/archive.cgi?noframes;read=35765. August 21, 2003.

Thomas, John P. "Is the U.S. Medical Mafia Murdering Alternative Health Doctors Who Have Real Cures Not Approved by the FDA?" https://healthimpactnews.com/2015/is-the-u-s-medical-mafia-murdering-alternative-health-doctors-who-have-real-cures-not-approved-by-the-fda/. 2016.

Thomas, Kenn. "Casolaro's Octopus." http://www.theforbiddenknowledge.com/hardtruth/casolaro_octopus.htm. June 7, 2001.

Thomas, Kenn, and Jim Keith. *The Octopus*. Portland, OR: Feral House, 1996.

Thomas, William. "Stolen Skies: The Chemtrail Mystery." http://www.earthisland.org/journal/index.php/eij/article/stolen_skies_the_chemtrail_mystery/. 2014.

"Timeline of the 7 July Attacks." http://news.bbc.co.uk/2/hi/uk_news/5032756.stm. July 11, 2006.

Tonnies, Mac. *The Cryptoterrestrials*. San Antonio, TX: Anomalist Books, 2010.

"Top 10 Illuminati Murders." http://www.illuminatirex.com/illuminati-murders/ April 21, 2015.

"Tor Project: Overview." https://www.torproject.org/about/overview. 2016.

"Transforming Our World: The 2030 Agenda for Sustainable Development." https://sustainabledevelopment.un.org/post2015/transformingourworld. 2016.

Travers, Peter. "V for Vendetta." http://www.rollingstone.com/movies/reviews/v-for-vendetta-20060317. March 17, 2006.

"Trilateral Commission." http://www.bibliotecapleyades.net/sociopolitica/atlantean_conspiracy/atlantean_conspiracy16.htm. 2016.

"True Conspiracies, the Illuminati, and One World Government." http://www.trueconspiracies.com/. 2016.

Trump, Donald, Speech, November 9, 2016.

"Trump Election: Clinton Blames Defeat on FBI Director." http://www.bbc.com/news/election-us-2016-37963965. November 13, 2016.

Tucker, Patrick. "The Military Wants Smarter Insect Spy Drones." http://www.defenseone.com/technology/2014/12/military-wants-smarter-insect-spy-drones/101970/. December 23, 2014.

"The 2016 GOP Record on Voting Rights." http://correctrecord.org/the-2016-gop-record-on-voting-rights/. 2016.

"22 Shocking Population Control Quotes from the Global Elite." http://www.fourwinds10.net/siterun_data/health/intentional_death/news.php?q=1291600521. 2014.

"25 Marconi Scientists, 1982–88." http://projectcamelot.org/marconi.html. 2014.

Twietmeyer, Ted. "Bush Replaced REX84 with New Martial Law EO." http://rense.com/general81/shadowgovt.htm. April 14, 2008.

"2003 Looting of the Iraq National Museum." https://web.stanford.edu/group/chr/drupal/ref/the-2003-looting-of-the-iraq-national-museum. October 20, 2008.

Tyler, Joshua. "V for Vendetta." http://www.cinemablend.com/reviews/V-Vendetta-1472.html. 2016.

"UK: Leveson Inquiry Report Welcomed and Criticized." http://humanrightshouse.org/Articles/18900.html. 2916.

"UN Troops Told to Kill Americans That Don't Give Over Their Guns." http://www.mrconservative.com/2013/11/28002-un-troops-told-to-kill-americans-that-dont-give-over-their-guns/. November 27, 2013.

"United Nations Global Issues." http://www.un.org/en/globalissues/water/index.shtml. 2016.

"The United Nations Is World Government." http://www.nwotoday.com/agenda/the-united-nations-is-world-government. 2016.

"United States Department of Justice Investigation of Recent Allegations Regarding the Assassination of Dr. Martin Luther King, Jr." http://www.justice.gov/crt/about/crm/mlk/part1.php. Department of Justice, June 2000.

"U.S. Concentration Camps: FEMA and the Rex 84 Program." http://www.theforbiddenknowledge.com/hardtruth/con_camps_fema.htm. 2016.

"US Family Gets Health Implants." http://news.bbc.co.uk/2/hi/health/1981026.stm. May 11, 2002.

Van Buren, Peter, and Tom Dispatch. "The Erosion of the US Constitution … and It Starts in the White House." http://web.alternet.org/civil-liberties/erosion-us-constitution-and-it-starts-white-house. February 16, 2014.

"Vast Majority of NSA Spy Targets Are Mistakenly Monitored." http://www.louisiana.statenews.net/index.php/sid/223558101/scat/b8de8e630faf3631/ht/Vast-majority-of-NSA-spy-targets- are-mistakenly-monitored. July 6, 2014.

Vaswani, Karishma. "The Chinese Yuan is Going Global." http://www.bbc.com/news/business-34961012. November 30, 2016.

Villasanta, Arthur Dominic. "Xi Calls for 'New World Order' Dominated by China and Russia and Elimination of the US." http://www.chinatopix.com/articles/98199/20160814/xi-calls-new-world-order-dominated-china-russia-elimination.htm. August 14, 2016.

Vorhees, Josh. "Obama Defends NSA Surveillance: 'Nobody Is Listening to Your Telephone Calls.'" *Slate*, June 7, 2013. http://www.slate.com/blogs/the_slatest/2013/06/07/obama_defends_nsa_surveillance.html.

Ward, Dan Sewell. "Are the Extraterrestrials Who First Came to Earth Still Here?" http://www.halexandria.org/dward359.htm. 2016.

Watson, Paul Joseph. "Ex-DARPA Head Wants You to Swallow ID Microchips." http://www.infowars.com/ex-darpa-head-wants-you-to-swallow-id-microchips/. January 7, 2014.

———. "Harvard Prof: Government Mosquito Drones Will Extract Your DNA." http://www.infowars.com/harvard-prof-government-mosquito-drones-will-extract-your-dna/. January 23, 2015.

Watson, Paul Joseph. "The Population Reduction Agenda for Dummies." http://www.prisonplanet.com/the-population-reduction-agenda-for-dummies.html. June 26, 2009.

Watson, Paul Joseph, and Alex Jones. "London Underground Bombing 'Exercises' Took Place at Same Time as Real Attack." http://www.prisonplanet.com/articles/july2005/090705bombingexercises.htm. July 13, 2005.

Watson, Traci. "Conspiracy Theories Find Menace in Contrails." *USA Today*, March 7, 2001. http://usatoday30.usatoday.com/weather/science/2001-03-07-contrails.htm.

W.E.B. "The Council on Foreign Relations (CFR) and The New World Order." http://www.conspiracyarchive.com/2013/12/21/the-council-on-foreign-relations-cfr-and-the-new-world-order/. December 21, 2013.

Weigel, David. "Ron Paul on the Trilateral Commission." http://www.slate.com/blogs/weigel/2011/12/23/ron_paul_on_the_trilateral_commission.html. December 23, 2011.

Wells, H. G. *The New World Order*. http://www.telelib.com/authors/W/WellsHerbertGeorge/prose/newworldorder/index.html. 2016.

"When Was Pearl Harbor, December 7, 1941, A Day That Will Live in Infamy!" http://beforeitsnews.com/alternative/2012/12/when-was-pearl-harbor-december-7-1941-a-day-that-will-live-in-infamy-2509294.html. December 6, 2012.

"Who Killed Off Star Wars Scientists?" http://www.ufoevidence.org/documents/doc826.htm. 2014.

"Why Was John Lennon's Doorman on CIA Payroll?" http://www.rumormillnews.com/cgi-bin/archive.cgi/noframes/read/86959. May 27, 2006.

Wilmut, Ian. "John Clark: Pioneering Scientist Whose Entrepreneurial Skills Paved the Way for Dolly the Sheep." *Guardian*, August 25, 2004.

Williams, Ray. "Anti-Intellectualism and the Dumbing Down of America." *Psychology Today*, July 7, 2014. https://www.psychologytoday.com/blog/wired-success/201 407/anti-intellectualism-and-the-dumbing-down-america.

Wilson, Julie. "Wave of Holistic Doctor Deaths Continues, as Florida Chiropractor Suddenly Dies Despite Being 'Hearty and Healthy.'" http://www.natural news .com/052975_holistic_doctor_deaths_thermography_cancer_detection.html. February 15, 2016.

Wolchover, Natalie. "Could the Internet Ever Be Destroyed?" http://www.live science.com/18030-internet-destroyed.html. January 20, 2012.

Wood, Robert M., and Nick Redfern. *Alien Viruses*. Rochester, NY: Richard Dolan Press, 2013.

Woolaston, Victoria. "We'll Be Uploading Our Entire Minds to Computers by 2045 and Our Bodies Will Be Replaced by Machines within 90 Years, Google Expert Claims." http://www.dailymail.co.uk/sciencetech/article-2344398/Google-futurist-claims-uploading-entire-MINDS-computers-2045-bodies-replaced-machines-90-years.html. June 19, 2013.

"The World Bank—History." http://www.worldbank.org/en/about/history. 2016.

Wozny, Andrew. "DARPA's Insight: New World Order Program to Watch Us All." http://www.bibliotecapleyades.net/sociopolitica/sociopol_DARPA02.htm. October 6, 2010.

Yadron, Danny. "Why Is Everyone Covering Up Their Laptop Cameras?" https://www .theguardian.com/world/2016/jun/06/surveillance-camera-laptop-smartphone-cover-tape. June 6, 2016.

Zetter, Kim. "April 13, 1953: CIA OKs MK-ULTRA Mind-Control Tests." *Wired*, April 13, 2010. http://www.wired.com/2010/04/0413mk-ultra-authorized/.

———. "How Does the FBI Watch List Work." https://www.wired.com/2016/06/fbi-watch-list-prevented-orlando-heres-works/. June 17, 2016.

———. "How to Keep the NSA from Spying through Your Webcam." https://www .wired.com/2014/03/webcams-mics/. March 13, 2014.

INDEX

Note: italicized page numbers indicates main entry.

A

Abbott, Tony, 60

Abraham, Larry, 220

Ackerman, Spencer, 181

Adachi, Ken, 54, 120

Adams, Scott, 186

Aerial Phenomena Research Organization (APRO), 338

Agee, Philip, 179

Agnew, Rosemary, 125

Alba, Duke of, 71

Alban, St., 76

Albert le Grand, 1

alchemy, 1–2, 187, 189

Aldrich, Richard J., 22

Alexander, M. C., 235

aliens, 110–12

Allah, 256

Allawi, Iyad, 163

Allen, Gary, 74, 157–58, 220–22, 381

Allen, Todd, 233

al-Qaeda, 215, 217

Alten, Steve, 215–16

alternative health care, 92–94

alt-right, 325–26

Alvarez, Luis, 337

Alzheimer's disease and the New World Order, 2–4, 3 (ill.)

American Civil Liberties Union, 19, 180–81, 364–65

American Vision, 4–5

Amerithrax, 5–7

Amrita, 148

The Andromeda Strain (Crichton), 309

Ansary, Alex, 315

anthrax attack, 5–7

anti-Christ, 256–58, 280

antidepressants, 208

anti-globalization movement, 7–8

Anti-Terrorism Act, 244

Apple, 155–56

Applied Digital Solutions, 193

Apuzzor, Matt, 195

Arachne, 37

Arbuthnot, Felicity, 259

Arctic ice, 191 (ill.), 191–92

Area 51, 9–12, 10 (ill.), 230

Arendt, Hannah, 46

Armageddon, 105–6

Arnold, Kenneth, 276

Arrigo, Sue, 121

Arulanandam, Andrew, 90

Asian Infrastructure Investment Bank (AIIB), 383

Assange, Julian, 12 (ill.), 12–13, 377–78

Astor, John Jacob, 71

Astor, Marissa, 378

Astor, Waldorf, 71

atomic weapons, 223–25, 391–92

Audrey (Reptilian abductee), 277–78

Austin, Jon, 23–24, 378

Austin, Stephen F., 127

Australian Signals Directorate (ASD), 116–17

Avian flu, 13–15

B

Bacon, Francis, 76

Bacon, Roger, 76

Baker, Michael, 184

Baker, Norman, 161, 162–63

Balko, Radley, 195

Ball, Kirstie, 194

banking, 379–83

banking deaths, 17–18

Bannon, Steve, 325–26, 326 (ill.)

Baraniuk, Chris, 153

barcoding the population, 18–20, 19 (ill.)
Barker, Brad, 58
Barroso, José Manuel Dura,o, 102
Barry, William, 167
Baxter, Irvin, 280
Beatrix, Queen, 71
Beatty, Frank E., 248
Becker, Hal, 316
Beckham, Alistair, 185
Beeston, Mark, 380
Behar, Alberto, 192
Bekkum, Gary, 106
Benedick, Richard, 61
Benjamin Franklin True Patriot Act, 20–21
Benson, Ezra Taft, 220
Berkner, Lloyd, 338
Berlitz, Charles, 32
Bernhard, Prince of the Netherlands, 21
Bernstein, Carl, 179
Berwick, Jeff, 38–39
Bible, 280–81
Biden, Joe, 214
Big Brother, 218–19, 237
Bilderberg Group, 21–23, 22 (ill.), 23–24, 70
Bilderberg's role in the New World Order, 23–24
Bin Laden, Osama, 23, 24–27, 25 (ill.), 217, 353
Bindon, Glyn, 269
biochips, 27–28
biological agents, 202–3
biological warfare, 176, 190
bioterrorism, 120
Birch, John, 157–58
Bishop, Greg, 333–34
Bissell, Richard M., Jr., 9–10
black helicopters of the New World Order, 28–32, 29 (ill.)
Black Nobility, 382–83
Blair, Tony, 32–34, 33 (ill.), 161, 313, 368, 369
blood types, 284–86
Blue Helmets, 344
Blumenfeld, Samuel L., 138
Blumenthal, Sidney, 76
Body Snatchers, 138

Boeche, Ray, 67–69
Boetticher, Johann Friedrich, 1
Bohemian Club and the New World Order, 34–36, 35 (ill.), 36–37
Bohemian Grove secrecy, 36–37
Bolton, John, 259
bombs, 89–90
Bonds, Ron, 231
border closings, 38–40, 39 (ill.)
Bosley, Walter, Jr., 290–91
Bosley, Walter, Sr., 290–91
Bovine Spongiform Encephalopathy (BSE), 2–3
Bowden, Keith, 182
Bowe, Rebecca, 279
Boyd, Jamie, 330
Boyd, Tim, 191
Boykin, William, 271
Boyle, Francis, 120
Brabeck, Peter, 367
brain, experiments on, 109–10
Brandt, Daniel, 341
Braun, Eva, 123
Brave New World (Huxley), 40–42, 41 (ill.), 297, 392
Bread of Presence, 148
Bresler, Fenton, 179
Bretton Woods system, 42–44, 43 (ill.)
Brexit, 44–46, 45 (ill.), 109, 173, 322, 342–43
Brimelow, Peter, 325
British East India Company, 69, 70 (ill.)
British royal family, 71, 274–76, 285
Brittan, John, 183, 184
Brooks, Jack, 282–83
Broucher, David, 161
Brown, Larisa, 149
Brown, Ryan, 279
Brown, Tim, 93
Brushlinski, Alexi, 190
Brussell, Mae, 179
Bryan, William Joseph, 171
Brzezinski, Zbigniew, 320
Buddha, 256
Buffett, Warren, 71
Bundy, McGeorge, 71

Bundy, William, 71
Bürgermeister, Jane, 14–15
Burke, Ryan, 145
Bush, Barbara, 47 (ill.)
Bush, George H. W., 47 (ill.)
  biowarfare agents, 121
  blood type, 285
  Bohemian Club, 36
  Committee of 300, 71
  Council on Foreign Relations, 73
  election against Clinton, 313
  Gulf War speech (1991), 48–50
  Kennedy, Robert F., 166
  New World Order speech (1990), 46–48, 214
  New World Order terminology, 64, 163
  Project for the New American Century, 259
  Putin, Vladimir, 260
  Robertson, Pat, 288
  Skull and Bones, 301
  water control, 367
Bush, George W., 14 (ill.)
  anthrax, 7
  Avian flu, 13–14
  Fort Detrick, 120
  genetic diversity, 285
  John Warner Defense Authorization Act, 187
  No Child Left Behind and Clear Skies Initiative, 238
  Orwellian, 237
  Patriot Act, 182, 245
  post-9/11 security state, 195
  PRISM Program, 304
  Putin, Vladimir, 260
  Reptilian, 275
  Rex 84, 283–84
  Skull and Bones, 301
  terrorism, 353
  weapons of mass destruction, 161, 368, 369
Bush, Jeb, 50, 50 (ill.), 356
Bush, Prescott, 71
Butler, Nicholas Murray, 235
Buxton, Charles R., 30
Byrnes, Sholto, 212, 383

C

Caladan, T. S., 140
Cameron, David, 44, 45, 45 (ill.)
Cameron, Grant, 268
Camp Alpha, 114
camps, 114
Camus, Albert, 314
Cantril, Hadley, 338
Cape Coral, Florida, 233
Carlin, John P., 374
Carlson, Darren K., 250
Carp, Ontario, 334–36
Carrington, Lord, 71
Carson, Ben, 39, 379
Carter, Jimmy, 73, 113, 288
Carto, Willis, 273
cashless society, *51–53, 52*
Casolaro, Danny, 229–30
Castro, Fidel, 164
Catcher in the Rye, 178–79
Center for Public Integrity, 21
Central Intelligence Agency (CIA), 199–200, 337, 340–42
Chadwell, H. Marshall, 336–37
Chaikin, Carly, 209
Chalabi, Ahmed, 163
Chalker, Bill, 251
Chan, Margaret, 120
Chan, Vincent, 153
Chapman, Mark, 177–79
Chardy, Alfonso, 282
Charles, Prince, 240, 274, 275, 276, 285
chemical warfare, 94–96
chemicals, 53–55
chemtrails, *53–55, 54* (ill.)
Chen, Tim, 318
Cheney, Dick, 5, 215, 220, 245, 367, 368 (ill.)
China, 150–51, 234
China and the New World Order, *56–58, 57* (ill.)
Chomsky, Noam, 8
Christianity, 375
Christie, Chris, 356
Chumley, Cheryl, 219
Church Committee, 197, 341
Church of Scientology, 341

Churchill, Winston, 71, 214, 248, 375
cities, spraying, 308–9
Citigroup Inc., 216
civil unrest, 58–59
Civilian Flying Saucer Investigators (CFSI), 338
Clark, Bruce, 330
Clarkson, Frederick, 288
Clayton, Patrick, 389
Clear Skies Initiative, 238
Clelland, Mike, 37
Clinton, Bill, 65 (ill.)
  blood type, 285
  Council on Foreign Relations, 73
  curfews, 78
  defense policy, 258
  federalism, 116
  Hussein, Saddam, 259
  militarization of the police, 195
  Putin, Vladimir, 260
  Reptilian, 275
  Talbott, Strobe, 313, 315
  Wolfensohn, James, 380
Clinton, Hillary, *61–63, 62* (ill.), 77 (ill.), 86 (ill.)
  election loss to Trump (2016), 329–30, 390–91
  militarization of the police, 196
  militia, 350
  Reptilian, 275
  Sanders, Bernie, 260, 329 (ill.)
  WikiLeaks, 13, 377–79
Cloonen, Kate, 330
Club of Rome, *63–64, 64* (ill.), 70
code-breaking, 247
Cohen, William S., 65 (ill.), 370
Cold War statements on the New World Order, 64–66, 65 (ill.)
Coleman, John, 66–67, 71, 382
Collins, Suzanne, 139, 140, 140 (ill.)
Collins Elite, 67–69

Colorado Bureau of Investigation (CBI), 29–30
Comey, James, 77, 373–74
Committee of 300, 66–67, 69–71, 70 (ill.)
Committee on the Atmospheric Effects of Nuclear Explosions, 224
Communications Security Establishment Canada (CSEC), 116–17
Communism, 221–22
Conyers, John, 245
Cooper, William, 272
Copeland, David, 23
Copeland, Miles Axe, Jr., 340–42
Coppens, Philip, 272
Corbyn, Jeremy, 293
Corsi, Jerome, 163
Costilla County, Colorado, 232
Cotard, Jules, 360
Cotard's Syndrome, 360–62
Coulter, Ann, 220
Council for National Policy, *72–73*
Council on Foreign Relations, 70, *73–74, 74* (ill.), 320
Count of St. Germain, *74–76*
coup d'état, *76–77, 77* (ill.)
credit card purchases, 318–19
Creutzfeldt-Jakob Disease (CJD), 3 (ill.), 3–4
Crichton, Michael, 309
Crites, Austyn Daniel, 329
Cro-Magnons, 286
Cronkite, Walter, 339
Cruz, Ted, 63, 322, 379
curfews, *77–78, 78* (ill.)
currency, 233–35
Czechoslovakia, 265, 266–67

D

Dajibhai, Vimal Bhagvangi, 183, 184
Dam, Harry, 35
Damon, Matt, 87
Daniels, Jonathan, 248
DARPA, 79–82
Daschle, Tom, 6, 7
Datura Starmonium, 95

Davis, Wade, 95
Deacon, John, 68
Dean, John, 328
Declaration of the Federation of the World, 236
Defense Advanced Research Projects Agency (DARPA), 79–82, 81 (ill.)
DeMar, Gary, 4–5
Demeny, Graham, 119–20
Democratic National Committee (DNC), 378–79
Denver Airport, 83 (ill.), 83–85
Department of Homeland Security, U.S., 85 (ill.), 85–86
Department of Justice, U.S., 229
Desert Shield/Storm, 49
Deutsche Bank, 17–18
Developing a Reliable and Innovative Vision for the Economy (DRIVE) Act, 38
Dewey, Thomas E., 236
Diana, Goddess, 87
Diana, Princess of Wales's death, 86–87, 86 (ill.), 275–76
Dias, Jason, 362
Dias, Simoni Renee Guerreiro, 123
Dick, Philip K., and the Nazi plot, 87–89
DiMaggio, Joe, Jr., 206
DiMaggio, Joe, Sr., 206
Dingledine, Roger, 317
dirty bomb, 89–90, 391
disarming the United States, 90–92, 91 (ill.)
Ditchley Foundation, 70
Doctorow, E. L., 273
doctors' deaths, 92–94
Doernberg, Ben, 279
Domestic Security Enhancement Act, 20
Doubleday, Portia, 209
Dragonfly drone, 149
drugs, 207–9, 208 (ill.)
Duclos, Susan, 321
Dugan, Regina, 81 (ill.), 81–82
Dugway Proving Ground, 94–96, 95 (ill.)

Duke, David, 326
Dulles, Allen, 109, 122, 123 (ill.), 163, 166, 308
Dulles, John Foster, 236
dumbing down the population, 96–98, 97 (ill.), 137–38, 315–17
Dumont, Santos, 376
Duncan, Thomas Eric, 100–101
Durant, Frederick C., 337, 339
Dutch royal family, 71
Dutton, Fred, 167

E

Ebola, 99–101, 100 (ill.), 190, 192
Economic and Monetary Union of the European Union, 101–3
education system, 96–98, 137–38
Edwards, Dane, 31
Ehrlich, Paul and Anne, 239–40
Eichmann, Adolf, 124
Einstein, Albert, 314
Eisenhower, Dwight D., 22, 73, 165, 285, 339
electromagnetic pulse disaster, 103–5, 104 (ill.)
electronic surveillance system, 27–28
Elizabeth II, Queen of England, 71, 212, 274, 275, 285, 383
Elliott, Tony, 62
Elliott Automation Space and Advanced Military Systems Ltd., 184
emergency exercise, 281–84
eschatology, 105–7, 106 (ill.)
Eskin, Harold S., 233
Esmail, Sam, 209
Estulin, Daniel, 23
e-tattoos, 82
European Black Nobility, 146, 382–83
European Central Bank, 381
European Monetary Union, 381
European Union (EU), 44–46, 101–3, 107–9, 108 (ill.)
experiments on the brain, 109–10

extraterrestrial New World Order, 110–12, 111 (ill.)

F

Facebook, 255
Falk, Richard A., 66
Farage, Nigel, 45, 343, 343 (ill.)
Fast Lightweight Autonomy program, 149
Fayed, Dodi, 86, 276
Fayed, Mohamed Al-, 276
Federal Emergency Management Agency (FEMA), 113–15, 114 (ill.)
Federalism, 115–16
Feingold, Russell, 245
Ferrell, Jeff, 55
Ferry, Peter, 185
Fifth Amendment, 349
Finletter, Tom, 66
Finney, Jack, 138
Five Eyes, 116–17, 117 (ill.)
Floyd, Rod, 93
fluoride, 117–20, 119 (ill.)
food stamp program, 52
Forbes, John, 71
Ford, Gerald, 73, 166
Foreign Account Tax Compliance Act (FATCA), 38
Foreign Intelligence Surveillance Act (FISA), 304
Fort Detrick, 120–22
Fourth Amendment, 278–80
Fourth Reich, 122–24
Fox, Vicente, 327
France, 152
Francis, Adolph, 144
Franco, Francisco, 237
Franklin, Benjamin, 127
Fraser, Ivan, 380
Freedom of Information Act erosion, 124–26, 125 (ill.)
Freemasonry, 70, 145, 375
Freemasons, 126–28, 127 (ill.)
Frieden, Thomas R., 120
Friedman, Stan, 289
Frost, Stephen, 161

G

G4S plc, 359–60
Gabb, Sean, 211
Galbraith, John Kenneth, 273
Gallagher, R. J., 31
Galperin, Eva, 374
Gandhi, Mahatma, 314
Gardner, Richard N., 65, 65 (ill.)
Garner, Eric, 357
Garner, Erica, 357
Gates, Bill, 192
Gates, Melinda, 192
George II, King of England, 127
Gephardt, Richard, 214
Giles, Katherine, 191
Gille, Jean-François, 252
Gingrich, Newt, 259
Giraldo, Greg, 208
Giuliani, Rudy, 76
glass, 388–89
Glass, Nicholas, 295–96
Glazyev, Sergei, 390
globalization, 7–8
Godfrey, Arthur, 338
gods, 256–58
Goepel, Eric, 250
Goff, Kenneth, *129–31*, 130 (ill.), 336, 341
Gohmert, Louie, 219
gold, 1
Golden Gate Bridge, 308
Goldsmith, James, 343
Goldwater, Barry, 158
Golin, Steve, 209
González, Mario Costeja, 152
Gooding, Stuart, 184
Google, 152, 255
Gorbachev, Mikhail, 47, 66, *131–32*, 132 (ill.), 214, 222, 267–68
Gore, Al, 71
Gottlieb, Sydney, 109, 308
Goudsmit, Samuel Abraham, 338
Government Communications Headquarters (GCHQ), 116–17, *133–34*

Government Communications Security Bureau (GCSB), 116–17
Graham, Robbie, 339
Grant, Ulysses S., 299
Grays, 110–11, 111 (ill.)
green glass, 388
Greenberg, Andy, 155
Greenhalgh, David, 184
Greenson, Ralph, 206, 207
Greenwald, Glenn, 156, 305
Greenwood, Arthur, 236
Greer, John Michael, 158
Gricar, Morgan, 145
Griffin, Andrew, 155, 355
Gritsch, Kurt, 212
Grogan, Leslie, 247, 248
Group of 20 (G20) summit, 56–57
Gulf War, 46–47, 48–50
guns, 90–92, 91 (ill.)

H

Haakon, King of Norway, 71
Hagopian, Joachim, 96
Halifax, Lord, 71
Hall, Manly P., 141
Halliwell, James O., 126–27
Halo Corporation, 58, 59
Hamilton, Chad, 209
Hamilton, William, 229
Hanks, Micah, 389
Harriman, W. Averell, 71
Harris, Kristan T., 345
Harris, Tom, 89
"Harrison Bergeron" (Vonnegut), *134–36*, 136 (ill.), 392
Haskell, Floyd K., 29–32, 31 (ill.)
Hastert, Dennis, 245
Hastings, Jay, 178
Hatten, Dennis, 357
Hawkins, Donald, 183
Hawks, John, 286
Hayden, Michael, 39, 58, 59
Hayes, Anna, 205
Head, Tom, 237
Hearst, William Randolph, 36
Hegel, Friedrich, 382

Heine, Henry S., 7
helicopters, 28–32, 29 (ill.)
Helldén, Anders, 361
Helms, Richard, 197
Helvetius, 1
Henderson, Dean, 382
Henningsen, Patrick, 52
Henry VII, King of England, 127
Herrera, Jon, 209
Hess, Moses, 287
Hesse, William, 71
Hewitt, John, 82
Hicks, Frederick C., and *The New World Order, 136–37*
Hill, Roger, 182
Hinckley, John, 178
Hitchens, Christopher, 237
Hitler, Adolf
    Dick, Philip K., 89
    fluoride, 117–18
    Fourth Reich, 122–24
    Jewish extermination, 253
    New World Order, 214
    revolution, 381
    Trump, Donald, reference, 186
    World War II, 246
HIV virus, 121–22, 190
Hockett, Guy, 207
Hodges, Dave, 61, 114, 322
Hohmann, Leo, 238
holistic doctors, 92–94
Holland, John Henry, 127
Holloway, April, 87
holograms, 256–58, 264
homeschooling, 137 (ill.), *137–38*
homosexuality, 5
Hoover, Herbert, 73
Hoover, J. Edgar, 220
Hope, Bob, 275
Hopkins, Herbert, 188–89
House, Mandel, 71
House of Hapsburg, 71
House of Orange, 71
House of Windsor, 212
House Select Committee on Assassinations (HSCA), U.S., 164

Howard, Clark, 301
Howard, Michael, 161
Howard-Browne, Rodney, 322
Hubbard, L. Ron, 340, 341
Hudson, David, 204, 205
human replacements, *138–39*
The Hunger Games (Collins), *139–41*, 140 (ill.)
Hungerford, Jean M., 265–67
Hunt, Nicholas, 162
Hunter, Greg, 321
Hurt, John, 351, 352
Hussain, Hasib, 294–95
Hussein, Saddam
    Bush, George H. W., 46–47, 48–49, 121
    Project for the New American Century, 259
    statue of, pulled down, 270
    weapons of mass destruction (WMD), 161, 162 (ill.), 367–69
Hutton, Lord, 161–62
Huxley, Aldous, 40–42, 41 (ill.), 71, 134–35, 297
hypnosis, 178–79

I

Icke, David, 145, 274, 275, 276, 285, 389
Illuminati, 24, *143–45*, 144 (ill.), 145–47, 388
Illuminati and the New World Order, 143–45, 144 (ill.), *145–47*
immortality, 74–76
immortality for the elite, *147–49*, 148 (ill.)
Indonesia, 14
Information Awareness Office, 80
Inhofe, Jim, 25–26
Inman, Bobby Ray, 36
Inouye, Daniel, 283
insect drones, *149–50*, 150 (ill.)
International Bank for Reconstruction and Development (IBRD), 380
International Center for the Settlement of Investment Disputes (ICSID), 380

International Development Association, 380
International Finance Corporation (IPC), 380
International Monetary Fund (IMF), 42–44, 214, 381
International Subversives, 12
internationalism, 236
Internet censoring, 150–52
Internet sabotage, 153 (ill.), *152–54*
Invasion of the Body Snatchers, 138
iPhone spying, *154–56*, 155 (ill.)
Iran-contra affair, 282
Iraq, 46–47, 48–49, 250, 367–69. *See also* Hussein, Saddam
Iserbyt, Charlotte, 98
Israel, 90
Itskov, Dmitry, 298
Ivins, Bruce Edwards, 6 (ill.), 6–7

J

Jackson, C. D., 22
Jacobs, Arthur P., 206
Jacobs, Jeffrey, family, 193
Jacoby, Susan, 97
Jam Handy Co., 339
James, William, 65
Japan, Pearl Harbor, 246–48
Jenkins, Jerry B., 105
Jesus Christ, 256–58, 280–81
Jesus Rifles, 270
Jewish extermination, 253
Jewish question, 236, 374–75
John Birch Society, *157–58*
John Warner Defense Authorization Act, 187
Johnson, Clarence "Kelly," 10–11
Johnson, Kim, 53
Johnson, Lyndon B., 125 (ill.), 170 (ill.), 273
Johnson, Vince, 106
Jones, Alex, 26, 36, 245, 381
Jones, Anson, 127
Jones, Clarence B., 98
Jones, Colman, 296
Jones, Nigel, 162–63

Jones, Steve, 386
Jordison, Sam, 237
journalism at risk, *158–60*, 159 (ill.)
Judicial Watch, 26
Juliana, Queen, 71

K

Kagan, Robert, 259
Karl Theodor, Duke of Bavaria, 145
Kate, Duchess, 285
Kay, David, 368
Keith, Jim, 28–29, 230–31, 333
Kelleher, Colm, 4
Kelley, Clarence M., 30
Kelley, Steven D., 90
Kelly, David, *160–63*
Kelo v. New London, 349
Kennedy, John F.
    assassination, 145, *163–66*, 165 (ill.), 170
    Council on Foreign Relations, 73
    Report from Iron Mountain, 273
    Rh negative blood type, 284, 285
    Skull and Bones, 301
Kennedy, Robert F., 164, *166–68*, 167 (ill.)
Kerry, John, 301
Khalilzad, Zalmay, 259
Khan, Mohammed Sidique, 294–95
Kim Jong-il, 151
Kim Jong-un, 151
Kimball, Ward, 339, 340, 341–42
Kinchen, Harold, 88, 89
King, Jon, 179
King, Martin Luther, Jr., *169–71*, 170 (ill.)
Kirk, Claude, 359
Kissinger, Henry, *171–73*, 172 (ill.)
    Bilderberg Group, 23
    Bohemian Club, 36
    Committee of 300, 71
    NATO, 213
    New World Order, 64, 66

population culling, 253, 346–47
Reptilian, 275
Trilateral Commission, 320
Knigge, Baron von, 144 (ill.), 144–45
Knight, Trevor, 185
Korb, Lawrence J., 250
Korshunov, Victor, 190
Kosovo, 212
Krishna, 256
Kristol, Irving, 259
Kristol, William, 258, 259
Krugman, Herbert, 315
Kucherena, Anatoly, 155
Kucinich, Dennis, 20
Kurzweil, Ray, 298–99
Kuwait, 46–47
Kyriazis, Marios, 297

L

Lafayette, Maximillien de, 76
LaHaye, Beverly, 72, 105
LaHaye, Tim, 72
Lane, Mark, 273
Langton, Edward, 68
Lawford, Peter, 206
Laxon, Seymour, 191
Leahy, Patrick, 6, 7
Lederberg, Joshua, 175–76, 176 (ill.)
Lehr, William, 154
Leibowitz, Annie, 177
Leipzig, Adolf, 123–24
Lenin, Vladimir, 381
Lennon, John, murder, 177–79, 178 (ill.)
less developed countries (LDCs), 254, 348
Leveson, Lord Justice, 159–60
Leveson Inquiry, 159–60
Levinthal, Elliott C., 176
Lewin, Leonard, 273
Lewis, Charles, 21
Li Ka-shing, 367
Libor scandal, 17–18
Library Connection, 180
library spying, 180–82, 181 (ill.), 244
Lieberman, Joseph, 367

Lincoln, Abraham, 313
Lind, Michael, 287
Lindsay, Germaine, 294–95
Lingeman, Richard, 273
literature
    Brave New World, 40–42, 41 (ill.)
    "Harrison Bergeron" (Vonnegut), 134–36, 136 (ill.)
    The Hunger Games, 139–41, 140 (ill.)
    1984 (Orwell), 217–19, 218 (ill.)
Lloyd, David, 351, 352
Lodge, David, 302
London, England, bombings (2005), 294–96
Lott, Trent, 259
Louis XV, King of France, 75
LSD, 199, 199 (ill.), 201, 201 (ill.)
Lully, Raymond, 1
Lurline, SS, 247
Luukanen-Kilde, Rauni-Leena, 27, 82
Lynn, Barry W., 270
Lynn, Matthew, 52

M

Maastricht Treaty, 381
Mad Cow Disease, 2–3, 3 (ill.)
Madison, James, 115
Magreta, Queen, 71
Maheu, Robert, 164
Makow, Henry, 146, 311
Malek, Rami, 209, 210
Mandela, Nelson, 215
Manna from Heaven, 148
Marcel, Jesse, 289
Marcello, Carlos, 164
Marchetti, Victor, 201
Marconi Electric Systems, 182–85
Marie, Philip, Sr., 55
Marquis, Don, 338
Marrs, Jim, 55, 204
Marrs, Texe, 321
Mars, 176
Marshall, John, 127

Marthews, Alex, 279
martial law, 185–87, 186 (ill.)
Martin, William H., 251
Masons, 126–28
Matthewson, Nick, 317
Maxim, Hiram, 376
May, Theresa, 45, 117
Mazzini, Giuseppe, 71
McCarthy, Kevin, 138
McCollum, Arthur H., 248
McDonagh, Melanie, 239–40
McDonald, Eric, 155–56
McDonald, Hugh, 165
McGovern, George, 214
McKeay, Martin, 154
McLeod, Judi, 329
McTeigue, James, 352
McVeigh, Timothy, 23
Meacher, Michael, 216–17
Men in Black (MIB), 187–89, 188 (ill.)
Mengele, Josef, 124
Merovinglians, 86–87
Metternich, Count, 213
Mexico border, 327–28
Micro Scope, 184
microbiologist deaths, 189–92, 191 (ill.)
microchips, 81–82, 192–94, 193 (ill.)
Microsoft, 255
Mikkelson, David, 18
militarization of the police, 194–97, 196 (ill.)
Military Religious Freedom Foundation (MRFF), 270, 271
militia, U.S., 349–50
Millegan, Kris, 299
Miller, Mark Crispin, 72
Milner, Lord Alfred, 71
Milosevic, Slobodan, 23
Milton, John, 353
mind control, 197–98
mind manipulation, 198–200, 199 (ill.)
MKDelta, 200–201, 201 (ill.)
MKNaomi, 202 (ill.), 202–3
MKUltra. *See* Project MKUltra
Mohammed, 256
Moloch, 37

Monast, Serge, 256–57
monatomic gold powder, *203–5*
monetary system, 51–53, 233–35
Monroe, Marilyn, *205–7, 206* (ill.)
mood-altering drugs, *207–9, 208* (ill.)
Mook, Robby, 378
Moon, Elizabeth, 19
Moore, Alan, 351, 352
Moore, Bill, 289
Moore, Michael, 245
Moore, Victor, 184
Moore, William, 32
Morange, Benjamin, 35–36
Morgan, J. P., 71
Morgan, William, 128
Morgan Stanley, 216
Morrison, Jim, 40
Moulden, Andrew, 191
Moulthrop, Roscoe E., III, 31
Moynihan, Daniel Patrick, 97
Mr. Robot, 209–10
Mubarak, Hosni, 215
Mulcair, Thomas, 27
Multilateral Investment Guarantee Agency (MIGA), 380
Munro, Ken, 302
Murray, Eunice, 206
Murray, Joseph, 45–46, 343
Muskie, Edmund, 340–41

N

Napoleon Bonaparte, 36
Narcisse, Clairvius, 95–96
National Aeronautics and Space Administration (NASA), 59–60
National Security Agency (NSA)
    Assange, Julian, 13
    Five Eyes, 116–17
    Snowden, Edward, 255, 303–5
    surveillance, 28, 133, 280
    webcam spying, 373
National Security Council, 337

National Security Letters (NSLs), 180
NATO, *211–13, 213* (ill.)
Navasky, Victor, 273
Navy (ONR), U.S., Special Devices Center, 338
Navy Seals, U.S., 24–25
Nazis, 87–89, 118, 122–24, 246. *See also* Hitler, Adolf
new security concept, 56
The New World Order (Hicks), *136–37*
New World Order in the 1990s, *214–15*
Newcombe, Tommy, 35
Newman, Alex, 172
Newman, Maurice, 60
Nichols, Larry, 321
9/11, *215–17, 216* (ill.)
1984 (Orwell), *217–19, 218* (ill.), 248, 303, 392
Nixon, Richard M.
    biological weapons, 203
    blood type, 285
    Bohemian Club, 37
    Council on Foreign Relations, 73
    Kennedy, Robert F., 166
    Kissinger, Henry, 172
    militarization of the police, 195
    Muskie, Edmund, 340–41
    New World Order, 64
    Watergate, 230
No Child Left Behind, 238
Noguchi, Thomas, 168, 207
None Dare Call It Conspiracy (Allen), *220–22*
North, Oliver, 282
North Korea, 151, 250
Norton-Taylor, Richard, 213
nuclear winter, *222–25, 223* (ill.)

O

Obama, Barack, 62 (ill.)
    anti-Trump rally, 329
    bioterrorism, 120
    Clinton, Hillary, 77
    Department of Homeland Security, 85

    disarming the United States, 90–91
    Federal Emergency Management Agency, 114
    Freedom of Information Act erosion, 124
    as "king," 321
    martial law, 186
    militia, 350
    Patriot Act, 182
    post-9/11 security state, 195, 196
    Putin, Vladimir, 390
    Rice, Susan, 315
    Robertson, Pat, 288
    United Nations Army, 345
    webcam spying, 372
obesity, *227–29, 228* (ill.)
O'Brien, Cathy, 205
O'Connell, Dan, 35
Octopus, 229–31
off the grid, *231–33, 232* (ill.)
Office of Scientific Intelligence, 197–98
Olson, Lee, 30
One World Government, 66–67
one-world currency, *233–35, 234* (ill.)
online purchases, 318 (ill.), *318–19*
Ono, Yoko, 177, 178 (ill.)
Openheimer, David, 257
Operation Big City, 308
Operation Cable Splicer, 283
Operation Garden Plot, 283
Operation Stand Up, 271
opioids, 208
Oppenheimer, Ernest, 71
Oppenheimer, Harry, 71
Orbitally Rearranged Mono-Atomic Elements (ORME), 204, 205
origins of the New World Order, *235–37*
Ormsby-Gore, David, 71
Orr, Christopher, 352
Orwell, George, 218 (ill.)
    New World Order, 134–35
    1984, 217–19, 303, 392
    Orwellian, *237–38*
    Patriot Act, 244

perpetual war, 248–51
police state, 61
Postman, Neil, 42
spying, 150
Orwellian, *237–38*, 238 (ill.),
  244, 372
Osbourne, Ozzy, 263
Oswald, Lee Harvey, 163–65,
  170, 178, 284–85
Oswald, Marina, 284–85
overpopulation, *238–41*, 239
  (ill.)
owls, 37
Oyster Card, 52, 52 (ill.)

P

Page, Dan, 187
Page, Ralph W., 237
Page, Thornton, 338, 339
Palast, Gregory, 360
Palin, Sarah, 220
Palmer, Bethania, 325
Pangilinan, Manuel V., 367
Paracelsus, 1
paranormal phenomena, 264
Parker-Bowles, Camilla, 275,
  276
Parkes, Simon, 24
Partridge, Robert, 30
Pasechnik, Vladimir, 190
Patriot Act, 20, 180–82, 243–
  45
Paul, Ron, 20, 245, 320
Payne, Michael, 218
Peapell, Peter, 184
Pearl Harbor and the New
  World Order parallels, *245–
  48*, 246 (ill.)
Peña Nieto, Enrique, 327
Pence, Mike, 323 (ill.)
Pentagon, 215–17
Perdomo, Jose Sanjenis, 178
Perez, Eddie, 77
Perle, Richard, 259
Peron, Juan Domingo, 124
perpetual war, *248–51*, 249
  (ill.)
Perry, Rick, 356
Peston, Robert, 377
Pham, Nina, 101

pharmaceutical industry, 191,
  207–9
Philip, Prince, Duke of
  Edinburgh, 71, 274, 275
Philips, Paul A., 177
phones, 154–56
Pickens, T. Boone, 367
Pine Gap, *251–52*, 252 (ill.)
Plessy, 184, 185
Podesta, John, 13, 314, 378
police, militarization of, 194–
  97, 196 (ill.), 392
population. *See* overpopulation;
  population culling
population culling, *252–54*,
  346–48, 354, 386–91
Portman, Natalie, 351
Posel, Susanne, 235
Postman, Neil, 42
Poteshman, Allen M., 216
Powell, Colin, 368, 369
Power, Peter, 295–96
Power, Samantha, 345
presidential election (2016),
  328–30, 330 (ill.)
Priebus, Reince, 326 (ill.)
PRISM Program, *255–56*, 304
prison camps, 283
privacy, 317
Privacy International, 116
Proclus, 76
Project Artichoke, 200
Project Blue Beam, *256–58*,
  264
Project Bluebird, 200
Project Chatter, 200
Project Derby Hat, 201
Project for the New American
  Century (PNAC), 70, *258–59*
Project MKUltra, 197, 198,
  199, 308, 341–42
Project Third Chance, 201
Prophet, Elizabeth Clare, 76
Protocols of the Elders of Zion,
  375
Prouty, Fletcher, 273
Puddy, Malcolm, 185
Pugh, Richard, 183
Purple code, 247
Putin, Vladimir, 260 (ill.)
  China, 57

Illuminati, 388
Talbott, Strobe, 314
Trump, Donald, and the
  New World Order, *260–
  61*, 389–91
World Order, 383–84

Q–R

Quayle, Dan, 259
Quayle, Steve, 192
Que, Benito, 190
Quetzalcoatl, 274
rabies, *263–64*
RAND Corporation, 70, *264–
  67*, 266 (ill.)
Randle, Kevin, 289
Rathenau, Walter, 70
Ray, James Earl, 170
Raytheon, 216
Rea, Stephen, 351
Readiness Exercise 1984 (Rex
  84), 281–84
reading habits, 180–82
Reagan, Annie, 88
Reagan, Ronald
  assassination attempt, 178
  Bohemian Club, 36
  Collins Elite, 68, 69
  concentration camps, 282
  Council for National Policy,
    72
  Gorbachev, Mikhail, 222
  Lennon, John, murder, 179
  militarization of the police,
    195
  UFOs, 267–69
  view of a world united by
    UFOs, *267–69*, 268 (ill.)
Regius Poem/Manuscript, 126–
  27
Reinikkaar, Allan, 120
religion, 236, *269–71*
religious miracles, 265–67
Report from Iron Mountain, *271–
  74*
Reptilians, *274–76*, 275 (ill.)
Reptilians and sex, *276–78*
Restore the Fourth, *278–80*
Retinger, Joseph, 21
Revelations, *280–81*

Rex 84, *281–84*
Reynolds, Diana, 282
Rh negatives, *284–86*, 285 (ill.)
Rhodes, Cecil, 71
Rice, Susan, 315
Rice University, 205
Riconosciuto, Michael, 230
Roberts, Paul Craig, 328
Robertson, A. Willis, 287
Robertson, Howard Percy, 337
Robertson, Pat, *286–88*, 288 (ill.)
Robertson Panel, 337–40
Robock, Alan, 224–25
Rockefeller, David, 71, 166
Rockefeller, Nelson, 64
Rockefeller Commission, 197
Rockefeller families, 381
Rockefeller Foundation, 355
Roland, Allen L., 293
Romero, Juan, 167
Roosevelt, Franklin D., 66, 214, 248
Rosack, Theodore P., 29, 30
Roselli, Johnny, 164
Rosenthal, A. M., 214
Ross, Chuck, 76
Rossi, David, 18
Roston, Leo, 338
Roswell, *288–91*, 290 (ill.)
Rothschild, David, 71
Rothschild, Evelyn, 71
Rothschild family, 287, 381
Round Table Group, 74
Royal College of Military Science, 184
Rubio, Marco, 356
Ruby, Jack, 164
Rudin, Mickey, 206
Rumsfeld, Donald, 259, 271
Russell, Bertrand, 71
Russell, William Huntingdon, 299–300
Russia, 57–58. *See also* Putin, Vladimir

S

Safire, William, 214, 245
Sagan, Carl, 176
Salazar, Adan, 377

Samsung, 301–3
Samuel, Prophet, 76
San Francisco, California, spraying, 308–9
Sanders, Bernie, 260, *293–94*, 326, 329 (ill.), 357
Sands, David, 184
Savage, Charlie, 377
Schevardnadze, Eduard, 267
Schiffman, Steve, 4
Schlafly, Phyllis, 158
Schlesinger, Arthur, 215
Schmitt, Don, 289
Schmitt, Gary, 258
Schmitz, John G., 221
Schneier, Bruce, 153
Scowcroft, Brent, 66
Sebesta, Donald, 30
Second Coming of Christ, 264, 280
Seiler, Wenzel, 189
Seltzer, Margo, 150
September 11, 2001, terrorist attacks. *See* 9/11
7/7, *294–96*
sex and Reptilians, 276–78
Shamsi, Hina, 364
Shanksville, Pennsylvania, 215
Shannan, Pan, 170–71
Shapiro, Ben, 325
Sharif, Arshad, 183, 184
Sheets, Nathan, 383
Shirreff, Richard, 212
Sholin, Dave, 177
Shultz, George, 71
Sieff, Martin, 56
signals intelligence (SIGINT), 116
Simon, Joel, 160
Simson-Kallas, Eduard, 168
Singel, Ryan, 319
Singh-Gida, Avtar, 183–84
singularity and artificial evolution, *297–99*, 298 (ill.)
Sirhan, Sirhan, 166, 167–68, 171
Sked, Alan, 343
Skeels, David, 184
Skousen, W. Cleon, 220

Skull and Bones, *299–301*, 300 (ill.)
Slater, Christian, 209, 210
Slaughter, Anne Marie, 378
smart TV spies, *301–3*, 302 (ill.)
smartphones, 154–56
Smith, Dan T., 106–7
Smith, Travis, 153
Smoot, Dan, 220
Snowden, Edward, *303–5*, 304 (ill.)
    iPhone spying, 155, 156
    PRISM Program, 255, 256
    Restore the Fourth, 278
    webcam spying, 373
Snyder, Michael, 97, 194
Social Security Administration arms purchases, 305 (ill.), 305–6
Socialism, 221–22
Soghoian, Christopher, 319
Soros, George, 57, 192
Space Brothers, 276
space race, 79
Spanish flu pandemic, *306–8*, 307 (ill.)
Spencer, Craig, 101
Speronis, Robin, 233
spraying cities, 308–9
Springman, Michael, 217
Sputnik 1, 79
Stalin, Joseph, 237, 381
Steiger, Brad
    alchemy, 1
    American Vision, 5
    Bohemian Grove, 36
    Freemasonry, 127–28
    Illuminati, 143, 144, 145
    John Birch Society, 158
    King, Martin Luther, Jr., 171
    Trilateral Commission, 320
Stephens, David, 188
Stephey, M. J., 42, 43
Stevenson, Adlai, 66
Stone, Jeff, 151
Stone, Oliver, 273
Stormer, John A., 158
Straub, Chris, 106
Stringfield, Leonard, 334

Stroll, Irwin, 168
Strong, Maurice, 71
Sullivan, Brendan, 282
Supari, Siti Fadilah, 14
superviruses, *309–10*
surveillance programs, 255–56
survivalists, 310 (ill.), *310–11*
sustainable development, 330–32
Sutherland, Donald, 138, 273
Sutherland, S. F., 35
Sutton, Anthony C., 300
SWAT unit, 195
Syrmopoulos, Jay, 232
Szymanski, Greg, 82

T

Taft, Alphonso, 299
Taft, William Howard, 301
Talbott, Strobe, *313–15*, 314 (ill.)
Tanweer, Shehzad, 294–95
Tarin, Haris, 270
tattoos, 82
Taylor, Jared, 326
television, 209–10, *315–17*, 316 (ill.)
television, smart, 301–3
Thatcher, Margaret, 352
Theosophists, 76
Third Reich, 122–24
Thomas, Augusto O., 235
Thomas, David E., 55
Thomas, Glenn, 192
Thomas, Kenn, 230
Thomas, Marcus, 372
Thomas, Norman, 236
Thomas, Richard, 194
Thompson, Reginald C., 68
Tonnies, Mac, 288–91
Tor Project, *317*
Toynbee, Arnold J., 314
tracking your online purchases, 318 (ill.), *318–19*
Trafficante, Santo, Jr., 164
Travers, Peter, 352
Trijicon, 269, 271
Trilateral Commission, 70, *319–20*, 320 (ill.)
Truman, Harry S., 66

Trump, Donald, *321–22*, 321 (ill.), 323 (ill.)
  children unable to vote for him, 357
  Clinton, Hillary, 378–79
  Hitler, Adolf, compared to, 186
  martial law, 115
  militia, 350
  New World Order, *324–27*, 343
  presidential election (2016), 62, 63, 76, 329
  Putin, Vladimir, 260–61, 389–92
  speech, *322–24*
  wall, *327–28*
Trump, Eric, 357
Trump, Ivanka, 357
Tucker, Patrick, 149
Turner, Karla, 334
Turner, Ted, 71
Turner, William, 230
Twietmeyer, Ted, 283
Twin Towers, 215–17, 216 (ill.)
2016 presidential election stolen, *328–30*, 330 (ill.)
2030 agenda, *330–32*

U

Uecker, Karl, 167
Ufologists and spying, *333–34*
UFOs
  Area 51, 9–12
  Collins Elite, 67–69
  eschatology, 105–7
  Goff, Kenneth, 130–31
  of the New World Order, *336–42*, 339 (ill.)
  Octopus, 230
  in Ottawa, *334–36*, 335 (ill.)
  Reagan, Ronald, 267–69
  Reptilians, 276–78
  Roswell, 288–91
UK Independence Party, *342–43*, 343 (ill.)
Ukraine, 89–90
UKUSA agreement, 116–17, 117 (ill.)
undesirables, 114

United Kingdom, 44–46, 159–60, 294–96
United Nations, 64, 214, 330–32
United Nations Army, *344–46*, 345 (ill.)
United Nations population plot, *346–48*
U.S. Air Force, 340, 370–71
U.S. Constitution erosion, *348–49*
U.S. militia, *349–50*
U.S.-Mexico border, 327–28
USA PATRIOT Act. *See* Patriot Act
Usborne, David, 77

V

V for Vendetta, *351–53*, 352 (ill.)
Valentine, Basil, 1
Van Zeeland, Paul, 21
variant CJD (vCJD), 3–4
Velikovsky, Immanuel, 388
Venetian Black Nobility, 382
VeriChip, 193
Verismo, Chris, 252
Verizon, 255
Veterans Today, 353
Vigenère, Blaise, 1
Vinson, Amber Joy, 101
Vintini, Leonardo, 389
Virgin Mary, 266, 267
viruses, 175–76, 190, 192, 306–8, 309–10, *354–55*
Volodin, Vyacheslav, 390, 390 (ill.)
Vonnegut, Kurt, 98, 135, 136 (ill.)
voting restrictions, *355–57*, 356 (ill.)

W

Wachowski, Andy, 352
Wachowski, Larry, 352
Wackenhut, George, 359
Wackenhut Corporation, *359–60*
Wadhams, Peter, 191
Waldbott, George L., 117–20

Walker, John, 68
Walker, Scott, 356
Walking Corpse Syndrome (WCS), *360–62*
wall and Donald Trump, 327–28
Wallström, Martin, 209
Walmart conspiracy, 353 (ill.), *362–64*
Walt Disney Inc., 339 (ill.), 339–40, 341
Wang Yi, 56, 57 (ill.)
War of the Worlds (Wells), 271–72
Warburg, Felix, 71
Warburg, Max, 71
Warburg, Paul, 71, 287
Ward, Chester, 73, 158
Ward, Dan Sewell, 204
Warren, Earl, 163
Warren, Shani, 184
Warren Commission, 163–64
Wash, Jonathan, 182–83
Washington, George, 127, 285
watch lists, *364–65*
water, fluoride in, 117–20
water control, *365–67*, 366 (ill.)
Watson, Paul Joseph, 82, 150
Watson, Traci, 55
weapons of mass destruction (WMD), *367–69*, 368 (ill.)
weather, 370–72

weather force support element (WFSE), 371–72
Weathermen, *370–72*
Weaving, Hugo, 351
webcam spying, *372–74, 373* (ill.)
Webster, Nesta Helen, *374–75*
Webster, William, 121
Weinstein, Michael, 270, 271
Weisel, William, 168
Weishaupt, Adam, 143–45, 144 (ill.)
Welch, Robert, 157, 158
Welles, Orson, 130 (ill.), 130–31, 271, 272, 338
Welles, Sumner, 236
Wells, H. G., 40–41, 71, 131, 271, *375–77, 376* (ill.)
White, Harry, 44
White Powder Gold, 148
WikiLeaks, 12–13, *377–79, 378* (ill.)
Wilder, Arizona, 275
Wiles, Rick, 322
Wiley, Don C., 190
William, Prince, 285
Wilmesher, Anna, 279
Wilson, Julie, 93
Wilson, Lawrence, 178
Wilson, Woodrow, 288
Wirth, Timothy, 61
Wolfensohn, James, 380
Wolfowitz, Paul, 259

Wood, David Murakami, 194
Woodward, Bob, 179
Woolsey, James, 259
World Bank, *379–83*
World Bank Group, 380
world government, 236
World Order, *383–86*
World Pax, 376
world peace, 272–73
World Trade Center, 215–17, 216 (ill.)
World Trade Organization, 214
World War III, *386–91, 387* (ill.), 390 (ill.)
Wozny, Andrew, 80
Wyden, Ron, 181–82

X–Z

Xanax, 208
Xi Jinping, 57–58, 151
Yahoo, 255
Yale University, 299–301
Yiannopoulos, Milo, 325
Young, Michael Henry de, 35
yuan, 233–34
Yudhoyono, Susilo Bambang, 14
zero hour, *391–92*
Zhou Xiaochuan, 234
Zika virus, 354–55
Zovirax, 361
Zuckerberg, Mark, 374